The Visual Imperative
Creating a Visual Culture of Data Discovery

The Visual Imperative
Creating a Visual Culture
of Data Discovery

Lindy Ryan

AMSTERDAM • BOSTON • HEIDELBERG • LONDON
NEW YORK • OXFORD • PARIS • SAN DIEGO
SAN FRANCISCO • SINGAPORE • SYDNEY • TOKYO
Morgan Kaufmann is an imprint of Elsevier

Morgan Kaufmann is an imprint of Elsevier
50 Hampshire Street, 5th Floor, Cambridge, MA 02139, USA

Notices

Knowledge and best practice in this field are constantly changing. As new research and experience broaden our understanding, changes in research methods, professional practices, or medical treatment may become necessary.

Practitioners and researchers must always rely on their own experience and knowledge in evaluating and using any information, methods, compounds, or experiments described herein. In using such information or methods they should be mindful of their own safety and the safety of others, including parties for whom they have a professional responsibility.

To the fullest extent of the law, neither the Publisher nor the authors, contributors, or editors, assume any liability for any injury and/or damage to persons or property as a matter of products liability, negligence or otherwise, or from any use or operation of any methods, products, instructions, or ideas contained in the material herein.

British Library Cataloguing-in-Publication Data
A catalogue record for this book is available from the British Library

Library of Congress Cataloging-in-Publication Data
A catalog record for this book is available from the Library of Congress

ISBN: 978-0-12-803844-4

For information on all Morgan Kaufmann publications
visit our website at https://www.elsevier.com/

Working together
to grow libraries in
developing countries

www.elsevier.com • www.bookaid.org

Publisher: Todd Green
Acquisition Editor: Todd Green
Editorial Project Manager: Amy Invernizzi
Production Project Manager: Punithavathy Govindaradjane
Designer: Matthew Limbert

Typeset by Thomson Digital

For my grandmother

Contents

Foreword

Nearly a year ago during one of many discussions regarding the impact of big data at companies struggling to realize its full potential, the topic of data visualization and visual communication became the centerpiece. While many companies had found proficiency in working with big data or even created data science and analytics initiatives, enabling people to work properly with data visualization tools was falling far short thus creating a roadblock for full realization of big data's potential.

This is the visual imperative, ultimately driven by every company's need to enable its people to analyze and communicate effectively in a data-centric world. Lindy and I started thinking about ways our research could help companies take something that started as a uniquely individual passionate and grass roots movement and turn it into an enterprise-wide program.

From there, Lindy's passion for the topic, depth of experience, extensive research, and practical application grew. The chapters in this book represent this body of research and ongoing mission, and as I consider the importance and potential value for readers, four pressing drivers rise to the top.

Imperative 1. Big data

Everyone might be a little tired of hearing about big data but it's a reality that there is so much more data for companies to leverage today, and it is increasing exponentially and coming at even faster speeds. *We simply cannot handle it all, crunch it all or make sense of it all with the techniques we have used in the past.* Business demands are driving technical innovation in computing power, storage density, and bigger faster distributed architectures, and the fact is that we are always trying to play catch up with the amount of data that is out there.

What we are experiencing now is similar to the industry-wide shift we saw 15 years ago when saying business intelligence was not just about the data warehouse. Then—and now—we go through the cycle, first trying to figure out how to manage all of the new data (an order of magnitude larger than what's currently in use) and then figuring out how to leverage that data for insights. Data warehousing gave birth to BI and performance management in this same way. The technologies and buzzwords have evolved, but going through a similar cycle now with big data (Hadoop) having arrived around 2008, followed by a growing need to leverage big data differently via advanced analytics (like the current machine learning and cognitive computing movement) and advanced visualizations and user engagement. While data is the key ingredient, computations and the ability to make business insights and decisions on the data is always the goal. It is not simply about having big data. It is what you do with it.

The cycle of technological innovation drives advances in both managing and analyzing the data. In recent years, the maturing and mainstream adoption of Hadoop has begun to stabilize the ability to acquire and manage big data sets as an extension of enterprise information management. Now we need to know how to work with, view, and understand all of it. In the BI era, visualizations had a well-defined role for communicating information reports, analyzing data dimensionally, and displaying goal-oriented dashboards. However, traditional data visualizations fall short in the big data era where the need to explore new data sets and discover insights is equally coupled with the ability to communicate all the patterns and relationships within the data in new ways.

What this means for data visualization is that there is no way to comprehensively look at, interact with, represent, and collaborate over that much data except to visualize it effectively. This is the imperative that will only increase with more and more data. New data sets are changing the landscape, and we are still only scratching the surface of what is possible. Internet of Things and machine data will take that an order of magnitude higher again. If you want to communicate with people or with machines, the way to do that will be through visual communication. If you are going to work with big data—today and in the future—you have to be competent at visualization, and that competency must be being taught, evolved, and monitored within companies today.

Imperative 2: The need to engage through design and user experience

The far-reaching impact of the technology revolution of 2007 with the launch of the Apple iPhone is not to be underestimated. Across every industry, Apple has had a profound influence through the psychological effect of how consumers expect technology to interact with them. People now expect good design as part of their visual communication and interactivity with information. In obsessing over simple, intuitive design, Apple sets a new standard for visual communication. It was necessary to design a completely original visualization experience because when converting from the real estate of a computer monitor to a 3.5-inch screen, smart choices must be made to effectively communicate visually and create intuitive interaction with the device. Not that Apple has always done this perfectly, but it has always focused on aesthetics and the user experience.

In fact, Apple went through a phase of "iCandy" with its photo-realism aspect. But then it adopted a whole new level of visual effectiveness that went away from what looks especially pretty and realistic, and went to flattened minimalism and straightforward iconography. The result may not be quite as pretty, but it is significantly more effective because it increases visual efficiency.

So you can see that whether it is massive amounts of data to work with or this new era of design we live in, the stage is set for what I think people have come to expect and perhaps even set the bar for acceptance criteria. People simply cannot go from the optimal visual designs and user experiences of iOS (or Android) and then be content with a laptop or tablet with a clunky interface. An earlier example of this was what I called the "Google Effect" when Google conditioned users to expect 100,000+ search results in 0.4 s. It was difficult that in my personal life I had ease of use and highly iterative and agile query and exploration or discovery ability, but at work I had to wait five minutes (or more!) for a standard sales report. Data visualization has become the new market to supplant where BI has not been able to meet user expectations. Apple did the same for visualization. The "Apple Effect" changed the expectation for aesthetics and interactivity. It influenced the entire product world across industries, as consumers now have exceptionally high standards for visual experience.

The important point here is that true visual efficiency is the expectation: stripping away everything so you are accurately facilitating discovery, enabling analytics with visualization, communicating an insight, or telling a data story and not being distracted because something is pretty or an artistic expression of data.

Imperative 3: Visual communication

With big data being managed and the latest generation of powerful data visualization tools on the market for companies to leverage, the real challenge then moves away from a technology issue to people and processes issue. Just because I exchanged your hammer for a nail gun and your hand saw for a cordless circular saw, does that mean you can build a skyscraper? When communicating data to any audience, proper data visualization and representation still does not guarantee accurate or effective communication. One must also consider the mode of the reader/audience and the language of visual communication for different kinds of conversations—sharing, understanding, exploring, persuading, and storytelling.

When creating a visualization for a lot of data, my task is not completely finished until I structure my presentation of the data to solicit a response or engage the viewer. I need to think through the flow of the visual experience and what the user will be seeking from the data. User experience design and visual communication go far beyond whether a bar chart or pie is the correct way to represent data. Proficiency is derived not only from a formal skillset but also from the narrative that we hear from the inner voice in our heads when we develop data visualization stories. The techniques come from a long history of humans telling stories and connecting with the audience. The way to be effective with big data is to be effective with visual communication through data visualizations and engagement.

Data storytelling is not always a classic story format, with a protagonist, antagonist, problem, and solution. That is one formula for storytelling. But I am not always sitting in an audience expecting a story with a happy ending. With data, sometimes I need to evaluate options and make business decisions—this is the probabilistic world prediction, prescriptive and cognitive computing with big data. I need to have everything in front of me—visually—to have the final decision and take action. If I am going to do discovery, I want to quickly see all the data and options on the screen and how they are related. And in the cognitive computing world, data visualizations are a critical component of helping machines make critical decisions quickly through simplifying visual communication and focusing on interaction efficiency—but not without the user assessing and validating the results

In order to communicate visually and correctly, whether in storytelling or visual discovery or whatever other visual communication method, it is absolutely necessary to do so without getting in the way of the user and what they are trying to understand from your message.

Imperative 4: Visual communication as a core business competency

When we talk about architecting for discovery, we are talking about managing data in all its different formats. When we talk about data visualization as a core competency, we are talking about user experience and technical design elements. When we talk about enabling visual discovery or visual analytics, that is bringing purpose to both. In order to realize the full potential of big data and its new capabilities, you have to unlock visual design and communication as an essential competency at every level of author and audience within the enterprise.

Consider this: You can read through a page of text, but what if you could have a really good visualization that you can understand 100× faster? Now imagine if your company could consistently communicate this way. The impact would change the way you do business—speeding the business strategy itself. This is not to say that data visualization is the only form of business communication, but done properly it is an effective, efficient way to discover and comprehend data and insights.

That is why this is so important. We are in the big data world and there is no going back, primarily because your competitors are not going backwards and your users have come to expect a new paradigm.

While proper technical visual design was in the past relegated to creatives and designers, it is now part of every business. Does everyone in your company know how to do visual design correctly? And once they know that, do they know how to communicate visually to deliver the point or solicit interaction—whether it is to convince me, help me discover, or help me make a decision? That is why the storytelling aspect is not just a hot trend; it is part of the big picture.

So, organizationally how do I create a company culture that recognizes and embraces these principles when you already have the tools? How do I make this part of the fabric of my business so everything runs 100× more efficiently and effectively? You cannot work with big data and work with numbers in a spreadsheet. You cannot have the best data visualization tools and let everyone do something different without proper training. As business leaders, change agents and champions in data driven organizations, you simply need to know.

That is why it is a visual imperative, and why the content of these pages is so relevant for every business leader, every analyst, and every businessperson today.

John O'Brien
CEO of Radiant Advisors

Introduction

When I was in college, I used to draw a distinction between where I was "from" and where I was "originally" from. I suppose it was a matter of semantics really—and looking back I doubt anyone actually ever cared what my answer was when they asked the question. Nevertheless, it was important to me to make the distinction between the place I had chosen to call home and the one my parents had, and I would give answers like "well, I'm *from* the Northwest, though my family is from the South" or "I live here, but I'm *originally* from Texas." Like I said: semantics. But, it was important to me, and seemed—at the time—a critical difference in the way in which I qualified my residential timeline. After all, I'd spent most of my formative years in the South, but it didn't feel right to say I was "from" there when I'd been in the Northwest since I'd toppled over into adulthood in my early twenties. I'd gotten married in the Northwest. My son had been born there. I'd graduated college, and grad school, there. I was *from* there, even if I had grown up elsewhere. In my eyes, origination and loyalty both were two sides of the same coin—me.

When I was new into the data industry, I did the same thing. And, for a while, it was true. My career began in the finance industry, and I stayed in banking for several years in a project management role before moving into another project management role in printing and advertising sometime during grad school. About a year before I finished my Master's degree I took yet another project management job as an education program manager at The Data Warehousing Institute (TDWI). Without knowing it, this move was the one that inadvertently began my journey into BI and all-things data. Still, for years I found myself falling back into the same old habit of distinction—of semantics. "I'm in the data industry now, but I come from finance… or banking…or (even though it was only a handful of months) advertising."

I said variations of the same type of thing for about five years until, at some point on the path from start to finish of this book, I realized that my go-to response no longer held true. I might have *originally* come from a background in project management in various industries, but today—almost a decade later—I am definitively *from* the data industry. And, I expect that no matter where my journey takes me, in the same way that I will forever say that I am "from" the Northwest even though I currently reside in the Northeast, that likewise no matter what role I fall into in the future, I will always say that I am "from" the data industry.

In the early months of 2011, when John O'Brien and I opened the doors to Radiant Advisors, I knew a whole lot about how to build project plans and Gantt charts, but next to nothing about business intelligence or data science. I had never heard of big data or of Hadoop, had rarely done anything more sophisticated with data than write the more simplistic of SQL statements in Microsoft Access. This was, frankly, somewhat surprising to me. I am (as I have often been reminded, usually with some degree of forced patience) a millennial. I've been using technology as long as I can remember; I have expectations of how I want to understand, receive, and work with information—and likewise I have requirements: fast, complete, and easy to consume. I wrote (and later published) my graduate thesis on how, as a disrupter, Netflix is a poster child for Hurst's theory of ethical anarchy and creative destruction, and how it used things like data and Long Tail theory to enable the transformation of an entire industry whose wake we are still seeing ripple today. Nevertheless, in those early days I found myself feeling like poor, oblivious *Game of Thrones'* Jon Snow, constantly second-guessing myself with the chant "you know nothing, Lindy Ryan." There was a good year of learning curve for me to establish a baseline comfort zone with some of the most established principles we take for granted in the industry—not to mention organize a mental glossary to hold the swarm of acronyms that dominate data industry vernacular—HDFS, JSON, EDM, ETL. And, it was not an easy thing to do, to rise up through the ranks from editor—armed with strong opinions on things like Oxford commas and parentheticals—to analyst—armed with years of insight and carefully crafted opinions. There was so much to learn, and I am still learning many new things each and every day as the industry continues to rapidly evolve, advance…change. It was (and still is) a time of exploration, understanding, and intrigue—and it has been a fantastic and rewarding voyage to bring a fresh perspective and learn from scratch, because as author Barbara Sher once said "You can learn new things at any time in your life if you're willing to be a beginner. If you actually learn to like being a beginner, the whole world opens up to you."

In late 2013, I started to get more hands-on with the technologies I'd spent the past few years learning about and developing an opinion on. Very quickly, I fell in love with—as I have come to affectionately refer to it—the subtle science and exact art of data visualization. And, having heard that "curiosity kills the cat" more times than I could ever count, it was only natural for me to gravitate to terms like "data discovery" or "information exploration." Even as a millennial, and even as someone who'd worked with data in every single one of my roles—from making sure projects were on time, schedule, and budget; to making sure that my clients were getting the most out of their print campaigns to meet targeted audiences; to making sure the analysis in my academic research was spot on—I had found that the most intuitive, compelling, and engaging way to truly see and understand information was through the power of visualization, and that—more important—sometimes the answers to questions you didn't even know to ask were there waiting for one to discover—to see—them.

Thus began my self-proclaimed love affair with data visualization and visual discovery, and why I believe so completely in the title of this book. Visualization is key to making data easier to absorb, more intuitive, more approachable, and more pervasive. With a tool like data visualization, everyone can be a data person if they have the awareness and wherewithal to use it to their benefit. A visual culture of data discovery is, as Oxford itself defines it, an imperative, noting that the visual dimension of culture is becoming increasingly dominant, and that spectacle and display are dominating cultural forms.

Numbers—data—don't speak for themselves; they need humans to interpret them. And, in my opinion, there is simply no better way to learn, comprehend, and appreciate data than to (literally) see it in action. Over the years, I have seen this statement ring true from the highest tiers of executive management, to the inner workings of the most innovative, to the most analytically oriented of data scientists, and down to the rungs of daily operations and performance management and beyond, trickling through the realms of higher education all the way to the earliest grade school years. I've watched my own son use the power of data visualization to understand parts to whole relationships in pie charts and, visually digging deeper into data, refitting it to tell a better story by leveraging industry tools (like Tableau, Qlik, and JMP) and then, empowered by his earned visual data literacy, embarking onto visual programming by coding his own interactive games and animations with MIT-based project Scratch. It's visual data literacy in action, and it's real.

Thinking visually is a universal, age-agnostic language to discovery, and it delivers immediate time to value every time it is simply given the opportunity to do so.

Today, in the age of "don't tell me, show me," we are becoming—from the personal to the enterprise—increasingly visual. To propagate and enable this shift, visual technologies are one way we are using the power of information to our advantage. This premium on visual data discovery and data visualization is part motive, part strategy. A quick Google search will yield a cornucopia of results from *Forbes*, *Harvard Business Review*, or even *The New York Times*—alongside a host of academic publications, conference presentations, TED talks, and more—with headlines like "Data Visualization is the Future" or "Visual Data Strategies Transform Information into Action," but even this is narrow. Visual data discovery is so much more, and fostering, nourishing, and cultivating visual discovery goes beyond motives and mechanics—beyond strategy. It truly becomes cultural, an essential part of the business fabric that amalgamates visualization as part of its collective beliefs, values, and attitudes. It influences management, drives decisions, and can be found in every nook and cranny of the infrastructure, from accounting to production to sales and marketing. Besides, as leadership expert Peter Drucker famously said, "culture eats strategy for breakfast." And, as we all know, breakfast is the most important meal of the day.

It is my hope that this book will do more than educate you on the various facets through which data visualization and visual data discovery add value to our lives. My hope is that it will inspire you to take action, to become an active participant in how data and visualization continue to refine and reshape the data industry and our organizations, how it affects us at work and at home. My hope is that by the end of this book you think differently, more visually, and find yourself joining the ranks of the many who consider themselves "from" a visual data culture.

About the Author

Lindy Ryan is a respected analyst and researcher in the confluence of data discovery, visualization, and data science. Her dissertation research focuses on addressing the technical, ethical, and cultural impacts that have continued and will continue to arise in a rapidly expanding big data culture. She is a regular contributor to several industry publications, as well as a frequent guest speaker at data conferences worldwide.

Acknowledgments

First and foremost, thank you to my partner, mentor, and friend, John O'Brien for everything—from the ideation process to taking the time to pen the foreword for this book. Without your ongoing support and constant and unyielding faith in me this project would never have been dreamed up, much less come to fruition. Thank you for always believing in me, from our earliest days to today and beyond. Your honesty and perspective have been invaluable and it's no exaggeration to say I wouldn't be where I am today without you. If I could put a *30 Rock* meme in this section to better express my adulation for you, you know that I would! Long live Jack and Liz!

Next, my sincerest thanks to Julie Langenkamp. I have been fortunate to know you over many years on the path from editor, to peer, and to friend. Thank you for being a willing and patient voice of reason and an editor extraordinaire, and for indulging some of my sillier anecdotes in these pages without taking them under the almighty red pen. I know that unscrambling my thoughts and ironing them out into written words is no small task, and I never recognized your superior diplomacy skills until I read your comments on each and every graf in this book. Just don't touch the dragon!

I would also like to thank the other members of my Radiant family. Natalie Whitney, for your unwavering positivity and enthusiasm, and for always keeping my wine glass—and my spirits—full. You have a knack for bringing out the good in people, even me, and even when it's three am and we're sitting in a hotel lobby in our housecoats. I love you for that. And, to Jason Cenamor, the unofficial fourth in the Radiant Advisors family, for always keeping it classy. You're a bloody brilliant friend.

To my team at Morgan Kauffman: Andrea Dierna for bringing me into the Elsevier family several years ago, Steve Elliott for believing in this project, and most especially Amy Invernizzi, for leading me through the publication process with grace and patience. To Krish Krishnan, Tolga Durdu, and Dr Nathan Halko for being willing to read the embryotic first scripts of the scope of this text and giving it your thumbs up. Additionally, to Nathan, for being a data scientist up for examination, and for putting that angry Lego kitty unicorn in your slide deck at Data Summit. I still smile when I think about that.

To a select few of my spectacular peers in the data industry, for each of your unique contributions in talking, thinking, brainstorming, or motivating me along the journey from Chapters 1 to 13—perhaps though you didn't even know it: Andrew Cardno, Richard Hackathorn, Suzanne Hoffman, Stephen Swoyer, Bob Eve, Rado Kotorov, Kim Dossey, Kerry Gilger, Craig Jordan, Frank Buytendijk, Ted Cuzzillo, David Napoli, and Robert Kosara. Over the course of this journey, I have humbly requested guidance and reviewers from those whose insights and opinions I value, and I am grateful for each of you.

To my colleagues, peers, and friends in academia—Barbara Wixom, Kelly Flores, Arron Grow, Pressley Rankin, Greg Price, Kyle Schlesinger, and Jason Brinkley— for support and guidance, and for keeping my academic integrity meter on high. To

Theresa Gehrig, my APA savior. And, without fail, thanks are owed to my long-time mentor, pen pal, and most cherished of professors, Robert "Dr. Bob" Brownlow, who once told me long, long ago, "Lindy, I'm going to push you to the breaking point in your work—and then push you even harder. You're going to hate it, but you'll thank me later." Do you remember that? I do. Thank you, again.

To all the various visual artists, designers, and sources of data-driven inspiration who allowed me to use samples of their work as illustrations in this text. The list is long, but a special thank you to everyone, including but not limited to Matt Brighton, Manuel Lima, Chelsea Carlson, Stefanie Posavec, Giorgia Lupi, Danny Fein, RJ Andrews, Scott Schwertly, Bill Shander, Jon Schwabish, Riccardo Scalco, and Marcin Plonka, I am privileged to know you and share your work. A special thank you to my friend, Dan Walters, who turned my doodles into drawings more than a time or two. Likewise, I am honored to have had the opportunity to interview, profile, and quote several experts in these pages, and learn from you and share your wisdom. Thank you, especially, to Deane May Zager for playing interview phone tag for no less than three months and then giving me one of the most inspiring conversations to date!

Last but certainly not least, to the people who take up the largest majority of my heart—my family. To my parents and in-laws—Mom, Dad, Paul, Dave, Korla—for not having a clue what I do for a living but being proud of me and buying this book anyway. To my sister, Lisa, for keeping my eyes big with dreams of Ted Talks. To Mike, for giving me room to write and being tolerant and supportive while I have pursued my dreams. To my brilliant, clever, and kind son, Wake. To Shon. To my purring fluff balls, Oskar and Ferrous, for keeping me company in long hours spent in my writing cave. It truly takes a village.

How data is driving business disruption, transformation, and reinvention

I

Focuses on how data is the driving force behind the reinvention, transformation, and disruption, impacting every industry today. This affects how companies benefit from improved agility and faster time to insight in visual discovery—and why data visualization is key to working with and understanding bigger and more diverse and dynamic data.

Separating leaders from laggards

"The world is being re-shaped by the convergence of social, mobile, cloud, big data, community and other powerful forces. The combination of these technologies unlocks an incredible opportunity to connect everything together in a new way and is dramatically transforming the way we live and work."
—Marc Benioff

Before we get too far ahead into data discovery and the beautiful science of data visualization—and how together these two concepts are reinventing today's approach to BI and emphasizing the need for organizations to create a visual culture of data discovery—it is worthwhile to frame the context for this book with a bit of a story about data. Specifically, about big data.

Once upon a time, several years ago, in a wee little Editor's Note I wrote for *RediscoveringBI* magazine, I managed to make the seemingly nonsensical leap of analogizing big data against my son's second favorite Avenger, the Hulk. Though that Note was written in the early months of 2013, my message still holds true today, perhaps even more so than it did before. Then—and now—"big data" is routinely being paired with proportionally "big" descriptions, like "innovative," "revolutionary," and (in my opinion, the mother of all big descriptors): "transformative." With the never-ending churn of cyber-journalism, industry events, and a growing body of analyst and academic literature on the subject, big data has spent the last couple of years firmly affixed atop buzzy headlines. Likewise, it has earned itself quite the reputation within the data community, replete with a stalwart following of pundits, early adopters, and those still eager to get their heads wrapped around how to use big data in their organizations. In fact, some might say that the whole "big data thing" has mutated into a sort of larger-than-life caricature of promise and possibility—and, lest we forget it, power.

So, at this point you can probably see where I am going with this Hulk analogy, but let us face it: big data is the Incredible Hulk of BI. It is gargantuan, brilliant, and—yes—sometimes even a bit hyper-aggressive. For many the mild-mannered, Bruce Banner-esque analyst out there, big data is—for better or worse—the remarkably regenerative albeit impulsive alter ego of the industry, eager to show with brute force just how much we can really do with our data—or, the tangible extent of all that big data power, so to speak. Yet, as with the inaugural debut of Stan Lee's destructive antihero in *The Incredible Hulk #1* in 1962, in 2016, we are only just now beginning to catch the first glimpses of what big data can really do.

While this is not a book about big data, it is almost impossible to write about data these days without talking about big data at some point, even if it is just a nod to the fact that not only big data is here, but it is here to stay—and it is going to keep getting bigger. More important, big data has ushered in an era of new opportunities to learn from and work with all this new and diverse information in new ways—and by a broader, more enabled group of people than ever before. Alongside the early mainstream adoption of big data, the data industry has also seen the emergence of data discovery as a complementary—if sometimes contradictory—component of traditional BI. Likewise, data visualization—along with visual data discovery and the growing concept of visual analytics—has leap-frogged from its resting place of those common, tried-and-true bar charts and pie graphs of old to a shiny new continuum of advanced data visualizations and a rekindled focus on the art of storytelling. With the Internet of Things quickly coming to fruition, it is no longer just a clever analogy—big data is the Hulk of BI and it is smashing apart the way we have been using data for decades.

This tidal wave of data is ultimately changing the way people experience data, and it is the catalyst that is spurring a period of rapid disruption, transformation, and reinvention that is fueling innovation in almost every industry today. In a nutshell, that is the focus of the first part of this book. We will begin with a look at how this era of disruption, transformation, and reinvention is mutating companies into visual, data-driven organizations, what the shift from BI to include discovery looks like, and how tools, technologies, and discovery-oriented cultures are expanding self-service into the realm of self-sufficiency for modern business analysts. And, because all of this change inevitably brings to light new concerns for the guidance of governance, privacy, and security in an increasingly data-dependent world, we will also touch on the emerging ethical quagmires and how to prepare incoming IT leaders and knowledge workers to navigate the data democracy, as well as how to gage the appropriate level of concern for big data ethical issues today.

1.1 AN ERA OF DISRUPTION, TRANSFORMATION, AND REINVENTION

Thanks to the digital business transformation, the world around us is changing—and quickly—to a very consumer- and data-centric economy, where companies must transform to remain competitive and survive.

Yes, it is a bold statement, but it is also very true. For companies today, it is a full-on Darwinian experience of survival of the fittest. Never mind the mass influx of new and diverse data flooding in from every direction—we all know that is happening. What we may not realize, however, is how much influence the Internet, mobile, and the toy box of highly interconnected social platforms have on the reinvention of industries all around us. From auto insurance to media and entertainment, today's most data-driven companies are proving, time and time again, that the entire body of industry is undergoing a period of explosive disruption that we simply cannot ignore. We see this in the way business models are changing, in how organizations are interacting directly with their customers, or even simply in the new breeds of companies that are springing up and changing the nature of their industries. To the latter, one top-of-mind example is Uber, a company that is—at least according to its website—"evolving the way the world moves." Unlike taxi services of the past, Uber connects riders to drivers through an app. In one tap, Uber uses your phone's GPS to detect your location and connect you with the nearest driver via a mapping and pricing algorithm that is often cheaper than metered taxis (unless you hit a surge pricing moment, like at rush hour or on a holiday) and generally always in a much cleaner vehicle. While Uber is changing the game for commuters needing a quick ride, it is also reshaping the taxi economy from the inside out, too. For example, cities like New York City sell a limited number of "medallions" that give car owners the right to operate taxis. These limited-supply medallions have been known to go for more than $1 million each. In the traditional model, taxi companies recoup their investments by renting their vehicles to drivers, gouging meter prices for riders, and giving as little monies back to their drivers as possible. Uber, instead, simply requires drivers to have a late model car and a clean driving record, and passes on a cut of each fare—no million dollar medallion needed. They give their drivers flexibility too: drivers can choose when they want to drive by simply switching their app on or off (Edwards, 2014). This is data-driven disruption, transformation, and reinvention, plain and simple.

If we boil it down to its simplest form, we could proclaim that companies looking to upsurge their disruptive fitness need to follow three steps: understand business disruption, build capabilities by design, and deliver a platform of speed. But first—and arguably more important—we need to approach the conversation by taking off the rose colored glasses of analytic possibility and thinking about how companies need to work in today's marketplace. This is the part of the conversation that should precede any decisions about action—the part about change and vision. We can talk all day about BI or big data or analytics, but the reality is that the business itself needs new capabilities in order to be competitive with those leading-edge companies that are paving the way of reinvention. This reinvention is not a by-product of technology either. Technologies—like Hadoop, the cloud (public, private, or otherwise)—is just that: technology. There are no silver bullet solutions to become suddenly a better data-centric company, and there are solutions lurking around the corner looking to sell you a magic bean for a problem that does not yet need solving. Instead, once you understand your business' disruption model, then you can design the most appropriate data architecture and bring in the technology you need to enable it as a platform.

It is the old wisdom of not putting the cart before the horse. To understand change, you must first understand why you need to change, and then how to make that change happen. Data and reinvention aside, this is the premise of change leadership, and reminds me of one of my favorite quotes from Simon Sanek's *Start With Why*, a book I encourage all of my graduate students studying leadership to read early on in their studies. In the introduction to his book, Sanek says "there are leaders, and there are those who lead" (Sanek, 2011, p. 5). Today's most disruptive consumer- and data-centric companies are not those who are merely seeking to be leaders in their respective industries. They are the ones who are looking to lead their industries.

With that in mind, let us talk about the power of disruption.

1.1.1 UNDERSTAND DISRUPTION

To understand the power of disruption, we first need to understand what a digital life looks like now, compared to what it looked like before. Most of us are connected to our devices (yes, plural devices) and sharing and generating much more data than we realize—and that data is being used. I would wager to bet that those of you reading right this second have at least one device on you, maybe more. Smart phones, fit bits or other wearables, tablets…? What about those of you readers who have chosen the e-book format of this text over the paperback? On top of that, how many readers are multi-tasking and juggling reading with some kind of social activity (if you are, please tweet "@lindy_ryan's new #dataviz book is G8"—just for fun)? This is not an idle guess: a 2012 Pew survey of 2,254 people found that 52% of all cell phone owners said that they multitasked on their mobile devices while watching TV. This is known as "media multitasking," and involves using the TV, web, radio, telephone, or any other media in conjunction with another in simultaneous use (Reardon, 2012). (It is not necessarily a good thing, either, with a growing body of research on cognitive distraction in multitasking springing up since 2009.)

Likewise, we have to understand the new generation of "connected consumers"— the digital natives and the millennials, who are staking a bigger claim in the influencer pool of innovation just as much as the surprisingly tech-savvy older generations. (I can say that because, before she passed away my 70-year old grandmother somehow had a larger Facebook following than I do. I tease about this number often, when giving data presentations at data events, and it never fails to get at least a few surprised looks from the audience.)

Of course, in theory this paradigm shift is not unlike those that have happened before. Consider back when getting an email address was all the rage. I remember staying up many late nights listening to the sound of dialup logging into AOL, just so I could troll chat rooms. It is a little traumatizing to realize that the first major commercial Internet Service Providers (ISPs) hit the scene in the early 1990s; 1995 was the year of AOL, Prodigy, and CompuServe, and webmail services (like Hotmail) starting coming around in 1996–97. By late 1996, about one in ten Americans were on the Internet (Manjoo, 2009)—and that was already twenty—yes, twenty—years ago. Today, one email address still is not the norm—but for a completely different reason. For example, between work, personal, university, and other various social email addresses I have something like half a dozen different digital contact methods (not including phone, SMS or MMS messaging, or social media handles). On the other end of the spectrum, some digital natives do not even bother with email addresses because there are so many "other" ways to connect with someone online: you can text, tweet, Facebook Message, Skype, Snapchat, etc. Who would have thought, in 1997, that email would be the old-timers digital communication method? Kids these days!

The point is, simply: today's digital natives are even more digital than we could have anticipated them to be before (and, often times also more digitally naïve about the risk of data and sharing too much information—the dark side of the Internet). Thus, we will need to learn how to experiment and move fast to meet those digitally demanding needs. Here, we can all take a lesson from learning to think like a start-up—something that is counterintuitive to many of us. But, we often hear about big companies that recognize how big they are, so they find a separate building down the street, rent it, and staff it with their creative thinkers. It is a haven for innovation—the "stay hungry for new ideas" model versus the "protect what we have" model. Think about it, big guys: your competitors are moving fast, and you do not have choice. As industry after industry is getting shaken out in the wake of change, you have to innovate before you can optimize. It is the time to move fast, find a market, hone a product, take advantage of lean product development, and worry about optimizing later. This is not the age of the tortoise and the hare, where the lovable, sluggish tortoise wins the race with diligence and determination. In the digital culture, speed—a necessary prerequisite for disruption—wins over perfection. It is an era of creative destruction: capture the market base with first mover advantage, move in and own it while your competitors try to catch up, and then create enough upheaval that when you leave—before anyone can show up second—you have made your success almost impossible to duplicate. That is the core premise of disruption: an unreproducible innovation that creates a new market or value network, eventually disrupting an existing market and displacing what came before.

Netflix, the subject of my graduate thesis on creative destruction, is the poster-child for this disruptive innovation—or, as Hurst (2002) calls it, ethical anarchy, wherein disruptors become pioneers and then owners of a market. In later examples of data-driven companies, Netflix will be at the top of our discussions. Of course, Netflix is not alone on the list of disruptive companies that have become impressively consumer- and data-centric and are now thriving in the very digital culture that they have created for themselves. There are so many familiar stories we could talk about that it is almost hard to choose a reasonable few. But, later in this chapter, we will talk about four—Netflix, Facebook, Starbucks, and Amazon—and I will share the data on why these companies are, arguably, the Fantastic Four of disruption.

1.1.2 BUILD CAPABILITIES BY DESIGN

In chapter: The Importance of Visual Design, we will discuss—in great detail—how today's data-centric companies are leveraging tools and technologies to capitalize on their data and earn a place as a disruptor by building data capabilities by design. Within that conversation, I will detail how these companies are balancing user intuition and self-service with high-performance for actionable insights; how they are facilitating increased time to data insight with tools that provide speed, agility, and self-sufficiency; and, how they are powering that discovery process with visualization, collaboration, and mobility. But, in this chapter the point I want to make is this: that building capabilities is—like the header suggests—by design. Transforming into customer- and data-centric organization does not happen by accident.

Disruptors are discovery-oriented. While we still need traditional data models and BI, discovery is that fail-fast, iterative, and agile process that takes us from information to insight in a more proactive, real-time, actionable way. And, it is experimental—a process of continuous learning and improvement.

One of the most data-driven, discovery-oriented companies out there is Google—the data giant with the search engine front-end that has ruined us forever with the expectation of typing in a search prompt and receiving 11 million records in less than one second. Do not believe it? Here is proof (Figure 1.1).

Here is what Google, in its technology overview, has to say for itself: "The software behind our search technology conducts a series of simultaneous calculations requiring only a fraction of a second. Traditional search engines rely heavily on how often a page appears on a web page. We use more than 200 signals, including our patented PageRank algorithm, to examine the entire link structure of the web and determine which pages are most important. We then conduct hypertext-matching analysis to determine which pages are relevant to the specific search being conducted. By combining overall importance and query-specific relevance, we are able to put the most reliable and relevant results first."

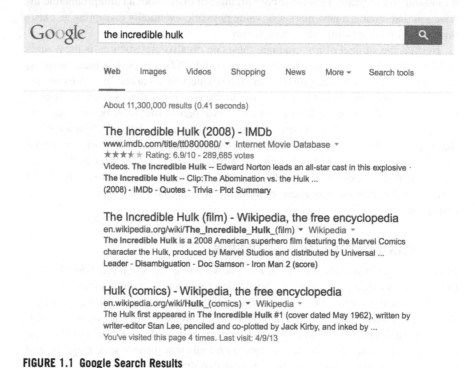

FIGURE 1.1 Google Search Results

A search prompt of "The Incredible Hulk" returned about 11,300,000 results in 0.41 s

The even crazier thing is that we are happy with what Google gives us—even if it is wrong! And, with every click on that back button and refinement of our search criteria, we are effectively helping Google, and its monster of a machine-learning algorithm, to learn.

Can you take this same psychological principle and apply it to BI? Or to discovery? The wrong answer is okay, when you can be iterative quickly enough to fail fast and try again. Failure is not typically a word that conjures up positive feelings, but in the discovery-oriented culture required for disruption, there is a change in mindset that needs to happen. In discovery, failure is okay—so long as there is learning and, therefore, increased value, involved. Google's search engine learns and improves its value with each "failed" search result that a human corrects the next time around. Google Translate—which is arguably better than other translation software that have had the benefit of decades of work and millions of dollars invested—follows this same approach: humans correct translation errors and Google learns at big data speed with human parallelism. This is that "not by accident" attitude—data-centric companies must be ready and willing to be exploratory and to play with new ideas and new paths. It is kind of like scouring the web via Google—half the time I put a prompt in with no idea what exactly I am looking for, but I know it when I see it. In many ways, data discovery is the same.

When we talk about building capabilities by design, there are a set of four core capabilities that you should keep in mind:

- *Designed for self-sufficiency*: Enable an environment where the business user is capable of acquiring, blending, presenting, and visualizing their data discoveries. IT needs to move away from being command and control to being an information broker in a new kind of business-IT partnership that removes barriers, so that users have more options, more empowerment, and greater autonomy.
- *Designed for collaboration*: Have tools and platforms that allow people to share and work together on different ideas for review and contribution. This further closes that business-IT gap, establishes transparency, and fosters a collective learning culture.
- *Designed for visualization*: Data visualizations have been elevated to a whole new form of communication that leverages cognitive hardwiring, enriches visual discovery, and helps tell a story about data to move from understanding to insight.
- *Designed for mobility*: It is not enough to be just able to consume information on mobile devices, instead users must be able to work and play with data "on the go" and make discovery a portable, personalized experience.

Ultimately, building capabilities by design is a mechanism with the purpose of increasing value generation not just from data, but also from the people working and interacting with the data. While there will be always be a population of people within your organization that just want to consume data, expand the potential of those who do want to strap on their fedoras of exploration and be insight discoverers.

Of course, as Spiderman's Uncle Ben famously said (and that is my last superhero reference, I promise) "with great power comes great responsibility," and questions of governance are inevitably going to come into play. This is not only the governance of people, roles, and responsibilities, but also governance of insights themselves, and—in my opinion—governance of data visualizations as unique information assets. But for now, let us put a pin in the governance conversation and save it for Part III.

1.1.3 ENABLE A PLATFORM OF SPEED

Lastly, as a criterion for disruption, let us again revisit speed, which is a recurring theme throughout the entirety of this book.

Alongside the awareness of the digital culture, and the capabilities needed to be a disruptor, today's customer- and data-centric companies keep three truths close to the heart. These are:

1. They collect data from everywhere. And, they start with the business goal, then work backwards to imagine the data needed to reach that goal.
2. They focus their analytics culture around four key areas: customer insights, product insights, optimization, and—obviously—innovation.
3. They act on analytics as a source of both continuous improvement and action.

So, what platform are you going to put this on? With Hadoop, an ever-increasing amount of As-A-Service models, and the expected differences in every IT culture—what do we do? Where do we even start? I mentioned before that technology is just technology, and that there will always be shiny new technologies available to play with to meet analytical goals. But, consider that speed is the most important element when evaluating technology decisions and drafting that architectural roadmap. Remember, speed does not just equal fast. Whatever the technologies chosen, a platform of speed must be (1) built to change, (2) should utilize the polyglot persistence approach (or, use the right database for its strengths), and (3) should put a premium on data unification to give users one "go to" place to navigate, understand, and access information. While there is not one platform to rule them all, there should be one cohesive platform of speed within your organization—or, as we call it: a true Modern Data Platform.

Think about it this way: we do not search the Internet for information. The Internet, while made up of millions of computers, from a platform perspective is a single (and proper) noun. This is how organizations need to think—not as silos of information, but as a Platform—with a capital P.

1.2 CHARACTERISTICS OF DATA-CENTRIC COMPANIES

In the section before we talked about the era of transformation and reinvention, about building capabilities for disruption, and about keeping the premise of speed at the top of the priority list. Much of this is not a simple recipe for change that, with a detailed ingredient list, we can stop off at the local market to scoop up. Instead, it hinges upon putting the right chef in the kitchen to make that vision a reality and change the way we think about our business, and our data. For example, Gordon Ramsey is not going to be the guy you get to run your hotdog and pretzel concession stand at the local ballpark. He is the master chef, who is going to have the skills, aptitudes, and mindset to launch that successful new five-star restaurant in Beverly Hills that all the A-listers flock to. For data-centric companies to earn the competitive advantage they need to survive in the era of disruption and innovation, a mindset change to thinking like a data-centric company is just as important as any tool or technology adopted to make it happen.

The mainstream adoption of Hulky big data is starting. Now, it is time to figure out what to do with all this data—and how to exploit it for competitive advantage.

Ultimately, companies use data—big or not—to solve business problems. The customer-oriented, data-centric company, however, does not just treat data as an asset—it treats data as gold—and they are willing to pay for it, too. Many data-centric companies do not even look like data-centric companies at first glance. Like Google's search engine or Amazon's online retail platform, which masquerade as "service providers" first, though what they are really doing is providing free services with the end goal of collecting data. Amazon pioneered this strategy of collecting and exploiting data by layering user data on top of open ISBN data to create new value—they do not own ISBN numbers, but they created the metadata to go on top and developed one of the best recommendation algorithms out there, killing off Borders (who outsourced its e-commerce model) in the meantime.

Other companies design loyalty programs to drive data collection. These are those customer rewards programs at grocery stores or gas stations, or at casinos or popular chain restaurants that are forever giving away free appetizers or desserts. By offering discounts on seemingly random products or by providing immediate 3-cent savings at the pump, they are literally paying their customers to provide data by enrolling in their user loyalty programs. Every time you swipe that card or stick it in a slot machine, you are telling that company where you are, how much you are spending, and what you like. (Conversely, you could look at opting-out—or, not signing up for the saver card—as incurring a privacy tax: you are paying full price to keep your data to yourself).

It might seem a stretched statement to say that data-centric equates to competitive advantage. However, there are competitive advantages earned by data-centric companies that are truly revolutionizing their respective industries. Here is how they do it:

1.2.1 THEY ARE DATA HARVESTERS

Data-centric companies collect and harvest data from everywhere. One of the "old ways" of thinking in BI was to ask what data was already available, and how to integrate the data to define metrics or map it to an already pre-defined metric. Data-centric companies tackle that question another way—instead of figuring out how to use what data is already available to answer metrics, they begin with first addressing the business problem that needs to be solved, then imagine the data needed—and then go out and find it or create it through new apps (like mobile) or collection agents. For these companies, data is not merely an asset. It is not even gold—it is (as my colleague John O'Brien often calls it) oxygen.

Data-centric companies are willing to do whatever it takes (ideally within ethical reason—more in chapter: Navigating Ethics in the Big Data Democracy) to get data. They leverage external public and purchased data, big data, …—whatever data through whatever means necessary, including internal sources, mobile apps, wearables, sensors, and so on.

They will buy data—they will even give away services for free, like Google's search engine or free downloadable apps for your mobile device that collect data every time you crush a piece of candy or check a movie show time in your neighborhood. Even a weather app can bring in untapped value. Being a data harvester is simply the willingness to collect every piece of data about your customers and people, any way you can, in order to gain insights about existing customers and relate that to future customers.

1.2.2 THEY LIVE AN ANALYTIC CULTURE

Data-centric companies create (and live and breathe, that oxygen metaphor from above) within an analytic culture—and they make it look easy, too. This analytic culture can be broken down into three categories.

Insight: Mining, clustering, and using segmentation to understand customers, their networks, and—more important—their influence, as well as product insights (for competing products too).

Optimization: Of business functions, processes, products, and models through the use of analytics.

Innovation: To discover new and disruptive business models that stay true to company brand but provide pathways to foster the evolution and growth of customer base throughout the entire customer lifecycle.

One of the mainstays of the data-centric culture is to drop biases. Look for the data, and derive correlations from there. Or, ask not what you can do for your data, but what your data can do for you. This is the reason that Best Buy is still here today while Circuit City is not: Best Buy embraced analytics to understand what their customer buy patterns were and recognized that an overwhelming majority of revenue was coming in from a relatively small segment of its customer demographic. Therefore, they started stocking the products that their customer demographic wanted to buy (like appliances), rather than what the store had previously been designed to sell (like CDs).

Two of my favorite examples of living an analytic culture come from the wearables community. Recently, Disney introduced its MagicBand, a bracelet-like device that provides an all-in-one room key, credit card, and FastPass (to skip those pesky waiting lines) for its wearers. They come in various colors (mine is orange, my son's is blue) and you can even have your name inscribed on them or accessorize them with little buttons of Disney characters. They provide value to the consumer, yes, but a considerably larger value to the parks. These MagicBands are a data-generating instrument system about everyone in the park for Disney to collect data and learn from. They can see where people are in the park, what they are buying, how long they are waiting in line—all kinds of handy information that Disney can use to improve the park experience and earn more revenue while nudging out their competition. Another example is what Apple is doing for scientific research with its devices, including the new Apple Watch. In March 2015, Apple introduced open-source software ResearchKit, which gives developers a platform for apps that collect health data by accessing the millions of bits of health data on users' iPhones (like the accelerometer) or the Watch (which can measure heart rate changes). In the press release, Jeff Williams, Apple's senior vice president of Operations was quoted as saying "ResearchKit gives the scientific community access to a diverse, global population and more ways to collect data than ever before" (Apple, 2015). The ultimate story point here: companies collect human behavior data to support analytics—and perhaps, as in the case of Facebook, to debunk so many psychology theories with the comment "who knows why people do what they do, we simply have the data to prove it."

1.2.3 THEY THINK LONG TERM

Data-centric companies find ways to perpetuate lifetime value through the acquisition of new, multi-generational customers. Remember: the data you have now only shows a snapshot of your current environment. Thinking data-centric is thinking long-term. It is looking for patterns in the data to see where your company is, sure, but more important to look at where it is going, and then developing a plan to work toward getting there.

To data-centric companies, thinking long-term means thinking about multigenerational customer engagement. These companies maintain a high brand-to-customer focus, where the brand itself is largely defined by the customer's sentiment and influence. For the customer, the relationship to the brand is a connection assembled through experience. Eventually brand loyalty becomes customer loyalty. Customer analytics should be used to identify and nurture potential valuable customers that can be engaged as lifelong customers. Further, data-centric companies should not expect customers to be loyal to the brand, but should instead focus on being loyal to their customers.

One industry in particular that is spending a lot of time thinking long-term about its lifetime customers is the casino and gaming industry. Think about all the different kinds of people you see in a casino: young and old, different ethnicities, cultures, income brackets. Each one of those people falls into a different customer segmentation, and yet each one is still having a great time and handing over their data to the casino. And, with customer analytics, the casino is able to keep all of those customer segments engaged through targeted offers, floor layout, game options, and so on. It is like that quote from *A Field of Dreams*: if you built it, they will come. With long-term thinking and a focus on lifetime customer engagement, data-centric companies can extend that to: if you build it, they will come—and if you build it right, they will keep coming back.

I am not much of a gambler, but this same type of long term customer loyalty from my brands is why I buy books from Amazon, though I spend weekends at Barnes and Noble perusing book shelves, flipping through titles, sipping coffee—and inevitably walking out the door with something in a green and white bag. I buy books on Amazon because I can trust that they will offer me the best price on the same book, but I still shop at Barnes and Noble because they are going to give me a great bookstore experience. They sell books, yes, but they are thinking long term about their customers by bringing in cafes, better Wi-Fi, in-store eBook kiosks, etc. and making sure to keep showing loyalty to customers through that more traditional in-store experience.

1.2.4 THEY TAKE ACTION

Finally, data-centric companies act on analytics. Data without action holds no value on its own: it is the action that drives the business value. Acting on analytics is not a one-time thing either, but instead a continuous process of experimentation and improvement. Improving analytic models is important as the data underneath is continually changing, too.

For a quick example, refer back to my earlier comment on the untapped value of the weather app. At a recent client event in Reno, Nevada, we asked attendees how many weather apps they had on their smartphones. Many—at least a quarter of the room—noted they had more than one. I have four, and I use them all—one for quick reference, one for detail, one to figure out what I should wear, and the other to evaluate whether I should be carrying an umbrella or not. Recently, I noticed that my quick-reference app started adding in more hour-by-hour data, and my what-to-wear app started adding accessories. Therein lies the rub: having multiple analytic engines drives competition, and competition drives improvement.

1.2.5 AND, THEY STAY CONNECTED

Becoming a data-centric company requires an inevitable cultural change to achieve competitive advantage. Through competing on analytic abilities, companies can build deeper understandings of customers and relationships. Think about the data you collect today—and then realize that the activity you capture today (probably) is not enough. Being data-centric means going the extra mile in the way you interact with your data.

And, last of all, data-centric companies stay connected to their customers. This is another tick mark in the pro-mobile column. The more mobile you can be, the more opportunity for data—the more access you have to a hyperconnected generation. Mobility is a way to instrument customers, too. Today, through mobile apps, customer's "public personas" are available through APIs. And, mobile is a "me"-phenomenon: it is a direct line to a customer's most selfish desires—what they like, what they hate, what they want, and what they are willing to say about it all. This social and behavioral data tells us about customer interests and actions, and thus the best ways to make them happy. Mobility provides a plethora of opportunities to influence and engage customers—by pushing advertisements, and offers, connecting in real-time on social media, or by being a part of their sharing experiences in hashtags and photos, or engaging directly online. One example is how true[X] Media (previously SocialVibe) is reimagining low-performing ads in a shorter, more interactive paradigm to engage directly with customers through digital ads. Through engagement advertising, true[X] delivers ad units that are self-selected by the viewer in exchange for unlocking online content (ie, music, videos, articles, etc.). Taking over the browser for approximately 30 seconds, the ad requires human participation (eg, a survey, like, share, or so forth) for completion. This quick and interactive mode was not only more preferred by the audience, but it also gave advertisers more ability to learn from the engagement data gathered by the online ad—and reduce fraud, a big problem in the digital ad industry (Kantrowitz, 2014).

Today's hyperconnected customers are always on the go, and they love to capture their experiences—this is why apps like Twitter, Snapchat, Instagram, etc. are so prolific. If you need any further convincing about the connected power of mobile, consider what happened to HBO and Showtime at the 2015 Floyd Mayweather and Manny Pacquiao fight. As the year's biggest fight, viewers could pay to watch the show for $100 on cable, or they could use Twitter's streaming business Periscope to broadcast unauthorized live feeds of the event for free. Naturally, this was not what Periscope was intended to be used for, but nevertheless, in a Costolo tweet, Periscope was pronounced the fight's winner (Shaw, 2015). (This was not the first time Periscoped usurped an event either: in April of 2015, Game of Thrones fans streamed the show on Periscope and Meerkat, too).

1.3 EXAMPLES OF DATA-DRIVEN COMPANIES

All this talk about customer- and data-centric companies might be for naught, if we did not take time to review how those Fantastic Four companies I identified earlier—Netflix, Facebook, Starbucks, and Amazon—are putting those principles into practice.

The next section of this chapter will take a deeper look into how each of these companies are capitalizing on creative destruction, market transformation, and customer-centric focuses to reinvent their respective industries. Many of these are familiar stories, but there may be some details you have not thought of before that lend a fresh perspective.

1.3.1 NETFLIX

Having spent a good six months of my life writing, editing, and polishing my graduate thesis on Netflix for publication, the on-demand streaming video service is one near and dear to my heart. And, there are so many interesting things about Netflix, and the way it is reinventing the media experience to talk about—starting with the fact that it was originally named Kibble.com (yes, like the dog food), as a reminder that "no matter how good the advertising, it's not a success if the dogs don't eat the dog food" (Randolph, 2011). To a 2015 study by the University of Texas that suggested a connection between binge watching streaming media, like Netflix, with behaviors associated with depression (though the survey only included a sample size of 316 people and "binge watching" was considered a measly two or more episodes (Rutsch, 2015)).

The entertainment industry is one that is not only rapidly reshaping, but is getting completely overhauled. From yesterday's broadcast, to cable, to online video and video on-demand, companies like Netflix, Hulu, and Amazon Prime have repioneered the way we watch television and movies. The first of these, Netflix disrupted its industry in a big way. In my thesis written in 2012, I wrote: "From humble beginnings as a dot.com startup in 1997, Netflix has redefined the video-rental market and become a giant-toppling industry leader with 24 million subscribers (Ryan, 2013, p. 429)." In January 2015—just a few years after the creative destruction of the "Qwikster disaster" that seemed like it would destroy Netflix's stronghold with an almost immediate stock landslide topping 57% (Ryan, 2013)—subscriber numbers have almost doubled, bringing the total number of Netflix subscribers to 57.4 million worldwide (Gensler, 2015).

Now that Netflix has reshaped how we watch media, it is reinventing what media we watch—or, orchestrating the full circle of the customer experience "from the moment they [customers] sign up, for the whole time they are with us [Netflix] across TV, phone and laptop" (Sweney, 2014, para. 3). With microsegmentation, Netflix is creating shows scientifically formulated to meet customer demands. Case and point for this is House of Cards—which Netflix reportedly sunk $100 million into production without even seeing a pilot (Sweney, 2014). It is not just Kevin Spacey that makes House of Cards such a win either: it is the data behind it—a meticulous analysis on subscriber data that basically guarantees its success.

One New York Times columnist called the show a Venn diagram of the director (David Fincher), the actor (Kevin Spacey), and the British version of the same show; another called it a data-driven holy grail for a hit TV show. Whatever you call it, on its release, House of Cards was the most streamed piece of content in the United States and 40 other countries (Carr, 2013).

1.3.2 FACEBOOK

If Benjamin Franklin might have been around in today's era of digital-dependency to coin that iconic phrase "there are only two things certain in life: death and taxes" he might have rephrased it to be "death, taxes, and social media." Like home computers and email addresses in the past, social media platforms—like Twitter, Instagram, Pinterest, and Facebook—are so ubiquitous in our every day lives that the absence of them in our social repertoires is almost counterculture to the highly inter-connected and social ways of communication today.

BOX 1.1 THE SOCIAL MEDIA ADDICTION

When graphic designer and self-proclaimed "casual Facebook user" Chelsea Carlson decided to quit Facebook, the results she got were not the ones she was expecting.

Curious if the size of a data set was less important than the question she was asking of it, Carlson first got the idea to deactivate her personal Facebook account when she thought she had stopped using it for social reasons—arguably the purpose of the platform to begin with—and was, instead, simply engaging out of habit and passively taking in information rather than participating in the social experiment. She wanted to collect a small, personal data set by hand and look for ways to improve or understand her decisions by tracking and visualizing various areas of her daily social habits. By collecting data on how she was really using Facebook, Carlson hoped she could apply the study on a tiny scale for personal impact and become more cognizant of her social interactions online.

The experiment was simple: Carlson deactivated her account—a bit of a hassle as Facebook does everything it can, from using pictures of friends to beg you to stay to putting you through the hoops of a deactivation questionnaire to convince you to stay—replaced her 3rd party social logins, and started to record every day and time she "needed" to log in, as well as the reason she was visiting the site (Figure 1.2).

The results of the experiment were interesting. When she began sifting through the data, Carlson found that it fit neatly within four core categories: absentminded visits, social visits, 3rd party logins, and missed news event. When she put her data into form, she chose to visualize her experiment as an outlet to present the personal data in a way that she found personally interesting—and that told a story about her experience. Thus, she chose a clock-type graph to display the rings of day and time to quantify the passing of time over her eleven days offline. By exploring the rings of her clock, it is easy to notice that the number one reason Carlson visited Facebook was simply out of habit.

While the data itself was interesting, the emotional journey through the experiment proved just as compelling. First, was Facebook's emotional plea to keep users online, which sparks the curious question of how many people abandon deactivation (perhaps an idea for another study?). Next, was the empowerment Carlson felt when she replaced all of her social logins to avoid sharing all that extra data with 3rd party sources. Freedom!

Of course, the short-term benefit for Carlson was that she effectively broke her absent-auto habit of logging into Facebook. The long-term benefit was that she is more aware of how she uses the social media platform, and it has provided her with personal guardrails to gage her social interactions.

More on Carlson's Facebook experience can be found online at: https://www.umbel.com/blog/data-visualization/11-days-deactivated/

It is not a big secret that Facebook is a stealthy data giant that has, in the decade since its inception, reinvented (or, perhaps more accurately, actively defined) what social networks are. The ability to connect with people we know—or once knew—meet new people, share pictures and details about our lives, stay updated on social news headlines, and so on tickles the very fancy of our intrinsically gregarious and attention-loving nature. It has become so engrained in our behaviors that we almost do not know how to live without social media and Facebook anymore (see Box 1.1 *The Social Media Addiction*). However, while Facebook's purpose is to help everyone connect, stay in touch, and meet new people within their ever-growing peer networks, it relies on data and algorithms—like the famous EdgeRank—to highlight and offer connections that may be most aligned with each individual's interests, and to publish ads that monetize the social media machine. With the overwhelming amount of data it has collected on its millions of users, Facebook has become one of

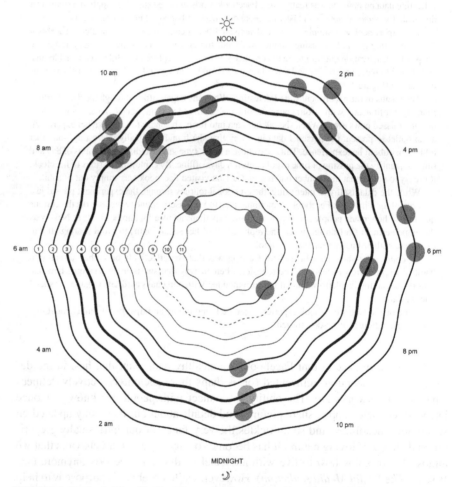

11 Days Deactivated

A little data visualization about what you actually miss when you quit Facebook for 11 days.

LEAST VISITS ┤├ MOST VISITS ⑦ DAY OF EXPERIMENT

● SOCIAL   ● SOCIAL LOGIN   ● NEWS   ● ABSENTMINDED VISIT

FIGURE 1.2 Carlson's Visualization Shows the Frequency of her Visits as Well as her Intended Reasons for Visiting the Social Media Site her 11 Days of Social Media Deactivation

(Source: With permission from Umbel, 2015).

the largest repositories of personal data. Let me put "largest repositories" into a bit more context. Facebook has its own modified version of Hadoop with geographically distributed clusters that store upward of 300 PB of Hive data, with an incoming rate of about 600 TB per day. In the last year alone, the warehouse has seen a 3× growth in the amount of data stored (Facebook, 2014).

Facebook has so much personal data, in fact, that a recent blog headline on (Newman, 2015) came with the title of *Big Data: Why Facebook Knows Us Better Than Our Therapist*. This was on the heels of an early 2015 social psychology study out of the University of Cambridge and Stanford University that concluded that Facebook could more accurately predict our personality than could a bevy of close friends, family, and even possibility our therapist(s)—all because of the power of intelligent insight into the data. This level of potentially invasive personal insight, however, is not too far from realizing those longstanding worries over Big Brother-esque privacy concerns, and the reason why things like Facebook's recent high-profile study on users' emotions sparked some heavy duty soul-searching and calls for better ethical guidelines and user privacy in an increasingly public online world (more on privacy and ethics in chapter: Navigating Ethics in the Big Data Democracy). Of course, remember again that we are actively—and willingly—giving Facebook that personal data through our click interactions: every time we like a page, make a post, or take one (or seventeen) of those addictive online quizzes.

1.3.3 STARBUCKS

Like most good American millennials and businesspeople, I love my coffee. Hot, cold, or blended, chances are most of us like coffee in one form or another. Or we like tea, whether it is mixed with milk or steeped in boiling water. If not coffee or tea, then we like pastries, or acoustic tunes, or working remotely in a relaxing atmosphere. Luckily for us all, one of the nation's largest coffee chains—Starbucks—is also an innovative, data-centric company that knows how to connect with its customers. And, while Starbucks may not take the "best coffee" blue ribbon from coffee snobs everywhere, what it may lack in flavor it makes up for in a coffeehouse experience. In fact, Starbucks is giving that experience to customers in over 20,000 places: a quick search online shows that Starbucks had 21,366 Starbucks stores around the world as of 2014.

From its newest products (like the mini Frappuccino, which is both cute and delicious), to its desirable Starbucks Gold Card, to scouting locations for its next retail stores, Starbucks is using data to dominate its market: the coffeehouse experience. Starbucks leadership has long considered their coffeehouse as the "third place" (Michelli, 2014, p. 158)—an environment positioned directly following its customer's first place—home—and their second place, work. Today, that third place view has been widened to engage customers in their first and second places (think home-brew and kiosk stores in high-traffic work zones, like hospitals and book stores), as well as via their mobile devices.

At the core of Starbucks' digital strategy are several interrelated areas: commerce; company-owned web and mobile channels, loyalty/customer relationship management and targeted databases; social media; and paid digital marketing (Michelli, 2014). But, the anchor of Starbucks' current mobile strategy is its loyalty program—the Starbucks Card—which itself represents a multibillion-dollar business as both a gift card and prepayment mechanism.

As of Q1 2013, Starbucks had a total of 6 million registered loyalty program customers profiled, with approximately 80,000 new members joining each week (Bashin, 2013). More important: a quarter of all transactions at Starbucks were made with loyalty cards, giving Starbucks more data than it knew what to do with but a whole lot of room to grow into. Joe LaCugna, director of analytics and business intelligence at Starbucks was quoted as saying, "We [Starbucks] know who you are. We know how you're different from others." And how is Starbucks using this data? Well, not in the way you might expect. Rather than targeting offers at its best customers, Starbucks has been doing the opposite: targeting customers—using a combination of data gathering, analysis, and modeling approaches—whose purchasing habits show they might not be returning anytime soon, and sending them offers (Bashin, 2013). Looking ahead, Starbucks plans to use this same approach to personalize the look and feel of the company's website and mobile app based on their knowledge of the individual customer (Michelli, 2014).

Another interesting element Starbucks is bringing to its mobile customer loyalty program is gamification—engendered through multiple reward levels and a progression tracker that visually gives loyal coffee lovers incentive to engage with the brand as they watch virtual gold stars fall into a cup to show their progress to the next member hierarchy. (As another non-Starbucks example of beverage gamification, think about the new Coke dispensing machines in restaurants that allow customers to customize their drinks at the touch of a button on-screen. This is fun and exciting for customers, while Coca-Cola uses this data to analyze new product development and recommend "other favorite creations" on its menu.)

1.3.4 AMAZON

There are buckets of stories in the media about Amazon's rise to greatness, and for good reason. As one of the world's largest booksellers, Amazon commands the largest slice of the book-selling pie—65% in mid 2014—for both print and digital units (Milliot, 2014). Through Kindle, they have an even larger percentage of the eBook market. Traditional booksellers, like Barnes and Noble, have had to reshape the book buying experience (and e-commerce models) to keep pace with Amazon's market position and discounted book prices. But the most innovative way that Amazon is using data is not just for its prowess as an online book retailer—in fact, buying books online is relatively minor in the scope of what Amazon is doing with data today.

First, Amazon has an unrivalled bank of data on online consumer purchasing behavior—data that we, as consumers, have given to Amazon through our activities while we browse their site. This is the horsepower behind Amazon's recommendation engine that suggests products to shoppers using data mined from its 150+ million customer accounts. Earlier in 2003, Amazon used item-item similarity methods from collaborative filtering to build this engine; today it is complemented with customer click-stream data and historical purchase data to give its users customized results on customized web pages. Amazon then monitors, tracks, and secures the 1.5 billion items in its retail store in a product catalogue data warehouse in Amazon S3. This catalog receives more than 50 million updates a week and every 30 minutes all data received is crunched and reported back to the different warehouses and the website. Then, there is Amazon Web Services (AWS), which—besides being used by large companies like Dropbox, Netflix, and Yelp—also hosts public big data sets. Some big data sets, including the data from mapping the Humane Genome Project, are even available for free public use in AWS cloud-based solutions.

Of course, Amazon has been criticized for some of its more ruthless business tactics, like introducing the price check app, which lets users scan barcodes from anywhere and instantly compare the in-store price to what is listed on Amazon. While its consumers are receiving the value of getting more information instantly, they are also contributing to Amazon's competitive intelligence model and providing the retailer with exact details on what their competitors are doing, too. And, because of what they are doing with big data (and how they are monetizing it), Amazon's top competitors—Google and Facebook—may not be the companies you expect.

1.4 FROM THE DATA TO THE DASHBOARD

If you want to distill the previous yarn about disruption, transformation, and reinvention in the wake of big data into a single bite-sized takeaway, you can easily say that big data is reshaping how we do business today—and, at least on one level, that is true enough. But, when it comes to customer- and data-centric organizations like those Fantastic Four above, data itself—big or otherwise—is not the only thing that is propelling these companies to greatness. Beyond being just data-centric, or more analytically minded, or even more daring and ready to boldly go where no company (or industry) has gone before, the most data-driven companies are also those that embrace an ethos of data discovery and data visualization. They focus on empowering everyone (or, as many people as possible) within the organization to take part in their data-driven success by establishing a democratic culture of data discovery and cultivating a competency on data visualization as core information assets.

To add a bit of color to this conversation, think of discovery in the larger landscape of data. With the continued democratization of data today, information is increasingly becoming available to everyone who wants to reach out and grab it—and without having to dig deep into budget pockets or employ robust IT departments (the previous Big Iron of Big Data). This is especially big for small businesses, where the democratization of data is helping them catch up to some of the bigger and more data savvy players. With bigger data now being more approachable, smaller companies are empowered to easily and affordably—and regardless of technical prowess—access, collect, and analyze data to create new opportunities to earn insights about their markets and customers. Data democratization, through the emergence of web-based data collection and analysis services, new technologies, and savvy social marketing, is giving fast access to actionable insights to companies big and small.

Now, let us distill that larger data democracy down in a way that can be rearticulated within the confines of one organization. Rather than an open data buffet for companies big and small, think instead of departments large and small. Of users from power users to business analysts. Of data scientists to data consumers. This data availability is a key element of data discovery, which requires the ability to get up close and personal with data to explore, play, dig through, and uncover new relationships and insights. It requires flexibility and agility, but most important, it requires more people hands on in the discovery process to realize its full potential. Discovery is a numbers game at heart. It may take 99 iterations through the data to find one meaningful insight. And, that type of "fail fast" mentality requires a new breed of self-service that gives as many people as possible—and along the full spectrum of data users—the ability to have the tools, environment, and access to the data that they need to create and consume on the fly without being hindered by IT handcuffs or avoidable friction-causing activities. This is part of IT's new role—enablement technology—and part of a larger shift we are going to continue to watch in the industry. And, it is part of building a true data democracy within the organization.

Beyond that culture of democratic data discovery is also needed a cultivated competency on data visualization—which is the collective group of graphicacy techniques that are the petri dish for visual discovery and insight and a critical part in a visual culture for data discovery. By all means, I am not going to try to convince you that data visualization is new. It is not. In his paper "Data Visualization for Human Perception," Stephen Few pointedly wrote, "We have been arranging data into tables (columns and rows) at least since the second century C.E. However, the idea of representing quantitative information graphically didn't arise until the seventeenth century" (Few, 2014). Some of today's most "historical" data visualizations—like Florence Nightingale's Coxcomb Plot or John Snow's London Cholera Map—are so impactful because they illustrate how data visualization is a timeless method to being able to see and understand data more clearly.

Data visualization is a key part of how we can earn insights into our data. On that note, I want to take the opportunity to sidestep the bubble-like kludge of definitions that seems to plague the BI industry and offer a clear, level-set understanding of what I mean when I say "data visualization within a visual culture of data discovery." Data visualization is the practice of presenting data in visual—and in increasingly interactive, engaging, and mobile-optimized—ways—via charts, graphs, and other analytical formats. But when I talk about creating a visual culture of data discovery, the core of this is extended to include a balance of art (read: design), science (read: information), and organizational culture with a focus on earning insights, discoveries, and being able to visually communicate and tell stories with our data. The visual dimension of culture is becoming increasingly dominant—the definition of visual imperative—and this is a force that is driving the need to create a visual culture of data discovery. Data visualization then is a tool—a mechanism, if you will—to enable visual data discovery.

1.5 NAVIGATING THIS BOOK

In his book, *The Visual Organization*, my friend and fellow author Phil Simon (2014) writes: "unleashing the power of dataviz and Big Data requires that organization do much more than pay lip service to these topics." Though he and I articulate it differently, both Phil and I are beating the same drum. To be a truly data-centric organization requires action, rather than reaction. With advanced visualization capabilities and the ability to harness, integrate, and interact with massive amounts of disparate data for discovery, discovery tools must balance user intuition with high-performance capabilities for real-time insights—coupled with a premium on IT-independent user self-sufficiency for the masses. However, the competent data-driven organization must recognize the influence of visual communication, and the importance of architecting for visual discovery in people, processes, and technologies.

This book is not intended to be a guide to data visualization. There are many who have contributed amazing work in the holistic body of data discovery and visualization, including people like Edward Tufte, Stephen Few, and Nathan Yau, who have all written extensively on the mechanics of data visualization. There are others too, who have contributed stellar material in the academic study and scientific research of data visualization, visual analytics, and the related fields of visual design and cognitive science that I can only offer superficial discussions of. Still more have written highly technical masterpieces on data architectures, big data technologies, and data governance methodologies. This book, however, is not intended to be an exhaustive guide on any of those. Instead, in the following pages, I want to take you on a journey through the revolution of data discovery and visualization, and explore how these practices are fundamentally transforming the capabilities of the data-driven organization.

The book is organized into four parts, designed to take you, the reader, logically through the compounding topics to provide a guided journey through the people, processes, and technologies of visual discovery.

> Part I focuses on how data is the driving force behind the disruption, transformation, and reinvention impacting every industry today. This affects how companies benefit from improved agility and faster time to insight in visual discovery—and why data visualization is key to working with and understanding bigger and more diverse and dynamic data.
>
> Part II begins with a brief history on visual communication and the reinvigorated role of data visualization as an analysis and storytelling mechanism. Key design principles and data visualization best practices will

be reviewed. This section will also explore the data visualization continuum, with emphasis on exploratory and explanatory graphics, as well as the power of pictures in infographics and iconography.

Part III dives into the technical and organizational aspects of building the foundation for data discovery through people, processes, and technologies focused on enabling a culture of visual data discovery.

Finally, Part IV concludes by setting our sights on the future and exploring the approaching Internet of Things. It will highlight the need for data visualization in advanced technologies, including streaming and animated data, human-centered design in mobile strategies, the interconnected web of wearable devices and personal analytics, and peek into gameplay and playful data visualization fueled by machine learning and affective computing technologies.

REFERENCES

Apple, 2015. Apple introduces ResearchKit, giving medical researchers the tools to revolutionize medical studies [Press release]. Available from: http://www.apple.com/pr/library/2015/03/09Apple-Introduces-ResearchKit-Giving-Medical-Researchers-the-Tools-to-Revolutionize-Medical-Studies.html.

Bashin, K., 2013. Starbucks exec: "We know who you are, we know how you're different from others". Business Insider. Available from: http://www.businessinsider.com/starbucks-exec-on-loyalty-card-data-tracking-2013-3.

Carr, D., 2013. Giving viewers what they want. The New York Times. Available from: http://www.nytimes.com/2013/02/25/business/media/for-house-of-cards-using-big-data-to-guarantee-its-popularity.html?_r=0.

Edwards, J., 2014. Uber has changed my life and as God is my witness I will never take a taxi again (where available). Business Insider Tech. Available from: http://www.businessinsider.com/uber-has-changed-my-life-and-as-god-is-my-witness-i-will-never-take-a-taxi-again-where-available-2014-1.

Facebook, 2014. Scaling the Facebook data warehouse to 300 PB. Available from: https://code.facebook.com/posts/229861827208629/scaling-the-facebook-data-warehouse-to-300-pb/.

Few, S., 2014. Data Visualization for Human Perception. In: Soegaard, Mads, Dam, Rikke Friis, (Eds.). "The Encyclopedia of Human-Computer Interaction, 2nd Ed.". Aarhus, Denmark: The Interaction Design Foundation. Available from: https://www.interaction-design.org/encyclopedia/data_visualization_for_human_perception.html.

Gensler, L., 2015. Netflix soars on subscriber growth. Forbes. Available from: http://www.forbes.com/sites/laurengensler/2015/01/20/netflix-soars-on-subscriber-growth/.

Hurst, D., 2002. Crisis and Renewal: Meeting the Challenge of Organizational Change. Harvard Business Review Press, Boston, MA.

Kantrowitz, A., 2014. Ad fraud creates worry for some, opportunity for others. Advertising Age. Available from: http://adage.com/article/digital/ad-fraud-creates-worry-opportunity/292565/.

Manjoo, F., 2009. Jurassic web. Slate. Available from: http://www.slate.com/articles/technology/technology/2009/02/jurassic_web.single.html.

Michelli, J., 2014. Leading the Starbucks Way: 5 Principles for Connecting with Your Customers, Your Products, and Your People. McGraw Hill, New York.

Milliot, J., 2014. BEA 2014: can anyone compete with Amazon? Publishers Weekly. Available from: http://www.publishersweekly.com/pw/by-topic/industry-news/bea/article/62520-bea-2014-can-anyone-compete-with-amazon.html.

Newman, D., 2015. Big Data: Why Facebook Knows us Better Than Our Therapist. Forbes. Available from: http://www.forbes.com/sites/danielnewman/2015/02/24/big-data-why-facebook-knows-us-better-than-our-therapist/.

Randolph, M., 2011. It isn't lying if you believe it. Fortune. Available from: http://fortune.com/2011/05/13/it-isnt-lying-if-you-believe-it/.

Rutsch, P., 2015. Does bing-watching make us depressed? Good question. NPR. Available from: http://www.npr.org/sections/health-shots/2015/02/04/383527370/does-binge-watching-make-us-depressed-good-question.

Ryan, L., 2013. Leading change through creative destruction: how Netflix's self-destruction strategy created its own market. Int. J. Bus. Innovat. Res. 7 (4), 429–445.

Reardon, M., 2012. Trend watch: we're using our cell phones while watching TV. CNET. Available from: http://news.cnet.com/8301-1035_3-57473899-94/trend-watch-were-using-our-cell-phones-while-watching-tv/.

Sanek, S., 2011. Start with Why: How Great Leaders Inspire Everyone to Take Action. Portfolio, New York, NY.

Shaw, L., 2015. Twitter's periscope disabled dozens of Mayweather fight streams. Bloomberg Business. Available from: http://www.bloomberg.com/news/articles/2015-05-04/twitter-s-periscope-disabled-dozens-of-mayweather-fight-streams.

Simon, P., 2014. The Visual Organization: Data Visualization, Big Data, and the Quest for Better Decisions (Wiley and SAS business series). Wiley, Hoboken, NJ.

Sweney, M., 2014. Netflix gathers detailed viewer data to guide its search for the next hit. The Guardian. Available from: http://www.theguardian.com/media/2014/feb/23/netflix-viewer-data-house-of-cards.

Improved agility and insights through (visual) discovery

2

"The most exciting phrase to hear in science, the one that heralds new discoveries, is not 'Eureka!' but 'That's funny'…"

—Isaac Asimov

The characteristics of data-driven companies and the proof points and case studies shared in chapter: Separating Leaders from Laggards, support the continued reinvention of traditional business intelligence (BI) today as data discovery and visualization continue to take an increasingly important seat at the BI table. Now, it is time to take a look at how the data industry itself is changing from the inside out.

Assessing change covers three areas: people, processes, and technology. In this chapter, I will focus on the expansion of traditional BI to include data discovery. This is part of the processes portion of the change in the data industry. And, while the role of data discovery is steeped in philosophical debate as the new kid on the block (though, as we will come to see, it is not really so new after all), it should be seen as a complementary process that drives BI going forward, rather than replaces it. As an extension of BI, data discovery supports the data-driven competencies for evolving data-centric organizations. This chapter reviews the role of friction in discovery and how to navigate the four forms of discovery to maximize the value of data discovery as a key strategic process—and what that means for those companies looking to adopt a discovery-centric culture today. With a foundational knowledge of what discovery is and how it differs from exploration, we will also briefly explore the emergence of visual discovery, a concept that will be paramount in later discussions throughout the rest of this book, as we continue to dive into the role of data visualization and its importance in visual analytics. Before moving ahead into the last piece of the organizations, process, and people trifecta—people—in chapter: From Self-Service to Self-Sufficiency, we will touch on the role of discovery in the days to come, and the unique challenges and opportunities that discovery will bring with it as it becomes an increasingly fundamental strategic process in data-driven organizations. You will find that many of these will shape later conversations in Part III of this book.

2.1 THE DISCOVERY IMPERATIVE

Data discovery—or, to use its previous moniker, information discovery (ID)—is not exactly new. In fact, the past has seen information discovery referred to, somewhat facetiously, as "one of the coolest and scariest technologies in BI."

Nevertheless, recently, discovery—like many other things in today's data intelligence industry is undergoing reinvention. Spurred into the spotlight with an influx of new tools and technologies, the new and improved approach to data discovery is fueled by slick intuitive user interfaces and fast in-memory caching, compressed, and associative databases—and by the realized affordability of Moore's Law that provides users with desktops that boast more capacity, more horsepower, and higher resolution graphics enabling desktop discovery tools that were not possible five to seven years ago—especially for mainstream users. The ability for people to effortlessly access data from anywhere, and then quickly and iteratively explore relationships and visualize information, has forever changed the way we think about data discovery in a world where analysts of all shapes and sizes (or, skill levels) get to play with data.

You could say that the entrance of discovery has erupted into a bit of a data discovery epidemic—but in a good way. Once introduced in an organization, information discovery tools spread like wildfire by those seeking to capture immediate value and insights—and, like opening presents on Christmas morning, they often do so without waiting on IT or BI teams (our analogous parents) to catch up. The tool vendors know this, too. For example, Tableau Software has a well-known "land and expand" strategy of trickling in with individual users (or user groups) and expanding to enterprise licenses within a short amount of time. Veteran BI professionals struggle with the "open-data" tenant that appears counterintuitive to decades of the traditional BI mindset of well-organized and properly controlled data and information usage. The overarching concern is the descent of BI into chaos and the inevitable discovery hangover: we should have known better. This is a worrisome shadow in the back of many of our minds that we are hoping never to face.

The rush toward new technologies that deliver instant gratification and value should be considered carefully. In the case of data discovery, I believe this is an undeniable and natural way in which humans learn, gain intelligence, and make better decisions. Being a species that relies on competition—figuring out things faster and better than others—we are practically bred to discover, and what better application to use that intrinsic drive of curiosity than with the thing that is becoming front and center in much of our personal and professional lives—data? With that in mind, let us explore some of the critical conversations that BI teams are having today—and those that you should carefully consider at some point in your adoption of discovery as a fundamental process alongside traditional BI.

2.2 BUSINESS INTELLIGENCE VERSUS DATA DISCOVERY

Now, let us not start out on the wrong foot. While it is common to hear that ominous phrase "BI versus Discovery" and get the impression that traditional BI and data discovery are somehow sworn adversaries or otherwise at odds, they actually have quite a lot in common. In fact, they should be seen, if anything, as companions rather than rivals. After all, sometimes the most unlikely of pairs make the best of friends.

Consider Nobel Laureate T.S. Eliot and the bawdy comedian Groucho Marx, who had a peculiar friendship that began when Eliot wrote Marx for a signed photograph and the two stayed pen pals until shortly before Eliot's death in 1964. Or the quick-witted Mark Twain and inventor Nikola Tesla, who became such good friends that each of them credited the other with having special restorative powers for the other—Twain's novels a tonic for Tesla's recovery from bedridden illness as a young man, and Tesla's electric wizardry a cure for poor Twain's severe bout of—shall we say—constipation.

Such an improbable companionship have BI and Discovery. Like Eliot and Marx's shared love for literature or Tesla and Twain's intellectual curiosity, at their cores both BI and discovery share the same intended purpose: to derive value from data. Their approach to that purpose is a matter of different perspective. When it comes to defining what really distinguishes discovery from BI, it boils down to a simple change in how we think about the data. Rather than relying on business people to tell us how the business works—the BI approach—discovery instead relies on using real data to show—to gain insights—on what is really going on in and around the business.

We can articulate the fundamental difference in BI and discovery in the following way: traditionally, enterprise BI has focused on how to create systems that move information in and around and up and down in the organization, while maintaining its business context. It focuses on keeping that *very important context* bubble wrapped tightly around the data so that the business consumer does not need to. It is "rely and verify:" a framework wherein the analyst role is embedded within the system and the end user does not have to be a data expert, but just has to be able to rely on the data presented to verify a business need is met. The end goal of BI is to create and predefine easily digestible information that is plattered up and served to the end user with the purpose of being consumed as-is. It is insight off a menu.

Traditional BI focuses on establishing predefined business goals and metrics that drive the necessary construct of business performance management and dashboards, and then transform data against them. The traditional BI process is designed to understand your data through a disciplined process of "analyze, design, and develop." It looks inherently backward to consume data as-is through reporting and analysis to achieve a rear-view mirror perspective into the business. It is reactive versus proactive.

Discovery, instead, is all about being proactive. It begins not with a predefinition but a goal to explore and connect unknowns—which is less a political statement and more aptly the whole idea behind collecting and storing all available data and looking to connect the dots and make associations between trends to see things that had not been known before—new insights. Opposite to the "rely and verify" approach of traditional BI, discovery approaches the data in an iterative process of "discover, verify, operationalize" to uncover new insights and then build and operationalize new analytic models that provide value back to the business. It is kind of like why buffets make for such a popular family dinner destination: everyone can personalize their dining experience with a seemingly endless combination cultivated from a diverse selection and amounts (I am looking at you dinner rolls) of food types.

Ultimately, the fundamental difference between BI and discovery is simple: one starts with a predefinition and expectation of the data, while the other ends with a new definition derived from new insights into the data.

When we talk about BI versus Discovery, we are not really putting them on opposite sides of the battlefield. Instead, what we are ultimately talking about is having the ability—the willingness—to iterate and explore the data without the assumptions and biases of predefinitions.

Consider this example: IT (or a BI team) asks the business to provide them back with the information that it needs to know. The business, in turn, answers with a metric—not what they need to know, but what they need to measure in order to calculate what they need to know. This, by the way, is how we have come up with things like dimensional modeling, OLAP cubes, and other slice-and-dice approaches to understanding and interpreting data to achieve a business goal or other key performance indicator (KPI). Whole generations of BI have fixated on understanding and defining how data needs to map into a metric. But here is the rub: (things like) OLAP are only as good as what you predefine—if you only predefine five dimensions, you will not discover the other twenty hiding in the data. You have to know that you do not know what you are looking for to be able to know how to find it—and no, that is not a riddle to the location of the Holy Grail. It is simply another way of thinking that supports the need for discovery—and for the environment in which to discover.

Discovery (which should not be confused with exploration—see Box 2.1) begins with a goal to achieve within the business, but it accepts that we simply do not know what the metrics are or what data we need (or have) to meet that goal. It requires living inside—getting all up close and personal with—the data. This is the investigative nature of discovery—exploring, playing, visualizing, picking apart, and mashing back together the data in an iterative process to discover relationships, patterns, and trends in the data itself. We may already know the context of the data, but the goal is to build new models to uncover relationships that we do not already know, and then

---

BOX 2.1 DISCOVERY VERSUS EXPLORATION

Discovery does not equal exploration, just as exploration—likewise—does not equal discovery. While interrelated, these concepts are not interchangeable—or, at least not in my opinion.

As I see it, data exploration is a process by which to systematically investigate, scrutinize, or look for new information. Within the discovery process, exploration is the journey that we take through each step, as we continue to seek a new discovery. To explore is a precursor to discovery: it is to set out to do something—to search for answers, to inquire into a subject or an issue. From the mid-16th century, to explore is to ask "why."

Discovery itself is the end game of exploration: it is to make known—or to expose—something that has been previously unknown or unseen, like an insight. Discovery moves beyond the "why" to that "what"—or, as from late Latin *discooperire*, to "cover completely." It finds something new in the course (or as the result) of exploration. It is the moment in which we become aware, observe, or recognize something new or unexpected—or, alternatively, at the moment when we realize that there is not something new to find. As the saying goes, "even nothing is something." When we talk about the discovery process, what we are really saying is the process by which you earn a discovery—it is an exploratory process primed for a happy discovery ending.

figure out how that information can provide value back to the business while always evolving and changing as the business does over time.

And, discovery is as much about prediction as it is about iteration. Analysts with an inherent knowledge of the data can look at the context and identify that it is not quite right—that it does not join with an established metric quite as anticipated—they can predict that and already have a plan in mind of what to try next. There is another critical component to context, too: each analyst must decide whether it is—and how it is—applicable to their situation. This has always been a conflict between enterprise data warehouse context and departmental data marts—now it is at the empowered individual level, too. Then, they can go forth and discover and derive further specific context from what is already known. They can iterate. It is agile, yes, but it misses some of the discipline that makes BI, well…BI. Data discovery has always been a part of the BI requirements gathering process, and included data profiling, data quality, data mining, and metric feasibility. Discovery does not have to be completely standalone or complementary to BI—it can also continue to aid those BI processes, which, years ago, required the assistance of agile methodologies.

To go full-on discovery mode requires this give-and-take ability to predict and iterate—to not be satisfied with one answer and to keep on searching for new information. We want to be able to fail fast—to take advantage of short shelf lives and get the most of our information when and how we can—and then move on. And that kind of iterative ability necessitates self-sufficiency, a new-and-improved breed of the old "self-service" that we will explore in detail in the next chapter. Analysts now need to not only have access to data, but they need to be able to create and consume on the fly, that is, without having to go and ask for help and without being hindered by avoidable friction in the discovery process. They need discovery tools, and they need discovery environments (see Box 2.2). This is part of IT's new role—enablement and consultative—and part of a larger shift we are going to start seeing happen in the industry.

2.3 THE BUSINESS IMPACT OF THE DISCOVERY CULTURE

I seem to have found myself sounding remarkably like a broken record in this chapter: discovery itself (as a function of learning more about available data) is not new, nor is the need for discovery environments. And, that is all true enough—these principles may be as old as the data industry itself. We have always wanted to push our data to the max and learn as much as possible from it, and we have wanted protected ways in which to do it. (It is a little reminiscent of that infamous canonical wisdom of the Biblical verse: there is nothing new under the sun.) What data discovery and its associated counterparts are, however—and you are welcome to pick your adjective of choice here—is changing. Being reinvented, evolving, modernized—the list can go on. It is a swing from the Old Testament—the old way of doing things, if you will—to the New.

BOX 2.2 PLAYING IN THE DISCOVERY SANDBOX

When you have great toys, the next thing you need is a great place to play with them.

Like discovery, the need for an environment to support it is not new. There have been "exploration data warehouses" for some time. More modern, the term "analytic sandbox" is being thrown into the vernacular to support the interactive nature of analytic models for business analytics. These analytic sandboxes can be a virtual partition (or schema) of existing analytic-oriented databases, independent physical databases, or analytic appliances. Other specialized databases are built inside out to support very human, intuitive discovery frameworks, too. Or, even more modern, these discovery sandboxes can be a section of the data lake, or a data "pond" even. Big data environments, like Hadoop, seem to intrinsically enable information discovery. Still, the data industry recognizes the information discovery category primarily as vendors whose desktop software enable users to leverage in-memory databases, connectivity, integration, and visualization to explore and discover information. Many of these vendors specialize and differentiate themselves by how they architect discovery-oriented sandboxes, as well as perform supporting tasks, like integration, preparation, or data acquisition.

The choice between enabling "desktop sandboxes" or "architected sandboxes" (or both) can center on choices regarding data movement, or location of the analytic workload, or user type. With a separate sandbox database, data collections from the data warehouse (and other sources and systems that contain additional data) can be moved via ETL (and a large number of other open source and proprietary data collection and integration technologies) to isolate analytic processing and manipulation of data without impacting other established operational BI workloads for the sake of discovery. Another advantage comes from the possibility of collaboration among business analysts, who can share derived data sets and test semantic definitions together. This kind of collaboration is not easily done when a business analyst works locally on their desktop and wants to perform other desktop functions, or requires the desktop to be connected off hours to execute data integration routines. Most discovery tools—visual or otherwise—now allow business analysts to publish their findings and data sets to server-based versions.

It was not too long ago that the discovery-inclined Hadoop environment lacked integration tool compatibility and was burdened by too much programming complexity, thereby limiting its use to specialized users like the data scientist. But, in the past handful of years, this has changed. Vendors new and incumbent have increased integration capabilities with Hadoop via HCatalog, Hive, and more. New platforms and frameworks, like Spark and the even newer Apache Flink, are squaring off to reduce complexity, eliminate mapping, and find even more performance gains. Whatever the tool of choice—and whether it is a single Hadoop cluster, a fully trenched data lake, or one of their more traditional on-premise counterparts—the choice is not whether to have a sandbox—it is where.

When picking your sandbox locale, consider the following:

- Who is doing discovery?
- Does all the data needed fit onto a desktop even with compression? (Excel can store millions or rows itself)
- Are users more likely to work isolated or collaboratively? What about now versus down the road?
- Is the same data being pulled of many desktops that would benefit from that one-time operation and enable many users to perform discovery? Or, is it more centralized?
- What types of sandbox ready architectures already exist—and do you need another?

Scottish poet, novelist, and purveyor of folk tales, Andrew Lang—who, consequently, is also "not new," seeing as how he passed away in 1912—has, amongst his writings, been credited with leaving behind a lovely quote that has since been used as an immortal critique of scholarly position (or of social progress): "he uses statistics as a drunken man uses lamp posts – for support rather than for illumination." Lang may have been speaking specifically on statistics, but his words hit on another thread—that of the need to see beyond the obvious and look toward the larger picture. Discovery—and the insights that we reach through discovery—should not be limited to face value alone, but should also be a part of a larger shift toward a discovery-oriented culture.

To recap our previous discussion into agreeable takeaways, we know that both BI and discovery rely on data. Likewise, they both require a high degree of business context and knowledge, and both pivot between analysis and verification to be actionable. However, while BI and discovery ultimately share the same mission of delivering derived insights and value to the business, they are—again—two uniquely distinct capabilities that are both concerned with analyzing, predicting, and discovering. And, all of these are part of the information feedback loop to measure the business, analyze, act, remeasure, and verify. To take advantage of data discovery for business value requires more than a pairing of two approaches to information management. It also necessitates a cultural change within the business. The fostering of a discovery culture—including embracing new mental models and fostering an iterative and agile environment—enables business users from analysts to data scientists to help organizations unlock the value of discovery. This was the salient point of an article I coauthored with Manan Goel for *Teradata Magazine* in 2014—discovery and BI each provide business benefits, but they are distinctly different. So what does that mean for your organization? Let us discuss.

2.3.1 FOSTERING A DISCOVERY CULTURE

Discovery organizations are different from those that are Business Intelligence Competency Center (BICC)-based, or those that are otherwise traditional BI-centric. Primarily this is because, unlike traditional BI, discovery is iterative. This is fundamentally different than BI, and thus it requires change to make it happen. And, like any organizational change, discovery cannot simply be given lip service as an organizational imperative: it must be embedded into the fabric of the business in order to live up to its potential of being a valuable process.

The discovery environment operates under the new mental model of "fail fast, discover more." It is highly iterative, focusing on providing the agility to access, assemble, verify, and deploy processes, wherein analysts can rapidly move through data to explore for insights. It is dependent on providing access and the ability to incorporate data, too, so that analysts can explore all data—not just that stored in the data warehouse—and leverage all forms of business analytics—from SQL, nPath, graph, textual, statistical, and predictive, among others—to achieve business goals.

Finally, the discovery process is collaborative and requires the ability to share and verify the findings. The discovery culture requires that the business users have some level of independence from IT, and that they have intuitive, visually optimized tools to support exploration, too.

The discovery culture is:

- Agile and iterative
- Failure-tolerant and experimental
- Collaborative and IT-independent

2.3.2 DISCOVERY CULTURE CHALLENGES

Enabling a discovery culture is not without its set of challenges. First, it is—or, it can be—difficult for successful BI delivery organizations to accept "iterative failures" as good cultural attitudes. This is a stark contrast to the traditional build-to-last mindset with the built-to-change mindset needed to be agile, discover opportunities faster, and capitalize on them before competitors. We are not typically programmed with the mindset that failure is acceptable—much less that it is actually okay, and a normal part of exploration. Instead, we hear "don't mess up," or "try harder," or "practice makes perfect." There was a recent Forbes article where the contributor wrote that failing—fast or otherwise—is an idea we think is a good one, but only when it applies to other people.

It is counterintuitive and an interesting psychological experiment to think about why failure is a good thing. Not only a good thing, failure is still decidedly undervalued as a technique for innovation. As an anecdote about the need to fail—and quickly—consider the story of British inventor James Dyson. Dyson like the vacuum company "Dyson"? Yes, exactly. One day, Dyson looked at his household vacuum cleaner and decided he could make it better. It took him 15 years and 5,125 failed prototypes for him to decide to fail (Dyson is quoted as saying "I thought I'd try the wrong shape…and it worked"). On his 5,126th prototype, Dyson found his winning design—winning to the tune of $6 billion to date in worldwide sales—and the improved Dyson vacuum is a great modern success story that speaks to the power of failure. This may seem like a lesson in perseverance more than anything, but when you do the math and realize that Dyson was creating an average of 28 prototypes per month, it becomes jaw-dropping to think about how quickly he was designing, experimenting, testing, iterating—how fast he was failing. Another rags-to-riches story about the power of failure could be J. K. Rowling, author of the multimillion dollar *Harry Potter* series. The story goes that Rowling received twelve publishing rejections in a row before being accepted, and was only then accepted after the eight-year old daughter of an editor demanded to read the rest of the manuscript (these are publishing rejections, mind you, and does not include literary agents rejections previous for which, knowing a bit about the publishing industry, I can only assume was even higher). Even after acceptance of *The Sorcerer's Stone* Rowling was advised to get a day job, which might be the most embarrassing comment that editor ever made to the woman, whose last four books in the *Potter* series have since consecutively set records as the fastest-selling books in history, on both sides of the Atlantic, with sales of 450 million—and this does not even include earnings from merchandising, movies, or the *Universal* theme parks, either. Burn!

The lesson, again, is that sometimes, failure can be a good thing. And the faster you fail, the quicker you can move on to that sweet, sweet win. Keep in mind that, as it becomes more data-driven, your company is/will be dependent on data discovery to stay competitive and alive, so the more people that are exploring in a field of data, the better.

Alongside the requisite mental "fail fast" models of discovery, a highly iterative and exploratory environment, and capable tools and wide-open access (more on these in the next chapter), embracing a discovery culture means that we also face new challenges in governing people, roles, and responsibilities. Aside from the mindset change of failure as a good thing, governance is arguably the second biggest challenge to be faced by the discovery culture. And, as if that was not enough on its own, we must be aware of the need to govern the results of discovery itself, and this applies both to the insight and the way in which we present—or visualize—the insight. Roles and responsibilities for accessing and working with the data should be established, as well as definitions of ownership and delegation for semantic context discovered. The discovery results themselves should also undergo governance, as well as monitoring the operationalization of discovered new analytic models. For the most part, BI has had the benefit of having governance baked in (as broad and optimistic as that may sound), while defining everything from extraction, transformation, and consumption of context. Discovery is driving governance to new levels and unexplored territories of policies and decisions to balance risks. That said, a conversation on governance cannot be constrained into a few measly sentences, so, I will devote an entire chapter later to this concept and move on for now.

2.3.3 DISCOVERY ORGANIZATIONS AS AMBIDEXTROUS BY DESIGN

Last of all, I just want to insert a brief tidbit on organizational design for the discovery culture, for those of you interested in such things. A strong case can be made that the discovery culture is one that is ambidextrous by design. These organizations attempt to create excellence—competitive advantage—by supporting entrepreneurial and innovative practices (Selcer and Decker, 2012)—hence, self-sufficiency (which I will introduce in greater detail in chapter: From Self-Service to Self-Sufficiency). Ambidextrous organizations—like data and customer-centric organizations—are adaptable and continue to mature and evolve as they react to internal and external challenges that contribute to the ongoing shaping of the organizational design. This can be top-down to strongly coordinate work for efficiency and productive, or it can be bottom-up and thus promote individuality and creativity.

2.4 THE ROLE OF FRICTION IN DISCOVERY

The role of friction in data discovery is much akin to that minimalist design mantra that will later on be the capstone of our visual design conversation: less is more.

Unlike traditional BI, discovery hinges on the ability to explore data in a "fail-fast" iterative process that cycles through repetitive steps of accessing the data; exploring it; blending and integrating it (or "interrogating it") with other data; analytically modeling the data; and finally, verifying and governing the new discovery before operationalizing it back into the enterprise. As an iterative exercise, discovery inherently places a premium on both the ability to quickly and agilely harness large amounts of varieties of data to explore, and also—equally as important—on speed. This is not just speed for the sake of speed, either: it is a fundamental prerequisite of truly enabling the discovery culture in your enterprise. The quicker you can move through the discovery process, the quicker you can arrive at insights that add value back into the business. Finding a worthwhile discovery—especially the first time around—is not guaranteed. This is the essence of fail-fast: if one discovery does not work, toss it aside and keep looking. Sure, it may take only one attempt to discover a valuable nugget, but it also may take 99 iterations through the discovery cycle before one valuable insight is uncovered (if at all). The value of speed, then, can be found at the intersection of actionable time to insight and the ease—or, the "frictionless-ness"—of the discovery process.

Friction is caused by the incremental events that add time and complexity to discovery through activities that slow down the process, like those that IT used to do for business users—many, if not all, of which can be reduced (or removed completely) with robust self-service, visualization, collaboration, and sharing capabilities. Friction, then, is a speed killer—it adds time to discovery and interrupts the "train of thought" ability to move quickly through the discovery process and earn insight.

Somehow every performance measurement seems to boil down to that same old 80/20 concept. When I was in project management, we applied it there: 80% time should be spent planning, 20% doing the work. Now, in discovery, it is here again. When it comes to discovery, we often hear that 80% of time is spent in data preparation, leaving only 20% of the time for data science and exploration (some have suggested this ratio is more closely aligned with a 90/10 split). The more friction that is added into the process, the longer it takes to yield an insight in the data. Removing friction reduces the barriers to discovery and subsequently increases time to insight—speed.

Think of it this way: would data discovery be nearly as worthwhile if analysts had to budget an hour of waiting time for each step of the discovery process? And, what if it does take 99 iterations to find one meaningful insight? Do the math: that is 5 steps at 1 hour each, 99 times, for a total of 495 hours or approximately 21 days to value. Yikes! But if we pick up the speed—reduce the friction—and drop that hour of waiting time down to 1 min per step, the time to value is significantly reduced: 1 min steps, 99 times, is a mere 495 min—8.25 hours—to value. How much time would you prefer to spend—two months or one day—before discovering an insight that adds value in your business? How much would you be okay with wasting?

Yes, sometimes there are unavoidable activities (like governance) that will inevitably add friction to the discovery process. However, the goal is to reduce the strain (and time sink) around those activities as much as possible—as illustrated by the math earlier, every second counts in discovery. Remember: the real value of discovery is to earn insights on data and facilitate interactive and immediate reaction by the business. Breaking down the activities that induce friction in each step of the discovery process reduces the barriers to discovery and subsequently increases time to insight. Speed, then, is a function of friction: the less friction in the discovery process, the more value speed can deliver to the business. As friction decreases, time to failures improves and subsequently time to insight increases—and the more valuable discovery becomes. Now, multiply that by ever-increasing amount of people in the enterprise (not just data scientists and analysts) to solve the challenges of the business. Compare that to the number of people using Google and Yahoo! to discover solutions to everyday life challenges, and how that has evolved over the past 5, 10, and 15 years—adoption has been proven.

Ultimately, it is a simple equation: less friction equals faster time to insight. The role of friction in discovery then? As little as possible.

2.5 THE FOUR FORMS OF DISCOVERY

Among their many other benefits, Hadoop and other big data playgrounds serve as a staging ground for discovery. This is not by accident, but by design: these ecosystems provide the ability to scale affordably to store and then search all data—structured and unstructured alike—enabling business analysts to explore and discover within a single environment.

Below I want to break down four identified forms of discovery, each of which is in use in organizations today, before introducing the concept of visual data discovery, which is the heart of this book. Each of the four forms of discovery below can be organized into two categories: traditional and advanced (or new). These traditional forms of discovery include commonplace, structured BI-discovery tools, like spreadsheets and basic visualizations, while advanced forms of discovery leverage multifaceted search mode capabilities and innovations in advanced visualizations to support new capabilities in data discovery.

2.5.1 TRADITIONAL FORMS OF DISCOVERY

First, both mainstay spreadsheets and basic visualizations—like basic graphs and percentage of whole (eg, pie) charts—are traditional forms of discovery.

2.5.1.1 Spreadsheets

Spreadsheets (like Microsoft Excel) remain the most popular and pervasive business analytics paradigm to work with data, in part because of their widespread and long-standing availability and user familiarity. However, with a wide range of analysis and reporting capabilities, spreadsheets can be powerful analytic tool in the hands of an experienced user. The original spreadsheet pioneers VisiCalc and Lotus 1-2-3 discovered a powerful paradigm for humans to organize, calculate, and analyze data that has proven to stand the test of time—though some of the companies themselves did not. Today, Microsoft Excel 2013 can hold over one million rows (1,048,576) and over 16,000 columns (16,384) of data in memory in a worksheet.

With spreadsheets, the real value is in providing access to data for the user to manipulate locally. With this tool, and the data already organized neatly into rows and columns, an analyst can slice and dice spreadsheet data through sorting, filtering, pivoting, or building very simple or very complex formulas and statistics directly into their spreadsheet(s). They can discover new insights by simply reorganizing the data. Some vendors, like Datameer, for example, have started to capitalize on the concept of "spreadsheet discovery." In this very Excel-esque spreadsheet user interface, analysts and business users can leverage the fluency of the Excel environment to discover big data insights. (This is not the only way vendors are reimagining the familiarity of intuitive Microsoft environments—some discovery tools (business user-based Chartio and statistical discovery solution JMP come to mind) have very wizard-like interfaces to guide users to discovery, too.) We might not always like to admit it, but Microsoft's mantra of technology for the everyday user has enabled nearly every company in the world today.

2.5.1.2 Basic visualizations

Basic visualizations, such as graphs or charts (including those embedded in dashboards)—whether generated through Excel or not—provide simple, straightforward visual representations of data that allow analysts to discover insights that might not be as easily perceived in a plain text format.

It is no small task to put a point on exactly what constitutes a basic data visualization as the range and breadth of visualizations is quite broad, but perhaps it is a simple description to say that basic visualizations are an effective means of describing, exploring, or summarizing data because the use of a visual image can simplify complex information and help to highlight—or discover—patterns and trends in the data. They can also help in presenting large amounts of data, and can just as easily be used to present smaller datasets, too. That said, basic visualizations fall short of their more advanced cousins in many ways. They are more often than not static, one-layered visualizations that offer little to no interactive or animated capabilities. Moreover, they are lacking in dynamic data content and do not offer abilities to query data, personalize appearance, or provide real-time monitoring mechanisms (like sharing or alerts).

2.5.2 ADVANCED FORMS OF DISCOVERY

The evolution of traditional forms of discovery has led to newer, more advanced forms of discovery that can search through—and visualize—multiple kinds of data within one environment. The two other forms of data discovery are what we classify as analytic forms of discovery.

2.5.2.1 Multifaceted, search mode

Multifaceted (or, "search-mode") discovery allows analysts to mine through data for insights without discriminating between structured and unstructured data. Analysts can access data in documents, emails, images, wikis, social data, etc. in a search engine fashion (like Google, Yahoo!, or Bing) with the ability to iterate back-and-forth as needed and drill down to dive deeper into available data to discover new insights. IBM Watson, for example, is a search mode form of discovery, capable of answering questions posed in everyday language. We will touch on other discovery-oriented languages, and how they are working to ready for the Internet of Things, in more detail in later chapters.

2.5.2.2 *Advanced visualizations*

Finally, advanced visualizations are everything that basic data visualizations are not. They are a tool for visual discovery that allow analysts to experiment with big data to uncover insights in a totally new way. These advanced visualizations can also complement or supplement traditional forms of discovery to provide the opportunity to compare various forms of discovery to potentially discover even more insights, or have a more complete view of the data.

With advanced visualizations, analysts can visualize clusters or aggregate data; they can also experiment with data through iteration to look for correlations or predictors to discover new analytic models. These advanced visualizations are interactive, possibly animated, and some can even provide real-time data analysis with streaming visualization capabilities. Moreover, advanced visualizations are multiple-dimension, linked, and layered, providing optimal visual discovery opportunities for users to follow train-of-thought thinking as they visually step through data and craft compelling data narratives through visual storytelling. While basic data visualization types—again, like bar or pie charts—can be optimized to be advanced data visualizations, there exists also an entire new spectrum on the visualization continuum devoted to advanced types of visual displays, such as network visualizations or arc diagrams, that can layer on multiple dimensions of data at once.

The inclusion of visual cues—like intelligent icons and waves of color in heat maps—are an emerging technique in advanced visual discovery that leverage principles and best practices in cognitive sciences and visual design. I will explore the "beautiful science" of data visualization in later chapters, when we talk about how to use color, perceptual pop-out, numerosity, and other techniques to layer visual intuition on top of cognitive understanding to interact with, learn from, and earn new insights and engage in visual dialog with data.

Remember, advanced visualizations are not simply a function of how the data is visualized, but are measured by how dynamic, interactive, and functional they are. Advanced data visualizations enable visual discovery by design—the core focus of chapter: The Importance of Visual Design (for now, see Box 2.3).

Later chapters will explore the anatomy of a visual discovery application and other technical details.

2.6 SQL: THE LANGUAGE OF DISCOVERY

For many the self-sufficient analyst, learning and being able to use SQL is not a skill prerequisite in the modern data analyst toolkit, as many self-service discovery-oriented tools are designed to take the scripting burden off of the user. Nevertheless, SQL remains a high-premium component of data discovery.

As organizations' transition more and more from traditional BI methods of querying, analyzing, and reporting on data to the highly iterative and interactive model of data discovery with new data in varying structure and volume, the ability to load, access, integrate, and explore data is becoming increasingly more critical. While

BOX 2.3 THE EMERGENCE OF VISUAL DISCOVERY

By now, we have nearly dissected every angle of discovery—how it differs from traditional BI, the nuances between traditional and advanced discovery, and so forth. We have begun to touch on a construct, which is the heart of this text as the phrase "visual data discovery" has started to materialize in paragraphs past.

It probably will not surprise you that there are many definitions of visual data discovery floating around out there. Such is the fate of buzzy new terminology when it first flies into the face of every vendor, marketer, and customer trying to wrangle out and differentiate on a piece of the definitive pie of definitions.

Rather than tossing another definition into the pool, I would like to cast my vote with one that already exists and try to achieve some degree of unification. Gartner Analyst Cindi Howson, a long-time data viz guru, has offered perhaps one of the most clear and succinct definitions of visual data discovery, stating: "Visual data discovery tools speed the time to insight through the use of visualizations, best practices in visual perception, and easy exploration." Howson also notes that such tools support business agility and self-service BI through a variety of innovations that may include in-memory processing and mashing of multiple data sources. To Cindi's definition, I would also like to add that visual data discovery is a mechanism for discovery that places an inherent premium on visual—perhaps more so than analytical prowess—to guide discovery and works to facilitate a visual dialog with progressively vast amounts of large and diverse data sets.

Thus, my definition of visual data discovery is this: visual data discovery is the use of visually-oriented, self-service tools designed to guide users to insights through the effective use of visual design principles, graphicacy best practices, and kinesthetic learning supported by animation, interactivity, and collective learning. Narrated visual discovery is the basis of true data storytelling.

technologies like Hadoop are gaining acceptance and adoption as data management systems built from the ground up to be affordable, scalable, and to flexibly work with data—and while many new languages are emerging to work with data in new, condensed, and more intuitive ways—the Structured Query Language (SQL) remains the key to unlocking the real business value inside new data discovery with a traditional method. Even SQL's little cousin MDX (multi-dimensional expression) language for OLAP will be empowered by big data.

The more users that are enabled to participate in the discovery process, the more value can be unlocked. This is in terms of both quantity of users, as well as the variety thereof. Every data user in the organization can be a vessel to discovery—from casual users (that represent 80% of BI users), to power users and business analysts (that represent 20% of BI users), to the few data scientists and analytic modelers in the organization. In addition to enabling more users within the organization to perform discovery, discovery-centric organizations should seek to extend the role of traditional data stewards. From traditional subject, process, unit (ie, sales and marketing) data, and project stewards, look to define new data stewards, including big data stewards (to include website, social media, M2M, and big transactions) and to leverage the role of the data scientists to recommend algorithms, verify and test analytics models, and—more important—research and mentor others in the organization. By the way, this includes C-level titles, too. We will explore the roles of Chief Analytics Officers or Chief Data Officers—or even Chief Storytelling Officers—in more detail in later chapters. However, even though these people may perhaps be less likely to dig in and work directly with the data, they are every bit as relevant to this part of the discussion due to their positions as leaders, mentors, and enablers within a visual discovery culture.

However, the very few data scientists in the organization—and even the enabled power users—can only scratch the surface of the business value of discovery, and that, too, will eventually flatten out over time. Going forward, we should position these users as the enablers for the enterprise casual users, who also need access—those "know it when they see it" discoverers who benefit most from having the ability to interact and explore data in a familiar and self-sufficient way. This is where SQL as the language of discovery comes in.

Today's self-sufficient analyst requires the ability to access data, to load it, and to iteratively explore and "fail fast" to discover insights hidden within data. This challenges traditional data management and data warehouses primarily through schema and controls. However, using SQL for discovery leverages decades of familiarity, adoption, and maturity that exists within tools already installed in today's technology ecosystems. For example, many spreadsheet raw-data formats and intuitive visualization tools are heavily dependent on the SQL word. Therefore, analysts and power users immediately benefit from having a highly iterative, high performing SQL capability within Hadoop—hence the rush to provide faster SQL access to schemas in Hadoop over Hive.

Unlocking big data value in discovery is heavily dependent on the ability to executive SQL because it is already so pervasive, coupled with functionality that has performance and capability. However, not all SQL engines are created equal. They are all maturing differently. They have a different history or a different DNA. And, some are starting fresh, while others are leveraging years of database capability. The following three areas are considerations when evaluating the power of SQL on Hadoop. Consequently, Radiant Advisors annually publishes independent benchmarks focused on the performance dimensions of speed and SQL capabilities, and are recommended reading for a look at how individual queries perform on today's leading SQL-on-Hadoop options.

2.6.1 SQL CAPABILITY AND COMPATIBILITY

First is SQL capability. We have learned through existing relational databases that not all SQL is the same. There are some vendor specific SQL, and while vendors can run SQL, it could be of many versions starting with SQL-92, and SQL-99 standards to the later analytic functions found in SQL-2000+ versions of the ANSI standard. If you have existing tools and reports that you want to connect to Hadoop, you do not want to rewrite a vast amount of existing SQL statements and make sure they are going to work in existing tools and applications.

Compatibility with standardized SQL—or more mature, advanced SQL, then—minimizes rework. And, without SQL capability and maturity, many analytic functions will be rendered unable to perform anyway. With this in mind, look at the vendor's roadmaps to see what analytic functions they have on tap over the next year or two.

2.6.2 SCALABILITY

Second is scalability. With a large cluster up to thousands of nodes, there is the assumption that the SQL engine runs on all the nodes in the cluster. However, be aware and cognizant of limitations. For example, if you are running 100, 500, or thousands of nodes, maybe the SQL engine is not capable of running on that and is limited to only run on 16 or 32 notes at a time. Some early adopters have sectioned off areas of clusters to operate SQL on Hadoop engines on, resulting in a tiered architecture in single clusters. Even more important recently is whether it is YARN certified or not.

Additionally, be aware of data duplication due to data file format inside of the HDFS (Hadoop Distributed File System). Is data stored inside an open file, like Text, Optimized Row-Column (ORC), JSON, or Parquet, or does it require extraction out of those files and into a propriety file format that cannot be accessed by other Hadoop applications—especially YARN applications? Beware of duplicating data in order to fuel the SQL on Hadoop engine.

2.6.3 SPEED

Finally, again, it is all about speed. Speed does matter, especially in interactive response time and especially for big data sets—especially from a discovery perspective, where the goal is to discover fast through iteratively "failing fast." If you know you are going to fail 99 times before you find the first insight, you want to move through those 99 iterations as quickly as possible. Waiting 700 seconds for a query return versus 7 seconds or for a batch process can be a painful form of analysis, wherein you can discover your patience thresholds before any insights into the data. When evaluating speed, look beyond response times to consider workloads, caching, and concurrency, too.

2.6.4 THINKING LONG-TERM

When choosing any SQL-on-Hadoop engine, take your broader data architecture and data strategies into consideration and make sure these align. The architecture for SQL-on-Hadoop will continue to evolve—it has already moved from a batch-oriented Hive on MapReduce in Hadoop version 1, to the current Hadoop version 2 that added the benefits of Hive and TEZ running on YARN for vectorized queries that brought orders of magnitude performance increases to Hive 13. Today, we see "architectural SQL," with Hive and TEZ running on YARN inside of clusters, and we can also begin bringing in other engines that can run directly with HDFS. Architecture is a differentiator between those SQL-on-Hadoop engines that are already YARN-compatible, and those that pick up performance by going directly to the HDFS core and looking for compatibility in long-term strategies. Of course, many new technologies and strategies continue to show up in the running for how to best manage and benefit from big data, but the one constant in a sea of change and invention remains SQL.

Ultimately, SQL is becoming more and more part of the story of unifying our data platform environment. Through SQL, we can bring together enterprise data, high-end analytics, and big data sets that live in Hadoop, and we can start to work with all of these through a unifying language.

2.7 DISCOVERY IN THE DAYS TO COME

This has been a long, somewhat nuanced, dissertation on the role of data discovery—and visual data discovery—alongside traditional BI and other forms of information discovery. Ultimately, we can distill the bulk of the chapter earlier into two capstone points: while discovery and BI share some commonalities, they are fundamentally different in approach and process yet intertwined. And, data discovery is expected to become the prominent approach to BI in the next several years.

Today data discovery is beginning to deliver on its all of its promise of capabilities and earned actionable insights (remember Netflix in the last chapter, which is basically the icon for discovery and empowerment as an organizations that has disrupted an entire industry)—especially those reached visually. However, there are still areas of improvement to close gaps and find balance in features and functionalities. One of these areas is in governance—both in the discovery process itself, and in how the data visualizations itself is utilized within the organization as an information asset. While discovery is good—and necessary—that does not mean it is a free-for-all. With intuitive, robust tools and wide-open access, we face the new challenges of properly governing roles, responsibilities and how data is used in the business. We do not want to return to the chaos of reports that do not match, garbage data, or mismatched information systems. Discovery is as strategic a process as any other in BI.

We will explore these issues of expanding data governance for discovery in more detail later in Part III. For now let us continue to explore the shift from self-service to self-sufficiency and the business implications of the big data democracy. Let us talk about people.

REFERENCE

Selcer, A., Decker, P., 2012. The structuration of ambidexterity: an urge for caution in organizational design. Int. J. Org. Innovat. 5 (1), 65–96.

From self-service to self-sufficiency

3

"Look up at the stars and not down at your feet. Try to make sense of what you see, and wonder about what makes the universe exist. Be curious."
—Stephen Hawking

In the previous chapter, we took a look at the foundational change happening in the data industry as organizations begin to include new thinking in data discovery as a fundamental complement alongside traditional BI processes. From an organizational perspective this is an important evolution in the larger way that data-driven organizations are beginning to think about—and approach—how they explore the untapped value hidden within their data to uncover new competitive advantages and insights. But, to realize the full potential of this change, we need to push the conversation a bit further down the rabbit hole. Rather than just looking at how organizations are cultivating a culture of discovery at the strategic top tier, we also need to consider how that shift is trickling down and changing the way various groups of people within the organization are working with data, too. After all, change does not happen in a vacuum of vision statements and good intentions. To realize changes requires the ability to take action—and while machine learning and other artificial intelligence technologies are rapidly reshaping our current perceptions of learning, humans are still our biggest data discoverers. Thus, they need to be empowered—and enabled—to be a part of discovery in a meaningful way.

One of my favorite leading ladies in the BI industry is Jill Dyché—and one of my favorites of Jill's quotes comes from her latest book, *The New IT*. In her book Jill eloquent writes, "IT is at a moment where its future is being redefined. And its cultural power is shifting to a new set of gatekeepers (Dyché, 2015, p. 13)." Going forward, Jill describes how IT is forging a new identity through its operations, connections, and innovations. Again, think back to chapter: Separating Leaders From Laggards and how traditional IT departments are recalibrating in the wake of disruption, transformation, and reinvention.

Luckily, I agree with Jill. In a December 2014 piece I wrote, entitled *From Self-Service to Self-Sufficiency: How Discovery is Driving the Business Shift*, I wrote pointedly about how self-service is being redefined to be less about service and more about sufficiency—thus, self-sufficiency—in terms of mindset, tools, and capabilities. I also wrote about the simultaneous shift of IT from Information Technology to Enablement Technology (or, ET) and how that is affecting the new types of modern data analysts and other data science professionals whose roles are materializing today in order to bridge the gap from self-service to self-sufficiency.

In chapter: Separating Leaders From Laggards, we took an overhead view into how business as usual is changing to become more data- and customer-centric. Likewise, in chapter: Improved Agility and Insights through (Visual) Discovery, we discussed how the data industry itself is changing in the way we think about data. Now, in this chapter, let us take a deeper dive into what self-sufficiency is and what it needs to thrive, as well as the new role of IT and how it is being refitted within the visual discovery culture today.

3.1 FROM SELF-SERVICE TO SELF-SUFFICIENCY

In the past several years, "self-service" has come to be understood as users simply having access to information they need, which is served to them in easily consumable ways for the most basic of slice and dice operations. Today, that definition is being redefined. Now, self-service is less about access and much more about ability: it is a fundamental shift from being able to consume something that has been predefined and provided to be able to develop it—to discover it—yourself.

As a quick aside, it is worth mentioning that self-service is a term that is applied more than generously in the data industry today. Everything is self-service and everyone needs self-service. It is the most versatile accessory you can find anywhere. But, I want to clarify that within our discussions on self-service to self-sufficiency, I am not talking about self-service for IT, developers, or even data scientists. I am talking about self-sufficiency for business users and modern data analysts. Self-service is an enabling term and previously meant for access to "information." Self-sufficiency is more about access to work with "data" independently without the need for requirements or developers to make it so.

To add a bit of color here, let me begin with a quick story. When I was a little girl, my favorite Disney princess was Ariel from *The Little Mermaid*. But, as it may surprise you, it was not Ariel herself who was my favorite character in the adaptation of Hans Christian Andersen's much darker tale. Sure, she was spunky and curious and determined—all qualities that I admire, but it was her curmudgeonly crustacean pal Sebastian the crab that reeled me in (no pun intended). Sebastian was a demanding, get-it-done kind of guy, who did not like to take no for an answer and who had an eye for finding solutions to the biggest problems under the sea. In one scene of the film, Sebastian—who by then had enough of that ditzy seagull and Ariel's other lovably inept companions—said, with a hint of seduction, if "you want something done, you've got to do it yourself." To bring this to life visually it, see Figure 3.1.

Now, I certainly do not want to implicate today's self-sufficient analysts as being the crabs of the industry—I am sure that title could be better applied elsewhere. But I do want to recognize the very Sebastian-like independent and Do It Yourself mindset because it is one that is being adopted with fervor across organizations

FIGURE 3.1 Sebastian Meme, Generated at Memegenerator.net

(not to mention society as a whole, with the surplus of DIY television shows and guidebooks and the appearance of crafting sites like Pinterest and Etsy). Now, let us apply this story back to our context. In the data science and analytics world, it is no longer enough to be like Ariel: inquisitive and eager to explore for new discoveries. Now, we are determined to find those answers—to earn those new discoveries, and we want the power and the abilities to do it ourselves. We are Sebastians.

The business user has changed, and that is possibly the most important driver shifting self-service to self-sufficiency. Like the business itself in an era of disruption, transformation, and reinvention, this change in the business user mindset is one of fitness. Users have had to adapt in order to respond to the evolving needs of data-centric cultures. Today's increasingly sophisticated predictive and operational analytics require users with business knowledge to become partners in discovery, not merely consumers of enterprise approved business information for decision-making. These users have the business context and tribal knowledge that gives them a unique position to contribute to collective learning in the organization and apply their insights into the larger discovery process. Equipped with better tools, users are also earning greater autonomy and compatibility within cutting-edge IT organizations. Where agility was a "codeveloper" before, self-sufficient business users can now do it all: they can connect, integrate, analyze, and visualize data without the central control and management of IT.

Alongside that attitude change has come a buffet of tools designed to support the demand. And, with the advent of increasingly robust technologies, there is no shortage of self-service tools on the market today. More important, these tools—BI and beyond—are good. In fact, they are more than good: these next-generation tools are the catalyst enabling business users to become increasingly more self-sufficient from IT in their data needs—if they so choose. While I will not spend a lot of time going through and comparing the different tools and solutions currently available in the marketplace, it is worth to take a look at a few leading players and the trends among them. See Box 3.1 for more.

Before I move on that last point—"if they choose"—warrants a small disclaimer. Self-sufficiency comes with a caveat. There will always remain those users within the business that simply do not want to be self-sufficient. Some—possibly even a majority—will want to stay dependent. They are not interested in all these new capabilities and are perfectly content to continue having information delivered to them—and that is okay. It is not about forcing 100% of users within an organization to be self-sufficient: it is about enabling those who want to be. Adoption will continue at its own pace that is nurtured and facilitated by how the business supports those early-movers and continues to encourage everyone else to follow suit. Again,

----

BOX 3.1 THE SELF-SUFFICIENT TOOL LANDSCAPE

You will not find much specific discussion on tools and technologies in the data intelligence vendor marketplace within these pages for one simple reason: they change too fast. It is a full-time job to keep up with all these updates and new releases—part of the reason analysts have such great job security—much less be able to preserve a moment in time in the confines of published text. But, even so, I want to take a snapshot of a select few of the tools in industry today to show how many are answering the need of self-service visual data discovery.

- Qlik, one of the first "all in one" BI tools, allows users to acquire and integrate, transform, and store the data in-memory on the desktop and provides mechanisms to visualize it. With the introduction of Qlik Sense in 2014, Qlik took self-service data discovery one-step farther.
- Birst's Visualizer solution has an embedded unification layer—which it calls a reusable semantic layer—built directly in to facilitate the adoption of self-service analytics.
- Tableau, a longtime supporter of what they call "self-reliant" business intelligence, provides a visual discovery-oriented solution that allows business users to analyze, visualize, and tell stories with data.
- GoodData is guiding self-service users to insights through the use of collective learning and its Guided Analytics, a discovery interface with a drag and drop visualization canvas that recommends next steps through data as it recognizes trends at each phase of users' analysis.
- Predixion Software's Insight is built to take traditional self-service to the next level by "democratizing analytics:" guiding the user from the creation of a predictive model to consuming predictive analytic insights.
- Datameer, with its Smart Analytics tool, extends self-service data mining functionality to let business users find patterns and relationships in their data.
- Composite Software—the data virtualization player recently acquired by Cisco Systems—has a unification layer to work with data without the need for code, although they had been missing that front-end piece that drives self-sufficiency. With the release of Collage in 2014, Composite now offers that much needed best-of-both duo.

this is part of the larger discovery culture change that starts at the top and works its way down throughout all levels of hierarchy in the organization. So, defining data provisioner and consumer roles—and, further, developing a user readiness assessment—is another key part of the access framework, too.

With the new business user credo "take care of thyself" that is reshaping user mindsets and ushering in an era of consumerized BI with a bevy of new self-sufficiency-oriented discovery tools, it should be no surprise that the role of IT is fast changing too. No longer that of command-and-control, IT is increasingly taking on the role of broker and consultant—of enabler. We simply do not need traditional IT anymore, at least not for discovery. Of course, this is not to say that IT itself is going away by any means. It is not. IT will always deserve a fundamental role in data management and continue to be a key player in information security, governance, and other stewardship facets.

Again, just so I am clear and there is no miscommunication, let me phrase this more explicitly. While self-sufficiency is about enabling more business users with more access to more data with more frequency and across more channels, it should not be enacted without putting governance at the forefront of the discovery process. I am not making a case for the Wild Wild West of data here, though I suppose I am suggesting a step out of the comfort zone for many. Governance is, actually, a topic that may now be more charged than ever because of self-sufficiency and discovery. However, we will save governance for discussion in later chapters, where I will take a magnifying glass to how to enable self-sufficient governed data discovery and a brand of governed data visualization, too.

Governance aside, traditional information technology must—and will—soon become enablement technology. And, as IT evolves into a role that is focused on enabling and supporting more information-hungry users, it must respond to the opportunity to educate the business on IT processes and governance.

Ultimately, the shift toward self-sufficiency is closing the gap between business and IT. It is a symbiotic relationship, now more than ever before. As Jill noted, the cultural power of IT is being shifted to a new set of gatekeepers. These gatekeepers are the data owners whose data is being used for discovery and also those self-sufficient business users—the demanding discoverers of new insights.

In the following sections of this chapter we will explore the core discovery capabilities for self-sufficiency as well as the shift of IT to ET and the arising roles in data science in greater detail. But first, let me share just one more story as an example to illustrate how self-sufficiency is changing the way we do BI and discovery.

3.1.1 A LESSON FROM FROZEN YOGURT

I am not afraid to say that the Big Data Culture hinges on self-sufficiency to be successful. I firmly believe that it does. Like discovery, self-sufficiency is a numbers game. The more data available and the more people that are actively enabled to work productively in the discovery process, the more insight potential and, therefore, the more valuable discovery. The less restriction and red tape we put on these self-sufficient users, the more discoveries they can uncover. They may not all be winners, but there will be the few golden nuggets, too.

At the Teradata Big Data Analytics Roadshow held in New York City in December 2013, Bill Franks, the current Chief Analytics Officer of Teradata, noted that changing small things about your policy and culture will achieve huge business impacts. Enabling self-sufficiency is one of these. As a way to explain his position, Bill pointed to yogurt shops and the customized frozen yogurt trend that is sweeping the nation and making the Ye Olde Yogurt Shoppes of the past more or less obsolete. This example has stuck with me ever since I heard it, and I want to share it with you.

To get the most out of this lesson, you have to know that there is a funny trick about learning how to dine with children. For example, over the years I have learned that trying to convince my eight-year old son to go to a fine dining establishment will have him bored to tears before I finish my first glass of wine. Likewise, he is never going to convince me to put anything that is handed to me out of a drive-through window into my mouth. But, the one thing he and I always agree on when we are looking for a tasty treat is our favorite frozen yogurt shop. At *Spooners* my son and I each grab a paper cup from the counter and take off in different directions. We each get to sample and experiment with different flavor blends by pulling the lever on any one of the dozen or so yogurt spouts lining the wall. We can fill the paper cup until it—or our eyes, at least—are satisfied. Then, we can further customize our creamy treat with sprinklings of candies, fruits, nuts, and other delicious toppings at will. When it is all said and done, we pay by the ounce for our dessert, eat, and enjoy while debating the merits of one froyo interpretation over the other.

Now, compare that experience against the traditional yogurt shop model. In the shops of my youth, I would be taken in and told to select from a menu of flavors that I would then watch the clerk measure into a cup. I had the option to select a topping that—for an additional cost per topping—could be, again, measured out and added to the cup by the clerk behind the counter. Then, we would pay per cup and per topping in a transactional, impersonal manner from a set menu of prices. As a kid, going with my father to get frozen yogurt was still a special treat that we enjoyed doing together, but it was inherently less…creative. In fact, when that particular chain went out of business, I had only ever tried one flavor of yogurt. I simply took what was served to me, and rarely had the opportunity (or the initiative) to think outside of the box.

This anecdote provides a simple, yet accurate allegory about self-sufficiency in our new data-driven culture. In the older model, the yogurt is the data, the clerk is IT, and the customer is the business user steadily requesting data. The old model—where IT prepares the data in a pre-defined way and delivers it to the business user—is self-service and it is traditional BI. I have access to the same basic ingredients—yogurt flavors and toppings—but someone else is measuring it out and giving it to me. All I get to do is consume. How would you feel if you realized you only got to play with one way of interacting with data—ever?

The new way—where IT provides access to the data and allows the user to explore, shape, and consume the data how they need to—is self-sufficiency and its discovery. Not only do I have access to all the ingredients that I need, but I also have the ability to measure my own yogurt, decide my own toppings, and toss in whatever types and amounts of either (or both) that I want to find new patterns and new tastes. Now, I get to customize my discovery experience to my own requirements. It is an endless supply of mix-and-match possibilities using the same basic elements to find new discoveries and insights while expectations and conditions are constantly envolving. That discovery environment gives business users the tools, the environment, and the access they need to shape their own experience in the data. And, that discovery environment (just like the new yogurt shops versus the progressively obsolete ones of the past) requires self-sufficiency to thrive.

3.2 DISCOVERY CAPABILITIES FOR SELF-SUFFICIENCY

As defined in chapter: Improved Agility and Insights Through (Visual) Discovery, discovery is—in a very simplified version—an iterative, revolving process where data is virtualized or modeled and then visualized to see insights into the data. Once new insights have been discovered (or not), discovery continues in an exploratory "lather, rinse, and then repeat" cyclical fashion until new insights are uncovered.

If we think of discovery as a process, then self-sufficiency is the charge—the battery, if you will—that sparks that process from a framework to an action. It is the mechanism that makes discovery "go."

For a visual example, think of self-sufficiency as a perfect triangle (as depicted in Figure 3.2), with tools, environment, and access each being one of its three points. Like any shape, the triangle requires its three points to retain its form. A failure in any of these three points becomes an Achilles Heel in discovery. If you care to revisit the discussion on friction from the previous chapter, you could

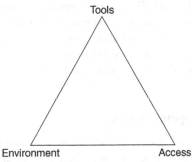

FIGURE 3.2 Self-Sufficiency Triangle

expand this idea in terms of slope, and consider that the addition of friction-causing activities in each of these three areas effectively steepens the angle between points, making the climb that much more uphill for the self-sufficient user. The less friction in discovery, the flatter the triangle, and the more enabled the self-sufficient discovery analyst is.

In the subsequent three sections, we will explore each of these points—tools, environment, and access—in further detail.

3.2.1 DISCOVERY TOOLS

The majority of business users are not ETL programmers. Many of them do not know how to write SQL or use other programming languages, and many of them are lacking any formal data analysis education or skills. Instead of considering this a weakness, consider it an opportunity to design from. Business users need tools that will work within the parameters of their roles, and that will allow them to discover without having to write programming code, or script, etc.—or, otherwise without the need for advanced training beyond their core function within the business. In later chapters, we will talk about the competencies and standards needed to architect governance and provide guardrails to users who lack formal data analysis and discovery training, however the emphasis in this section is simply on the tool capabilities needed to enable self-sufficient user discovery.

Bells and whistles aside, business users hunting self-sufficient discovery tools are looking for two things. First, they need agile, iterative tools that propel them beyond limited self-service capabilities and provide more opportunities to interact with the data. Second, along with best practice design, guided discovery, and other mechanisms to preserve the integrity of the discovery process and insulate the business from risk, these discovery tools also need to be visual, and invite visual discovery and storytelling to foster train of thought thinking and compelling communication of insights. Together, these are two basic criteria that are requisite for self-sufficiency: best-of-breed BI coupled with best-of-breed data visualization. Cumulatively these give users the ability to integrate and abstract data, visualize it, analyze it for insights, share discoveries—and then go back and do it all over again.

Tools are not the end-all-be-all for self-sufficiency. Along with these tools, business users need an environment to work with data—not just a local data set to tinker with offline. Some organizations are building their own environments some are turning to the cloud. Either way, what is needed is a discovery environment that responds to and leverages the capacities of self-sufficient tools.

3.2.2 DISCOVERY ENVIRONMENT

In the previous chapter, we discussed sandboxes, and their role in discovery. This type of discovery environment is important because the discovery process has to live within the business: business users are the drivers with the inherent knowledge to detect context (ie, predefinitions) and know what they are looking for. They are also the ones who may not know what they are looking for, but can—and will—know it when they see it. Discovery requires a leap of faith. Think of your discovery environment—whether in the cloud or within an architected sandbox or otherwise—again like that glorious baseball diamond in *Field of Dreams*: if you build it, they—insights—will come.

This optimistic, forward-looking mentality is a key distinction between BI and discovery. While both focus on deriving value from data, BI and discovery are differentiated in that BI relies on people to tell us what is going on inside the business, while discovery uses the data to gain insights that show us what is happening. These value opportunities typically fall into one of four categories—customer insights, risk avoidance and compliance, business optimization, and/or business innovation—and self-sufficient users are one vehicle to champion discovery in the business.

At the end of the day, providing self-sufficient users with the tools and the environment in which to use them is not just a shift we should do or react to: it is something that we have to. A 2013 IDC and ComputerWorld study found that 10–15% of organizations say that their environment consists of established discovery sandboxes. There is a good reason behind that: if you do not give people a place to innovate, they will find a place—and that place may bring unnecessary (and unknown) risk into the business. After all, "shadow IT" scenarios (a term used to describe IT systems and solutions build and used inside the organization without explicitly organizational approval) persist primarily in those companies where IT does not embrace becoming a discovery enabler for the business (in addition to their data management and governance responsibilities).

3.2.3 DISCOVERY ACCESS

Finally, the third point on the self-sufficiency trifecta, is access. Self-sufficient data discovery requires not just tools and technologies, but it also involves creating a culture of exploration and embedding analytics into the fabric of the entire business. Self-sufficient users thrive within a data culture that does not shy away from innovation, or of empowering business users to explore the data. We have to move away from the habitual hoarding of information into little silos or slapping up so much red tape to get access to nonregulated or otherwise protected data that the business user ends up just forgetting it and moving on. It is not an "unleash the firehose" mentality, but we should at least be turning on the sprinklers. Self-sufficient data discovers need more access to more data with more frequency to have as much opportunity to discover new insights as possible.

Having this data discovery environment requires overcoming that long-suffering information barrier and giving business users access to information they need—and want—to explore for new insights. No, it is admittedly not the easiest change to make, but access is a critical ingredient of self-sufficiency and it has to be resolved, governed, and set up responsibly. Whether this access is given via the cloud or the internal environment is irrelevant: self-sufficient users just need the freedom to take their toys and go play.

3.3 (INFORMATION) ENABLEMENT TECHNOLOGY

Self-sufficiency is such an important part of the new Big Data Culture because the real value of big data is utilizing it to discover new insights—and uncover new patterns or questions that we do not know already and sometimes do not even know that we are looking for—in the data. Thus, our business users and modern data analysts need self-sufficiency, enabled by discovery capabilities, including tools, environments, and more frequent and open data access, in order to truly maximize the value proposition of data discovery. And, as mentioned already, enabling business users in discovery is part of IT's new role. In fact, that is IT's new role: they need to become information enablement technology, not just information technology. IT—or, ET—is (and will continue to be) responsible for helping enable more self-sufficient opportunities for business users to explore and do more so that we discover more and, as a result, gain more actionable insights that bring value back to the business.

More enabled users results in reduced demands on IT to endlessly perform tasks that users can now do for themselves (again, this is the concept of friction and "frictionless" that was introduced in chapter: Improved Agility and Insights Through (Visual) Discovery). When IT takes business requirements there is a big challenge in distinguishing between generalization (for many) and personalization (for one). Self-sufficiency enables personalization and governance guides generalization. Yes, IT's role is going to change, but within this change comes the perfect opportunity for IT to step up and educate the business on IT processes and governance. The business does not have the background (or interest) in systems and data management—knowledge about the maintenance of systems, about standards and management and service-level agreements, and so on. And, with reduced business user needs, IT has more time to focus on navigating governance, security, and other quagmires that keep popping up for data and platform management—especially in an ecosystem driven by self-sufficiency.

Really, it is a win–win for IT—and there is little need for IT to become defensive or insecure about the reshaping of their role. Instead, ET needs to take the initiative to educate the business on (1) how technology works, (2) what to expect, and (3) how to properly articulate their requirements and needs. Because of IT's proven capability to standardize and efficientize information, as much as they will become an enabler, they will also take the role of a technology administrator. We will analyze this further in a later chapter on the joining of governance and discovery.

Of course, not everyone in IT will see this as a win–win. For example, if traditional IT now has a new focus, one next question becomes: what will become of all the IT developers in this new era of self-sufficiency? What is going to happen to them? I think many IT folks would be quick to argue that they have plenty of other things to be setting their minds to. But, discovery is not prototyping. IT developers will still productionize; they will find a home, write the code, optimize, and harden designs into processes. They will still develop and build, it is just going to get started a little differently is all— with discovery and governance in addition to (or in lieu of) requirements gathering processes.

As with any change, there was inevitably be doubt, potential reservations, and resistance. However, now is not the time to sling around the Borg mantra "resistance is futile" but instead to work together collaboratively to migrate through those changes as they come. There will be early adopters and there will be late adopters. There will be champions and naysayers. This is to be expected and should be approached with a keen sense of change leadership.

Along with the revised job description of business users and IT, there are also new roles working their way into the organizational charts of companies across virtually every industry vertical. Beyond "new" some of them are even super sexy. And when we think of sexy data science jobs, there is one that immediately pops in our mind. This is the role of the Data Scientist.

3.4 THE DATA SCIENTIST: THE SEXIEST OF THEM ALL

While the original credit for the concept of "sexy statistics" goes to Google's chief economist Hal Varian (2009) perhaps it all started—the romance and the legends alike—in a *HBR* article by Tom Davenport and DJ Patil (2012). In the breath of one headline—*Data Scientist: The Sexiest Job of the 21st Century*—Tom and DJ managed to upgrade the mental image of the geeky math guy from pocket calculators and too-short pants to one of a hipper, cooler guy (or gal) in a t-shirt. Thick-rimmed black glasses somehow came back into style. In fact, those hipster frames somehow became the logo of the data scientist, regardless of whether any actual data scientist has ever worn them or not (I still have not met one that does). For myself, the memory that comes immediately to mind when I think of the data scientist is one event where a respected industry analyst, participating on stage in a dueling keynote with another analyst, put on a pair of black spectacles and pronounced himself a data scientist in front of the audience's eyes. When I renewed my eyeglasses prescription I even subconsciously chose a pair of the black frames—and statistics have been my nemesis since high school.

But, just like in high school, once we all heard that the data scientists were hot, they got really, really popular—and really, really fast. Suddenly, they were the stuff of dozens of articles, infographics and, on occasion, the beneficiary of a zinger or two about ponytails and hoodies. At *Teradata PARTNERS* in October 2013, one analyst called them new versions of old quants. They have been firmly denied any of thought-leader Jill Dyché's affections according to her blog post *Why I Wouldn't Have Sex with a Data Scientist* (Dyché, 2013). And, my personal favorite: industry writer Stephen Swoyer labeled them unicorns—fantastical silver-blooded beasts of folklore and impossible to catch. If there was a home-coming king/queen of the data industry in 2012, it would have, without a doubt, been the data scientist.

In the wake of their first appearance, some of the craze surrounding the data scientist has, admittedly, died down a bit—though by no means has it settled into the cozy comfort of urban legend. Just about everyone still has something to say about the data scientist, and for good reason: finding one is hard, retaining them even more difficult. For all their allegorical appeal, to a large degree the data scientist is something of a rare creature. This is partly because the genetic makeup of the data scientist is a hybrid mix of both skillset and mindset. And, that skillset itself is blended—and one that is still difficult to find as educational programs and experience with brand new (and intrinsically fluid) tools and technologies are almost impossible to keep up with (this will be the focus of chapter: The Data Science Education and Leadership Landscape). After all, it is hard to be an expert in something that just appeared on the market 6 months ago—or less.

3.4.1 THE BLENDED APTITUDES OF DATA SCIENTIST, PhD

First, let us talk skillset. One often-disputed characteristic of the data scientist is their educational background. Some say that the data scientist is a PhD statistician or mathematician with business acumen and a knack for communicating technical info. Others believe it is an MBA graduate with tech savvy aptitudes. And, still some say it is both…or neither, or that the data scientist is a myth, or that it is really the everyday analyst that holds the real value. The jury is still out.

Regardless, one question that manages to always bubble to the top is: does the data scientist need a terminal degree—or, to put it another way, should our data unicorns be limited to data scientist, PhD? While I cannot answer that question definitively, I would like to provide at least some kind of practicable advice for you. Here is what a tiny sample of de facto data scientists in my network had to say:

> *Data Scientist #1*—has a PhD in engineering and data management—said that a PhD student with statistical skills is typically a good candidate for a data scientist role—so long as he or she is willing to engage with the business context.
>
> *Data Scientist #2*—has a PhD in applied mathematics—said that math teaches the ability to abstract problems and dive into data without fear. And, while a business background is important, it does not give a data scientist the skillset to execute a data problem.

Granted the sample size was miniscule and seeing as how both the data scientists above happened to have doctorate degrees (although in different fields), I will gladly admit that their positions on the issue were probably biased. But, that aside, if you look closely we can tweeze two very interesting pieces of insight out of those comments. Does having advanced mathematics education give some a better ability to execute—turning business ideas into solutions that can be delivered to others? Or, perhaps data people simply can more easily understand what the business needs than a businessperson can understand what the data is capable of? I am not suggesting any answers, but it is definitely food for thought.

Either way, competency in mathematics (especially statistics) is unanimously important for a data scientist—perhaps even more so important than having a business background. Yet, there is also a common sentiment that it is (typically) easier to interface with someone who has a business background, as opposed to one highly technical. And that is where we shift to a business-education skillset: clear, effective communication delivered in a simple format that business executives expect—and that lacks mysterious data jargon. Equally as important for the successful data scientist is the ability to translate and engage between both business and IT, and have a firm understanding of the business context in which they operate.

So, business acumen and statistical skills—got it. These two competencies are complementary, even if they are imbalanced. But, maybe a data scientist does not need a degree that says data science any more than they need an MBA. What the data scientist does need is a foundational understanding of these concepts. More important, these unicorns require a third skillset that is a little more intangible: an eagerness to explore and discover within data. Beyond their educational background, the characteristic that really seems to set the data scientist unicorn apart from the data user herd is their personality. This is the other half of the blended aptitude: the mindset to go along with the skillset. A true data scientist possesses a suite of hidden skills, including things like innovative thinking, the readiness to take risks and play with data, and a thirst to explore the unknown—and he looks to see how these skills are embedded within the integrated whole of education and experience.

The best data scientist(s) who you will find out there today are not just the ones with the right skills to do the job, but the ones who think about the job the right way, too. These curious unicorns are the ones who are able to divorce the idea that formal education is simply on the job training and keep their humanity intact. Being a data scientist is not about checking off a list of qualifications and adding buzzwords to a resume. It is about becoming a data scientist—having the eagerness and hunger to dig deep inside data and find value. That is aspiration, and it is an intrinsic characteristic not taught in any program.

Remember: the key to discovery is curiosity. Not just in curiosity-enabling technologies, but more important, in curiosity-driven personalities. This is, ultimately, the demystification of the data scientist. It is not limited to a dissection of their skills, academic pedigree, or depth of business knowledge, but an innate component of their personality type. The discovery culture in the business as it relates to the people, then, is a function of matching personality to possibility.

That said, there are some essentialities to being a good data scientist who are becoming more and more ubiquitous in the data scientist job description. If you are hunting for the perfect data scientist resume, consider the below. They must:

- Be of an analytical and exploratory mindset
- Have a good understanding of how to do data-based (quantitative) research
- Possess statistical skills and be comfortable handling diverse data
- Be clear, effective communicators with the ability to interact across multiple business levels
- Have a thorough understanding of their business context

Ultimately, it is not just about the knowledge the data scientist brings with them. It is about the willingness to keep learning. Regardless of what works for your particular organization or job description, the key is this: hire for capability, not for skill set. The skillset will change; the mindset, however, will not (Box 3.2).

At the end of the day, we have got to get beyond the sex appeal of the data scientist and start thinking of data science more broadly—not as a particular set of technologies or skills, but as those people who have a set of characteristics: curiosity, critical-thinking, and the ability to communicate insights and assumptions. And this does not necessarily mean we have to look outside of our company walls. Those naturally inquisitive people already living and breathing the data within our businesses are every bit as much capable of being the next data scientist, even if they do not have the fancy job title.

One thing is for certain: data scientists come in as many colors as the rainbows that their fantastical counterparts dance upon. But data scientists, no matter how sexy or rare they are, are not the only source of discovery within the organization, especially with the rapid increase of self-sufficient discovery tools allowing everyday business users to explore their own data. The lone data scientist does not scale,

BOX 3.2 DO PhDs WANT TO WORK OR TEACH?

Certainly, the data scientist is no stranger to this question—nor is any PhD who is not in a full-time academic position. Yet, in my experience, just as soon as someone asks the inevitable, "What are you going to do with a doctorate degree?" they almost immediately answer their own question with another, "Teach?" Indeed, academics are a very competitive sport and top positions are relatively few, however today's data-driven companies cannot afford to be without people thinking and solving problems at the intersection of mathematics, data analysis, and computer science. The price tag alone—never mind the aptitudes or availability—of a data scientist can be one of the ways in which they are nearly impossible to capture by some companies.

"I know of a handful of people in my [statistics] program [at University of Colorado] that are now data scientists, researchers, and machine learning experts in industry rather than professors," says Boulder-based data scientist Dr. Nathan Halko. "I don't know what the industry scene was like 10 years ago as I was blissfully studying math for the fun of it. I didn't know that the data scientist would emerge as such a key role in industry/business, but from what I gather that has been changing only recently."

Yes, there are many opportunities to work on interesting problems outside of academia, and the data scientist is willing to tackle them, too.

and if you define data scientist community as a set of skills, you are missing out on a ton of people who already exist in your organization—and who can contribute a ton of value, too.

3.5 **MOVING FORWARD**

Whether it is supporting the enablement of self-sufficient business users with internal training, support, and opportunities; or harnessing the educational opportunities brought to light by the surplus of powerful and intuitive tools already available to business users; or simply looking to hire and retain the rarest of data scientists, the simple truth is that continuous learning and improvement are the main source of competitive advantage in an era of business disruption and reinvention. And, as the next-generation of knowledge workers and information leaders, millennials are on course to become the most educated generation in American History. In fact, they will have overtaken the majority representation of the workforce by the end of 2015—last year (Pew Research Center, 2010). Building a blended education model that connects research and academia with experienced professionals, and hands-on practicable experiences facilitates a knowledge transfer that will not only empower the individual, but continue to bring value into the next-generation of the organization. Further efforts in this space should include an increased focus on mentorship between incoming and retiring workers to facilitate knowledge transfer, as well as the continued availability of more internship opportunities for incoming graduates.

However, merely educating incoming knowledge workers is not the answer to developing future technology leaders. Likewise, innovation cannot be a reactionary Measure. Reinvention is an intentional and proactive process designed to reimagine leadership potential (Gallagher et al., 2010). This leadership potential dives much further than the internal affairs of IT, academic research, and business acumen: it becomes a process of developing competent data leaders and equipping them with the skills they need to be successful.

The term "leadership" commands a broad umbrella of competencies and capabilities, including leadership styles, models, coaching, and more. But one thing I want to give special consideration to is ethics. Today, leaders are expected to adhere to ethical standards in the way they interact with the business and how the businesses they champion interact with and impact society. This is especially relevant in the world of data, and analysts and researchers in the business intelligence and big data industry have written extensively on the need for ethics in various aspects of the emerging data-centric culture. Whenever technology innovation—such as big data—moves faster than society, business, and people can handle, the question of ethics inevitably comes up. Business ethics have always been an issue, and today this includes the business use of data with known—and unknown—customers and consumers.

As we start to consider the governance, privacy, security, and other ethical quagmires that face the big data democracy that is gaining momentum with every advancement the importance of ethical conduct becomes increasingly more imperative. This will be the lens for how we approach the next chapter.

REFERENCES

Davenport, T.H., Patil, D.J., 2012. Data scientist: the sexiest job of the 21st century. Harvard Bus. Rev 90 (10), 70–76.

Dyche, J., 2013. Why I wouldn't have sex with a data scientist. Available from: http://jilldyche.com/2013/01/03/why-i-wouldnt-have-sex-with-a-data-scientist/.

Dyche, J., 2015. The new IT. McGraw-Hill, New York, NY.

Gallagher, D., Dadone, T., Foster, S., 2010. Reinventing Leadership Development: Proactive and Progressive Strategies. [Books 24x7 version].

Pew Research Center., 2010. Millennials: A Portrait of Generation Next.

(2009). Hal Varian on how the Web challenges managers. Available from: http://www.mckinsey.com/insights/innovation/hal_varian_on_how_the_web_challenges_managers.

Navigating ethics in the big data democracy

*"Ethics is knowing the difference between what you have a right to do
and what is right to do."*
—Potter Stewart

4.1 INTRODUCTION

This chapter begins, ironically as ethics could (and does, often) easily provide enough fodder for a book on its own, with one of the simplest introductions in this book.

With the arrival of big data, companies have a huge opportunity to capitalize on—or even exploit—information for business value in new ways. By this point in our discussions (as well as your general understanding of the data industry), this should not come as a bombshell of new insight. It should be more of an accepted truth. We have more data, with more diversity, from more sources, and with more people contributing to the pool of information available than ever before. We have more ways to work with this data, too, and more motivation to use it in novel ways to disrupt industries and transform our businesses. However, we still have to figure out *how* to do this—both in the operational sense (through technologies, architectures, analytical models, and so on) as well as philosophically. Many of these are new and emerging questions that we are only just beginning to consider. I like to refer to these as a new generation of ethical quagmires—how we can (or should) approach navigating ethics in the big data democracy.

Ethics is one of those conversations that has the tendency to either get people fired up or to do the exact opposite—bore them to death. I happen to be among the former. In fact, discussions regarding big data ethics are actually some of my favorite discussions to have, and those that generally get the most animated when I have the opportunity to engage in them with live audiences. Often these bleed over into more in-depth conversations on peripheral (and just as important) topics, such as governance, privacy, best practices, and so on, and how we can combat ethical ambiguities by anticipating them in our system designs. However, for this chapter we will stick to ethics and the morality of the collection and use of big data, how these affect our data-driven decisions, and how we communicate these with data visualization. Primarily, we will explore these through personal applications of potentially sticky ethical data situations, case studies, and by engaging in real-life, thought-provoking exercises.

4.2 AFTERSHOCKS OF THE BIG DATA REVOLUTION

Like so many things top-of-mind in the data industry, this conversation begins with focusing, again, on big data. In chapter: Seperating Leaders From Laggards, we paid homage to big data as the Incredible Hulk of BI, though it has been little more than an undercurrent in the previous few chapters without any concentration. This was intentional, as I have reserved the big data conversation for now. Definitions offer good starting points, so let us begin there.

Big data is a term used to describe the massive data sets (and related analytical techniques) that are too large and too complex to rely on traditional data storage, analysis, and visualization technologies. It is shaped partly by ultra-fast global IT connections, the development and deployment of business-related data standards, electronic data interchange formats, and the adoption of business database and information systems that have facilitated the creation and disbursement of data (Hsinchun et al., 2012). Contributing to this, the willingness of consumers to directly share information about themselves and their preferences through web services and social media has further enhanced the volume and variety of complex unstructured and customer sentiment data available for interpretation and use (Nunan and Di Domenico, 2013). The widespread and robust amount of data generated has led to an increased reliance upon data by the business, and big data strategies are now a critical component of business objectives as organizations seek to maximize the value of information.

To capture this surplus of ever-generating information, the advent of new technologies—such as cloud storage and new database types—has made collecting, storing, and analyzing big data increasingly more cost-efficient and manageable for the business. This has been accomplished in part by what is commonly referred to as Moore's Law: the steady continuance of technology capacity—that is, computing hardware—to double every two years, complemented by simultaneously improving efficiency and cost reduction of hardware (Ramana, 2013). For the business and its bottom line, this is good: the need to garner and exploit insights from collected information is a foundation of most business strategies, providing a key-in-lock mechanism to reach established business metrics and quantify strategy efforts. We now have more technology to truly make use of our data in ways we never could before.

It would be fair to say that "big data" has been the linguistic power couple of the data industry for the past decade or so. This is for good reason. It was not too long ago that large volumes of information were available only to the selected few able to afford the expensive IT infrastructure to collect, store, manage, and analyze it. These were the big budget companies with seemingly bottomless pockets, or the Internet companies that built empires on collecting and interpreting data—those with the Big Budgets to invest in Big Iron. But now, with new technologies and through the realized effects of Moore's law as described earlier, along with the consumerization of BI and analytics tools, this big data is increasingly available to everyone—and without having to dig deep into budgets or employ robust IT departments. This is especially important for small (and newer) businesses that need access to data to survive and thrive. Widespread access to data is empowering these organizations to easily and affordably access, collect, and analyze data to create new opportunities within their markets and customers. This is the quiet momentum of "data democratization" that has emerged in the wake of the big data revolution. Through the emergence of web-based data collection and analysis and richer self-service technologies, this data democracy is enabling fast access to actionable insights. As a result, organizations, from the massive to the miniscule, are racing to get a handle on their big data.

Race they should. Big data equals more information and information, as we all know, is power. Access and insight into data drives innovation and competition. Likewise, it is the ability to index and integrate information to improve performance and create opportunity. It is the grease that oils the gears that spur innovators to innovate, creators to develop, and marketers to market—what GoodData CEO Roman Stanek aptly termed "the oil of this century." More important, individual consumers are becoming the new market research companies—and they are ready to capitalize on their data. There is a greater emphasis on mobile engagement and a mainstream willingness to share data online, including behavioral data. Users themselves are generating a huge chunk of all the new data that we are using in our advanced analytic efforts today. In practice, this is where that visual imperative becomes so worthwhile: sometimes the best—or only—way to truly make sense of this big data is via the power of data visualization. We have to literally see it to understand it.

However, the continued proliferation of big data does not simply offer promise and opportunity. It has also raised concerns over privacy, security, and the guiding principles surrounding the collection, storage, aggregation, distribution, and use of sensitive information. While big data presents a convergence of technological and strategic capabilities that provide significant potential for data-driven organizations to squeeze the value out of information, it also brings the potential to use this data unethically. Because of this, one of the most pressing concerns in the development of future information leaders is the focus on developing ethical competencies to engage in an increasingly data-dependent business environment. And it brings top-of-mind unique questions on how users contribute to and participate in the big data democracy, too.

One of the most salient themes in these concerns relates to the nature of knowledge and its connection with power. Along with the "Power of Knowing" comes the obligation to use this knowledge responsibly. While laws will set the legal parameters that govern data use, ethics establish the fundamental principles of "right and wrong" critical to the appropriate use of data in the technology age—especially for the Internet of Things. Unfortunately, though the concept of ethics is important, it rarely receives much attention until someone does something perceived as "unethical." The black and white guidelines of laws and regulations typically appear in hindsight—until we know something is "wrong" to do (or, until we do something that has what are generally agreed to be widespread negative consequences), it is unlikely that such rules will appear.

Therein lies the rub: now that we have the chance to get our hands on all kinds of new and exciting data, what can we do with it? And more important, what *should* we do with it? While ethics in big data is bound to get more complicated as data-dependency, data democracy, and technologies advance, if we do not institute ethics cultures, education, and policies now it will only become more difficult down the road.

Big data exists in an environment of duality, with one side the potential and opportunity embedded in the untapped value of information and insights learned in analytical discovery processes, and the other a mixed bag of concerns for privacy, quality, and the appropriate use of information, and its impact on society-at-large. Data-driven companies must proactively implement a culture of ethics that will set precedents in how it approaches the appropriate use of, responsibility for, and repercussions for data's use by leaders who rely on data to make decisions and take action within their organizations. Providing future technology leaders with a foundation in ethical responsibility and accountability will support the emergence and nurturing of complementary leadership competencies in emotional and cultural intelligence; transformational and adaptive leadership; and critical thinking and decision-making. We will discuss this leadership aspect in greater detail toward the end of this chapter, but first let us talk through a few key areas that may have an especially big ethical footprint.

4.3 BIG DATA'S PERSONAL IMPACT

One of the most effective ways to make a philosophical conversation about ethics impactful is to make it personal. In this, big data ethics are no different. Big data opens up opportunities to use customer and consumer information in new ways, many of which pose the potential for exploitation. However, it would be a mistake to think that all this data is stuff that is being collected about us. As mentioned earlier, much of this is data that we are generating about ourselves. Through our digital activities, people are one of the biggest contributors to the ever-deepening pool of big data, and we are generating an avalanche every minute of every day. Don't believe me? Let us quickly review some of the data on big data.

Take a look at the infographic (Figure 4.1), which was presented by Domo in 2012. As you can gather from its title, the infographic was intended to illustrate how much data is generated by people every minute of every day. And, it does what an infographic is designed to do: it allows us to see some immediate takeaways into very big numbers. For example, we can see that for every minute of the day in 2012, we pinged Google with over two million search queries. We collectively sent about 204,166,667 emails. We spent a lot of time building and sharing content, with hundreds of new websites and blog posts per minute. We were also starting to really get into the groove of social media: 3,600 photos on Instagram per minute; 100,000 tweets, and so on.

The problem with this data—as is so often the problem with data these days—is that the 2012 infographic very quickly became outdated. Thus, Domo updated its infographic in 2014 (Figure 4.2). More than just an update on our digital activities, in the mere space of two years we can already spot some major trends in how we are behaving digitally.

Between 2012 and 2014, we started to send slightly fewer emails (a small decrease from 204,166,667 emails to only 204,000,000). We apparently got a lot more curious—twice as much in fact: our Google searches doubled from 2 million a minute to 4 million. We also spent less time building content online and more time sharing content and details about our lives and our opinions. Tweets per minute nearly tripled and Facebook, Pinterest, Tinder, and other social platforms all leap frogged. Take a look at Instagram, which grew from 3,600 new photos a minute in 2012 to 216,000 new photos in 2014—that is an increase of 6,000%. Flipping between these two visuals suddenly that 2012 infographic just seems...*so* 2012. I am willing to bet that when Domo produces an even more updated infographic (which I hope they do), 2014 is going to look pretty historical already, too.

We have been busy generating a massive amount of data—all that digital activity—about ourselves, on top of all the other data that is coming in from everywhere else, like sensors and wearables, or our sales transactions at the super market. And it is safe to assume that all that data is not just languishing in some ignored data warehouse somewhere (though some probably is until we can figure out how to use it). How is all that data about us being used? And, beyond just the sum of the data points, what does it say about us—the users?

This was the question I asked a room full of attendees in a recent session at the 2015 TDWI Boston Analytic Experience conference, where we enjoyed a lively, open dialog about the emerging technological, commercial, and moral issues surrounding big data. In that session, we focused on five key areas in which big data may impact the lives of people without their immediate knowledge, from protecting their social relationships to preserving individual privacy in a public world. Let us explore those briefly now.

4.3.1 SOCIAL GRAPHS

Social graphs are our network of interconnected relationships online—from our LinkedIn professional networks to our personal Facebook networks, and everything in-between. To truly appreciate the complexity and connectedness of social graphs, we have to first quantify how many people are on social networks.

Of the near 3 billion people on the Internet (some numbers say this number is 2.4 billion, others put it closer to 2.95 billion), 74% are active social media users. In January 2014, the Pew Research Center released its Internet Project Omnibus Survey.

FIGURE 4.1 Data Never Sleeps, Infographic by Domo

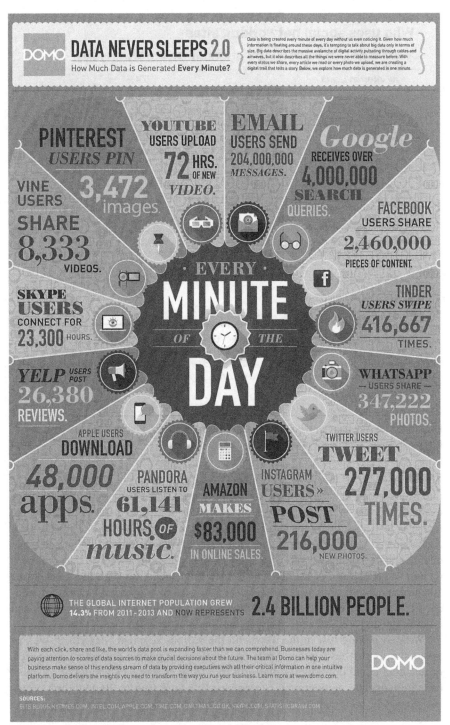

FIGURE 4.2 Data Never Sleeps 2.0, Infographic by Domo

Who uses social networking sites

% of internet users within each group who use social networking sites

All internet users	74%
a Men	72
b Women	76
a 18-29	89cd
b 30-49	82cd
c 50-64	65d
d 65+	49
a High school grad or less	72
b Some college	78
c College+	73
a Less than $30,000/yr	79
b $30,000-$49,999	73
c $50,000-$74,999	70
d $75,000+	78

Pew Research Center's Internet Project January Omnibus Survey, January 23-26, 2014.
Note: Percentages marked with a superscript letter (e.g., [a]) indicate a statistically significant difference between that row and the row designated by that superscript letter, among categories of each demographic characteristic (e.g., age).

PEW RESEARCH CENTER

FIGURE 4.3 Survey Data on Who Uses Social Networking Sites, Presented by the Pew Research Center's Internet Project January Omnibus Survey

This survey and its takeaway percentages is outlined above in Figure 4.3. What is interesting about this data is how surprisingly even all of the percentages are. For example, there is no significant gender gap amount social media users, with 72% of men and 76% of women engaged. The same type of spread appears through levels of education and income. The only statistically significant differences are in age range demographics, but these come with a few caveats. First, there was no data collected on users under the age of 18. Likewise, a noticeable lag in use evidences in the over-50 age demographic, but there are a wide number of environmental factors that influence this segment, too (including mortality rates, familiarity with technology, and other health and medical concerns that limit Internet access).

Without getting lost in the weeds on the various segments described, we can assert simply that, as a general rule of thumb, most people are online. It is pretty much an equal opportunity platform that truly encourages people of all ages, backgrounds, and demographics to connect, making true on its longtime promise. However, we need to be able to put this in a more personal context. One

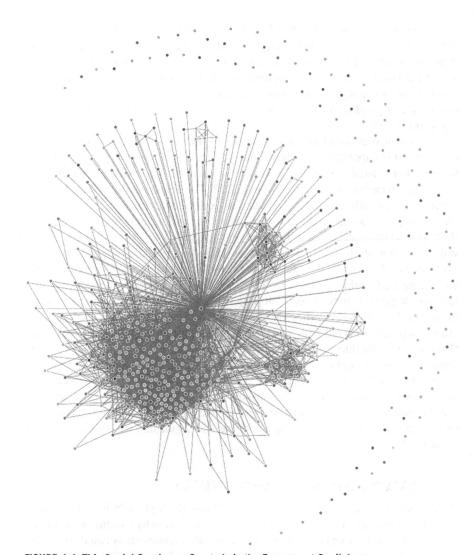

FIGURE 4.4 This Social Graph was Created via the Free app at Socilab.com

It visualizes the first 500 of my personal LinkedIn connections

way to really be able to recognize just how complex and interconnected your social network is to visualize it. Take a look at Figure 4.4. This is an example of a
social graph. Using Socilab—a free online tool—I visualized the first 500 of my
personal LinkedIn connections. From a personal perspective, what I find interesting is what I can infer about my relationships via these connections. I can make
certain assumptions about the denser portions of my network and assume that
these gray areas are my friends, colleagues, peers, and associates in the greater
business intelligence industry. Likewise, I would guess that similar clusters might

be various academic networks that I am heavily involved with. What is even more curious is interpreting the disconnect outliers at the outer ring of my network. Who are those people, and why are not they connected to at least one other person? I am usually fairly discriminatory on whom I connect with and would not expect to see so many disconnected "connections." Do you see the same patterns in your social graphs? What do these connections say about me, and what does it say about them?

Looking at your social graph is a fun personal exercise, but in the scope of big data ethics it is important to remember that you are not the only one looking at your network. For example, Facebook is somewhat infamous for its Graph Search, a semantic search engine introduced in March 2013. This feature combined the big data acquired from its billion-strong user base and external data (including that from Microsoft Bing) into a search engine to provide user-specific search results (eg, it could show you which restaurants in London your friends have visited). Graph Search was met with a whirlwind of privacy issues (including its share of hoaxes, like one that announced that the app made private Facebook content visible to strangers) and after being made public to users in July 2013, Facebook changed its graph search features, dropped its partnership with Bing, and eliminated most search patterns by the end of 2014. However, while Facebook's Graph Search did not exactly take off, other companies working with social graphs as a part of marketing research, are. One example is Boulder, CO-based startup Spotright, which has developed a patent-pending social graph platform—GraphMassive™—that maps billions of consumer relationships and interests across social media with individual-level offline data (ie, demographics). Using data and relationships provided from analyzing your personal social networks, social graphs can be a tool for marketers and data-driven companies to amp up their efforts in targeting marketing and segmentation. How do you feel about that?

4.3.2 DATA OWNERSHIP AND DATA MEMORY

Data ownership refers to who owns—or *should* own the legal right to and complete control over data. Data memory compounds data ownership by looking at the length of time data can be stored or recalled. These are often addressed as two distinct categories, but for the sake of brevity I will combine them here.

In the scope of data ownership and memory, what is perhaps most interesting is the juxtaposition between who we—as consumers—*think* should have ownership and access to data versus who actually does. Figure 4.5 on the next page is a data visualization of the 2013, J.D. Power and Associates Consumer Privacy Research Study. Notice how noticeably different ideas our ideas are about who we think should access data—from our friends and families to the government—and how even our own ideas about this change across different devices and activities.

It would appear that for our cell phone data—texts, pictures, or maybe even game app data—we are basically okay with our family members having access to all that data. However, we do not want that same group of people to look into

Graph 4: Who Should Have Access to Online Data

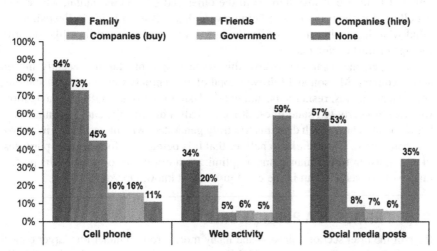

FIGURE 4.5 Results of the 2013 J.D. Power and Associates Consumer Privacy Research Study

our web browsing history. In fact, we do not really want anyone to access our web activity data, especially not the government. I suspect that we are okay with companies we work for (hire), having more access to our cell phone data because so many of us use company-provided or BYOD programs at work. Other than that, we really do not want companies—whether those we work for or buy from—to have access to our data.

It is worth mentioning, too, that data that is private now may be public later. Facebook—this time its Timeline—is again a perfect example for this scenario. With changing privacy settings, what is posted as a private post to be shared with only friends, family, or a defined group, could very likely be changed to a public, globally-shared post at some point in the future. It is up to the user to continuously stay abreast of privacy policy changes, as well as new platform updates that can alter the way their data is openly viewed by the public. This brings up many questions regarding the longevity of data and the statute of limitations on how long the data you generate can be used for—or against—you.

4.3.3 PASSIVE DATA COLLECTION

Passive data collection is one that has the potential to go from really cool wearable devices (the focus of a later chapter) to really creepy Big Brother behavior—and really fast. In a nutshell, we can articulate this concept as data that is being collected without the express consent of the user at the time of collection. This includes everything from mob-mentality—or, opt in once and "fugget about it"—passive data collection (such as data that is collected via an app that has a one time opt-in clause at installation) to the other end of the continuum, where data is collected without the person being aware that it is even being collected, never mind what it is being used for. In the latter we could group things like security footage or traffic cameras.

As a personal example to give this some shape, my family recently moved across country. My son and I drove a total of 1600 miles, stopping at gas stations, convenience stores, restaurants, and hotels. Using my in-dash GPS for navigation, we crossed nearly ten state lines, drove on half a dozen toll roads. I cannot even begin to guess how much data this trip truly generated, who has access to it, or how it is being used. I would like to believe that it is being used for altruistic purposes, like to assist in traffic management optimization efforts or to measure the performance of my vehicle, but in the end I just do not know. Do you?

4.3.4 PRIVACY IN A PUBLIC WORLD

Each of the brief sections above—and many more—roll up under one larger ethical umbrella: privacy in a public world. It begs the question, how much privacy do we have when almost everything is public? Privacy itself is a bit of a paradox, as the concept of privacy is often cultural or based on geography (eg, Europeans have different perceptions of—and rules around—privacy than the United States), it changes over time, and is largely subjective. It is an understatement to say that digital activity is pervasive. It has become a way of life. Companies are taking to social media to communicate directly with customers. We are being forced to rely on apps and our devices in every day interactions—like urgent travel update notifications (delays/cancellations), confirming doctors' appointments, or even refilling prescriptions. With so many things "going online," if we choose not to engage with technologies in certain ways—that is, if we are not on Facebook or if we buy a car without a GPS— are we on our way to being excluded from everyday social interaction? For example, without the digital services offered by a smartphone app for local traffic, we are often excluded from seeing real-time traffic updates, which can make our work commute or other travel needs suffer, if we are unable to see potential roadblocks in our path. What about every day social needs hosted through Facebook group or event pages that make having a profile a requirement? How connected is too connected?

4.4 EXERCISE: ETHICAL DATA SCENARIOS

Ethics is deceptively simple in the abstract. When given a choice between two actions, most of us can quickly identify—on the surface—the difference between one that is "right" and one that is "wrong," however, most matters are not that black and white. Ethics exist on a continuum of shades of gray. So, let us have some fun and try out an exercise. In the next few sections, I will present you a few potential (and very realistic) ethical scenarios. I invite you to play along in this experiment, and consider how you might respond in the following situations. Would you feel differently if you were on the opposite side of the table in any of these—if your role changed from the head of analytics to the consumer demographic in question? Why, or why not?

4.4.1 SCENARIO ONE

Imagine you are the head of analytics at a major insurance provider. Your CDO asks you to create a social media presence to connect with customers' (and their networks') publically shared data. So, you do. Your CDO then asks you to mine social activities of customers to identify those who engage in extreme sports. Is it ethical to use this kind of customer data to adjust policy rates?

Considering this scenario from the consumer perspective: You are a Facebook user and "like" your insurance company online. Recently, you uploaded pictures to your page of you and some of your friends base jumping off of Royal Gorge Bridge, 956 feet in the air of Canon City, Colorado. By liking your insurance company's page, you are helping them to build a deeper view of the customer (you) as well giving them permission to engage with you on the platform. By tagging your friends, you are also inadvertently sharing insights into your social network—some of which may or may not also be customers. They see your pictures and upgrade your risk category.

But what if you tried base jumping once, hated it, and vow never to do it again? The pictures are a one off, bucket list thing and not an indicator of your every day behavior (or is it—maybe it is a prediction of what you might try later). Is that one experience enough to change your risk category? Should you have to worry about what you post on your personal Facebook page in fear that you might be subject to negative consequences by an agency that is supposed to help you? And, what about base jumping customers who are not on Facebook? They do not get the policy increase simply because they are not engaged in social media? That certainty does not seem right. So, if your online connection with the insurance company penalizing me, maybe you should not "like" them and they need to rethink their engagement model?

4.4.2 SCENARIO TWO

You are the head of analytics at a major retailer. You are asked to create a mobile app to engage customers in the store with promotional offers, coupons, etc. Your company also wants to sell its app data to its partners for targeted advertizing and cross-selling opportunities. How would you feel about exchanging customer behavioral data with third parties for the opportunity to gain better insight?

Again, here is a context to consider: I am your customer, in your store, using your app. Thanks to the location sensors in the app, your system notices that I am hovering around in the formalwear section and pushes me a coupon for 20% off on any formalwear purchase. I use the coupon, so you can be reasonably sure that I bought some type of fancy new attire. I might need shoes to go with it, and your partner shoe company is located in the storefront next to you. Is it okay for you to give them my data so they can send me offers, too?

This one is a little more complicated than the previous. Many customers might actually be quite happy if this happened: it saves them money on things they likely want or need, it is prompt and timely, and it is easy to ignore if they do not need it. When I have shared this example, eight out of ten people seem agreeable to it. However, there are still those who think it infringes on their privacy and will bring up the big data "creep factor" at being stalked while shopping. Sure, using the app is voluntary, but if—like many stores—the only coupons available are on the app, it makes it hard not to use it. Again, it is almost a privacy tax not to use the app (and thus not have access to the money-saving coupon). Is this a situation where, as Mr Spock so famously said, the needs of the many outweigh the needs of the few? Is there a way to keep both the majority and the minority happy shoppers, or is that small percent worth losing?

4.4.3 SCENARIO THREE

You are the head of analytics at a social networking site. Your CDO wants to allow researchers access to user-generated data in order to alter the user experience to conduct experiments on user sentiment and behavior. Is it ethical to manipulate user emotions even if it is for academic or medical research?

This scenario never fails to elicit some kind of immediate, visceral response from an audience (I think it is that word "manipulate"). No one seems to be fond of the idea of turning over data to researchers and letting them play with it, especially when we do not know it is happening and there is the real possibility that they are literally toying with our emotions. But, with things like cyber bullying constantly making headlines, what if these researchers do find an insight on how teenage suicides can be linked to what they see on social media and this discovery can save lives? Does it make a difference if we know the end goal of the research or not—the idea of informed consent? What about if we know that it is going on versus finding out about it later?

4.5 DATA ETHICS IN THE NEWS

If this last scenario presented in the earlier section sounds strangely familiar to you, it is probably because it is not hypothetical. In fact, something very similar happened in 2014. Moreover, these kind of sticky ethical data circumstances creep to the top of tech news very often. This section will look briefly to a sample of situations of companies not-so-ethical use of big data that have made big headlines.

4.5.1 FACEBOOK

The fact that we can pick on Facebook so much as an example of all things good and bad about the most data-centric companies is a testament to just how much Facebook is pushing the envelope when it comes to operationalizing its customers' data. As of the second quarter of 2015, Facebook had 1.49 billion active users worldwide. To put that in perspective, consider that the population of China—the entire country—is just shy of that number at an estimated 1.39 million (as of July 2014 by Worldometers). (If you are inclined, there is an interesting static timeline visualization that shows the increase of active Facebook users from 2008–15 at http://www.statista.com/statistics/264810/number-of-monthly-active-facebook-users-worldwide/.)

With that amount of people contributing data with every click and scroll, one can only imagine just how much data Facebook really has. And, just like its user community, we can see a similar growth curve in the amount of infrastructure Facebook needs to manage all of that data. Exact details are proprietary and this is not the place for a technical discussion on how all of this data is managed, but reports from 2014 quantify the amount of data Facebook stores as some 300 PB in addition to a daily intake of about 600 TB (Cohen, 2014). (It also boasts a staff of over thirty data scientists—see research.facebook.com/datascience.)

Facebook is a hub for market (and other types) of research. In summer 2014, researchers associated with Facebook, Cornell, and the University of California-San Francisco participated in a social media-based emotion experiment (Waldman, 2014). The paper, which was published in the *Proceedings of the National Academy of Sciences*, revealed that the researchers intentionally manipulated the Facebook news feeds of nearly 700,000 of its users in order to study "emotional contagion through social networks" (Kramer et al., 2014). For the study, researchers tested the affect on user's emotions by either reducing the number of positive or negative posts that were visible on users' news feeds. This experiment raised a number of red flags, including whether university's or Facebook financed the survey. Here is the nutshell version of the research design: certain elements were hidden from 689,003 peoples' news feed (about 0.04% of users, or 1 in 2,500) over the course of seven days in 2012. The experiment hid a "small percentage" of emotional words from peoples' news feeds, without their knowledge, to test what affect that had on the statuses (including likes, commenting, or status sharing) that they posted or reacted to. The expectation was that news feeds did not affect users' mood and were simply social content hovering on the Internet. Contrary to this expectation, the researchers instead found that peoples' emotions were significantly affected by their news feeds. This phenomenon is what the researchers dubbed as "emotional contagion, or the ability for emotions to be contagious and spread virally through social content" (Arthur, 2014).

The most significant criticism of the emotion study is that it did not conform to the principles expressed in the widely regarded cornerstone document on human research ethics, the Declaration of Helsinki, which mandates that human subjects be adequately informed of, among other things, the potential risks of the study and any discomfort it may entail. This is the premise of informed consent. Because it affected users' moods (both positively and negatively), this "unethical experiment" harmed participants, and it forms the basis of widespread malcontent of the study. However, one of the researchers noted in a lengthy defense (which was published on Facebook) that the primary purpose of this study was altruistic. Kramer wrote, "The reason we did this research is because we care about the emotional impact of Facebook and the people that use our product" (Kramer, 2014).

The end result of the Facebook emotion study is that we learned that social media exposure *does* affect people's moods. We can now use this information to avoid or address certain issues, perhaps such as cyber bullying or other social problems. While that is the result, the question still remains: does this benefit overshadow the fact that a percentage of Facebook users were unknowingly subjected to emotional experiments?

4.5.2 TARGET

As the name behind one of the biggest urban legends in predictive analytics history, retailer Target is widely believed to have predicted the pregnancy of a 16-year old girl before even her father knew—which was a big surprise when coupons for baby wares arrived in the family's mailbox.

The legend began when a conspicuously titled story—*How Companies Learn Your Secrets*—by Charles Duhigg went live in a February 2012 New York Times article, followed by many similar titles that reported on the same topic. The story was largely theoretical, and detailed the work of statistician Andrew Pole (and Target's Guest Marketing Analytics team), who did indeed design a pregnancy prediction model (starting with the information and behavioral data of women enrolled in Target's baby registry). Pole's work, by the way, was not too terribly different than research from the 1980s by a team of researchers led by a UCLA professor, who undertook a study of people's most mundane shopping habits to predict major, albeit predictable changes that might impact purchasing behavior. All in all, simply understanding how habits work makes them easier to control—and predict. Nevertheless, as Pole crawled through the data, he was able to identify a few dozen products that when analyzed together, gave him the ability to assign a shopper a "pregnancy prediction" score, along with the ability to estimate a delivery date by taking buying trends and timelines into consideration. These analytics were not aimed at predicting when pregnancy would occur and proactively try to secure consumer loyalty with personalized offers, but on sending relevant offers to customers during specific stages *of* pregnancy.

Then, as many may recall, there was the story of the dad that reportedly walked into Target armed with a mailer of baby coupons and upset that his daughter had received them. He later recounted and—somewhat abashedly (per quotes printed from here to Mars)—admitted that he had not been aware of all things happening under his roof and his daughter was indeed pregnant. After this incident, according to Duhigg's article, Target went quiet and no further communication was contributed to his article—in fact, from reading his article you would get the idea that Duhigg was forcibly silenced by Target's cold-shoulder. The trail went cold, but the public spotlight only grew brighter—due in part to a second article, Kashmir Hill's *How Target Figured Out A Teen Girl Was Pregnant Before Her Father Did* (2012), which was published on the same day as Duhigg's but in short-form. Hill's article cut through the fat of the longer *New York Times* cover piece with some carefully tweezed quotes that left readers with one clear message that went viral: Target is watching you.

What was not made clear in the original article is that this was not a piece of investigative journalism. It simply reported on work presented by Pole himself in 2010 at the Predictive Analytics World Conference (PAWCon) entitled "How Target Gets the Most out of Its Guest Data to Improve Marketing ROI" (which is still available and free to view online at www.pawcon.com/Target).

So, *did* Target really predict that teenager's pregnancy and take advantage of the opportunity to send targeted marketing offers to a soon-to-be teen mom? As Eric Siegel (founder of PAWCon) wrote in his book, *Predictive Analytics: The Power to Predict Who Will Click, Buy, Like, or Die* (2013), this *probably* is not how it actually happened. This is for two reasons, according to Siegel. One it took an implication and made it fact, and two, Target "knows" consumers value privacy and thus might not enjoy being marketed to on such a private matter, and the retailer actively camouflages such product placements among other nonbaby-related products.

Thus, we are left with two different questions—*can* Target predict a customer's pregnant, and *did it* do so (and will it continue to so/do it again)? The ethical implications of either question are likely as fundamentally different as the questions themselves.

4.5.3 ASHLEY MADISON

One of the most recent data hacks you may be familiar with is that of online adultery site, Ashley Madison. With the tagline of "Life is Short, Have an Affair," Ashley Madison had amassed a user base of over 37 million users worldwide (including about one million from the UK). In July 2015, a hacking group calling themselves The Impact Team hacked Ashley's Madison database, stealing the personal and private details of those using the website and threatened to release the data to the public if the website was not taken down. As evidence of its threat, 40 MB of data was initially released, which included internal files and documents from the parent company, Canada's Avid Life Media (ALM) (Kharpal, 2015). The motivation for The Impact Team's hack was ideological in nature: the group said they targeted the ALM and its subsidiary sites because they do not agree with the morality of the service (one statement from The Impact Team referred to the site(s) as prostitution/human trafficking for rich men to pay for sex (McCormick, 2015)), as well as the fact that it is supposedly littered with thousands of fake female profiles which prey on other users.

In August 2015, after Ashley Madison's website owners, ALM (which also runs sister sites Cougar Life and Established Men, both of which are designed for users to arrange sexual encounters), refused to shut down operations, just under 10 Gb of data was released, including the names, email addresses, passwords, and bank details of accounts of users associated with the site (Tidy, 2016). The data dumped online, which by all accounts by investigators and data experts looks completely legitimate, includes some interesting names and affiliations. Personal data—including the names and, in some instances, credit card information, of approximately 10,000 email addresses that appear to be associated with government (including political party members) and military accounts (Williams, 2015) were also included in the data dump. The site users themselves were caught in the crossfire, and when Ashley Madison ultimately refused to shut down the site, the hackers made good on their threat to dump the 9.7 GB of stolen data if the site was not shut down as demanded. However, they dumped it in a place were the average person would not find it: the "dark web," which is only accessible through the Tor network (Dark Reading Staff, 2015).

Some call the act by The Impact Team "hactivism," the art of gaining unauthorized access (or "hacking") into a computer system for a politically or socially motivated personal goal. Others say that it is simply one of criminality. There are those, like Ashley Madison CEO Noel Biderman, who has been quoted as saying that "cheating is like the secret glue that keeps millions of marriages together" in order to justify hi-tech infidelity (Kharpal, 2015). Still, morality issues aside, the data hack is an illegal act against the individual members of AshleyMadison.com as well as against personal privacy and freedom to engage in lawful online activities. What do you think?

4.6 THE DATA VISUALIZATION HIPPOCRATIC OATH

Before we move forward into assessing the type of leadership competencies needed in an ethically-aware big data culture, it is worth a quick aside to realign the conversation thus far to data visualization and the visual data culture which is the heart of this text. One of the most potent applications of ethics to data visualization is through data journalism. Armed not only with more data but also with data visualization, data journalists wield an incredible amount of power into how to mislead with numbers. There have been numerous examples of "good data viz gone wrong" by news organizations that have unintentionally—or perhaps intentionally—produced faulty data visualizations (The *New York Times* has been criticized for this in a number of occasions). We will discuss data journalism more in a later chapter on visual data storytelling, but a brief mention here provides the perfect opportunity to briefly make a meaningful connection of ethics to data visualization.

Many in the data visualization industry have suggested—even demanded—the need for a sort-of data visualization Hippocratic Oath to guide data journalists and other types of business users generating data visualizations. This oath is intended to go beyond things like data visualization best practices to offer a simple and succinct essence of responsible visualization. While there is no officially recognized (or sworn) Hippocratic Oath for data visualization, at VisWeek 2011 Jason Moore of the Air Force Research Lab suggested an oath that has since been accepted by many, echoed on the blogs of data visualization galleries, practitioners, and even a few vendors and creative services.

Moore's Oath is written simply as thus:

> *"I shall not use visualization to intentionally hide or confuse the truth which it is intended to portray. I will respect the great power visualization has in garnering wisdom and misleading the informed. I accept this responsibility willfully and without reservation, and promise to defend this oath against all enemies, both domestic and foreign."*

Taking Moore's Oath one step further, I would like to add the following: I will engender the continuation of best practices and awareness of design principles in data visualization, and I will view visualizations first from the perspective of the receiver than of the creator.

The latter plays an important part in the newly formed Data Visualization Competency Center™ that I introduced at Radiant Advisors in 2015. However, this cursory mention of ethics and data visualization accomplished, let us put a pin in this topic for now and continue to narrow our focus on ethics and data leadership.

4.7 ETHICS REQUIRES LEADERSHIP

Coming from a background in leadership studies, I could not resist the urge to spend time talking about leadership in the context of ethics. One of my favorite quotes from the literature on leadership comes from New York Times best-selling business and management author John Kotter and is readily applicable to our current state of disruption and innovation in the data industry. In *A Sense of Urgency* (2008), Kotter writes that creating a sense of urgency is the "first step in a series of actions" critical to avoiding stagnation and achieving success in a rapidly changing world. To achieve this sense of urgency, leaders must commit to identifying and resolving issues that create obstacles to success. They must foster change initiatives, celebrate short-term wins that open pathways to larger goals, and they must make changes stick by incorporating them into the organizational structure, processes, and culture (Kotter, 2008). This statement resonates profoundly when applied to the ethical quagmires faced by big data. We must first and foremost embrace a sense of urgency in developing future technology leaders by fostering growth in critical leadership competencies needed for a strong foundation of ethical leadership in a dynamic data economy.

This ethical foundation begins with perspective. Developing leaders must be aware of their ethical responsibilities not only to their organization, but also to the people inside the organization, those it impacts, and society as a whole. However, an organizational structure itself (including the requisite policies and codes of ethics) does not guarantee ethical behavior unless the leadership actively demands that those policies are followed and values demonstrated.

Therefore, ethical leaders must have the courage to take action when the organizational acts unethically, even if it damages profits or has an otherwise unfavorable result on the business. As part of what Freeman and Stewart (2006) defined as a "living conversation" of ethics within an organization, just as important as the ability for leaders to take action against organizational objectives or actions perceived as unethical are mechanisms for leaders—and others within the organization—to voice concerns or "push back" too. These processes, which can be anonymous to avoid any perceived barriers or retaliation responses, are critical to avoiding the likelihood of values becoming stale or overlooked. Additionally, having this living conversation about ethics and behaviors throughout all levels of the organization provides a measure of accountability and transparency (Freeman and Stewart, 2006), reinforcing the organizational culture of ethical responsibility.

Continuous research is devoted to the study of big data and ethical implications—including the creation of best practices and incorporating mechanisms for feedback—however preparing future technology leaders to speak as advocates in the ongoing conversation on ethics, and the potential ethical issues surrounding big data is a vital component of educating emerging leaders. This begins first with the fostering and refinement of emotional intelligence as well as cultural intelligence and diversity appreciation. We will quickly review these next.

4.7.1 EMOTIONAL INTELLIGENCE

Seminal research by researchers Peter Salovey and John Mayer (1990) posited that, as humans, we have developed an emotional system that helps us to communicate problems. They coined this system "emotional intelligence" (commonly referred to as EQ). EQ is defined as the ability to monitor one's feelings and those of others, and to use that information to guide thinking and action (Salovey & Mayer, 1990). Later evangelists built upon Salovey and Mayer's original work, and "[added] in components such as zeal, persistence, and social skills" (Caruso et al., 2002, p. 307). It is now considered part of the set of multiple intelligence, and proselytized by management guru Daniel Goleman (2011) who noted that IQ and technical skills are "threshold capabilities" and that true leadership edge comes from knowledge and acceptance of emotional intelligence.

4.7.2 CULTURAL COMPETENCE AND DIVERSITY IN DATA

Diversity has an especially important impact on the assemblage, storage, and usage of big data for several reasons that extend beyond an appreciation and awareness. A primary reason is because the data itself is nearly as diverse as the mechanisms for collecting, generating, and analyzing it. There is a wide disparity in data types and origins, and the discovery capabilities of recognizing and adapting to data anomalies by many types of data users within an organization (Jonker, 2011). The commercial value of big data likewise requires a diverse application. Because much of the growth in data is due to the sharing of information directly by consumers there are implications as to the ownership of data and respecting privacy in a public environment (Nunan and Di Domenico, 2013). There is also a wide array of attitudes toward the data that is shared, and this is dependent on the social culture of where the data originates and the expectations of what data can—and should—be used for, how long it should be retained, etc.

Emerging technology leaders should be instructed in the responsiveness to a multicultural vision that assesses the cultural competence and empathy of leaders in order to help them thrive in diverse business environments. In fact, it is worth a mention that legislation for data collection, use, retention, and so forth vary worldwide as well. Thus, a widespread understanding and insight into different cultures, motivations, and norms will provide leaders with the skills to make ethical decisions when dealing with the realities, opportunities, and challenges of working in diversity and also provide them with insight into the behaviors and expectations of outside cultures (Cortes & Wilkinson, 2009).

4.7.3 ADAPTIVE LEADERSHIP AS AN APPLIED APPROACH

With the rapid rate of change, complexity, and uncertainty in the business intelligence industry, adaptive, transformational leadership is paramount to driving organizational success. The ability for organizations to mobilize and thrive in new business environments is critical, and the solutions to these challenges reside in the collective intelligence of leaders (Heifetz & Laurie, 2011). Adaptive leadership—an approach to command based on situation and factors like mission, strategy, etc.—is a trait requisite of successful leaders, however it is somewhat counterintuitive because leaders must be able to see a context for change or create one rather than respond to a need. Adaptive leadership is about leading change that enables the organization to thrive. It is the practice of mobilization, and it occurs through experimentation and requires diversity (Heifetz, Linsky, & Grashow, 2009).

Because adaptive and transformational leadership—wherein a leader is charged with identifying needed change and creating a vision to guide the change through inspiration—is individually considerate and provides followers with support, mentorship, and guidance (Bass & Riggio, 2006), it is tied to the construct of emotional intelligence. This connection between transformational leadership and emotional intelligence has been supported by several empirical studies that report a positive correlation between the two, with analysis indicating that both emotional intelligence and transformational leadership are emotion-laden constructs (Lindebaum & Cartwright, 2010). That said, the principal difference between these two theories is that emotional intelligence is applied primarily to the leader, while adaptive leadership is applied primarily to the organization. Adaptive leadership requires that a leader embrace a learning strategy to address challenges that are adaptive, or for which there are no known solutions and which require a shift in thinking (Granger & Hanover, 2012). This, in turn, denotes a need for emotional intelligence in the capacity to be self-aware and self-managing (Goleman, 2005). A transformational leader must shift perspectives in order to adapt to changes that are happening, and leverage emotional intelligence skills to motivate and inspire others to engage when confronting a challenge, adjusting values, changing perceptions, and nurturing new habits—or, behaving ethically (Heifetz & Laurie, 2011).

4.7.4 FINALLY, CRITICAL THINKING COMPETENCE

Leaders who exhibit strategic decision-making analyze ideas in a nonsuperficial way to discover logical connections for reasoning and effective judgment

(Patterson, 2011). This is particularly relevant in the era of big data, as organizations must work to harness data and uncover insights and business value within that can then be implemented into business use and part of the organizational fabric.

Remember, no two leaders are the same (Bennis and Townsend, 2005). Nevertheless, developing future technology leaders, knowledge workers, and—yes—big data experts from a foundation of ethics will contribute to how we collectively approach constructing an ethical framework for leadership behavior in an increasingly murky culture of data overload.

And, while specific practices to prepare future leaders will vary for any given industry, the inclusion of a blended education model of technical and leadership skills alongside the provision of prescriptive, applicable, and practicable experiences are paramount. Leadership is an ongoing process: learning and growth happen perpetually, and sharing these cumulative experiences provide educators with the input needed to prepare ethical, next-generation leaders—regardless of industry. This will be our focus in the next chapter.

4.8 CLOSING THOUGHTS

A few years ago, I wrote a book review on *Big Data: A Revolution That Will Transform How We Live, Work, and Think* by Viktor Mayer-Schönberger and Kenneth Culkier (2013). During that review, I had the opportunity to interview Mayer-Schönberger, and in one of our exchanges, he wrote something that has stuck with me over the years (and a quote which I included in the original review). Speaking of his book, Viktor wrote, "[We] try to understand the (human) dimension between input and output. Not through the jargon-laden sociology of big data, but through what we believe is the flesh and blood of big data as it is done right now." As a closing thought, I would like to propose that it is our human traits of creativity, intuition, and intellectual ambition that should be fostered in the brave new world of big data. That the inevitable "messiness" of big data can be directly correlated to the inherent "messiness" of being human. Most important, that the evolution of big data as a resource and tool is a function of the distinctly human capacities of instinct, accident, and error, which manifest, even if unpredictably, in greatness. And, in that greatness is progress. That progress is the intrinsic value of big data, and what makes it so compelling—but it comes at a price.

Ultimately, no one expects ethics to ever become a simple, black and white issue, and nor should it, really. However, as data and innovative technologies becomes increasingly more and more an embedded part of our every day lives, we must pay attention to the circle of interrelated ethical quagmires that we face and approach them carefully, or—as Jaron Lanier (2011) writes in his book *You Are Not a Gadget*, we should approach these as if they were *a part of* nature rather than from an externalized perspective.

REFERENCES

Arthur, C., 2014. Facebook emotion study breached ethical guidelines, researchers say. The Guardian. Available from: http://www.theguardian.com/technology/2014/jun/30/facebook-emotion-study-breached-ethical-guidelines-researchers-say.

Bass, B., Riggio, R., 2006. Transformational Leadership, second ed. Lawurence Eribaum Associates, Inc., Mahwah, NJ.

Bennis, W., Townsend, R., 2005. Reinventing Leadership: Strategies to Empower the Organization. HarperBusiness, New York, NY.

Caruso, D., Mayer, J., Salovey, P., 2002. Relation of an ability measure of emotional intelligence to personality. J. Pers. Assess. 79 (2), 306–320.

Cohen, D., 2014. How Facebook manages a 300-petabyte data warehouse, 600 terabytes per day. Social Times. Available from: http://www.adweek.com/socialtimes/orcfile/434041.

Cortes, C., Wilkinson, L., 2009. Developing and implementing a multicultural vision. In: Moodian, M.A. (Ed.), Contemporary Leadership and Intercultural Competence: Exploring the Cross-Cultural Dynamics Within Organizations. SAGE, Thousand Oaks, CA, pp. 61–73.

Dark Reading Staff, 2015. Hackers dump Ashley Madison user database…where most people won't find it. Information Week. Available from: http://www.darkreading.com/attacks-breaches/hackers-dump-ashley-madison-user-database-where-most-people-wont-find-it/d/d-id/1321810.

Duhigg, C., 2012. How companies learn your secrets. The New York Times. Available from: http://www.nytimes.com/2012/02/19/magazine/shopping-habits.html?_r=0.

Freeman, R., Stewart, L., 2006. Developing ethical leadership: Business Roundtable Institute for Corporate Ethics.

Goleman, D., 2005. Emotional Intelligence: Why It Can Matter More Than IQ, tenth ed. Bantam, New York, NY.

Goleman, D., 2011. What makes a leader? HBR's 10 must reads on leadership. Harvard Business Review Press, Boston, MA, pp. 1–21.

Granger, K., Hanover, D., 2012. Transformational performance-based leadership: Addressing non-routine adaptive challenges. Ivey Business J. 76 (1), 41–45.

Heifetz, R., Laurie, D., 2011. The work of leadership. HBR's 10 must reads on leadership. Harvard Business Review Press, Boston, MA, pp. 57–78.

Heifetz, R., Linsky, M., Grashow, A., 2009. The practice of adaptive leadership: Tools and tactics for changing your organization and the world. Harvard Business Review Press, Boston, MA.

Hill, K., 2012. How Target figured out a teen girl was pregnant before her father did. Forbes. Available from: http://www.forbes.com/sites/kashmirhill/2012/02/16/how-target-figured-out-a-teen-girl-was-pregnant-before-her-father-did/.

Hsinchun, C., Chiangm, R., Storey, V., 2012. Business intelligence and analytics: from big data to big impact. MIS Quart. 36 (4), 1165–1188.

Jonker, D., 2011. Data marts can't dance to data's new groove. Eventdy 24 (10), 10–12.

Kharpal, A., 2015. Adultery site Ashley Madison hacked, user data leaked. CNBC. Available from: http://www.cnbc.com/2015/07/20/adultery-site-ashley-madison-hacked-personal-data-leaked.html.

Kotter, J., 2008. A Sense of Urgency. Harvard Business Press, Boston, MA.

Kramer, A. [Adam], 2014. OK so. A lot of people have asked me about my and Jamie and Jeff's recent study published in PNAS, and I wanted to give a brief public explanation. The reason we did this research is because we [Facebook status update]. Available from: https://www.facebook.com/akramer/posts/10152987150867796.

Kramer, A., Guillory, J., Hancock, J., 2014. Experimental evidence of massive-scale emotional contagion through social networks. Proc. Natl. Acad. Sci. 111 (24), 8788–8790.

Lanier, J., 2011. You are not a Gadget. Vintage Books, New York, NY.

Lindebaum, D., Cartwright, S., 2010. A critical examination of the relationship between emotional intelligence and transformational leadership. J Manage. Stud. 47 (7), 1317–1342.

Mayer-Schönberger, V., Culkier, K., 2013. Big Data: A Revolution that will Transform How we Live, Work, and Think. Eamon/Dolan/Houghton Mifflin Harcourt.

McCormick, R., 2015. Ashley Madison hack could expose 37 million cheaters. The Verge. Available from: http://www.theverge.com/2015/7/20/9002185/ashley-madison-hacked-data-37-million-users.

Nunan, D., Di Domenico, M., 2013. Market research and the ethics of big data. Int. J. Mark. Res. 55 (4), 2–13.

Patterson, F.J., 2011. Visualizing the critical thinking process. Issues 95, 36–41.

Pew Research Center, 2014. Internet Project January Omnibus Survey.

Ramana, A., 2013. Applying Moore's Law to business processes. Ind. Eng. 45 (11), 33–36.

Salovey, P., Mayer, J.D., 1990. Emotional intelligence. Imagination, cognition and personality 9 (3), 185–211.

Siegel, E., 2013. Predictive Analytics: The Power to Predict Who Will Click, Buy, Lie, or Die. Wiley, Hoboken, NJ.

Tidy, J., 2016. Ashley Madison adultery data "dumped online." Sky News. Available from: http://news.sky.com/story/1537943/ashley-madison-adultery-data-dumped-online.

Waldman., 2014. Available from: http://www.slate.com/articles/health_and_science/science/2014/06/facebook_unethical_experiment_it_made_news_feeds_happier_or_sadder_to_manipulate.html.

Williams, K., 2015. Head of Louisiana GOP among those in Ashley Madison data dump. The Hill. Available from: http://thehill.com/business-a-lobbying/top-gop-official-in-ashley-madison-data-dump-hack.

The data science education and leadership landscape

"Education is the most powerful weapon which you can use to change the world."
—**Nelson Mandela**

5.1 INTRODUCTION

We left off the last chapter discussing ethics in the ongoing Big Data Revolution, closing on a brief yet detailed discussion on the need to instill critical ethical competencies on emerging IT leaders and knowledge workers. However, that begs the question: who are these incoming data science professionals? Where are they coming from and what do they look like? How *else* are we preparing them to take on roles in an ever-changing and fluid data economy? And, perhaps even more thought provoking: how are *they* contributing to the next-generation of changes in how we work with and expect results from our technologies? When we think of both the new people and the new technologies emerging in the data industry, we can imagine a very interesting future indeed.

While most of this book is dedicated to talking about the people, processes, and technologies that will enable and drive a visual culture of data discovery, this chapter focuses solely on the people impacted and affected by the aforementioned disruption, transformation, and reinvention of the data industry at large. Likewise, it closes out a few very necessary conversations that are important as we consider the future of the data-driven organization itself. We will focus on new data science programs cropping up across the world (both in academia and in industry), as well as various other key areas concerning the new landscape of digital natives and millennials quickly overtaking the data workforce.

5.2 THE NEW DATA SCIENCE STUDENT

Let us start first with the educational portion of this conversation. Business as we know it is changing. Business users, too, are changing and becoming more empowered. IT is becoming less about control and more abut enablement. New data science job descriptions—like, for example, the data scientist—are springing up. Like so much else going on in today's data intelligence industry, the landscape of data science education is every bit as fluid and dynamic. After focusing on the internal group of self-sufficient business users and the role of the data scientists, let us broaden our view to take a look at what the data science workforce may look like in years to come.

Over the past few years, we have been reminded that data workers are in demand—likewise, we have seen how limited the current supply is. If we are thinking purely in terms of those elusive unicorns with a terminal degree in hard maths, we can find little comfort in the results of a 2014 study by the National Center for Education Statistics that revealed just 1669 people graduated in 2012 with a PhD in statistics or related math degree—and only 323 were true statisticians. Don't count on a big graduation day boom, either, as the need for qualified candidates is nowhere near keeping pace with the demand. When it comes to forecasting the number of computer science jobs in the next few years, the numbers are staggering. The US Bureau of Labor Statistics estimates that by 2020 there will be 1.4 million computer science jobs available. More specifically, a recent McKinsey Global Institute (2014) study estimates that there will be 140,000–180,000 unfilled data scientist positions in the market in 2018. Naturally, demands drives prices. A data scientist can currently command a salary upward of $300,000, making even one data scientist a hefty investment (without any guarantee of delivering usable business insights). Ouch is an understatement.

Don't yet lose hope. Beyond the earlier disclaimer that data scientists are not the only ones who can bring discovery value to organizations, the paradigm shift in the data industry has not left the academic community untouched as they, too, are recalibrating to develop new educational programs that can develop the skills and education needed by incoming data science professionals. These University Information Science programs—whether labeled business intelligence, business analytics, data analysis, systems analysis, computer science, or any of the other dozen or so terms used by academia—are only just now beginning to be sorted out, much less keeping pace with the rapid rate of change happening in the industry. Nevertheless, alongside that slow-churning process of clarification, new programs are emerging to meet the increasingly complex demands of data science education.

Different universities are taking different approaches to craft a new kind of data science education. Some are reshaping existing curricula by unifying across academic silos to better integrate courses across disciplines of study. Others are forming academic alliance programs in deeper ways to give students learning experiences with contemporary industry tools and creating projects that expose students to analytical problems within real-world business context. Other universities are attempting to hone the skills of current workers through experiences, such as through on-line advanced degree programs or Massively Open On-line Courses. These are affectionately referred to as "MOOCs," a general term that applies to simpler and more impersonal ways of education made possible by "outsourcing agreements between the educational sector and external providers of multimedia materials" (Baggaley, 2013, p. 368). (Beyond this, a number of organizations run bootcamps and independent training programs (eg, mentorships, certifications, etc.) or informal programs through web seminar series and partner-vendor training, too. However, a word of caution is in order. These programs still suffer from a lack of accreditation, and with such high demand organizations are jumping on the bandwagon to address these needs with less qualified courses and certificates.)

All universities are listening to campus recruiters—who are clearly saying that we need people with more and deeper data skills and knowledge. The new generations of knowledge workers need programs that offer practical applications through real-life situations and tools used to improve learning. Students who enter the workforce with only a study-based education will lack the hands-on skills that they need to be successful. Therein lies the rub: are the new academic programs being developed to meet the next generation of BI knowledge workers applicable to the jobs available, and will they be able to answer the business challenges industry segments are grappling with today?

Academics and industry alike need sharp criteria on what will make good business intelligence and business analytics programs for the next generation of BI students. Here a few points worth of consideration:

5.2.1 MANAGING COMPLEX SYSTEMS

Today's data intelligence industry is not merely about information: it is about understanding and managing complex systems. Data discovery environments are an iterative process of moments of execution followed by celebration. This is not new—and it is been a focus for many information science programs of the past—but it is particularly relevant for data science today.

Understanding complex systems is about modeling, more so than describing or predicting. It is about understanding relationships and discovering them. While on the surface, data science looks like a lot of calculations, what is underneath are the end products of a long process that struggles with trying to understand complex systems.

5.2.2 CONTINUOUS LEARNING

Innovations in data science and their success stories may give the perception of "if you apply tool/algorithm to <insert business problem> you will be successful," but it does not work that way. Under the covers in a lot of those tools and algorithms are a lot of "I gotchas:" hundreds of assumptions that are made about what the data is really telling you and the validity of applying certain algorithms to data.

More so than ever, business intelligence and data science is a craftsmanship challenge that is focused on continuous learning—this time of learning art, rather than *only* science (because the scientific aspects of the equation are still and will continue to be, important). The industry is accompanied by a new wave of technology that has a lot of aspects of immaturity: it is not ready for prime-time to the masses. The implication, then, is that it is a very eclectic area, able to come up with new ideas from a very diverse spectrum. We talk a lot about agility in the industry these days, and that is a now nomenclature that applies as readily to business, as it does to people and technology. There is a challenge in operationalizing analytics where data science needs to monitor and tweak analytic models on a regular ongoing basis with the IT authority to do so. This is a different mindset than traditional BI.

The challenge for the new data student is to come out of a program and present themselves to a prospective employer as capable to confront new business challenges with a very wide array of ideas, insights, perspectives, and tools in their repertoire. Academia likewise is challenged with delivering an eclectic education, rather than installing a clean box around a rigid subject matter.

5.2.3 BLENDING RESEARCH AND PRACTICE

To move forward, the whole area requires a blending of academic research and industry practice—not either/or. Reflecting on the past ten years shows excellent innovation in creativity, and while that process needs to continue, we also need to define the kinds of data problems we are confronting today and the kind of data problems we see on the horizon.

One example is machine learning: this emerging discipline is counterintuitive for a traditional statistician or systems analyst, and it is very counterintuitive to an intelligence engineer designing dashboards. The classic black box approach of jumping in, turning the crank, and popping out numbers no longer applies. With a blend of academic research and industry practice, we can construct a very effective pile of algorithms to sort through a pile of very messy data.

True data science leaders need to assume responsibility of educating and nurturing a variety of people in their ecosystem. There are a lot of ways of doing that: luncheons, symposiums, and mentorship—to name a few.

5.2.4 THE REALITY

It is an unfortunate truth that partnering between academia and the outside world does not always work. Traditional academics simply do not embrace industry in a cuddly fashion, and business does not typically invest in the kind of research that satisfies academic standards. In the end, it can result in something of a philosophical standoff.

Even so, educators are responding to a sense of urgency to meet the changing leadership demands in information technology and data science by developing new academic programs focused on continuous, prescriptive learning, and an integrated education model between academia and industry. However, preparing next-generation technology leaders does not stop at technical competency and business acumen alone. In addition, educators must also recognize the ethical implications of the emerging big data era, and foster the development of ethical leadership through a competency framework of ethics, emotional and cultural intelligence, adaptive and transformational leadership, and critical thinking, as discussed in chapter: Navigating Ethics in the Big Data Democracy.

5.2.4.1 A snapshot of integrated education in technology

We talk about "best of breed" technology approaches all the time. Let us not be shy about applying this to the concept of new types of data science and business analytics education. Many researchers in the academic literature have proposed the use of an engaged, interdisciplinary approach between industry and academia to enable a blended model of education. And, the good news is that we are starting to take action on that prescription. In December 2012, the Association for Information Systems (AIS) Special Interest Group on Decision Support, Knowledge, and Data Management (SIGDSS) and the Teradata University Network (TUN) cosponsored the Business Intelligence Congress 3 (BIC3) research and companion surveys to assess the current state of business intelligence education (Wixom et al., 2014). This research resulted in five notable findings: program offerings in BI/BA have dramatically increased; access to and use of pedagogical teaching resources has increased; demand for students continues to outplace supply; foundational skills—including communication, SQL and query, basic analytics, data management, and business knowledge—remain the most critical; and, employers are unsatisfied with the practical experience of graduates (Wixom et al., 2014).

5.2.5 NEW UNIVERSITY PROGRAMS AND VENDOR PARTICIPATION

New university programs are emerging to meet the complex, yet specific, demands of a data science education. The number and depth of new business analytics and data science program offerings has seen significant increase since 2010: as of the publication of the BIC3 research findings, there were a total of 131 confirmed, full-time BI/BA university degree programs, including 47 undergraduate level programs (Wixom et al., 2014). Today, that number continues to rise dramatically, with programs at the undergraduate and graduate level alike springing up at accredited institutions across the country.

Take a look at Figures 5.1 and 5.2. Created by visual artist Ali Rebaie, these graphics—representing the United States and the world, respectively—show the new

FIGURE 5.1

Data science programs in the US

(Source: With permission from Rebaie Analytics Group, 2015).

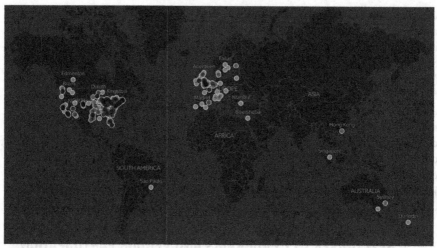

FIGURE 5.2

Data science programs across the globe

(Source: With permission from Rebaie Analytics Group, 2015).

data science programs cropping up to meet the demands of data science education to prepare incoming knowledge workers. The darker the bubble, the more densely packed the availability of newly created data science programs in that region. Note that this visualization shows both undergraduate and graduate level degree programs only.

BIC3 survey findings also reported that 296 out of 319 university professors (based on survey responses) are leveraging one or more business intelligence or analytics software programs to support teaching efforts in the classroom, coinciding with increased investments by vendor organizations to offer resources to academia at free or reduced costs (Wixom et al., 2014). The academic alliance programs measured by BIC3 responses included Microsoft, Teradata University Network (which includes solutions from KXEN and MicroStrategy), IBM, SAP, SAS, and Oracle. Other industry vendor organizations are also providing substantial support to the educational efforts in the academics. For example, among its many education-focused programs, Tableau Software, an interactive data visualization vendor, provides Tableau for Teaching, a free, course-long license for instructors and students when the technology used is part of the curriculum (Tableau, 2014). Currently, Tableau for Teaching is in use by more 800 classes worldwide—including institutions in South Africa and Singapore—in any given semester.

Another vendor organization doing their part to add to the collective knowledge of the blended education model is SAS, which supports a wide array of STEM initiatives in both K-12 and higher education. JMP, a division of SAS that produces interactive software for desktop statistical discovery, also has roots deep inside the statistical community and education, and we will look at a specific example of how JMP has contributed to advancing visual data literacy in chapter: Visual Communication and Literacy.

5.3 THE NEW DIGITAL NATIVE

It would be fair to say that a new kind of education and approach to train incoming knowledge workers is not the only factor affecting the change in the data science education landscape. Nor are new technologies and business needs are not the only disruptors of business as usual today. With the rapid entrance of millennials inside the business, the very face of business is literally changing. It is getting younger, smarter (more educated), and, most important, more digital. This will (and already does) initiate a ripple effect, as it is an important contributor to how BI-as-usual continues to evolve and change across all verticals of industry now and in the years to come.

The revolution of technologies like the Internet, mobile devices, and social media has created a new digital ecosystem most adopted, understood, and exploited by millennials—a term used to describe the generation born after 1980 (typically assigned the range of birth years that occurred between 1982–93) and to the first to come of age in the new millennium. As the largest cohort of demographics, the millennial generation is the biggest in US history according to the US Census Bureau—which makes them even bigger than the Baby Boomers (Check out the interactive visualizations on Goldman Sachs that tells the Data Story of Millennials at http://www.goldmansachs.com/our-thinking/pages/millennials/.) What is more, is that now millennials are not only reshaping the workplace and all that comes with it, but they are also generating the new crop of tech users, too. In 2014, millennials gave birth to 85% of the new babies in America (Mims, 2015). Thus, expect the rapid advancements and changes that are happening now to increase exponentially in the future.

Self-identified as "digital natives," millennials have fused technology with their lives and are increasingly more and more mobile, as well as utilizing personalized analytics provided through wearables and other mobile technologies (more in chapter: Visualization in the Internet of Things). A 2010 Pew Research Center report noted that the use of modern technology is 24% of what makes the millennial generation unique from its predecessors. However, millennial workers are not merely tech savvy—they are tech hungry. They have an inherent appreciation of—and an innate curiosity in—the way we approach and understand technology. They are eager to innovate and pioneer new ways of thinking and doing. They expect to use technology, too, and have little patience when it is overlooked or not used to its fullest capability. This translates directly into how millennials expect to see information, how they communicate and understand data, and how they explore data to uncover insights that translate into business value. Other recent statistics give more insight into how millennials affect the design of technologies of tomorrow, especially interactive and social technologies from smartphones to websites to mobile and SaaS apps that need to be more usable, self-guided, hiccup-free, and offer more efficient user experiences than ever before. By 2017—next year—millennials will not only have a big chunk of the workforce in their hands, but will also comprise the largest online audience with more buying power than any generation before them. This will only add to the already 50% of e-commerce coming from smartphones and tablets—this is now designated as m-commerce ("m" being mobile) (Wobbrock, 2014).

Millennials are on course to become the most educated generation in American history, partly because of the demands of an increasingly knowledge-based economy. According to Pew Research estimates, this new breed of knowledge worker will have overtaken the majority representation of the workforce by 2015; by 2030 they will make up 75% of the workforce—or the Millennial Majority Workforce, as it has come to be called. In other words: get ready. Looking at these numbers, the odds are pretty good that if you are reading this book, you may even be a millennial yourself.

In September 2014, Elance-oDesk and Millennial Branding (a Gen Y research and management consulting firm) commissioned an independent research study led by Red Brick Research to better understand how millennials are positioned to take over the workforce and the key business skills required to remain agile and innovative, while keeping up to date with the emerging technology. According to the official press release of the study, the survey was fielded in the United States among 1,039 millennials aged 21–32 years old, with a bachelor's, master's, or postgraduate degree, and 200 hiring managers aged 33+ years and responsible for recruitment or HR strategy within their various industries and business. For clarification, for the purposes of this survey—which weighed millennial results to ensure demographic representation across the sample—birth year ranges for millennials was 1982–93 consistent with the range given previously while Gen X was within the birth year bracket of 1959–81. Let us look together at a few key findings of the research, and how they fit into the context of this conversation and support various points made so far:

Millennials are seen as bringing unique skills to the table—especially since they are the first generation of "native technologists" (whereas the following generation, Generation Y, and even younger generations are growing up in pure Internet access and telecom enabled world, having never known life before texting or smartphones and tablets)

- 68% of hiring managers agree that Millennials possess certain skills that previous generations do not have
- 82% of hiring managers agree that Millennial are more technological adept

Millennials have skills that drive innovation, including hot STEM skills

- Millennials can learn things more quickly (74% of millennials and 60% of hiring managers agree)
- Millennials are more likely to come up with fresh ideas (71% of millennials and 57% of hiring managers agree)
- IT is the highest-ranked skills in terms of shortages. However, skills in 3D printing, cloud computing, wearable technologies, Internet of Things, and Data Visualization are among the highest emerging skills possess by millennials (Box 5.1)

BOX 5.1 WHY I TAUGHT MY SEVEN-YEAR OLD DATA VISUALIZATION

Beginning in 2009, March has been home to National Pi Day (cleverly 3/14)—a day meant to celebrate the mathematical concept of Pi. (Pi Approximation Day—or 22/7, is observed less ceremoniously on July 22.) Ever since its earliest official observance by physicist Larry Shaw at the Exploratorium in San Francisco in 1988, Pi Day has been celebrated in many ways—including eating pie, throwing pies, and discussing the significance of the number of Pi. MIT even uses the day to send out its formal acceptance letters. Coincidentally, Pi Day is also the birthday of Albert Einstein, who was born on March 14, 1879.

In the data industry, Pi Day is also the birthday of the #onelesspie movement by vendors SAS and JMP. In the world of data viz, #onelesspie uses Pi Day as the hokey-but-fun motivation to clean up the data visualization world one pie chart at a time (especially those Wikipedian pie charts that have a nasty habit of finding a place at the top of the Worst Data Visualizations list). This is something I think we all can agree is a mission worthwhile!

In celebration of Pi Day 2015, I took the opportunity to kill two pies with one viz. First, by making a new data visualization from a pie chart of old, and second, by asking my (at the time) seven year old, Wake, to do it with me. With the need for visual data literacy continuing to be more and more important as we prepare younger generations to engage in a new data culture, and with more and more tools actively working to become more self-service for nontechnical users, this seemed like the perfect opportunity to share in the movement in a meaningful—and unique—way. It is never too early to start teaching younger generations the important math, data, and analytical skills that will serve them well in their data-driven future. And, having access to some of today's leading self-service data visualization tools was a great opportunity to give him some hands-on experience with the tools already being used in organizations today (not to mention assess just how self-services these tools really are to the inexperienced user).

My son's first actions were the ones I expected. He took to Google to search around to find a small set of sample data and a traditional pie chart worth reworking, and then start thinking about fun ways to visualize it. To begin his analysis, he stumbled across a foodie blog, which featured a traditional pie chart that had been made using data from a 2008 Schwan nationwide poll on America's favorite pie flavors. His analysis of the chart was (and you cannot argue with kid logic): "that doesn't even look like a pie." As he explored different ways to look at the data, I was intrigued to hear his untrained, innately curious mind thinking up new ways to tell a compelling story with the data. Eventually, the data made its way into Tableau, where he created a packed bubble chart to more easily "see how many people liked a pie by the size of its bubble." The data revisualized, his inner artist was released and he then moved on to Adobe Photoshop, where he used stock photography images of the corresponding types of pies to layer images of each pie flavor over the bubble to tell a much more "delicious" data story (see Figure 5.3).

Sure, there may be some technical flaws with Wake's visualization, and it is by no means comparable with some of the breathtaking and highly curated advanced data visualizations out there today. I dare say there may not really be statistical significance to his chart, either. But, the mechanics aside, as a first time experiment by a seven year old just beginning to dabble in data analysis and visualization, it is an example of how we can (and should) train young minds to think about, visualize, and tell stories about data in new, compelling, and meaningful ways.

I thought the Pi Day experiment would end there, but it did not. Inspired by his newfound love for data visualization, Wake has continued to revisualize other data sets to continue telling his delicious data stories using a handful of viz tools—including Tableau, JMP, and Qlik Sense. He is even started to build his own surveys to collect and work with his own data, too. I might be unknowingly raising a future data scientist.

See more of Wake's "pies" at www.WakesPis.com or follow along with the social conversation at #wakespis.

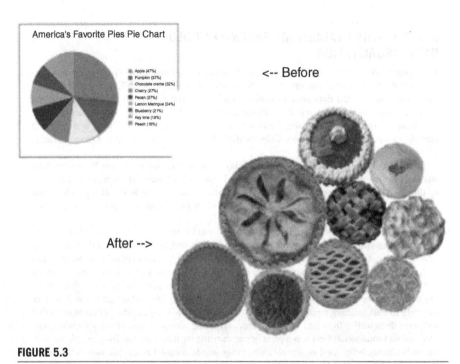

America's Favorite Pies Pie Chart

- Apple (47%)
- Pumpkin (37%)
- Chocolate creme (32%)
- Cherry (27%)
- Pecan (27%)
- Lemon Meringue (24%)
- Blueberry (21%)
- Key lime (18%)
- Peach (16%)

<-- Before

After -->

FIGURE 5.3

The before and after images of America's favorite pie chart in its original form, compared to the revisualized "Pie" chart on www.WakesPis.com

These numbers and findings provide the insight and framework we need to build up new workers and empower them to be successful—and make our new era of reinvention even more successful. However, effectively doing business in today's highly digital world requires more than just data scientists and big data—it requires an eagerness to continue to be disruptive and create new ways of thinking about how, why, and for what purposes we use information to be competitive. Likewise, it requires just as much insight into how millennials see and interpret insights into data, and how they use new approaches—including those garnered by being brought up in an era of visual technologies—to discover business value within data. I would expect to see many new changes over the next few years as some of these predictions become a reality and timing milestones are met.

5.3.1 LEADERSHIP QUALITIES OF THE MILLENNIAL LEADER

Ultimately, hard skills reign as millennial data workers are expected to be equipped with technological competencies and business acumen—those learned skills that we can teach through new models of blended education. A bare majority of hiring managers (55% of the Elance-oDesk and Millennial Branding study) say that they will be even more skills-focused in the new workforce, which is a shift from previous research (as recent as 2013) that put soft skills more important than hard technical skills. However,

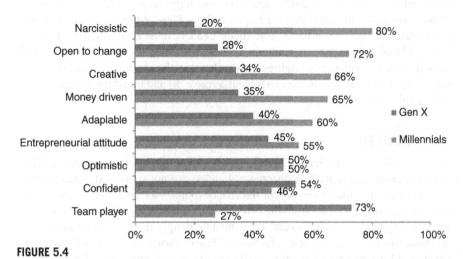

FIGURE 5.4

The perceived personality attributes of the millennial generation compared against their Gen X predecessors

personality and leadership skills will always be important, and these attributes are expected to bubble back to the top of the hiring criteria, as skills become more evenly distributed and obtained through the new workforce. Unfortunately, for as creative and optimistic as millennials are perceived to be, there still remains an unflattering belief that millennials are more narcissistic, money-driven, and self-centered than previous generations (see Figure 5.4). Naturally, millennials widely disagree with these blemishes on their character (who would not). This begs leadership capabilities back to the forefront of the conversation, perhaps even earlier than hiring managers expect.

Having a background in leadership (a course of study wherein I earned my graduate degree) and fitting nicely into the millennial age group myself, several years ago I blogged regularly for a website focused on leadership topics for the millennial (aptly named MillennialLeader.com). One of the blogs I wrote in mid-2012 focused on what I called the H-Qualities for new leaders, which paired leadership capabilities with the set of special considerations we touched on already in the previous chapter to reinforce ethical and mindless leadership skills in new leaders—regardless of industry. As the tide of techy skills swells and then inevitably begins to retreat, let us take the opportunity to repose those same characteristics here so that we can keep them in mind going forward.

5.3.2 HUMILITY

One of the most desired leadership traits is confidence. We want leaders who are confident in themselves, in their followers, and who have the oomph to lead us through the peaks and valleys of life. However, over-confidence can mutate into arrogance and stall a leaders' progress. Leaders must have the emotional intelligence to keep their confidence in check and stay humble (before it bleeds over into ego and narcissism). They must remember that the responsibility of leadership is not only to guide and motivate others, but also to serve them. Leaders must be confident enough to lead, but humble enough to remember why they are leading. Leadership theories and models including emotional intelligence (explored in the chapter previous), servant leadership (formalized by Robert Greenleaf's research) and transformational leadership readily apply here.

5.3.3 HUNGER

Today's leaders must be hungry. They must be eager, growth-oriented, and willing to go the extra mile to make a difference. Leaders are not spoon-fed opportunities. They must go after them, looking for the chance to make a change, to be innovative, and to set themselves a part from the herd. Leaders must have courage and ambition, and be ready to take on challenges. They must be hungry for new opportunities, for the chance to lead, and for new information. Recall earlier discussions for chapter: Separating Leaders From Laggards, on disruption, transformation, and reinvention. Hunger for new information, new insights, and new ideas drive these into reality. Creativity is one of the resonating personality traits of the millennial leader, and hunger is a function of that.

5.3.4 HAPPINESS

Finally, it is a matter of taking grit with grace. Being a leader is not an easy job, and it can be filled with trials and setbacks. It is important for a leader to remain focused, stay positive, and have the capacity to persevere in challenging times. Maintaining a positive mental attitude and modeling this behavior aids in keeping the morale and loyalty of followers high. Leaders should approach the world from a "half-full" perspective, and stay positive as they continue to drive change in a positive way. An alumni article from New England-based business school Bentley University dubbed this the "unbridled optimism of millennials," and it will be a motivating force going forward with continued complexity, privacy, and governance challenges.

5.4 ADDRESSING THE GENDER GAP—WOMEN IN IT

For all intents and purposes, it would seem that we at least have a handle on taking the appropriate next steps to work to mitigate the impending deficit for knowledge workers. Along with awareness and research into the needs and trends of the industry and the emerging workforce within it, we have made an incredible amount of headway in implementing new educational programs to meet these needs, with both academia and industry actively contributing to this goal. This is no small feat, and it is a big step forward. However, there is—as always—more work to be done.

Even with these advancements and a mass availability of computer science jobs coming in the near future, there are still some big issues that we need to address to maximize their potential and find new and improved ways to source more talent and make sure we are tapping into all available sources of next-generation knowledge workers. One of these is to recognize the continued gender gap between men and women actively working (and pursuing both STEM education and careers) in the larger data industry. As contrary as it may seem, women continue to be underrepresented in current positions and are likewise not enrolling in programs to nurture their development along this path, perhaps due to long-standing biases or ongoing socialization deficiencies. While high-profile women in the technology industry—like Yahoo! President and CEO Marissa Mayer or Facebook COO Sheryl Sandberg have vocalized some of the struggles of women in IT, it is not enough. In fact, it is not even at a point where it is steadying out with the possibility of improving and new trends beginning to climb upward. It is actually going down, though there is no ready explanation as to why. Nevertheless, today women are still sliding along a downward trend in their opportunities to move into these positions. Beyond the gender gap issue, simple math says that with less bodies going into programs and preparing for new roles and jobs in data science, that filling these jobs will be further impacted.

To catch up supply with demand for knowledge workers, educational organizations are working to meet this need by developing new undergraduate and graduate level courses—we went through these numbers already. Reiterated again here, another layer of insight is that though the numbers (both in types and accessibility) of these programs increase, the number of women in rolling in these programs is actually decreasing. According to the National Center for Women & Information Technology (NCWIT), in the mid-1980s, 37% of computer science majors were women compared to only 18% in 2012 (Gilpin, 2014). This directly translates to how many women are actively working in computer science professions, both in the United States and abroad. For example, in the US in 2013, women held 26% of computing jobs, down from 35% in 1990 (American Association of University Women, 2015). In the UK, only 16% of the 1,129,00 people working in IT were women in 2013 (Ranger, 2014). Similar trends were seen in other countries, such as Australia and Japan. Thus, we can infer this as not only a US problem, but a global one.

The simple truth is that women are hired into IT professions at significantly lower rates than men (McKinney et al., 2008). One explanation for the underrepresentation of women in computer science jobs is their inability to hire into these positions. But why? For one, prejudices and biases contribute to the hiring process, as women are perceived as less competent in math and tech than men (Peck, 2015; Reuben et al., 2014). Some companies are working to overcome this by focusing on diversity in the workplace, however it has yet to make the leap from lip service to practice. Discrimination continues to contribute to the low percentage of women in STEM careers, with men twice more likely to be hired than women (Reuben et al., 2014). Another possible explanation for lack of career entry is the fact that women appear to be under-socialized in IT positions, with a fear for job security and flexible working conditions stalling their entry into the field (McKinney et al., 2008). Moreover, women with less access to female role models along their learning and career maturity pathways, especially around the technical or social aspects of the profession, may be less likely to remain or succeed (McKinney et al., 2008). Therefore, women with less access to role models or lower levels of learning may be less likely to succeed in IT careers, which offers a plausible explanation for their continued—and downward—representation. (So, while such strong female leaders like Mayer and Sandberg are leading the charge, this is a mission that should be echoed throughout all tiers of the organization, as well as academic institutions, to drive change from the bottom up). Ironically, once in a position women surveyed have said that they do feel supported by supervisors related to their careers (at least, their perception is more so than that of their male counterparts, though this finding was supported by only a p-Value of .05).

While understanding women's motivations to or not to pursue computer science education—or advance in education—is ongoing, it is worthwhile to note that studies that have sought to understand differences between male and female perspectives (regarding socialization, experience and attitudes of experience) in the IT profession have uncovered very little that could be considered statistically significant. However, in a set of 2008 findings, the two most significant imbalances were in comfort with technical language and confidence in technical skills (these last two were supported by p-Values of .001, which many revere as the holy grail of statistical significance).

All of this said, younger girls have demonstrated remarkable proficiency and interest in computer science. This is evidenced by programs such as Hour of Code, a campaign to advocate for more computer science education launched in late 2013 by Code.org. By the end of its first week, 15 million students had written more than 500 million lines of code, and over 50% of the participants were women (Gilpin, 2014). Further, to support early data socialization, an insurgence of gender-neutral "Learn to Code" books have begun to be marketed toward early learners, including titles like *How to Code in 10 Easy Lessons: Learn how to design and code your own computer game* by Sean McManus, that helps young readers get familiar with computer coding and write simple code in HTML, or *Coding for Kids* from the Dummies Series, designed to teach elementary-to-middle-school-aged students core concepts to building games, applications, and other tools (Box 5.2).

BOX 5.2 LEADERSHIP PROFILE: A WOMAN IN A MAN'S IT

If you are a seasoned fellow in the BI industry and hail from Orange County, California, then chances are you might have heard of Deane May Zager. Deane (and her business partner Diana Turner) did the unthinkable as two young women in the early 1960s: they opened the first data processing service bureau in Orange County, California—and were wildly successful. Zager's new book, *The Highest Rung of the Ladder: Achieving the American Dream* (2015), is a testament to her success, a memoir of her experience, and a legacy of her determination to persevere, when all outward signs stacked the odds against her. Today we see the continued gender gap of women in data, but we are putting effort into overcoming it—whether through education, socialization, or efforts of organizations like Women in Technology International (WITI)—we are working to correct and counter that. Unfortunately, this was not the case when Deane set out and opened her small business in 1962.

"It was a real experience," she told me in a recent phone conversation, "because there were no women at all in the field – in any type of management position, supervisors, or anything like that when we started. Women were pretty much at the very bottom." Nevertheless, a friend invited Deane and Diana to join the Data Processing Management Association of Orange County (a group then comprised of men from sixty different companies across Orange County and Los Angeles), and much to her surprise, they were welcomed—if for no other reason than because they were an anomaly. "We were like a phenomenon," Deane admitted to me on our call, with a good-natured laugh to follow. "We were such mavericks [that] I think they didn't really know what to do with us."

Ford Motor Company awarded Deane and Diana their first major contract. And, on orange stationary, the pair built a name for themselves, being careful to make friends along the way. "Each company [we worked with] would be Number 1. Each company we worked for got our personal attention. We learned as we went," Deane says. They made contact with everybody, and, more important, they made friends. And when the 1970s brought a period of economic stagnation and recession, these relationships and their generally optimistic, people-oriented way of doing business, kept them afloat. Sure, they made mistakes—but even those carried their silver lining as Deane is quick to remember them fondly as learning experiences.

I asked Deane her thoughts on the disparity of women still in IT. About this, she is puzzled. "I don't know why more women don't venture out," she said. "The percentage is just too low!" After all, things seemed to be on the upswing in Deane's era. They'd been in business about two years when she noticed companies in LA starting to bring in more women into the ranks. "We'd go to 'mahogany row' and see a sprinkling of women, but by the time we sold [our company] there were just about as many women as men at that point. I'm not saying they reached the top of the ladder, but they were there. That was something."

"With women, it doesn't pay to be sensitive, and it doesn't pay to be pushy," Deane offered me as a final word of wisdom in our brief chat. "You can't take anything as a personal insult; you have to take it as a stepping stone."

Ms. Zager was president of Orange County Data Processing, Inc. for 30 years. She was honored as the Outstanding Business Woman of the Year in 1991 by the American Business Women of America, Orange County California Chapter.

5.5 NEW ROLES FOR NEW LEADERS

Data scientists are not the only new job title that will be (or is already) on the list of those persons most in demand in our new data economy. With new types of leaders and new types of business to lead, there are—as you would expect—also new types of roles emerging within organizations (Box 5.3). And, like understanding how new types of workers will affect, how we work in the future in general, understanding

BOX 5.3 MILLENNIALS, HIPSTERS, AND YUCCIES – OH MY!

Self-proclaimed *millen-intelligensia* David Infante (2015) wrote a brilliant article on Mashable entitled "The hipster is dead, and you might not like who comes next." If you find yourself either in or trying to understand the millennial demographic, Infante's article would likely spark your interest—after all, one nitpicky requirement of this generation is that they do (as Infante notes) prefer to be snarked in precise terminology (probably because a lot of us are English majors).

We know what millennials are. We are all familiar with the hipster trend (for the record, there are two types of hipsters—those real and their marketed facsimiles). So, what are yuccies? According to Infante, these are Young Urban Creatives (YUC), "borne of suburban comfort, indoctrinated with the transcendent power of education, and infected by the conviction that not only do we deserve to pursue our dreams; we should profit from them." These are the segment of millennials that are hopelessly creative to the point of creative entitlement in their flavor of art and flourish with new technology. Yuccies define themselves by how much something validates their intellect. In short, if you are looking for your next-generation, digitally-native, and rapidly visual new artists, thought-leaders, and innovators within the millennial generation, you might be looking for a yuccie.

As a sidepiece along with Infante's article, Mashable released – as it is want to do – an Are You a Yuccie quiz. Of course, I took it. According to my results, I am such a yuccie, "it's insane" (Figure 5.5).

Lord of the yuccies, we bow to you and your kind -- all of whom have made the Forbes 30 under 30 list. Chomp down on your artisanal donuts in celebration, but be sure to despise yourself for it.

FIGURE 5.5

A snapshot of my personal yuccie quiz results

what kind of people are currently "doing" data visualization will help us to see trends and patterns that may influence the new types of roles that we can expect to see starting to emerge, too (Figure 5.6).

While new data roles will be plentiful, many, like the data scientist (or, the new "data wrangler") will more than likely be highly technical in order to work with new modern data technologies, architectures, and programming languages. Many other new positions will begin to blend these analytical skills with other highly-sought after creative talents—like graphic design and visual artistry—and still others will arise in the communications arena to continue to help making visual information meaningful. Going forward, we can expect to see new roles in data that blend science, art, and communication—and we can see them in layers of organizational hierarchy ranging from the lowest levels to the most senior of executives (Box 5.4).

Here are a few that are beginning to gain traction and recognition now, as well as some that you can expect to add to your payroll within the next few years:

5.5.1 THE DATA VISUALIZATION ANALYST

With more emphasis on data visualization than perhaps ever before, along with the expectation that these visualizations are—at a minimum—animated, interactive, and highly curated, the role of the data visualization analyst is to take vast amounts of information and condense it down into the appropriate graphs, charts, maps, or other

What kind of people do #dataviz?

These are the full results of a highly unscientific one-question survey asking:

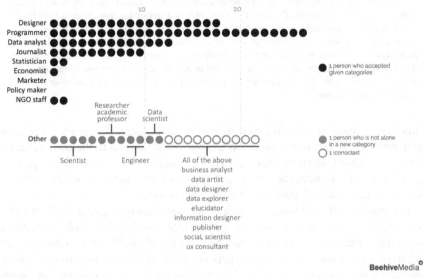

FIGURE 5.6

This chart, created by Beehive Media, might surprise you as you discover what kind of people do data visualization. Likewise, it provides food for thought on the data viz jobs of tomorrow

(Source: With permission from Beehive Media, LLC, 2015. Data collected via an online survey on May 13–14, 2015. The link to the survey was shared via Twitter, Linkedin, and Google+ and RT's and Fav'd a bit, resulting in some respondents outside my personal network. There were a total of 95 responses as of 12:00 pm EDT, May 14, 2015).

BOX 5.4 WILL TECHNOLOGY REPLACE JOBS?

On the cover of its July/August 2015, issue, *The Atlantic* featured a cover story that could jar the attention of many. "Technology will soon erase millions of jobs," the cover shouted in bold, serif font. "Could that be a good thing?" This rhetorical question was accompanied by a bright red stamp that said simply, "The end of work." The actual article, penned by Derek Thompson, began with the tale of Youngstown, Ohio, a town unraveled by the shut down of its once-prosperous steel mills, and how this could be but a predecessor of what we can expect in an even more technology-dependent culture. There are, according to Thompson, reasons to cry robot as technology could exert a slow but continual downward pressure on the availability and value of work that leads, eventually, to a loss in labor, of a spread of unemployment (especially in men and youth), and a second machine age. To toss some validation in there, Oxford researchers have forecast that machines might actually take half of all US jobs within the next two decades.

But could technology usurp the total workforce as we know it, and lead to a no-job future? Not likely. Instead, we could see the next wave of automation return us to an age of craftsmanship and artistry. This is a good thing. People could return to their "callings," rather than their "jobs." With machines doing the dirty work for us, our "third places"—separate from homes and office—could become central to growing up, learning new skills, discovering passions. Rather than a religious devotion to overworking, we could devote more our time to nurturing our interests, our families, our social structures. Or could we?

Ultimately, predicting the future is probably a job (no pun intended) better left to soothsayers than to journalists. However, Thompson's article provided fodder for thought on a long flight. Technology has—and will always continue—to change the status quo of our normal daily lives. What we do, how we do it, and how productive and dependent we are on it, are all intertwined paths that will continue to be affected by technological advancement. The question we have to decide is how we want that change to be reflected in how we approach the two things that arguably give us, as people, the most personal fulfillment: what we do, and what we wish we were doing. The future is ours.

data-driven infographics to effectively display the information. Of the roles I will call out in this section, this role is the most technical in skillset, with the need to have a sufficient depth of understanding of analytics and analytics tools to be able to process data from various sources (as well as extract, transform, and load the data into the required form) to make it meaningful and within context.

This person will need fairly sophisticated programming language skills to either build (develop) or at a minimum use self-service oriented user tools to design a proper data visualization, and thus may be more readily pulled from a data science background and trained up on user experience (UX) skills. Unlike a true visualization curator or designer, this analyst will likely be the one using commercial visualization software or hand-coding them in JavaScript.

5.5.2 THE VISUALIZATION CURATOR/DESIGNER

This is a job title I have seen thrown around throughout academic institutions (sometimes calls a "Data Visualist" or the more ambiguous "digital information media designer") and within various journalism fields. Ms. Kennedy Elliott, currently a Visual Journalist from The Washington Post, spoke at the 2015 Tableau Tapestry conference, leaving behind this inspiring quote: "Whether journalists know it or not, [we] are increasingly moving toward human-centered design in data narratives, and applying this [human centered-design] will explore uknowns."

Typically, these job roles are nested somewhere in the media arts and design functional groups, and focus on experience and interest in data visualization and infographics across platforms (including web, video, print, and mobile). The typical candidate is/will be someone who has a journalistic or storytelling background, along with a level of expertise in graphic design and other artful considerations. Usually, this role would also have an applied interest and contribution to visual communication with specific expertise in certain media area (one job announcement I saw for this position, located in Berlin, was looking for a visualist who had experience with both infographic designs and geoscience tools—or their "weapon of choice"). While the position tends to err on the side of graphic design, expect to see a blend of computer science and data analysis education, too.

5.5.3 **THE DATA STORYBOARD ARTIST**

The data storyboard artist is a role first conceptualized by a colleague and friend at American Family Insurance. When creating a film, a storyboard is central to conveying the expected flow and climaxes of the script. Though not as detailed as a script—nor as visually complete as a true data visualization—it still has the power to convey points of view, visual perspective, and pace. Various types of data teams (whether BI teams, analysts, or other data workers), like directors, benefit from a role geared toward converting dry data requirements into compelling storylines and keeping the team on track to achieve the value of finding and applying analytical insights.

The goal of the storyboard is to communicate how the story around a solution to working with new data can (or should) unfold. It is not a pixel perfect user interface prototype or set of sample reports. Its emphasis is simply on the interactions necessary to achieve a solution to a business problem. They are decidedly low-tech, but require some visual skills. Thus, the data storyboard artist is comfortable with visual communication, and likely has some illustration skills of some sort (whether drawing or diagramming). Since the storyboard will be used in a variety of settings with both technical and nontechnical audiences, it is important to pick someone who is adept at working and communicating with a wide variety of people. This person should be familiar with the technical aspects of the solution, and the business functions that will use it.

5.5.4 **THE CHIEF STORYTELLING OFFICER**

The title of a 2002 book by David Armstrong, the role of the chief storytelling officer (or CSO) is a thoroughly modern title that is currently gaining corporate momentum. As of May 2015, LinkedIn listed two dozen executives who have held CSO positions, a trend that is cropping up more and more but may have actually begun at Nike in the 1990s (their then CSO Nelson Farris was attributed with the following quote in a 1999 Fast Company article: "Our stories are not about extraordinary business plans or financial manipulations…They're about people getting things done" (Grothaus 2015).

Like the data scientist—which is part business and part mathematician—the CSO is another twofold role that is part editorial and part graphical. These are the story champions of the organization that align the informational goals of the business alongside a virtual library of relevant stories that translate information goals and needs into meaningful communications. Of course, organizations are by no means strangers to telling stories, especially those internal (think press releases or when a new organization launches or goes through major change). But, a CSO is a role that is more than simply sharing information. This requires crafting a true, simple, and emotionally impactful story. This role must carry the ability to engage and inspire loyalty from both employees and customers; it should be a compelling narrative that articulates the organization's mission and vision, and makes it memorable. The exercise of storytelling is—as we will soon discuss—a creative way to think about strategy.

As you might have noticed, these roles are a heuristic blend of art, science, and communication. That will be the new norm. And within them there is a certain theme that seems to invariably rise to the top. No matter how visually driven, or how data-oriented, or even how strategy-focused, we keep seeing the word storytelling become a critical element in positions of the future. This is where we will spend a future chapter: exploring the art of storytelling, and what it can and must do to contribute to a visual data culture.

5.6 THE STEPS BEYOND

Moving away from specific discussions on demographics and emerging leadership, and as we begin to level off into a stabilized and tactical approach to visually working with the massive data sets in big data, we can expect to see a few major themes in both our new knowledge workers and our new roles that are at the core of the conversations of the first section of the book as a whole. These themes are specialization, education, automation, and the true emergence of modern visualization.

The first, as hinted at in the job roles listed previously, is specialization. What is currently somewhat of a niche field (or, at least somewhat indistinct) will becoming more defined—and ever more blended as people join the field and delineate skill sets to nurture the needed expertise in different functional areas and hierarchy. Larger or more specialized firms may build a strong internal data visualization department, or they may deploy a Data Visualization Competency Center (we will touch on both of these in chapter: Data Visualization as a Core Competency), while smaller or more niche firms may reach out to the broad pool of freelancers and agencies that concentrate in these areas. Customers and internal users demand more because they are exposed to such high standards of design in visualization in their everyday lives—business or personal. The most successful visual companies will have to compete with the best designers on the market even with internal visual communication competencies.

Next is education. While data science education is fundamentally based on math and statistics and on the rise already, some cutting-edge universities are already bringing in curriculum to support data visualization education. Traditional visual media or graphic design programs will continue to become more enriched with technologies and education on foundational data analysis principles; likewise data analysis education will put an additional premium on visual design and data visualization mechanics and evolving best practices.

Automation—or the continued evolution of self-service and self-sufficiency—will continue to automate a best practices-led data visualization process for users of varying skillsets and experience. Many visualization tools will continue to build guardrails to support users, while embedding educational components to foster continued growth and competency in these areas.

Finally, we will see the emergence of a truly modern visual culture. While data visualization has only recently received a serious rejuvenation from its ancient roots, we are just now beginning to really tap into the potential of data visualization in a big data-centric economy. Much confusion or inconsistencies still surround the use of data visualization, and how it can be used for visual discovery and visual analytics. Eventually, these pervasive changes will ironically be the death of data visualization, as what is now considered "good" data visualization will cease and turn instead into an expectation that data visualization *is*. To close the circle on discussions begun in chapter: Separating Leaders From Laggards, this is where we find the tipping point of the visual imperative. As the visual dimension of culture becomes increasingly dominant, driving the need to create a visual culture of data discovery, we must prepare for even greater changes with new data opportunities brought by the growing Internet of Things and advanced by a brave new world of knowledge workers.

REFERENCES

American Association of University Women, 2015. Solving the equation: the variables for women's success in engineering and computing.

Baggaley, J., 2013. MOOC rampant. Dist. Edu. 34 (3), 368–378.

Gilpin, L., 2014. The state of women in technology: 15 data points you should know. TechRepublic. Available from: http://www.techrepublic.com/article/the-state-of-women-in-technology-15-data-points-you-should-know/.

Grothaus, M., 2015. Why companies need novelists. Fast Company. Available from: http://www.fastcompany.com/3045216/why-companies-need-novelists.

Infante, D., 2015. The hipster is dead, and you might not like who comes next. Mashable. Available from: http://mashable.com/2015/06/09/post-hipster-yuccie/?utm_cid=mash-com-fb-main-link#rYDrjIXoJOk9.

McKinney, V., Wilson, D., Brooks, N., O'Leary-Kelly, A., Hardgrave, B., 2008. Women and men in the IT profession. Commun. ACM 51 (2), 81–84.

McKinsey Global Institute, 2014. Big data: the next frontier for innovation, competition, and productivity.

Millennial Branding, 2014. The 2015 Millennial Majority Workforce Study. Millennial Branding. Available from: http://millennialbranding.com/2014/2015-millennial-majority-workforce-study/

Mims, C., 2015. How aging millennials will affect technology consumption. The Wall Street Journal. Available from: http://www.wsj.com/articles/how-aging-millennials-will-affect-technology-consumption-1431907666.

Peck, E., 2015. The stats on women in tech are actually getting worse. The Huffington Post. Available from: http://www.huffingtonpost.com/2015/03/27/women-in-tech_n_6955940.html.

Pew Research Center, 2010. Millennials: A portrait of generation next. http://www.pewsocialtrends.org/files/2010/10/millennials-confident-connected-open-to-change.pdf.

Ranger, S., 2014. Women in tech: under-represented and paid less. TechRepublic, European Technology. Available from: http://www.techrepublic.com/blog/european-technology/women-in-tech-under-represented-and-paid-less/.

Reuben, E., Sapienza, P., Zingales, L., 2014. How stereotypes impair women's careers in science. Proc. Nat. Acad. Sci. USA 111 (12), 4403–4408.

Tableau, 2014. Tableau for teaching. Available from: http://www.tableausoftware.com/academic.

Thompson, D., 2015. A world without work. The Atlantic, 51–61.

U.S. Bureau of Labor Statistics, 2015. College enrollment and work activity of 2014 high school graduates.

Wobbrock, J., 2014. How millennials require us to design the technologies of tomorrow. Wired. Available from: http://www.wired.com/insights/2014/09/millennials-design-technologies/.

Wixom, B., Ariyachandra, T., Douglas, D., Goul, M., Gupta, B., Iyer, L., Turetken, O., 2014. The current state of business intelligence in academia: the arrival of big data. Commun. Assoc. Inform. Syst. 34 (1), 1.

Zager, D.M., 2015. The Highest Rung of the Ladder: Achieving the American Dream. Archway Publishing, Bloomington, IN.

Communicating data visually

Data-driven organizations are becoming increasingly visual in how they see and interact with data. This section begins with a brief history on visual communication and the reinvigorated role of data visualization as an analysis and storytelling mechanism. Key design concepts and data visualization best practices will be reviewed. This section will also explore the data visualization continuum, with emphasis on exploratory and explanatory graphics, as well as the power of pictures in infographics and iconography.

Visual communication and literacy

6

"If students aren't taught the language of sound and images, shouldn't they be considered as illiterate as if they left college without being able to read or write?"
—George Lucas

In the first few chapters of Part I, we set the tone of the book by focusing on today's emergent discovery imperative and exploring the unique needs and characteristics of the data-driven organization in an era of disruption and invention. We reviewed the adoption of business-driven discovery to complement traditional business intelligence; the emergence and enterprise adoption of visual discovery from the data to the dashboard; and the maturation of self-service, self-sufficiency, and user enablement for data discovery as IT shifts to ET, or enablement technology. And, last but certainly not least, we engaged in a practical albeit philosophical conversation on how next-generation information leaders must navigate the complexities of today's big data democracy and prepare for ever-increasing interconnectedness and ethical challenges of the Internet of Things.

As we move into Part II we will begin to dig deeper into the premise of visual discovery and the elements—communication, storytelling, design, and application—that make it so compelling. To frame our next series of conversations, I would like to begin with a brief history on the genesis and evolution of visual communication and data literacy. With these as foundation, we can better apply a larger, more integrated perspective to the role of data visualization and data discovery today, as well as how we use visual-based approaches to interact with information in the big data ecosystem that offers more variety, volume, and velocity of data than ever before.

Keep in mind that this discussion is not meant to be all encompassing. Each of these areas easily deserves (and already commands) its own body of dissertation. Instead, this perspective is intended to provide a mere potsherd of distilled information on the history of visual communication by which to broker a larger context of understanding for the impact of data visualization and data science. The discussions in this chapter will, too, be by far the most academic in the book, as we will be discussing communication, cognition, and literacy from a scholarly perspective and visiting a small sample library of available academic literature. In the subsequent chapters of Part II, we will expand these constructs to explore storytelling psychology and how various narrative frameworks can be applied to tell meaningful, actionable, and inspiring data stories.

In the preface to his seminal research on the history of visual communication and graphic design, American graphic designer, professor, and historian Philip B. Meggs begins his discussion with one word: zeitgeist. A German word with no direct English translation, zeitgeist roughly translates to mean the spirit of the times, or the intellectual or dominant school of thought that influences the cultural trends characteristic of a given era. "Since prehistoric times," writes Meggs in *The History of Graphic Design*, "people have searched for ways to give visual form to ideas and concepts, to store knowledge in graphic form, and to bring order and clarity to information" (Meggs, 2011, preface). If we consider the evolution of visual communication from a historical relevance perspective—from prehistoric cave drawings, to the Sumerians who invented writing, to Egyptian artisans and medieval illuminators, and throughout the aesthetic movements that have propelled us to today's contemporary design artists—we can better inform and position ourselves (as Meggs rightly claims) to continue a legacy of beautiful form and effective communication.

Visual communication is, at its simplest, the act of engaging in direct or indirect communication through a visual aid. It is the conveyance of ideas and information in forms that can be looked upon, and thus relies on vision—whether the image itself is communicated through typography, drawings, designs, illustrations, animations, and so on. The study of visual communication also explores the idea that a visual message and accompanying text has a greater power to inform, educate, or persuade (Smith et al., 2004). Visual communication, when focusing on information transfer and the distillation of complex (often mathematical) concepts, can be further articulated as a function of visual data literacy—a critical component of the multiple intelligences theories that we will explore later in this chapter. And, both visual communication and data literacy impact how we analyze imagery and how visualization is used within the larger storytelling paradigm—the subject of the chapter to come.

Paying homage to "iconic" artist Ivan Chermayeff, who has created hundreds of memorable commercial logos and icons, let us begin our brief journey in cultural anthropology where "the design of history meets the history of design."

6.1 THE HISTORY OF VISUAL COMMUNICATION

From the earliest cave drawings and cuneiform languages to the first alphabets and typologies, visual communication has been among the most primary ways that humans have communicated over thousands of years (see Box 6.1). By tracing the history of visual communication back through its roots from simple, elementary symbolic pictures to convey basic information, to how it has evolved through written languages, illustrated manuscripts, photography, modern graphic design movements, and advanced data visualization, we can clearly see the influence of visual communication throughout the ages.

BOX 6.1 STUDYING COMMUNICATION AND BEHAVIORAL MODERNITY

The study of communication is a broad field of study that encompasses a vast range of topics. Included in these are the studies of the origins of language (separate from speech) (Box 6.2), writing, and communication traits and mechanisms—all intertwined yet distinct areas encompassed under the umbrella of behavioral modernity. Behavioral modernity is the set of traits that distinguish present day humans and our recent ancestors from other primates, as well as other extinct hominids. Though hotly contested, there are two main theories regarding when fully modern behavior may have emerged: as the result of some sudden event around 50,000 years ago, or as the gradual result of accumulated knowledge, skills, and culture over thousands of years of human evolution.

BOX 6.2 THE ORIGINS OF LANGUAGE AND THE ORIGINS OF SPEECH

With the exception of a relatively brief prohibition by the Linguistic Society of Paris that began in 1866 and remained influential throughout most of the twentieth century (Stam, 1976), the study of the origin of language has long been the subject of scholarly discussion. Today, with still much speculation, hypothesis, and theory, the discussion has no ultimate consensus. In fact, determining exactly when, where, or how spoken human language came to be is considered by many to be "the hardest problem in science" (Christiansen & Kirby, 2003). Linguists, archaeologists, psychologists, anthropologists, and others studying this field are continually stumped by a shortage of empirical evidence. Instead, they are left largely to depend on an incomplete fossil record and other archeological information to compare systems of communication.

The fossil record of the Upper Paleolithic shows the development of fully human speech anatomy, which was previously absent in the remains of Neanderthals and earlier humans (Lieberman, 2007). The FOXP2 gene—or, the "language gene"—has been isolated and identified as the gene which governs the embryonic development of the subcortical structures that support the neural circuits necessary for human speech, language, and cognition. Based on molecular genetic techniques, the human form of the gene seems to have appeared sometime in the last 200,000 years, suggesting that it may be the necessary catalyst by which modern humans have earned increased motor control that made human speech possible (Lieberman, 2007).

A precursory exploration into the genesis of visual communication will show that it has taken an interesting and somewhat parallel journey alongside that of the history of writing. As the primary means of visually conveying ideas and information, visual communication had its beginnings in manmade markings found in Africa that date to over 200,000 years old (Meggs, 2011). In our archeological discoveries, explorers have discovered rock and cave painting dating from the early Paleolithic to Neolithic periods (35,000 BCE to 40,000 BCE). While the examples are many, one particularly remarkable finding is the Chauvet-Pont-d'Arc Cave in southern France, discovered in 1994, which is home to the earliest known and best preserved figurative cave paintings. These paintings feature renderings of several animal species with spectacular anatomical precision and are lauded as being of exceptional aesthetic quality (UNESCO, 2015). The next time you visit your local natural science museum, pause to look at the many markings on pottery or other objects and reflect on their potential not as mere decorative embellishment, but as the earliest forms of visual communication. What stories about their lives were our earliest ancestors trying to tell us?

When they eventually came, our first written languages were inherently visual—from ancient Eastern ideogrammatic writing systems, where a single image represented a word or a morpheme (a meaningful unit of words) to the first pure alphabets (properly known as "abjads" and which only represented consonants) of ancient Egypt that mapped single symbols to single phonemes. These visual languages later inspired the Phoenician and Greek alphabets, and eventually the Aramaic alphabet, which is credited for being the ancestor of nearly all of the modern alphabets of Asia. One of the later (and perhaps best-known if controversial) picture-based writing systems is Early Indus script, a corpus of symbols developed by the Indus Valley Civilization dated to have emerged somewhere between the 35th and 20th centuries BCE (Whitehouse, 1999).

Without oversimplifying the continued (and largely subjective) scholarly disagreement on the factors that distinguish "proto-writing" (systems of writing which used ideographic and/or early mnemonic symbols to convey information yet were probably devoid of direct linguistic content) from "true writing" in visual communication history, we can note succinctly that conventional writing systems follow a series of developmental stages that provide a maturity framework that illustrates how the arrival of picture writing (whether mnemonic or ideographic) moves forward to transitional systems and ultimately to phonetic systems wherein graphemes are represented by sounds or spoken symbols, and finally, elements like alphabets are introduced. (Curiously, these defined stages of alphabet maturity are not too unlike the developmental stages of children learning to write, who similarly transition from scribbling, to the emergence of letters and symbols to represent ideas, to the inclusion of sound clouds, and then eventually words as they move from drawings to represent ideas to sentences by which to tell them.)

The invention of the alphabet took place in an era of experimentation in writing, and brought with it an easier opportunity for literacy (Millard, 1986). Thus, on the continuum of the history of writing and its convergence with the history of visual communication, the advent of the alphabet was the catalyst that propelled us into the realm of written communication. Eventually, this led to the conception of what we consider today as written storytelling and literature. Of course, while writing and storytelling are interconnected but not synonymous concepts, their histories are nonetheless paramount in the history of visual communication. Medieval Europe brought about the first visual storybooks in the form of illuminated manuscripts—beautifully and ornately illustrated books that often took several (short) scribe lifetimes to complete (the earliest surviving of these manuscripts are from CE 400 to 600). From these manuscripts, next came technology that enabled movable type and Gutenberg's mechanized printing press that began to spread across Europe in the early 16th century (Febvre and Martin, 1976). Alongside the printing press appeared the art of calligraphy, the illustrations of Da Vinci, and those known as the Masters of Type, including Claude Garamond and John Baskerville (we will explore typography as an element of design in future chapters) that carried storytelling through the 18th century.

The Industrial Revolution of the late 18th and early 19th centuries spread major technological, socioeconomic, and cultural change throughout the world unlike anything witnessed since perhaps the Neolithic revolution (which propelled human advancements in agriculture). Production machines for manufacturing enabled mass production of text-complementary illustrations through lithography, which, within a few years of its invention, allowed for the creation of multicolor printed images, as well as free running type, a process called Chromolithography. This era was also marked by another major innovation in visual communication: photography. From the first photo image produced in 1826 by French inventor Joseph Nicéphore Niépce to the Daguerreotype of 1839, to the invention of film in 1886 to replace the photographic plate, photography became an unprecedented and innovative mechanism of visual communication. Eventual mass-market availability of photography was made possible with the introduction of the Kodak Brownie in 1901, effectively making visual communication a self-service endeavor with the most advanced technology of the time. With the ability to pair the written word with self-service visualization (and, of course, the benefits of postal mail) came perhaps the first method of "modern" visual communication and storytelling: the postcard (see Box 6.3).

The Arts and Crafts movement—a major English and American aesthetic reaction that occurred in the transitional years between the 19th and 20th centuries—closed the gap between the eclectic historicism of the Victorian era and the machine-made production milieu of the Industrial Revolution. This movement brought visual communication back to the forefront of storytelling. One of the principal founders of Arts and Crafts was William Morris, an English artist, writer, social activist, and ecosocialist pioneer. Morris later founded the Kelmscott Press in London to produce examples of printing and book design that led the press to become the most famous of the private presses due to its integration of type and decoration (or, visual illustration). From there, we dove into periods of visual-based art, with movements in eclecticism, art nouveau, and the invention of posters paving the way for new graphic design styles, such as constructivism, futurism, Dadaism, Bauhaus, and De Stijl. Moving ahead, these initial steps forward in graphic design and visual storytelling have led to the age of the computer and digital (or, inkless) graphic design—which has dramatically changed the game in how we interact with visual communication in the age of modern visual communication, and what is now being referred to within the industry-at-large as data storytelling.

As inconsequential and meandering as it may seem, this bit of history can be distilled into one simple takeaway (see Figure 6.1): from prehistoric cave paintings to today's modern data visualizations, we have stayed true to our roots of using visual communication as a primary means of interacting with and communicating about information (see Box 6.4).

BOX 6.3 THE DEAR DATA PROJECT

When New York-based Giorgia Lupi and London-based Stefanie Posavec met at the 2014 Eyeo Festival in Minneapolis and bonded over a mutual passion for hand-drawn data visualization, they had no idea that they would be soon embarking on a year-long, analog data drawing project together. Their project, Dear Data, is (per the website) "an art project that challenges the increasingly widespread assumption that big data is the ultimate key to unlocking, decoding, and describing people's public and private lives." And, it is a working example of how visual communication is technology-influenced without being technology-dependent.

Each week for the length of the project, Lupi and Posavec have collected and measured a type of data about their lives; hand-drawn a custom data visualization generated from manual data collection and analysis on a postcard-sized piece of paper; and dropped it in the post on its way to the other side of the world. The visualization is drawn on the front of the postcard, and an instructional "how to" legend for guiding understanding and interpretation is rendered on the back. Once received, the images are uploaded weekly on dear-data.com, as Lupi and Posavec share their beautifully illustrated—and deeply personal—journeys through their everyday lives as quantified in personally curated analog data visualizations (Figure 6.2).

A design project at heart, Dear Data is a compelling way that two women are working together to humanize data. But, it is also a foray into continuing visual, nonanalog communication with data visualization. Each postcard is an exploration of small, incomplete, and imperfect data. More important, Dear Data is a way to visually communicate and share personal experiences through data in a way that makes it possible to physically experience data from the interaction they share in collecting, designing, and using the postcards.

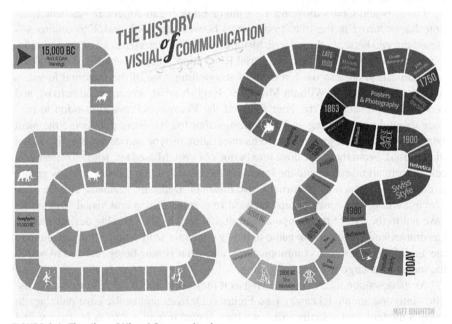

FIGURE 6.1 Timeline of Visual Communication

Created by visual artist Matt Brighton, this visualization represents the journey of visual communication from its earliest known roots to today's approach to graphic design.

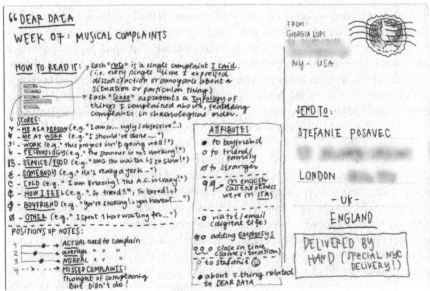

FIGURE 6.2 Dear Data Week 7: Musial Complaints.

This data visualization, told through musical scales, shows the type and frequency (or tune!) of Lupi's complaints over the course of one week.

BOX 6.4 THE EVERGREEN TREE DIAGRAM

In his book, *Book of Trees: Visualizing Branches of Knowledge*, Manuel Lima (2014) writes, "From powerful metaphors with divine associations, tree diagrams have slowly become pragmatic and are nowadays predominantly the tools of computer science and the mathematical field of graph theory." Indeed, we can see the use of tree diagrams as powerful visualization tools for more than 800 years—from illuminated manuscripts in medieval Europe to today's intricate data visualization. Thus, the use of graphical, symbolic data visualization like the tree diagram as a visual communication tool is a trend that transcends time.

6.1.1 NOTEWORTHY FIGURES IN VISUAL COMMUNICATION

Before we move on and shift our discussion to the role of human cognition in visual literacy, and further, visual storytelling as a form of data communication, it would be a disservice to overlook the contributions of two notable figures in the relatively recent study of visual communication. These influential figures are author and philosopher Aldous Huxley (1894–1963) and psychologist Max Wertheimer (1880–1943), respectively.

Perhaps most well-known for his dystopian novel *Brave New World*, Aldous Huxley is a highly regarded explorer of visual communication and sight-related theories. In *The Art of Seeing*, his critique of orthodox approaches to corrective vision and the resulting dehumanizing aspects of the scientific process (Huxley became nearly-blind as a teenager as the result of an illness and used the Bates Method to improve his vision to the point where he was capable of reading without the use of glasses), Huxley posits that there is more to seeing than simply sensing imagery—that there is more to visual communication therefore than making an image for the eyes to perceive, but that it must also accommodate the mind of the person being communicated to (Huxley, 1943). We will see the wisdom of Huxley's assessment later in discussions of visual design (Box 6.5).

Along with Kurt Koffka and Wolfgang Köhler, Max Wertheimer is a founder (and said to be the father of) Gestalt psychology. In a nutshell, Gestalt (the German word for form or shape) theory is the study of whole processes and their interactions which we experience (Humphrey, 1924), and springs from experimental work that has—in over nine decades since its inception—proved fruitful in presenting hypotheses. The study of Gestalt psychology emphasizes simplicity in shape, color, and proximity, and looks for continuation, closure, and figure-ground principles. Today, studiers of visual communication can expect to learn about Gestalt psychology alongside color and perception theories, design principles, semiotics, etc. Again, like Huxley, the Gestalt principles will prove to be a pivotal piece of the conversation when we later discuss how visual design hinges not on embellishment, but on removing and simplifying until nothing stands between the visual's message and its audience.

6.2 VISUAL MEMORABILITY AND RETENTION

Moving forward, let us apply the previous brief anthropological summary of the genesis and progress of visual communication as a communication mechanism, art form, and psychological perspective to the role of human cognition in visual memorability

BOX 6.5 SPECTRUM OF SIGHT

Recently, I was sitting in my local planetarium celebrating the 25th anniversary of the Hubble telescope, and found myself engaged in an intense conversation with the resident astronomer on the aptitudes and uses of color and how we perceive them in visualizations. (If you did not already know, the Hubble telescope cameras produce images in shades of black and white—color is added during image processing as a tool to simulate the colors our eyes might see if we visit outer space, to use representative color for scientific study, or to enhance or visualize details not visible to the human eye. More info at www.hubblesit.org).

While color and its influence on data visualization will be explored within the context of visual design in a later chapter, vision and the visible spectrum itself is worth a brief mention within this context because "what we see" is equally as important as "how we see." The visible spectrum is the portion of the electromagnetic spectrum that is visible to the human eye, which, interestingly, does not contain all of the colors that the human eye and brain can distinguish. Some unsaturated colors—like pink and purple variations—are absent. Likewise, color displays—like that of your desktop or mobile device—cannot reproduce all colors either. Many colors, like spectral colors (colors evoked by a single wavelength of light in the visible spectrum, or by a relatively narrow band of wavelengths, including red, orange, yellow, green, blue, and violet) can only be simulated by projecting a spectrum of colors onto a uniform gray background.

and retention. In an effort to disentangle the myriad compounding factors that affect visual cognition, we will save discussions that explore human cognition in the context of visual design—including perceptual pop out, pattern recognition, numerosity, etc., for a later chapter and stick simply to the basic cognitive elements of visual memorability, recall, and retention in this chapter.

As you may suspect by our long history of visual communication, humans are extremely good at remembering thousands of pictures and a vast amount of visual detail. In fact, the number of remembered images and context has been measured to be somewhere in the ballpark of 10,000 images with a recognition rate of approximately 83% (Standing, 1973).

In recent years, attributes-based visual recognition has received a lot of attention in computer science literature. And, this attention has not been in vain. With numerous in-depth studies providing clear data and learning opportunities, we now definitively know that visualization that blends information with influential features (such as color, density, and content themes, like recognizable icons or imagery) significantly and reliably increases learning, memorability, and recall (Borkin et al., 2013). Further, seeing and interacting with an image in combination with traditional written and verbal instruction has, too, been consistently associated with higher levels of retention and understanding of salient ideas. While research into the human cognitive capacity to remember visual stimuli has been ongoing, in the past few years researchers have worked to systematically study the intrinsic memorability of images and the interface between human cognition and computer vision. This body of study is ultimately intended to help understand the predictive ability of visual memorability and how visuals can be designed to take best advantage of our visual recognition system.

Today there is ongoing debate in the visualization community regarding the role that visualization types play in data understanding and memorability. And, like all great scientific debates, those who seek to understand the role of visual attributes in memorability are not unique in that there are convincing pieces of research on both sides of the topic. The conventional view, supported by visualization purists, argue that visualizations should be devoid of chart junk and curated with as few design elements as possible to create a clean visualization and increase memorability and information saliency. While this view is supported by many psychology lab studies, there is, naturally, still a body of research that argues the opposite—that chart junk can possibly improve retention and force a user to expend more cognitive effort to be able to understand and learn from the visual, thereby increasing both their understanding and recall of the data in a deeper way. That said, let us call attention to two specific studies that provide really interesting—and very opposite—takeaways into visual memorability to provide a deeper understanding of the recurring themes and their points of contention.

First, a recent collaborative research project by computer scientists from Harvard and cognitive scientists from MIT—whose findings were later presented at the IEEE Conference on Computer Vision and Pattern Recognition—explored cognitive memorability of visualizations in hopes of finding empirical evidence to support the theory that while our memories are unique, we have the same algorithm embedded in our heads to convert visual communication to memory and thereby learn—and retain that learning. In other words, regardless of the memory being stored within our brains the same algorithm—a standard baseline that does not vary much from person to person—commits these to memory. To test their theory, these researchers used a publically available memorability dataset, and augmented the object and scene annotations with interpretable spacial, content, and aesthetic image proprieties (colors, shapes, etc.) (Isola et al., 2011). While the finding that images containing people are more memorable than images of settings (places and/or locations) is not particularly surprising, their other finding—that unusualness and aesthetic beauty are not associated with high memorability and are, instead, negatively correlated with memorability—is. This would seem to challenge the popular assumption that beautiful images—more aesthetically pleasing ones—are more valuable in memory currency. Another interesting find of the Harvard/MIT study is that visualizations are instantly and overwhelmingly more memorable if it includes a human-recognizable element—such as a photograph, person, cartoon, or logo—items that, in essence, provide our memory with a visual cue to build a story around, linking back to our most primitive of visual communication methods: symbolism, or the practice of representing things by symbols. This is a compelling case for the use of icons in visualizations like infographics that rely on symbols to communicate mass amounts of complex data in simple and meaningful ways.

In a later study on what makes a visualization memorable, another group of researchers built a broad, static visualization taxonomy to cover the large variety of data visualizations in use today, and then collected nearly 6,000 visual representations of data from various publications. The scraped visualizations were then categorized by a wide range of attributes. The researchers were able to expose the images to participants via Amazon Mechanical Turk and test the influence of features like color, density, and content themes on participants' memorability. The results of the study again validated previous findings that faces and human-centric scenes are more memorable than others—specifically, people and human-like objects contributed most positively to the memorability of images. This again confirms that certain design principles make visualizations inherently more memorable than others, irrespective of a viewer's individual context and biases (Borkin et al., 2013). However, an interesting find of this particular study was that, contrary to the popular mantra of "less is more" in data visualization, these researchers found that visualization with low data-to-ink ratios and high visual densities (or, in the common vernacular: more chart junk) were actually more memorable than minimalist data visualizations (Borkin et al., 2013). Unique visualizations that left a lasting impression were more memorable than traditional, common graphs—like bar charts or line graphs—which likewise is a direct contradiction to the previous study, which found that uniqueness of visuals was actually associated with lower levels of memorability. This is part of the experience of looking at a visual, which we will explore more later.

While the intrinsic—and predictive quality—of visual memorability continues to be an ongoing area of inquiry, there are a few key takeaways that are of paramount importance:

- We have a high memory capacity—we can remember thousands of images for a long time with a high degree of recall
- Memorability is an intrinsic feature of visual information, and likewise, is reproducible across a diverse spectrum of visual taxonomies
- Memorability is a tool that can be used as a metric for quantifying information and presenting it in visually meaningful ways
- Certain design principles make visualizations consistently more memorable than others, irrespective of a viewer's individual context and biases
- Visuals that blend information with influential features (like color, density, and content themes of recognizable icons or imagery) are significantly more memorable

Of course, as many researchers and data visualization pundits (myself included) have pointed out, it is crucial to remember that a memorable visualization is not necessarily a good visualization. Data visualization does not equal data analysis, and poorly designed data visualizations that misinterpret or misrepresent data may very well be memorable—but for all the wrong reasons (and even potentially make visualizations dangerous). Going forward, we will discuss how to avoid this paradox and leverage design considerations and visualization best practices, as well as learn from a few examples of memorable, beautiful data visualization gone wrong.

6.2.1 IMAGERY ANALYSIS

There is an old age that says, "the more you know, the more you see."

In his book *Visual Communication: Images with Messages*, Paul Lester—a professor of Communications at California State University—writes, "An image…is forgotten if it isn't analyzed…Meaningless pictures entertain a viewer only for a brief moment and do not have the capacity to educate. But an analyzed image can affect a viewer for a lifetime" (Lester, 2010). If we reflect independently on Lester's wisdom, we can each bring to mind certain images—photographs, paintings, or other works of art—that have greatly impacted us in a personal way. For example, who cannot immediately conjure up a mental image of da Vinci's Mona Lisa or that iconic photographic rendition of the RMS Titanic as it plunged into the North Atlantic? What about the photo of American soldiers raising a flag in Iwo Jima during World War II, the famous portrait of a scowling Winston Churchill, or Marilyn Monroe's skirt-blowing pose over a New York City subway grate? Likewise, from a data visualization perspective, those who have seen Florence Nightingale's area chart—the Coxcomb Plot—that analyzed the causes of morality of soldiers in Crimean war, or Gapminder's Wealth and Health of Nations global trend animated visualization are not likely soon to forget either the visual or the information it presented. Analyzing imagery is ego-driven (at least, according to author and literary critic, David Lodge). How we approach this analysis moves through our initial assessment, to an emotional one, and then to a subjective personal reaction before making the transition to a rational, objective response. Through this process we learn and reveal, first and foremost, something about ourselves (or the person making the analysis) before the actual image itself.

There are many perspectives to analyzing imagery. Lester himself emphasizes six perspectives—personal, historical, technical, ethical, cultural, and critical—while others, like David Lodge—list up to 14 different analytical perspectives. However, rather than discuss perspectives by which to analyze a visual image, I would like to suggest four simple steps to guide image analysis. We will walk through these next.

First, make an observation. Focus on the image to draw out what immediately catches your eye as significant. Then, transform those observations into connections by drawing in additional elements in the visual that could affect or influence your first observation in a new way. Then, make an educated guess that is grounded in observation and critical thinking as to what the image is trying to communicate. Finally, arrive at an interpretive conclusion that leverages observations, connections, and inferences to form a hypothesis on the message the image is conveying. Critical thinking is a very satisfying intellectual endeavor. As a thinking exercise, apply these steps to any of the visual examples listed above and see what results you come up with.

To walk you through the exercise, consider Figure 6.3. At first glimpse, we see a young girl from the back looking into a circular window through a wall with peeling paint. She is wearing a white dress with a shawl draped over her shoulders and arms, and a hat resting on her back. These are high-level take aways from what you may immediately notice when you look at the picture. There is very little analysis; it is pure observation. Following the fours steps outlined above, next draw in additional elements that influence that first observation—notice, perhaps, that the girl is standing awkwardly in a somewhat tentative pose with her bare right foot overlapping her left. Or, notice that her right hand disappears into the void of the window as she investigates whatever she is looking at. Now, make an educated guess about what you are seeing in the photograph. Like many of Alvarez's photos, this one invites several interpretations. One is that the girl is a symbol of the innocence of childhood, looking at a world of unknowns in her future. Another is that the peeling paint and the girl's bare feet speak to a "hardness" of the world outside, and that the window is an escape. Arriving at the final step, it is time for you to arrive at a conclusion that leverages these observations, connections, and inferences, as well as your personal opinions

FIGURE 6.3 The Daughter of the Dancers by Manuel Alvarez Bravo, 1933

and experiences. If you are familiar with Alvarez's work or with Mexican reliefs and carvings, your analysis of the photograph may yield one conclusion, and if you are looking at this photo for the first time, you may see something different. (As a side note, in this visual we see many repetitions of shape, patterns, contrast, and balance—themes we will explore in more detail in chapter: The Importance of Visual Design).

Upcoming sections on visual data literacy will add more substance on the bones of this framework, but for now it is important to understand the process of image analysis and the experience of looking at a visual.

6.3 EXTENDING VISUAL LITERACY TO VISUAL DATA LITERACY

Before we make the transition from visual communication and cognitive hardwiring to visual literacy, it is useful to note that the insistence on visual literacy is not new. In fact, it is an argument that is both old and perennial (George, 2002). Consider this quote from a turn of the 20th century text on English composition: "In some respects...words cannot compare in effectiveness with pictures. The mere outlines in a Greek vase painting will give you a more immediate appreciation of the grace and beauty of the human form than the pages of descriptive writing. A silhouette in black paper will enable you to recognize a stranger more quickly than the most elaborate description in the world (Gardiner et al., 1902)."

As early as the beginning of the twentieth century, right about the same time as the world's first self-service cardboard camera—again, the Kodak Brownie—made photography accessible to everyone who could afford the modest price tag (which, by the way, at a price of between one and two dollars is roughly equivalent in today's value of a few bucks short of $800 dollars), the construct of visual literacy was hot on the list of multiple literacies that complemented the traditional three R's—reading, writing, and arithmetic—of traditional education. The Dick and Jane elementary reader alerted teachers to the need to pair visual cues with written instruction, and fifty years later the New London Group, finally identified the ability to both read and use visual information as primary among multiliteracies, stating: "literacy pedagogy must account for the burgeoning variety of text forms associated with information... This includes understanding and competent control of represpresentational forms" (New London Group, 1996).

Even with a vast amount of scholarly literature and academic examination, there still remains much confusion over visual communication, visual rhetoric, and the role of "visual" as a pedagogical construct—what it is, and where and whether or not it belongs in composition. This is particularly relevant as an evolving understanding of the cognitive style construct continues to emerge with today's advances in multimedia and visual technologies (Stokes, 2002; Mayer & Massa, 2003), making literacy increasingly visual. Earlier in this chapter, visual communication was proposed as a form of communication: the act of engaging in direct or indirect communication through a visual aid that provides the means by which to convey an idea and/or information in forms that rely on seeing (including typography, drawings, designs, illustrations, animations, etc.). Likewise, visual rhetoric is a theoretical framework that describes how such visual images are used to communicate. Both visual communication and visual rhetoric fall under the umbrella term of visual literacy, or the ability to read, interpret, and understand information presented in nonword form (Wileman, 1993) (Figure 6.4). Using visualization approaches, coupled with a focus on increasing information understanding and analysis, leverages our visual cognitive hardwiring and extends visual literacy to cultivate visual *data* literacy, and furthers the construction of critical and higher-level thinking, encourages data-driven decision-making, and provides the deeper degree of data fluency requisite for data analysis and communication.

6.3.1 VISUAL LEARNING KEY TO DATA LITERACY

As we have discussed in the previous sections, visual learning is part and parcel to intrinsic human cognitive hardwiring as a communication, learning, and memorability mechanism. Further, established learning theories outline how learners acquire

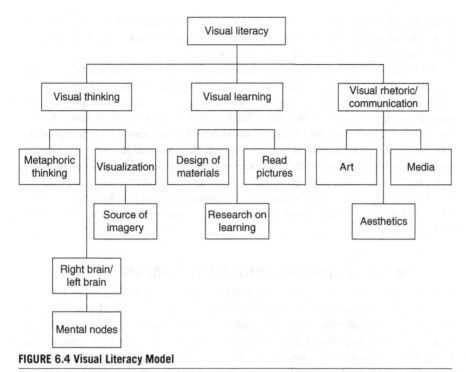

FIGURE 6.4 Visual Literacy Model

This model is modified from Sandra Moriarty's diagram in her essay *A Conceptual Map of Visual Communication* and expanded to include the role of data visualization and rearticulated within the context of visual data literacy.

different types of information and through which processes (including classic conditioning, behavior theory, functionalism, sign learning, mathematical learning, information processes models, and/or neuron-linguistic programming and cognitive sciences) (Penrose, 2006). As a core construct, many of these support the role of visualization as a key component of learning and retention—visual literacy. The ability to visually learn from and consume information is a core construct of the deeply engrained visualizer–verbalizer hypothesis (wherein learning is a combination of verbal and visual elements) (Stokes, 2002).

Today, visual learning may be tipping the scales of this hypothesis, in terms of both cognitive ability (human capabilities) and cognitive style (how people process and represent information by preference). One possible explanation for this shift could be attributed to the globalization of classroom education increasingly directed to both English speaking and nonEnglish speaking audiences that reduces dependency on verbal instruction and places more emphasis on visual methods of interactive learning to span language and cultural barriers. Another reason for the use of visualization is to compensate for a documented drop in vocabulary, especially across younger generations into the workforce today. It is estimated that the vocabulary of a 14-year old dropped from 25,000 words in 1950 to only 10,000 words in 1999—a reduction in verbal lexis of 60% (Penrose, 2006).

With increasing technological competencies (eg, more advanced statistical and/or visualization tools used in educational settings), the ability to place emphasis on visually-oriented approaches in learning has evolved from an information presentation mindset to the integration of interdisciplinary approaches, designed to cultivate data literacy and critical thinking to support the needs of an increasingly data-dependent and analytical culture. Incorporating more visual elements into learning helps to foster interdependency between the two modes of thought, balancing verbal and visual learning (Stokes, 2002). This approach to learning complements previous research, which has proposed multiple literacies are necessary to meet the challenges of society, including print, visual, aural, media, computer, and ecoliteracy (Kellner, 1998; Stokes, 2002).

6.3.2 INCORPORATING DATA INTO VISUAL LEARNING

In later chapters, we will explore the need for and role of formal data analysis education in data visualization, in addition to statistics and analytical modeling and the convergent relationship of visual analysis and data discovery. Here, within the context of cultivating visual data literacy, the intent is to simply understand that as the need to gather, examine, and explore data becomes increasingly more fundamental across all verticals of industry, it brings alongside it a growing need to introduce and establish data literacy skills to build capabilities for understanding data (Brinkley, 2014). This does not merely support current knowledge workers and business analysts working with data, but is extremely pertinent to next-generation workers entering the workforce and students learning to apply analytical concepts to information. Building on the framework of visual literacy, we can achieve various learning objectives for data literacy by directly leveraging data visualization tools that include elements of design, statistics visualization, and communication. Each of these provides benefit to expanding visual data literacy, including enabling current and emerging visual analysts to think creatively and map conceptual and physical space; helping to examine changes and hypothesize reasons for change; and providing the ability to create persuasive visual representations to support arguments or recommendations (Hitchcock et al., 2014).

To achieve data literacy through visualization, visual learning should be extended to project data in a way that reduces complexity while capturing important information in a meaningful and memorable way. Many case studies in the literature provide the design, prototypic implementation, and evaluation of a framework for contextualized visualization as a learning support mechanism for ongoing, informal (or not focused on a particularly educational objective or provided through formal academic processes), and visually supported learning. However, there are many less academic and more practicable examples of using data visualization mechanisms to foster data literacy, irrespective of subject appeal and within a broader educational context. To meet this need, two major approaches to visual data literacy have been proposed as extensions of traditional visual literacy models. They are, respectively, decode and encode.

6.3.3 DECODE

The first is to leverage visualization to read and decode, thus assisting learners with various analytical techniques that includes teaching mathematics and statistics. While students have traditionally been taught to draw graphics to visualize mathematical information, the growth of user-friendly computing technologies has spurred a trend to teach statistical concepts using interactive data visualization tools (Forbes et al., 2014). Further, pictorial vision is a prerequisite for the understanding of the concepts of statistical inference (Moore as cited in Forbes et al., 2014). Putting this theory into practice, an enrichment program for high school students interested in a career in science of mathematics was designed by researchers from North Carolina General Assembly in partnership with JMP Software, an interactive software tool for desktop statistical discovery and division of business analytics software leader SAS. As an experiment, this program was intended to expose students to data in a unique and exciting way by allowing them to engage with information and describe, visualize, and critique data sets from health care, education, and business. With a very limited focus on material covered in traditional mathematics curriculum, students were invited to explore data critically and visually to structure information for summary analysis (Brinkley, 2014). At the end of the program, students had developed a proven capacity to visually work with and understand data, as well as understand the role of data in decision-making.

6.3.4 ENCODE

The second proposed method to visual data literacy is to encode visuals with data as a communication mechanism. One particularly popular type of visualization applicable under this concept is the infographic, which visually communicates complex quantitative and/or qualitative information through the combination of data displays, lists, graphics, and other data elements (including words) (Toth, 2013). Infographics, which we will explore in detail in a later chapter, have been integrated into collegiate level business courses to highlight literacy concerns and teach students what information is valuable and how to use it effectively. In one study, students were directed to design a meaningful infographic as part of the learning process. Results showed an increase in student engagement and a deeper understanding for the visual data design process, while the production approach of the infographic supported traditional pedagogical elements, such as writing proposals, performing research, and meeting citation and documentation requirements (Toth, 2013).

6.3.5 SPECIAL CONSIDERATIONS FOR VISUAL DATA LITERACY EDUCATORS

Visual data literacy is a core competency in the days to come, both for knowledge workers and for educators. To recap, in chapter: From Self-Service to Self-Sufficiency, we discussed the changing academic landscape to facilitate the emergence of new data science roles, how universities and companies alike are addressing a noticeable STEM worker shortage, and the continuing challenges being faced in talent acquisition and retention. In chapter: Navigating Ethics in the Big Data Democracy, we explored how educators are preparing future IT leaders with the ethical competencies they will need to navigate an increasing data-dependent culture. Within the discussion on cultivating visual data literacy, as academics align with the needs and demands of industry for emerging workers, there is an increased expectation to deliver graduates with enhanced knowledge and technical skills that leverage advanced visualization techniques for critical business competencies and data-driven decision-making (Hitchcock et al., 2014). This is driven by a progressively data-reliant and analytical business culture, wherein workers are expected to use data visualization techniques to graphically see business data to clearly interpret meanings, patterns, and trends, and make decisions that affect the business, internal and external stakeholders, and society-at-large. Thus, while the majority of this text is geared toward business and technical audiences, there are special considerations to be paid to those educators interested in integrating visual data literacy as an exemplary educational practice. Many of these considerations will also apply to the methods organizations can employ to provide guided data visualization, which we will explore in the appropriate context later.

Like any use of data visualization, the use of visualization to promote data literacy should be carefully planned. Applying the use of visualizations depends largely on the content, and thus must be used in the appropriate context. While many forms of graphics exist, visualizations that incorporate illustrations and text (the verbalizer–visualizer hypothesis) depict patterns of concepts and ideas that service as frameworks to promote learning, whereas those that steer learners toward exciting presentation can interfere (Stokes, 2002). This includes using visualization in photographs for realism, drawings, diagrams, or maps, as well as deciding when to use visualizations for the effective visual support of data and information (Penrose, 2006). Additionally, visualization must be used within the proper larger educational context, as visualization alone does not maximize achievement (Stokes, 2002).

When using data visualizations to support visual data literacy, highlight connections between visualization, design, and elements of science, and engage students in group critiques to explore and develop a position of personal insight and experience with data visualizations (Dykes et al., 2010). As an intellectual endeavor, providing guided visualization examples has also been acknowledged as a catalyst for creative thought and problemsolving, and offers an innovative pedagogical format for teaching ethics and decision-making alongside complementary frameworks like Six Sigma, which involves the continuous and systematic use of data (Honey-Roses et al., 2013).

6.4 FROM COMMUNICATION TO CONVERSATION

As humans, we are hard-wired to communicate, to learn, and to remember visually. From this, we develop the capacity for visual dialog, or as conceived by Nathan Knobler (1972), the exchange that must occur between the artist, his work, and its consumer. Building upon the basis of visual memorability and literacy, cognitive psychologists describe how the human mind, in its attempt to understand and remember, assembles bits and pieces of experiences and information into a story. To aid in this story-building process, we automatically conjure images—visual cues—associated with the story. Stories, then, are not only how we learn, but also a key ingredient to how we remember—visually.

Award-winning writer and director, Robert McKee, said that ultimately the most powerful way to motivate people to action is by "uniting an idea with an emotion." The best way to do that, McKee says, is by telling a compelling story—where you can not only weave in a lot of information, but you can also arouse the listener's emotion and energy. He argues that a good story "fulfill[s] a profound human need to grasp the patterns of living—not merely as an intellectual exercise, but within a very personal, emotional experience." The value of a good story, then, is an experience that inspires more stories. It turns a onesided narrative into a living conversation.

Don't buy in to the value of a good, visual data story as a vehicle primed for learning and memorability? Good—let me tell you a story to change your mind! At the 2014 Tableau User Conference, astrophysicist and science communicator Neil deGrasse Tyson reminded an audience five thousand strong of data visualization lovers that our human brains are built for learning from graphics rather than pure scientific data. In his keynote, Tyson gave a tour of scientific topics—from the continued disgruntlement abut Pluto's declassification as a planet to the spectacular rendition of Tyson's own starry vest in a recent *Superman* comic book. He debunked the Super Moon idea, showed us the power of correlations in data, and showed the audience a simulation of galaxies colliding and how data and computer modeling was used to deflect Apophis. By the end of his speech, Tyson moved the room to standing ovation—which is not such an easy feat when talking about data.

This, of course, was not the first time that Tyson has used storytelling to help communicate scientific information to the masses. For example, in his National Geographic miniseries *Cosmos: A Spacetime Odyssey* (a follow-up to Carl Sagan's 1980s television series of a similar name), Tyson distilled the 14-billion year history of the universe into a digestible 12-month calendar and used it as a visual guide—or, as he was quoted as saying "vehicle of storytelling"—for each of the series' 13 episodes.

How effective were these vehicles of visual data storytelling? Well, *Cosmos* won the 4th Critics' Choice Television Award for "Best Reality Series" and Tyson himself won the award for "Best Reality Host." The show received a multitude of other nominations and awards, including several Emmys and a 2014 Peabody Award for education. But—more important than awards—what makes Tyson such a celebrated storyteller? It is because he accesses mental models for scientific education, and layers these—along with a fair amount of levity and clever puns—to make the data accessible to a nontechnical audience. He engages the audience in learning that is visual, memorable, and fun. This is the heart of McKee's quote: uniting an idea with emotion.

Stories engage us: they create bonds through a compelling narrative that help us to learn, connect, retain, and relate information across communities over time. A good story is memorable by design, and, if history proves anything, we tend to share good stories over and over again. Stories spread, and they nurture the interest in future storytelling. However, storytelling alone does not provide the value that we need and using visualization to communicate supports stories in an increasingly more complex world (see Box 6.6). Thus, in the next chapter, we will discuss how narrative visualization differs from other forms of storytelling and the key elements of story structure for telling meaningful data stories with data visualization.

BOX 6.6 STORYTELLING THROUGH ART

What do you get when you pair the love of books with widely used, general-purpose programming language Python? For entrepreneur Danny Fein, the answer is Litographs, an innovative Massachusetts-based startup that designs projects to lift the text of a literary classic off of the page and transform it into a stunning piece of visual art (Figure 6.5).

Fein left UPenn with a degree in evolutionary psychology and went to work in applied science at a DC-based software company, where he became interested in data visualization. While teaching himself Python through self-written and abstract, slightly-modified script, Fein knew—that he wanted to create something creative while promoting literacy, both at home and abroad. With his creative director, the pair drew up a couple of silhouette concepts and wrote a Python script to translate a raw image into a text data image—and Litographs was born. Today, the company has found its niche in telling stories in a new way, and doing its part to promote global literacy: as of this writing, Litographs offers over 140 titles, and for each poster, t-shirt, and tote bag sold, a new, high-quality book is donated to a community in need.

Through its work, Litographs is helping to keep the beauty of classic literature alive and well to continue to tell traditional stories in an increasingly digital era. "As books become more electronic," says Fein, "Litographs gives us a new opportunity to find innovative ways to bring people back to the beauty of a classic text."

In its first major departure from their bread-and-butter business of representing complete texts in a single image, Litographs launched The World's Longest Tattoo Chain™ as an interactive, community-based project intended to tell Lewis Carroll's enchanting tales via temporary tattoos. Powered by Kickstarter, and inspired by projects like Shelley Jackson's SKIN Project (who published a 2,000 word novella across participants' bodies in single words) and other literary tattoo movements, The World's Longest Tattoo Chain is an ode to the connection between a reader and a book told in 5,258 unique—and randomly-selected for the recipient—phrases.

"This project provides a new way to visually collaborate with thousands of people in a way that transcends the temporary nature of tattoos and creates a powerful, forever concept," says Fein. "It's a visual way for people to come together through literature and art—to stamp themselves as a book lover and participate." And, it is a project wherein each person is a part of something larger than themselves—telling a global narrative through their personal interpretation of a seemingly out-of-context, mysteriously chosen few words.

In what feels like a natural tie back to the idea of creating artwork from book text, the outcome of The World's Longest Tattoo Chain project will be a permanent collection commemorating Carroll's work through the bodies and photos of each participant. Meanwhile, Litographs is already working on the next tattoo chain, hoping to continue finding books that resonate in a new format to produce interesting results and continuing telling stories through beautiful photos.

FIGURE 6.5 Litograph's Alice T-Shirt

The average litographs t-shirt contains approximately 40,000 words—the length of a short novel.

REFERENCES

Borkin, M., Vo, A., Bylinski, Z., Isola, P., Sunkavalli, S., Oliva, A., Pfister, H., 2013. Proceedings from IEEE INFOVIS 2013: What Makes a Visualization Memorable? Atlanta, GA: IEEE.

Brinkley, J., 2014. Proceedings from JMP Discovery Summit 2014 Using JMP as a Catalyst for Teaching Data-Driven Decision Making to High School Students. Greenville, NC: JMP SAS.

Christiansen, M. H., Kirby, S., 2003. In: Language evolution: the hardest problem in science? Morten H. Christiansen, Simon Kirby (Eds.) Language evolution. Oxford; New York: Oxford University Press.

Dykes, J., Keefe, D., Kindlmann, G., Munzer, F., Joshi, A., 2010. Proceedings from IEEE VizWeek: Perspectives on Teaching Data Visualization (Best Panel Award). Minneapolis, MN: University of Minnesota.

Febvre, L., Martin, H.J., 1976. The Coming of the Book. (D. Gerard, Trans.). Feinberg, London (Original work Gerald (1977) What is the World Made of).

Forbes, S., Chapman, J., Harraway, J., Stirling, D., Wild, C., 2014. Use of data visualization in the teaching of statistics: a New Zealand perspective. Stat. Educ. Res. J. 13 (2), 187–201.

Gardiner, J.H., Kittredge, G.L., Arnold, S.L., 1902. The Mother Tongue: Elements of English Composition, Book III. Ginn & Company, Boston, MA.

George, D., 2002. From analysis to design: visual communication in the teaching of writing. Coll. Compos. Commun. 54 (1), 11–39.

Hitchcock, W., Miller, F., Pontes, M., Wieniek, D.,1, 2014. Proceedings from the Marketing Management Association Fall 2014 Teaching Data Visualization.

Honey-Roses, J., Le Menestrel, M., Arenas, D., Rauschmayer, F., Rode, J., 2013. Enriching intergenerational decision-making with guided visualization exercises. J. Bus. Ethics 122 (4), 675–680.

Humphrey, G., 1924. The psychology of the Gestalt. J. Educ. Psychol. 15 (7), 401–412.

Huxley, A., 1943. The Art of Seeing. Chatto & Windus, London.

Isola, P., Xiao, J., Torralba, A., Oliva, A., 2011. What makes an image memorable? IEEE Conference on Computer Vision and Pattern Recognition (CVPR), 1, pp. 145–152.

Kellner, D., 1998. Multiple literacies and critical pedagogy in a multi-cultural society. Educ. Theor. 48 (1), 103–122.

Knobler, N., 1972. Visual Dialogue: An Introduction to the Appreciation of Art, second ed. Holt, Rinehart & Winston of Canada Ltd.

Lester, P.M., 2010. Visual Communication: Images with Messages, fifth ed. Cengage Learning, Boston, MA.

Lieberman, P., 2007. The evolution of human speech. Curr. Anthropol. 48 (1), 39–66.

Lima, M., 2014. The Book of Trees: Visualizing Branches of Knowledge. Princeton Architectural Press, New York, NY.

Mayer, R.E., Massa, L.J., 2003. Three facets of visual and verbal learners: cognitive ability, cognitive style, and learning preference. J. Educ. Psychol. 95 (4), 833–846.

Meggs, P.B., 2011. Meggs' History of Graphic Design, fifth ed. Wiley, Hoboken, NJ.

Millard, A.R., 1986. The infancy of the alphabet. World Archeol. 17 (3), 390–398.

New London Group, 1996. A pedagogy of multiliteracies: designing social futures. Harvard Educ. Rev. 66, 60–92.

Penrose, J., 2006. Teaching the essential role of visualization in preparing instructions. Bus. Commun. Q. 69 (4), 411–417.

Smith, K.L., Moriarty, S., Kenney, K., Barbatsis, B. (Eds.), 2004. Handbook of Visual Communication: Theory, Methods, and Media. Routledge, New York, NY.

Stam, J.H., 1976. Inquiries into the Origins of Language. Harper and Row, New York.

Standing, L., 1973. Learning 10,000 pictures. Q. J. of Psychol. 25 (2), 207–222.

Stokes, S., 2002. Visual literacy in teaching and learning: a literature perspective. Electron. J. Integ. Technol. Educ. 1 (1), 10–19.

Toth, C., 2013. Revisiting a genre: teaching infographics in business and professional communication courses. Bus. Commun. Q. 76 (4), 446–457.

UNESCO. Decorated Cave of Pont d'Arc, known as Grotte Chauvet-Pont d'Arc, Ardèche, 2015. Available from: http://whc.unesco.org/en/list/1426.

Wileman, R.E., 1993. Visual Communicating. Educational Technology Publications, Englewood Cliffs, NJ.

Whitehouse, D., 1999). Earliest writing' found. BBC News Online (BBC).

Visual storytelling
with data

7

"To write it, it took three months; to conceive it three minutes; to collect the data in it, all my life."
—F. Scott Fitzgerald

First off, take a deep breath. We made it through chapter: Visual Communication and Literacy. I know the information was dense, but I assure you that an understanding of the long and winding evolution of visual communication will only serve you in the future as you put these concepts into practice within your organization and ground how data visualization is made an important part of your visual communication strategy. Thus, I will end our prior discussion on visual communication and literacy with a quote from American poet, novelist, and contributor to the founding of New Criticism, Robert Penn Warren, who infamously wrote that, "History cannot give us a program for the future, but it can give us a fuller understanding of ourselves, and of our common humanity, so that we can better face the future." Going forward, we will see the echoes of Penn's words as we not only apply the context of the evolution of visual communication to storytelling, but also to cognitive and artful design considerations necessary in a visual data culture.

I intentionally ended the previous chapter with a bit of a cliffhanger, talking about the power of stories as a mechanism to move information from communication and into understanding. We saw, too, in chapter: The Data Science Education and Leadership Landscape, how the ability to tell meaningful data stories will be of paramount importance in new roles in data science and data visualization going forward. Storytellers like Robert McKee or Neil deGrasse Tyson or even Francis Ford Coppola (from whom I will share an anecdote later in this chapter) are masters of their craft. They (to again reference the previous McKee quote) "unite idea with emotion." They have embraced the storytelling paradigm to engage their audiences in learning complex information in a way that is visual, memorable, and fun—something we can learn from as we build a storytelling strategy around how we see and understand data and information. Storytelling is a skill and it takes (copious amounts of) practice.

As humans, we are hard-wired to communicate, to learn, and to remember visually, a premise we have touched on already and will continue to explore deeper in the chapter to follow. Storytelling leverages these native cognitive characteristics, yet alone it does not provide the value that we need when using visualization to communicate in an increasingly more complex world. The most interesting thing about storytelling—visual or otherwise—is not simply the actual story we are telling: it is *how* we tell it. Storytelling is not just about scripting a compelling narrative to exchange ideas and information, but it is about painting the narrative into a picture that effectively communicates the story itself in a meaningful, memorable, and inspiring way. Yes, it is uniting idea with emotion, but it is even more important for data—even visual analytics expert and technical evangelist Andy Cotgreave (2015) remarked it so in a *Computerworld* article pointedly entitled "Data without emotion doesn't bring about change."

When we think about storytelling in the context of data, we should first and foremost understand that narrative visualizations *should always* put data at the forefront of the story. However, data stories differ from traditional storytelling that typically chains together a series of causally related events to progress through a beginning, middle, to arrive at an end. Data stories, instead, can be similarly linearly visualized or not, or they can be interactive to invite discovery, solicit new questions, and offer alternative explanations. However, while today's robust visualization tools support richer, more diverse forms of storytelling, crafting a compelling data narrative requires a diverse set of skills. In this chapter, I will clarify how narrative visualization differs from other storytelling forms and identify elements of story structure for telling data stories with visualization—including nuances of genre, visual narrative design, and narrative structure tactics best suited for the complexity of the data, the intended audience, and the storytelling medium. First, let us examine exactly what the data story *is*.

7.1 THE STORYTELLING PARADIGM: DEFINING THE DATA STORY

The storytelling paradigm—or, the narrative paradigm—is a theory proposed by Walter Fisher, a 20th century philosopher, who believed that all meaningful communication is a form of storytelling or of providing a narrative report of events and information. According to Fisher, human beings experience and comprehend life as a series of ongoing narratives. Each has its own conflicts, characters, beginning, middle, and, ultimately, an ending. Additionally, all forms of human communication are to be seen, fundamentally, as stories shaped by history, culture, and character. And, it is important to note that these narrations are not limited to nonfiction, but rather, we tend to gravitate toward fiction more so perhaps than anything. It is, as Newman University provost Michael Austin writes in his book *Useful Fictions,* one of humanity's most defining paradoxes: that we cannot survive without a steady flow of information, but that it does not necessarily have to be accurate. We need myths to help comprehend life's mysteries, as well as stories that thrill and scare us without any true or factual basis, just as much as we need comedic, dramatic, or otherwise fantastic stories to entertain and inform us. Stories—of fact or fiction—help us navigate the world around us.

The storytelling paradigm meets the data story where good ideas fall victim to the melee of buzzwords. Recently, the word "storytelling" has been applied in the data industry everywhere from a tool feature or functionality, to part of the skillset of a visual analyst, or even to a job role itself. One can rarely talk about data visualization without the word storytelling cropping up somewhere in the conversation. This leads to a larger problem: as Segal and Heer (2010) have rightly pointed out, though data visualization often evokes comparisons to storytelling, the relationship between the two is rarely articulated. And firsthand research supports this: in our recent research at Radiant Advisors wherein we surveyed the end user market on their priorities in tool evaluations and purchase decisions, we found that storytelling ranked right in the middle as both the "most important" and "least important" feature of data visualization tools. Among other things, this tells us that it is likely that the concept is still largely ambiguous. Outside of data journalism where data storytelling has become the new bread and butter of the editorial and news world, the rest of us have yet to quite figure out how to use data storytelling in our increasingly data-dependent and visual organizations.

While data stories do share many similarities with traditional stories, they are, in fact, quite different. Visual storytelling could be thought of, if anything, as a visual data documentary. By definition, these are quantitative visual narratives told through sequential facts and data points. While it bridges the gap between the data and the art (both of storycraft and of design), in visual storytelling we use visualizations primarily as purveyors of truth. What makes data visualization itself different from other types of visual storytelling is the complexity of the content that needs to be communicated. Thus, data storytelling is essentially information compression—smashing complicated information into manageable pieces by focusing on what is most important and then pretending it is whole and bound entirely within the visualization(s) used to illustrate the message. Later in this chapter, we will review a few examples to help illustrate this point.

To facilitate storytelling, graphical techniques and interactivity can enforce various levels of structure and narrative flow (for example, consider an early reader picture book, which illustrates salient points with a visual—sometimes interactive—to emphasis key points of learning). And, though static visualizations have long been used to support storytelling, today an emerging class of visualizations that combine narratives with interactive data and graphics are taking more of the spotlight in the conveying of visual narratives (Segel & Heer, 2010). In the sections that follow, we will focus on the frameworks for narrative visualization as well as a few key steps to telling stories with data visualization.

7.2 A BRIEF BIT OF STORY PSYCHOLOGY

Humans have a deep-seeded need for stories, data-driven or otherwise. Let us take this opportunity to briefly review both an anthropological perspective on our love of stories, as well as how this is supported by our cognitive hardwiring.

7.2.1 AN ANTHROPOLOGICAL PERSPECTIVE

Stories give us pleasure; we like them. Stories teach us important lessons; we learn from them. We think in stories—it is how we pass information, through myths, legends, folklore, narratives. Stories transport us—we give the author license to stretch the truth—though, in data storytelling, this license extends only as far as it can before the data loses its elasticity and begins to break down. (Data stories have a certain degree of entropy, the unpredictable ability to quickly unravel into disorder if not told properly.)

Storytelling has been called the world's second-oldest profession, and, alongside visual expression is an integral part of human expression. All human cultures tell stories, and most people derive a great deal of pleasure from stories—even when they are not true (honestly, perhaps the more fantastical they are, then more pleasure they induce—think of fairy tales set in enchanted lands, or the far reaches of space in science fiction). Not only are we drawn to fiction, but also we are willing to invest significant resources into producing and consuming fictional narratives. How significant? The 2011 adventure flick *Pirates of the Caribbean: On Stranger Tides*, staring Johnny Depp and Penelope Cruz, currently holds the rank of the most expensive movie ever made by Hollywood (a title formerly held by James Cameron's *Titanic*) at $397 USD (Gibson, 2015). Likewise, The Hobbit series earns the top spot of a back-to-back film production with combined costs up to $745 million USD in 2014, and still counting (Perry, 2014).

So, why do we tell stories? Well, it is all part of the anthropological evolution of communication, one that, as Michael Austin wrote in the introduction to *Useful Fiction*, is very young yet already crowded with books and articles attempting to explain the cognitive basis of all storytelling and literature. In fact, there is no shortage of contributions to the field of story psychology that try and tweeze out the exact underpinnings of the importance of a good story. We could, however, venture to provide two possible contenders for why we tell stories: the need to survive and the need to know.

7.2.1.1 Survival of the fittest

As much as philosophers might like to suggest, human reason did not evolve to find truth. Rather, it evolved to defend positions and obtain resources—often through manipulation. Likewise, natural selection does not care if we are happy, but only that we survive (Austin, 2010). Our cognitive architecture is designed through instinct and evolution to have anxiety—worry about death, pain, etc. These are drivers for natural selection. Thus, predation narratives get our attention very quickly. Think of some of the earliest classic texts that are still popular today that focus on overcoming the most seemingly unbeatable of characters or situations (ie, Dracula or Frankenstein)—they have some degree of predation, many playing on intrinsic chase-play psychology that is universal in many breeds of animals, including humans.

As a precursor to survival, one thing we have always had to do is to understand other people. In fact, the most expensive cognitive thing we do is to try and figure other people out: predict what they are going to do, understand relationships, and so forth. And, when (or if) we succeed, this is an important part of survival—winning—another narrative that gives us pleasure because it brings much needed confidence back to our abilities to dominate and prevail. In this light, our stories are almost predictive in quality: if we know what worked in the past, it might help us to imagine what might happen in the future. Stories are guides.

7.2.1.2 *The cliffhanger*

Another reason for telling stories is because we all need resolution to ongoing questions and curiosities. It does not have to be a happy ending, but we need *an* ending—we simply cannot handle cliffhangers. This is known as the Zeigarnik effect, named for the Soviet psychologist Bluma Zeigarnik, who demonstrated in the early 1900s that people have a better memory for unfinished tasks that they do for finished ones (Austin, 2010). From its initial home in the annals of Gestalt psychology, the Zeigarnik effect is now known as a "psychological device that creates dissonance and uneasiness in the target audience."

Basically, this Zeigarnik effect speaks to our human need for endings—for closure. It is why television shows go to commercial breaks with cliffhangers, or why we will hang on through a Top 10 radio show and listen to songs we do not like just to get to that week's #1 hit. We come back, almost unfailingly, for resolution. Theoretically, a story ends with two simple words—the end—but even that does not always mean the story is over. Sometimes we are not ready emotionally for an ending, and we develop things like sequels. No matter the story's purpose—to focus, align, teach, or inspire—we build narratives the way we do to foster imagination, excitement, speculation—and successful narratives are those that introduce (get attention) and then resolve our anxiety (give a satisfactory ending). Thus, stories are therapeutic.

7.2.2 A COGNITIVE PERSPECTIVE

Stories are not just fun ways to learn or pass the time—they are a little bit like metaphorical fireworks for our brain, or at least a certain percent of it.

When we are presented with data, two parts of our brain respond: Wernicke's area—responsible for language comprehension—and Broca's area—responsible for language processing. Consider this: when you share facts and information—pure data—your audience will do one of two things. They will either 1) agree or 2) disagree. They will make a decision, a judgment, and move on. Hence, only the above named two parts of the brain have to bother to react to this—it is a simple input and respond transaction. However, when presented with a story, five additional areas of the brain are activated, including the visual cortex (colors and shapes), the olfactory cortex (scents), the auditory cortex (sounds), the motor cortex (movement), and the sensory cortex/cerebellum (language comprehension).

In a presentation on the neuroscience of storytelling, Scott Schwertly, the author of *How to Be a Presentation God* and CEO of Ethos3, said that the best way to

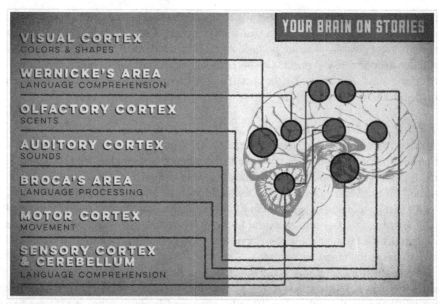

FIGURE 7.1

Your brain on stories. This visual illustrates which parts of the brain activated by a story

engage your audience—no matter what you are presenting—is by telling a story. It is the most efficient way to activate and ignite the often-elusive audience brain. Figure 7.1, created by Schwertly, illustrates the brain on stories.

7.3 THE DATA NARRATIVE FRAMEWORK

Storytellers through the ages have recognized that successful narratives can be shaped into recognizable structures. American writer Kurt Vonnegut is quoted, somewhat famously, as having said that "there is no reason that the simple shapes of stories can't be fed into a computer – they have beautiful shapes." Indeed, the structure of a narrative—whether it is a fictional novel or a data documentary—is beautiful in its growth, form, style, and message (even if that beauty is somewhat chaotic, which is something many writers may attest to, too). Similar to how traditional storytelling strategies vary depending on genre and media used, data stories can also be organized in linear sequences or otherwise constrained to support richer and more diverse forms of data storytelling and through more forms of storytelling media. However, with fiction, the goal is to draw people in through various psychological tactics— developing character, plot, storyline, etc.,—yet a documentary is more interested on concentrating on every element that success is dependent on the viewer deriving a larger understanding about the topic. It worries itself over building an argument based on *evidence*.

In his book *The Seven Basic Plots*, Christopher Booker (2004) established seven plots that are the basics of plotwriting. Booker classified these as: overcoming the monster (Dracula); rags to riches (Cinderella); the quest (Iliad); voyage and return (Odyssey); comedy (Much Ado About Nothing); tragedy (Macbeth); and rebirth (A Christmas Carol). You can relate these plot types to some of the points made in discussions this far in this chapter already. For the purposes of storytelling, the basic "plots" of visual data stories can be rearticulated as the following:

- *Change over time*—see a visual history as told through a simple metric or trend
- *Drill down*—start big, and get more and more granular to find meaning
- *Zoom out*—reverse the particular, from the individual to a larger group
- *Contrast*—the "this" or "that"
- *Spread*—help people see the light and the dark, or reach of data (disbursement)
- *Intersections*—things that cross over, or go from "less than" to "more than" (progression)
- *Factors*—things that work together to build up to a higher level effect
- *Outliers*—powerful way to show something outside the realm of normal

Beyond story plots, the other half of the data narrative framework equation is visual narrative tactics and design space considerations. While the chapter next is devoted to design considerations for data visualization, we could also consider how story genre can affect the nature of a visual data story as a distinct subject. To this point, Segel and Heel (2010) organized data stories into eight genres of narrative visualization that vary primarily in terms of the number or frames and the ordering of their visual elements. These genres, illustrated in Figure 7.2, are the magazine style, the annotated chart, the partitioned poster, the flow chart, the comic strip, the slide short, and finally, the conglomerate film/video/animation.

Data visual narratives are most effective when they have constrained interaction at various checkpoints within the narrative, allowing the user to explore the data

FIGURE 7.2

Genres of narrative visualization by Segel & Heer (2010)

without veering too far away from the intended narrative (the wisdom of guiding the reader versus allowing the reader to define their own story, like those "choose your own adventure" books you may remember from your childhood). Visual cues for storytelling include things like annotations (labels or "story points" as they are often called) to point out specific information; using color to associate items of importance without having to tell them; or even visual highlighting (ie, color, size, boldness) to connect elements. As a necessary aside, it is important to note that some data visualization tools are being enhanced with storytelling capabilities. Tableau, for example, has its storypoints; Qlik storytelling "snapshots"; YellowfinBI its storyboard. With these tools and more building capabilities intended to be used to facilitate data storytelling, visualizations are designed—or at minimum, intended to be designed—to feel less like data and more like story illustrations.

7.3.1 INVERTED JOURNALISM PYRAMID

One simple shape that can be used to tell a data story is that of an adapted model of the inverted journalism pyramid. The inverted pyramid is primarily a common method for writing news stories and as such is widely taught to mass communication and journalism students to illustrate how information should be prioritized and structured in a text. It is also a useful mechanism to tell a meaningful data story—or to activate belief with as little information (or as much information condensed) as possible.

Drawn as an upside down triangle (see Figure 7.3), the inverted journalism pyramid teeters with the tip of the triangle at the bottom of the shape. The most important, substantial, and interesting information lives at the widest portion of the triangle (the inverted "top"), while the tapering lower portions show how other material—like supporting information and background information, respectively—illustrate the other materials' diminishing level of importance. Ultimately, this system is designed so that information less vital to the reader's understanding comes later in the story,

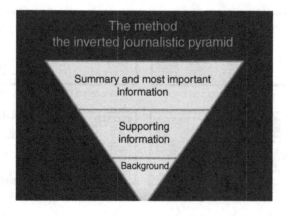

FIGURE 7.3

The inverted journalism pyramid

where it is easier to edit out for space or other reasons, and where the audience already has the knowledge to make new connections and draw their own conclusions. This also gives the story the ability to end with a call to action and spur decision-making. The same technique applies to data stories.

7.4 FIVE STEPS TO DATA STORYTELLING WITH VISUALIZATION

Today's visual narratives, according to a recent article in *The Economist*, "meld the skills of computer science, statistics, artistic design, and storytelling" (Segel & Heer, 2010). Building upon that sentiment, at a recent annual data storytelling and visualization conference, Tableau Tapestry, hosted by data visualization vendor Tableau, Hannah Fairfield, Senior Graphics Editor for the New York Times began her keynote presentation by saying, "Revelation is always based on prior knowledge." These two quotes speak to the compounding nature of crafting a compelling data story, which we can break down into five pertinent steps requisite of storytelling through data visualization:

7.4.1 FIRST, FIND DATA THAT SUPPORTS YOUR STORY

The first step in telling a useful data narrative depends on finding the data that supports your story—as both supporting background material and as fodder for stoking the fire of inquiry and discovery. Part of the revelation of storytelling is testing a hypothesis—of going through the scientific process to ask questions, perform background research, construct and test one or many hypotheses, and analyze results to draw and communicate a conclusion. However, finding data to support a story does not necessarily require scientific data. As an example, see Figure 7.4. This visual, produced by the *New York Times* builds upon itself in a series of five compounding animations that move the data story one step farther with each click. Using individual faculty member data from Harvard Business School (HBS), this visualization shows the tenure pipeline at HBS over the span of the next 40 years: the darker circles represent the currently tenured faculty members for men and women; the open circles show the pipeline of that gender equity over the next four decades.

This data, while not scientific, is nevertheless meaningful and applicable to a scientific process that melds data and storytelling to produce revelation. If you visit the visualization online and watch as it builds upon itself, it is easy to see that it is unlikely that the gender imbalance in tenured faculty will shift in the near future. In fact, that very revelation is the story of the graphic that we can discover throughout the scientific method of exploring the question of gender equity in academia—"what will tenured faculty look like in the future?" We start out with one level of knowledge—the current situation of tenured faculty at HBS—and through a series of steps that add more data and information to the scenario, this allows us to form

The Tenure Pipeline at Harvard Business School

But **the pipeline for women is small.** Fewer than a third of untenured faculty members are women, making it unlikely that the gender imbalance in tenured faculty will shift in the near future.

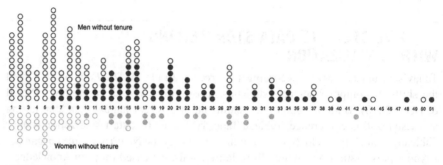

FIGURE 7.4

The tenure pipeline at Harvard Business School, produced by the New York Times. Step through the visualization online at http://www.nytimes.com/interactive/2014/02/27/education/harvard-tenure-pipeline.html

(Source: Harvard Business School; individual faculty members).

a hypothesis (that it likely will not change dramatically), and then test that through even more data until we reach an informed enough point that we can share our discovery.

7.4.2 THEN, LAYER INFORMATION FOR UNDERSTANDING

There is no shortage of information or data sets floating around that we can use to tell data narratives. But, like any craft, storytelling is not dependent on plucking out some random information and weaving a tale around it. Instead, it is more precise: figure out the story you want to tell, and then look for the data that supports or challenges that story. In other words, find a story you are interested in telling. Then, make sure that you understand your data. Remembering the inverted journalism pyramid above, think like a journalist: interview your data, ask it questions, examine it from different angles. Look at the outliers, the trends, and the correlations. These data points often have a great story to tell by themselves.

As the first step above hinted at, knowledge is incremental. Every piece of information that we learn is founded on something we have already learned before (for a simple example, we learn letters, then words, then phrases, and then sentences). Thus, layering information is incredibly critical: it is a tool you can use to bring your audience through a fairly complex story by guiding them step-by-step. If you viewed the above visualization on the *New York Times* website, you will easily see how each step in the series builds upon previous interpretations of the data. However, compounding builds in visualization are not the only technique to achieve this layering of insight and understanding. We can also achieve this effect through sequencing types of visualizations, or by drilling deeper into one single visualization, too.

7.4.3 THE GOAL IS TO DESIGN TO REVEAL

It should go without saying that data visualizations cannot be relied upon to tell the story for you. As tools, charts cannot do it all. Rather they should act as an aid—the illustrative accompaniment to your narrative. Likewise, various types of visualization can present the data properly, but still fail to tell a story. Visual data storytelling should give analysts and audiences a nugget of information that can continue to be refined and expanded to tell or receive a story. Thus, you must choose your data and your visual form carefully so that the two work together toward communicating one message.

To accomplish this, start by stripping out information that is not necessary, and design the data story in a way that leaves the audience with a single, very potent, message. Focus on the most powerful elements; however, understand that these are not always the most obvious trends or elements. To illustrate this example more clearly, see the snapshot of another *New York Times* graphic in Figure 7.5.

This graphic shows the difference in mortality rates between women of color and white women with breast cancer, and through animation (which you can watch at the URL provided) emphasizes how this gap has widened since 1975. While the overall occurrences of women's deaths due to breast cancer have gone down, the more powerful element of the story is the continued gap between women of color and white women. (This visualization shows, too, how motion and animation can be extremely powerful in data visualization as a way to tell a story through movement. We will look at this further in chapter: Visualization in the Internet of Things.) Thus, the thing to remember is that when we use data visualization with the goal to design to reveal, we have to focus on the message we are trying to communicate. There is not always one truth in data, and this is where context becomes a huge element of how to tell a data story.

7.4.4 ...BUT BEWARE THE FALSE REVEAL

A false reveal—one that leads the audience to a false understanding of cause and effect—can be a dangerous thing. It can incite the audience to draw the wrong conclusions or take an incorrect action; it can also damage the effect of the data itself. As a visual data documentary, our data stories should be engaging and entertaining, but they should also focus on sharing the truth. Sanity checking a story is paramount to making sure stories are meaningful and compelling, but that they also make sense. While a little levity is important in data visualization and storytelling to keep the audience engaged (see Box 7.1), data stories are not the place to practice comedy. As the adage goes, correlation does not imply equal causation, though admittedly, it does make for some pretty silly stories and visualizations. Think of some of the funny data stories you have probably heard where the data, for all intents and purposes,

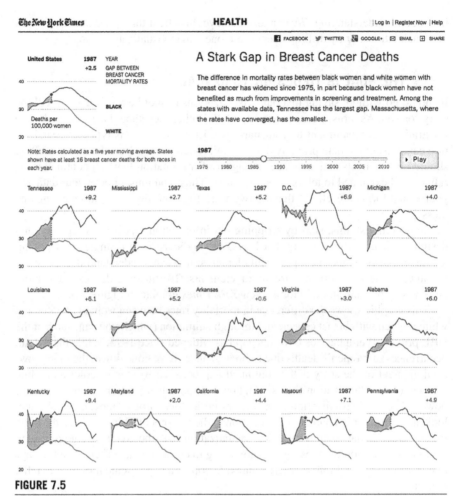

FIGURE 7.5

A stark gap in breast cancer deaths, produced by the New York Times. Animated visualization online at http://www.nytimes.com/interactive/2013/12/20/health/a-racial-gap-in-breast-cancer-deaths.html

seems to support the tale but are nothing more than nonsensical correlations. Like, for example, the parallel upward journey of amount of ice cream eaten and a rise in crime rates over the summer months. There is no causal relationship between ice cream consumption and crime; they just both happen to go up when another variable—temperature—goes up. Another fun example is the familiar beer and diapers story—a popular data mining parable now firmly enshrined in BI mythology that says that some time ago, Wal-Mart decided to combine the data from its loyalty card system with its point of sales system and discovered, unexpectedly, that, on Friday afternoons, young American males who buy diapers also have a predisposition to buy beer

BOX 7.1 COMPUTATIONAL HUMOR

If charts could talk is an interesting concept. What would a chart say if we could add dialogue inside the graphic? More important: would it (could it/should it) make us laugh?

I mentioned earlier that a smidge of levity is important in data visualization and storytelling. Humor is, after all, an integral part of the human experience. So much so that data industry researchers Dafner Shahaf and Eric Horvitz of Microsoft and Robert Mankoff of the *New Yorker* worked together to study the influence of language of cartoon captions on the perceived humor of a large corpus of cartoon submissions to a *New Yorker* contest. The researchers believed that understanding humor defines an intriguing set of challenges for computer science in general, and, more specifically, how this ties into and can enhance human-computer interaction, collaborations, and sentiment. More important, the researchers were curious as to how humor can be harnessed in computer science functions—like data visualization or data storytelling, or even predictive algorithms—to increase attention, retention, and engagement—and how we can apply these contributions to computational humor prototypes (Shahaf, Horvitz, & Mankoff, 2015).

While humor is well studied in linguistics and psychology, there is substantially less in computer science. One, however, is that of the JAPE punning-riddle generator, another the HAH Acronym project.

As a result of their research, Shahaf, Horvitz, and Mankoff developed a classifier that was successful in deducing the "funnier" of two captions 64% of the time. They used this to find the best captions for New Yorker cartoons and reduce the load on contest judges. What is next? Future directions for this research could include more detailed analysis of the context and anomalies represented in the cartoons, as well as their influence on tension, questions, and confusions. Make way for computer-generated humor!

(Whitehorn, 2006). Another interesting tidbit is that the number of people who drown by falling into a swimming pool correlate almost exactly with the number of films actor Nicolas Cage appears in (for more of these with accompanying data visualizations, check out Tyler Vigen's site, "Spurious Correlations" at www.tylervigen.com) (Box 7.1).

Of course, faulty correlations are not the only danger of a false reveal—there is also the element of bias, or intent, to tell a data tall tale. After all, we can force the data to tell the story we want it to, even if it is the wrong one. Or, we can do this inadvertently through the process of dramatizing. Engaging and inspiring storytelling is, at least in part, a function of entertainment. We are tasked not only with the need to tell a story, but to make it *our* story and to make it interesting. We are invited to add our opinion and spice it up a bit—add a creative flavor that spurs response and reaction. But, in addition to making sure that we do this with accuracy we should temper it with, shall we say, decorum. We can always find a way to make the data more interesting, but should do so with tact. As a rule of thumb, perhaps, we might take give more lenience with business or economics data, but should shy away from amusement factor in things like healthcare data. Again, think of building this visual story as scripting a data documentary: a nonfiction work based on a collection of data. Do like Disney in its Nature documentary series and make it interesting and emotional, but without compromising truth and relevance (Box 7.2).

BOX 7.2 FRANCIS FORD COPPOLA ON STORYTELLING

Today, visualization and storytelling are hot topics in the data industry, and Hollywood is an inherently visual place. Through various forms of visualization (sets, costumes, props, special effects, green screens, and so on), Hollywood has been telling us stories for years. And while it is not accurate to call Hollywood the "original storyteller," it may not be too far from the truth to call it the original, high-tech storyteller.

At the 2015 Gartner BI and Analytics Summit held in Las Vegas, Academy Award-Winning filmmaker and founder of American Zoetrope, Francis Ford Coppola took the stage to share his views on the data age, how technology is changing Hollywood, and—as you might expect—the art of storytelling. While, I did not have the opportunity to ask any questions to Mr. Coppola directly (though I did get to into a similar conversation with actor Cary Elwes, which I will share later, he nevertheless gave me the answers I was longing to hear: how we—the data industry at large—can learn from the world's best storytellers.

"There's a story connected with everything," Mr. Coppola noted pointedly, speaking specifically on his entrance into theatre, wine, and technology though this statement was arguably the theme of his entire keynote. He then told us his story, through a series of questions and answers, captivating the audience with his tale of life as a young filmmaker and how he pursued many avenues to make money and films while staying focused on doing things that he loved. This itself was a bigger lesson that Mr. Coppola translates to how he does (and we should do) business: the things you love other people love, and from that passion (they) can sense authenticity.

On storytelling, "Don't let the mathematics outweigh the art of storytelling," he said. Storytelling is not about a formula—one that he believes that Netflix has already cracked—but more about savoring the words on a page. He colored this statement with humorous anecdote about a time when he and Star Wars creator George Lucas picked up, rented U-Hauls, and moved to California. "Take risks," he encouraged a room of hundreds of data users, analysts, experts. "Transform areas of passion into areas of opportunity."

To be honest, I lost track of my original questions listening to Mr. Coppola on stage, entranced by how he—unscripted and off the cuff—wound threads of stories together that touched upon everything from his beginnings, successes, to his leadership beliefs, wine, family, collaborations ("learning is the most profound activity…and also maybe music"), and even predictive technologies. This I attribute not to any flaw in Mr. Coppola's session (or my ineptitude at taking notes), but something else—something in sharp contrast: the power of engaging storytelling. For an hour and a half, I did not realize I was even being told a story—I was expecting a back and forth dialogue, or interview, which I got, too—but it was a story nonetheless. I left feeling inspired, rejuvenated, and like I had learned something intensely insightful in a personally meaningful way.

This session served not only as a learning experience about Hollywood with a few bits about data and technologies thrown in, but also as a testament to the power of stories. After all, how do we know that a story is great?" according to Mr. Coppola, it is when it is all you can think about. "A good story stays in your mind," he said. "It sticks."

7.4.5 TELL IT FAST – AND MAKE IT MOBILE

Stories, of any kind, have an inherent amount of entropy as mentioned before. Whether it is because of timeliness (in either topic and data), audience attention span, or market need, they can quickly unravel and fall apart. Stories have the most potency when they are happening (as events occur). Data journalists are taking this to heart in live models that keep track of events as they happen in real time—think political elections or disaster scenarios. The timestamp on when data is reported—or a visualization created—can be a big difference in how it is interpreted or the impact it makes.

Second, mobile requires wise editing. We have to be aware of form factor limitations and rethink the way storytelling via mobile devices happens. Mobile has already been a game changer in data visualization design in many ways and we can expect to see even more impacts in the coming years. This means that we have to change the way we think about storytelling—can we tell the same story through various mediums, including desktop, print, and mobile? It is unlikely.

7.5 STORYTELLING RECONSIDERED, THE PROBABILITY PROBLEM

As you can tell from the above, we make sense of our world by telling stories about it. We could rightly even speak of a human predisposition to think and to know in terms of stories. Storytelling is in our DNA, and it has worked pretty well for us for thousands of years.

However, what if the structure of a story, like the schema of a data model itself, embodies a kind of a priori representation or understanding of the world? We are all aware of the shortcomings of the data model as a structure. By imposing a rigid schema and organizing data in specific ways, a data warehouse data model attempts to optimize for most BI workloads. It is able to tell a certain kind of story—but it is much less adept at telling others. Have we ever thought about the similar trade-offs and optimizations that go into structuring the stories that we tell every day?

These questions were the focus of an article penned by industry writer Stephen Swoyer in a 2013 issue of *RediscoveringBI*, for which at the time I was still Editor-in-Chief. Like many of Stephen's pieces, this article has stuck with me because it does what so little articles seem to do these days, or what I have even provided thus far in this chapter. It hints not to the value of data storytelling, or how to do it, but instead it tackles something bigger that often gets overlooked: the problem of storytelling. Perhaps even more important, it poses a question were were not expecting: what if the very structure of the story itself—with its beginning, middle, and end; its neatly articulated sequencing and its emphasis on dramatic developments—is problematic?

Rather than recreating his piece, Stephen and I updated, edited, and condensed the original article and have repurposed it within the context of our discussions in this chapter.

7.5.1 THE STORYTELLING PARADOX

Certainly, in telling stories we have been known to exaggerate, to misrepresent, or to invent events. That is the very stuff of dramatic flair. However, for data storytelling, the problem is much deeper than this. It has to do with the structure of the story itself. To put it in the language of probability theory, our tendency to interpret events by telling stories about them is a way of imposing a deterministic structure on something that is not properly deterministic.

For most of human history, this was not a problem. We simply did not have the means to identify, qualify, or quantify its effects. Today, the combination of statistics and data gives us this means. As a tool for interpreting and understanding events, storytelling can, in some cases, be unhelpful or disadvantageous.

For example, consider the 2012 Presidential contest, when we had two different kinds of storytelling—deterministic and probabilistic—telling two very different stories about the state of the race. The former depicted an exciting, leapfrogging, neck-and-neck contest; the latter—plotted over a protracted period—suggested a mostly ho-hum race, with periodic volatility ultimately regressing over time. And that is the point. Probabilistic stories tend to be much less exciting—with fewer surprises, dramatic reversals, or spectacular developments—than those stories more deterministic and narrative-driven. In a probabilistic universe, for instance, there is a vanishingly small chance (let us say 0.00001 probability) that vampires or zombies can exist, let alone live among us (which puts a serious damper on letting our imaginations run wild—stories are pleasure-inducers, remember?). Likewise, we tend to need to give more weight to anomalies than we probably should. After all, we like stories to be exciting in some capacity—thrills, adventures, insights, suspense…again, those trappings of dramatic flair.

Statistical storytelling is probabilistic, not deterministic. In this sense, it is fundamentally at odds with the deterministic story craft, we have practiced for all of human history. The two are not irreconcilable, but they do not tell quite the same story (pun intended).

The long and short of it is this: human beings are super bad at thinking probabilistically—even when the issue is not something fantastic, like the existence of vampires or zombies. Most of us cannot properly interpret a weather forecast, especially one that calls for precipitation. If the forecast for the La Grange, GA, for example, predicts a 90% chance of rain, this does not mean there is a 90% chance, it is going to rain across all or most of La Grange; nor does it mean that 90% of the La Grange region is likely to get rained on. It is rather a prediction (with 90% probability) that rain will develop in some part of the forecast area during the stated period. This might well translate into widespread precipitation. It might not. This is not the way most of us tend to interpret a weather forecast, however. (Or, if you are like me, you can ignore this altogether and check an app, like the aptly named Umbrella, which tells me in a glance if I should grab my umbrella.)

The problem, then, is two-fold: (1) human beings seem to have a (hard-wired) preference for narrative or deterministic storytelling; (2) human beings likewise tend to have real difficulty with probabilistic thinking. In most cases, we want to translate the probabilistic into deterministic terms. We dislike open-endedness, indeterminacy—we want to resolve, fix, and close things. We have this nasty habit of wanting our stories to have tidy conclusions, resolute endings (remember the cliffhanger?).

We need to be especially mindful of these issues, if we expect to use analytic technologies to meaningfully enrich business decision-making. Viewed narrowly through the lens of data, statistical numeracy—that is, the application of statistical concepts, methods, and (most important) rigor to the analysis of data—promises to contribute to an improved understanding of business operations, customer behaviors, cyclical changes, seemingly random or anomalous events, and so on.

Our embrace of statistics will count for little—regardless of the size of our data sets, the complexity of our models, the power of our algorithms, or even how we visualize it all—if we fail to account for that most critical of variables: the human being who must first conceive of and then interpret (the results of) an analysis. Professional statisticians pay scrupulous attention to this problem: it is a critical aspect of research and preparation—of rigor—in statistics.

But even professionals can make mistakes. What is more, with the rise of big data analytics and the insurgence of commonly called self-service technologies, we are attempting to enfranchise nonprofessional users—business analysts, power users, and other savvy information consumers—by giving them more discretion to interact with and visualize information. This usually means letting them have a freer hand when it comes to the consumption, if not to the selection and preparation, of data sources and analytic models. In a sense, then, practices such as analytic discovery propose to enlist the business analyst as an armchair statistician, giving her access to larger data sets—compiled (or "blended") from more and varied sources of data—in the context of a discovery tool that exposes algorithms, functions, visualizations, and other amenities as self-servicable selections.

We will get into more technical discussion on architecting for discovery later, so let us put a pin in this digression for now and stick to storytelling. This last bit is not to dismiss or undermine the potential value of analytic discovery as a means to data storytelling. It is rather to emphasize that our ability to make use of information is irreducibly constrained by our capacity to interpret it. We are projecting our own biases, desires, and preconceptions into the "insights" that we produce. We must be alert to the possibility of hidden or nonobvious human factors in analysis: this as true of interpretation as it is of preparation and experimentation.

When we are counting on our ability to make a data story sing with meaningfulness and prompt an appropriate action (or reaction), we must control for our all-too-human love of a good story. This means recognizing the storytelling capacity of the tools (such as metaphor, analogy, and idea itself) that we use to interpret, frame, or flesh out our stories. Metaphor and analogy have the potential to mislead or confound. Ideas, for that matter, can have irresistible power.

To this point, consider the "meme," which was conceived by Richard Dawkins to describe an idea that gets promoted and disseminated—in evolutionary terms, selected for—on the basis of its cultural or intellectual appeal. If you think memes cannot mislead (for emphasis, see Figure 7.6) look to that most versatile of memetic constructs: Malcolm Gladwell's "tipping point," which has by now been interpreted into...almost everything. The "tipping point" even enjoys some currency among sales and marketing professionals, chiefly as a promotional tool. This is in spite of the fact that researchers Duncan Watts and Peter Dodds penned an influential paper ("Influentials, Networks, and Public Opinion Formation") that raised serious questions about Gladwell's theory. From a sales or marketing perspective, the tipping-point-as-meme has unquestionable promotional power; its usefulness as an analytic tool is altogether more suspect, however. No matter: as memes go, the "tipping point" is the very stuff of what American philosopher William James dubbed "sensational tang:"

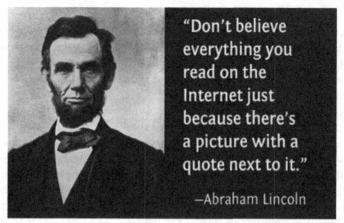

FIGURE 7.6

I am pretty sure Mr. Lincoln did not actually say this

the kind of idea that is simply irresistible to the intellect, regardless of its validity or veracity.

It is an illustrative lesson: if we expect to arm nontraditional users with statistical tools and techniques, we must attempt to control for "effects" like sensational tang. It will not be easy (Box 7.3).

BOX 7.3 CITIZEN DATA STORYTELLERS

At 2015s Tableau Tapestry event, creator of Info We Trust RJ Andrews presented his take on the art of storytelling and the heroes of interpolation. These heroes—including names like American mythologist Joseph Campbell, science storyteller Neil deGrasse Tyson, and documentarian Ken Burns, do that thing that only good stories do: create an experience. "At the best of times," remarked Andrews, "we create an experience. We offload some of the story processing to listeners, readers. We give them nodes of information and let them connect – not show but don't tell, but show in a way that let's them tell themselves."

Practicing what he preached, Andrews then showed the audience some of his own visual data stories that he tells through his blog Info We Trust, like Bloom, a data visualization that visualizes the life of all 212 flowers in Jefferson's Monticello Garden told through vector art and animation. He has also done a series of three charts on the USS Constitution, on the creative routines of people like Charles' Darwin and Dickens, and his newest—a language analysis project on Donald Trump to William Shakespeare. Many of his visualizations are compelling both as static images with an additional layer of detail added in through interaction. For example, Endangered Safari (Figure 7.7) shows at a glance all of the large African mammals, using visual cues like size, color, and shape to signify their IUCN threatened species status. The interactive version online (found at http://www.infowetrust.com/endangeredsafari/) includes, among other things, individual animal range maps. You can also buy prints of some of Andrew's digital creations.

For Andrews, an engineer and MIT graduate who works at Duke by day, Info We Trust was born as a "sandbox to play in before breakfast." From there, it has grown to become a billboard of sorts for Andrews' ideas. Today, Info We Trust is online as a "data adventure exploring how to better humanize information." It even took home the Kanter Information is Beautiful Award for infographics in November 2014.

Following his speaking session at Tapestry, I caught up with Andrews to learn more about how he approaches putting together a data narrative to tell a compelling story. He spoke so much on the creative routines of others in his session that I was curious to understand his. I was intrigued to find he starts mostly with nondigital media: colored pencils and markers. His goal is to blend the creative process with the scientific process of working with data in a new way. And, he often believes that most of the interesting data is locked away and it is his goal tom move from "wouldn't it be cool to see this" to a sketch of brainstorms that he can take into the digital world of bits.

For data storytelling, Andrews' words of caution are simple. (1) Recognize—and avoid—bias. (2), To have enough information to tell the whole story you want to tell.

FIGURE 7.7

A static image of endangered species by RJ Andrews, Info We Trust

(Source: With permission from INFOWETRUST.COM, 2015).

7.6 STORYTELLING'S SECRET INGREDIENT: THE AUDIENCE

As you can by now tell, there is a lot that goes into creating a good—hopefully great—story—from plot, to genre, to media. Depending on the story you are trying to tell, and the insight you are trying to share, shaping up your story can be like cooking a favorite recipe from memory—a little of this, a dash of that, a bit of intrigue and an element of surprise! And, like any favorite recipe, there is at least one secret ingredient. As we close out this chapter, let me share with you what I think it is by telling a story of my own.

One of my favorite storytellers of all time is Garrison Keillor, whose name you might recognize from the popular radio show *A Prairie Home Companion* or any number of his brilliant narrative monologs capturing the goings-on of fictional Minnesota town Lake Wobegon. If you have never heard Garrison Keillor tell a story, you are missing out on one of the finest things in life. I encourage you to switch over to NPR on weekend mornings (though it has been rumored that Mr. Keillor is neigh on retirement, so act fast!), or pick up a copy of one of his works at your local bookstore. Keillor's steady, rhythmic storytelling style is one that has the power to weave narration like Rumpelstiltskin spun straw into gold: one strand a time. And, while Keillor is somewhat known for offering a goldmine of witticisms and words of wisdom, he has one quote of particular brilliance that we should raptly apply to our data storytelling strategies. He says, "I don't have a great eye for detail. I leave blanks in all of my stories. I leave out all detail, which leaves the reader to fill in something better."

At first take, this may seem contrary to everything that has come before. And, while I am certainly not suggesting that, as a data storyteller, you leave out the details, there is a golden nugget of wisdom—that secret ingredient, if you will—in Keillor's quote. "I leave blanks in all of my stories…which leaves the reader to fill in something better." This is the essence of reader-driven stories.

Ultimately, one of the most important aspects of a great story is its ability to invite the reader to become part of the discovery. As a storyteller, your job is to give your audience all the data pieces needed to assemble the insight, and then sit back and wait for it to unfold. This is the "ah-ha!" moment of a great story, when your audience goes from passively listening to thinking (or saying), "oh my goodness, *that's* what's going on." American film director M. Night Shyamalan has a fastidious knack for this special brand of user-oriented storytelling to lead up to the moment of discovery (usually accompanied by some kind of bizarre plot twist). For example, when we all realize that there are not really monsters roaming *The Village* or that moment at the end of *The Sixth Sense,* when the audience suddenly realizes that Bruce Willis has been dead *the whole time.* We had listened to the story for a good while, seen all the little hints and clues dropped along the way, and layered them on top of each other to reveal one, jaw-dropping insight: the kid can only *see* dead people, and no one else seems to acknowledge Bruce Willis the entire movie. Oh my sweet, sweet climactic moment: Bruce Willis is a dead guy!!! It is satisfying, gratifying, and the best way to end a story—when you (the viewer, listener, or otherwise raptly engaged recipient of the story) are a part of telling it.

REFERENCES

Austin, M., 2010. Useful Fictions. University of Nebraska, London.

Booker, C., 2004. The Seven Basic Plots. Bloomsbury Academic, New York, NY.

Cotgreave, A., 2015. Data without emotion doesn't bring about change. Computerworld. Available from: http://www.computerworld.com/article/2988444/data-analytics/data-without-emotion-doesnt-bring-about-change.html.

Gibson, S., 2015. The 10 most expensive Hollywood movies ever. Highsnobiety. Available from: http://www.highsnobiety.com/2015/06/24/most-expensive-hollywood-movies/.

Perry, N., 2014. Cost of making "Hobbit" movies goes up to $745 million. Associated Press. Available from: http://bigstory.ap.org/article/9f10f14bf21e4c899405fc609f7e7970/cost-making-hobbit-movies-745-million.

Shahaf, D., Horvitz, E., Mankoff, R., 2015. Inside jokes: identifying humorous cartoon captions. In: Proceedings of the 21st ACM SIGKDD International Conference on Knowledge Discovery and Data Mining. ACM, pp. 1065–1074.

Segel, E., Heer, J., 2010. Narrative visualization: telling stories with data. IEEE T. Vis. Comput. Gr. 16 (6), 1139–1148.

Whitehorn, M., 2006. The parable of the beer and diapers. The Register. Available from: http://www.theregister.co.uk/2006/08/15/beer_diapers/.

The importance of visual design

8

To set the tone for this chapter, I borrowed a few wise words from Hollywood icon Orson Welles. But, perhaps another quote that adds spice to this rhetoric comes from a more unlikely place: *Harry Potter*'s Professor Severus Snape, brought to life in film by the incomparable Alan Rickman. Potter-fans may remember many of Snape's feisty oneliners, however it was upon Harry's first day of potions class in his first year at Hogwart's School of Witchcraft and Wizardry that, speaking of potion-making, the Professor enigmatically says to his class, *"You are here to learn the subtle science and exact art of potion making."*

The potion master's words echo the essence of the complex and beautiful science of data visualization. It is both subtle and exact—and it is perhaps even a little bit mysterious. There are many elements that go into designing an effective data visualization, from the appropriate use of color and counting techniques, to the affect of typographies and other visual design building blocks, like lines, contrast, and forms, and many more beyond—not to forget, of course, the also very important (and evolving) data visualization best practices that tell us how to visualize different types of data and which features to emphasize visually. Many of these are "science" because they take advantage of preattentive features of our visual brains or other levies of cognitive horsepower. Others are more exact and depend on the mechanics of design and other affective properties, like cultural biases or contingencies in the way different people perceive colors. In any case, it is fun to imagine a visual analyst standing over a bubbling cauldron, tipping in bits from various vials to brew that perfect blend of all the above.

Our discussions in Part II of this book have thus far focused on data visualization primarily as a mechanism for visual communication—one who taps into generations of cognitive hardwiring custom built to understand, learn, and communicate visually. We have also rummaged into story psychology, and the various nuances of genre, narrative design, and storytelling tactics best suited to tell a meaningful data story. All of these are valuable conversations that guide us in how we can visually and simply articulate the complexity of data to its intended audience and through its intended storytelling media, whether information visualization or otherwise.

153

The best data visualizations are, somewhat like potions, a carefully curated blend of art and science. And as such, data visualization requires equal attention to be paid to both the visualization method as well as to how the data is visually presented. Visual design and data visualization mechanics are separate yet highly interrelated concepts that work together to visually create meaning from data. Applied in data visualization, these elements can exploit our brain's cognitive functions to help us better see and understand information. This chapter will tackle the first half of the equation and provide a visual design checklist of core design considerations applicable to successful data visualization.

But first, allow me to serve up a few disclaimers and level set expectations. Many researchers, colorists, and other visual design experts have devoted entire texts (and careers) on studying each of the design elements we will cover in this chapter. Thus, I can offer only a very distilled introduction to the beautiful science of data visualization within the confines of one chapter. Consider this chapter a crash-course on visual design with only a sample set of design issues—or, Visual Design 101. For further study into one of these areas, I recommend you to source more comprehensive texts.

Second, is a more practical concern: this book is printed in black and white. In a chapter devoted to design—wherein our conversations naturally gravitate to things like color—you might see how this can be problematic and a challenge to showcase the true effects of visual elements. Therefore, I am limited by what I can show you versus what I can tell you.

8.1 DATA VISUALIZATION IS A BEAUTIFUL SCIENCE

Right off the bat, when you think of data visualization, you likely think of the artistic elements first—things like color and shape are often what come to mind before the mechanics of visualization, like which type of chart, graph, or other form of analysis best suited for the type of data and the intended insight. It is actually the most logical approach if you think about it, because we are visual creatures by nature. In fact, the human visual system has—by far—the highest bandwidth of any of our senses. Our visually evolved brains are our best tool for decoding and making sense of information.

It is fitting to say that as people, we love pictures. Whether they are art, captures of memories, or merely illustrations for instructional or other educational purposes, pictures are powerful. As an example, think again about the evolution of photography (as mentioned in chapter: Visual Communication and Literacy). In the late 19th century, photography emerged as an expensive, labor-intensive process, quickly matured into a mass-market (or, self-service) endeavor in the early days of the 20th century, and has since continued to evolve, adapt, and become more and more a part of every day life with its current position of digital daily documentation. It is an image explosion: some research has estimated that we took over one trillion photos in 2015. And, that is just photographs, and does not include other forms of visual communication—like data visualization.

We have already discussed image saliency, drawing on seminal research that quantified our ability to remember and recall upward of 10,000 images at one time,

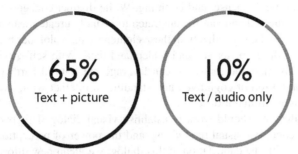

Picture superiority effect

Memory retention after 3 days

FIGURE 8.1 The Picture Superiority Effect

This visual depicts memory retention after 3 days. The first circle shows text/audio only at 10% after 3 days, juxtaposed at 65% after 3 days for information learned via text and picture

and at an 83% accuracy rate. Even more important, as we have seen established in recent research, is that people remember pictures better than words—and we remember images long after we have forgotten the words that go with them. We can describe this as the "experience" of looking at an image, or as it is more formally known, the Picture Superiority Effect. Simply, this is the notion that concepts that are learned by viewing pictures are more easily and more frequently recalled than those learned purely by textual or other word-form equivalents (which also includes audio words). One prominent way of articulating the particulars of the Picture Superiority Effect comes from developmental molecular biologist John Medina (2014), who succinctly qualified it in the following way: when we read text, in three days we only remember 10% of the information. In contrast, information that is presented visually gets a much heftier earmark in our remembrance. Text combined with a relevant image is more likely to be recalled at 65% in three days. The above visual is both a representation of this concept and a practicable example of it (see Figure 8.1).

Without getting too caught up in the details, we can simply say that it is a cognitive truth: our visual system is enormously influential in our brains. The best data visualizations are designed to properly take advantage of "preattentive features"—a limited set of visual properties that are detected very rapidly (typically within 200–250 ms) and accurately by our visual system, and are not constrained by the display size. With that mindset in place, let us explore few of those special ingredients of design that contribute to the visual curation of data.

8.2 KEY COGNITIVE ELEMENTS IN VISUALIZATION

Any work of art relies on core visual design principles and elements. When we say, "design principles" what we are really saying is shorthand for the list of guidelines that help improve viewers' comprehension of visually encoded information. Though there is a long list of visual design principles within the scope of the larger conversation of designing data visualization, we will limit this conversation to what could be considered the three most important cognitive elements of visual analysis. These are pattern recognition, color use, and counting. While distinct concepts on their own, they are interconnected and can be integrated to visually create meaning from data. Applied as a unit in data visualization, these elements can exploit our brain's intrinsic horsepower to help us better see and understand data. With self-service and user-oriented data visualization tools, we can leverage our natural hardwiring to layer visual intuition on top of cognitive understanding to interact with, learn from, and reach new insights from our data.

Data visualization should work to establish visual dialog. This two-way dialog leverages our cognitive visual hardwiring–and the power of perception—to have a "conversation" with the data. Through this dialog, we glean new information in salient, memorable, and lasting ways. And, this conversation is incremental: it builds on what came before to construct layers of learning and insight upon itself. It is also expressive, adding meaning, emotion, and understanding to transform information form mundane data to a creative palette by which to present it. The data visualization is the tangible byproduct of when art and science come together to facilitate a visual discussion of data. And, this is how data visualizations can be storytelling mechanisms to communicate quantitative visual narratives, told through sequential facts and data points.

Not to beat a dead horse, but again, there is wisdom in the old adage that says, "The more you know, the more you see." Understanding and awareness of the elements discussed above are intended to help us to craft data visualizations that balance art and science while keeping a wary eye on the power of pictures and visualization constraints. On its own, we should never mistake beautiful data visualization for effective data visualization. In fact, many memorable, beautiful data visualizations are those now infamous for being flawed in terms of data analysis. Thus, there exists the need for guidance in analyzing imagery and making sure that visual dialog is a worthwhile, accurate conversation between the visual and its audience.

8.2.1 PATTERNS AND ORGANIZATION

The way we perceive patterns is one of our most interesting cognitive functions. Patterns—the repetition of shapes, forms, or textures—are a way of presenting information help our brains discriminate what is important from what is not. There are patterns around us every day that we may not even recognize—for example, the way television show credits list actors in a series (generally the top star first and the second last, making the first and final data points in the pattern the most significant). Patterns are how our brains save time decoding visual information: by grouping similar objects and separating them. The Gestalt principles of design emphasize simplicity in shape, color, and proximity and look for continuation, closure, and figure-ground principles. In fact, the German word *gestalt* literally translates in English to "shape form," or pattern. Gestalt psychology assumes that visual perception is a holistic process (a la "the whole is worth more than the sum of its parts") and that humans tend to perceive simple geometric forms.

When we look at any data visualization, one of the first things that the brain does is look for patterns. We discriminate background from foreground to establish visual boundaries. Then we look to see what data points are connected and how (otherwise known as perceptual organization)—whether it is through categorical cues like dots, lines, or clusters, or through other ordinal visual cues like color, shapes, and lines.

Typically, there are four core ways in which we apply pattern recognition to data visualization (see Figure 8.2). Though only a subset of the Gestalt Laws, these are:

Proximity: Objects that are grouped together or located close to each other tend to be perceived as natural groups that share an underlying logic. *Clustered bar graphs and scatter plots utilize this principle.*

Similarity: This principle extends proximity to include items also that are identical (or close). This gives the brain two different levels of grouping: by the shared, common nature of objects, as well as how close they are. *Geospatial and other types of location graphics utilize this principle.*

Continuity: It is easier to perceive the shape of an object as part of a whole when it is visualized as smooth and rounded – in curves –, rather than angular and sharp. *Arc diagrams, treemaps, and other radial layouts use this principle.*

Closure: Viewers are better able to identify groups through the establishment of crisp, clear boundaries that help isolate items and minimize the opportunity for error (even if items are of the same size, shape, or color). *This effect would be applied, for example, in a clustered bar chart to add additional organization to the pattern by alternating shading the area behind groups of bars to establish boundaries.*

Patterns help to establish clear visual organization, composition, and layout. Once we can see patterns in information, we can next coat visual intuition on top of

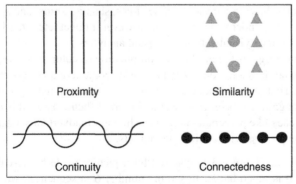

FIGURE 8.2 Four Core Ways We Apply Pattern Recognition to Data Visualization

cognitive understanding to come to new conclusions. This is where color and counting come in.

8.2.2 COLOR USE

Colors and shapes naturally play a large part in patterns. Color (or the lack thereof) differentiates and defines lines, shapes, forms, and space.

However, the use of color in design is very subjective, and color theory is a science on its own. Colorists study how colors affect different people, individually or in a group, and how these affects can change across genders, cultures, those with color blindness, and so on. There are also many color nuances, including overuse, misuse, simultaneous and successive color contrast, distinctions between how to use different color hues versus levels of saturations, and so on. At the moment, let us focus simply on when and how to use color in visualization to achieve unity. We will discuss the basics of color theory and a few select color contingencies a bit later in this chapter.

In *The Functional Art*, Cairo (2013) writes, "The best way to disorient your readers is to fill your graphic with objects colored in pure accent tones." This is because pure colors—those vibrant "hues of summer" that have no white, black, or gray to distort their vibrancy—are uncommon in nature, so they should be limited to highlight important elements of graphics. Subdued hues—like gray, light blue, and green—are the best candidates for everything else. Most colorists recommend limiting the number of colors (and fonts and other typography) to no more than two or three to create a sense of unity in a visual composition. Unity is created when patterns, colors, and shapes are in balance.

When thinking about color use in your data visualization, first focus on how well (or poorly) you are applying your color efforts as visual targets. Be especially cognizant of:

> *Color and Perceptual Pop-Out* or the use of color as a visual beacon or target to preattentively detect items of importance within visualization. The shape, size, or color of the item here is less important than its ability to "pop-out" of a display. Color differentiates and defines lines, shapes, forms, and space. (This theory has come under some criticism, however it nonetheless has been very influential for data visualization and visual analytics.)
>
> *Conjunction Target* is the inefficient combination of color and shape. Rather than giving target feature one visual property, conjunction targets mix color *and* shape. That distracts and causes visual interference, making visual analysis and other cognitive processes slower and more difficult. Thus, it is prudent to maximize cues like perceptual pop-out, while not inadvertently interrupting the preattentive process with conjunction targets.

As illustration, Figure 8.3 is inspired by a picture made by visualization guru Stephen Few. It is much harder to see the number 6 in sequences without the benefit of shading. Likewise, we can take advantage of perceptual pop-out by adding

14362684622327386392037 3

34887632394713087326320 7

234327432771673934083478

14362684622327386392037 3

34887632394713087326320 7

234327432771673934083478

FIGURE 8.3 Perceptual Pop-Out

Inspired by Stephen Few, this visual shows the immediate impact of perceptual pop-out

an additional color element into the picture. It is much more fun to add some wow factor to this example and throw in some red or other primary color to bring some zing, but in the humble black and white example we can show this—very simply–by using gray scale to show the number six in black against a background of gray. This example shows how elements of pattern recognition, color, and shape can be used together while avoiding the clutter of conjunction targets.

8.2.3 COUNTING AND NUMEROSITY

Color and counting work in tandem, as do counting and patterns. Relatively new research shows that the brain has an ordered mapping, or topographical map, for number sense, similar to what we have for visual sense and other preattentive features.

There are two relevant counting conversations within the scope of data visualization. First is how data visualizations try to reduce counting by clustering or similar approaches designed to replace similar data objects with an alternative, smaller data representation. *Histograms take this approach. Visual spacing on linear scales versus logarithmic scales is another example.*

Second is numerosity—an almost instantaneous numerical intuition pattern that allows us to "see" an amount (number) without actually counting it. This varies among individuals (people with extreme numerosity abilities are known as "savants"). Numerosity itself is not an indicator of mathematical ability. In fact, it is an important note to understand that numerosity only applies to numerical count, and is different from mathematical ability or symbolism. For most of us, numerosity gives us the ability to visually "count" somewhere between one and ten items. We can further enhance numerosity with visual elements like color. As an exercise, glance quickly again at Figure 8.3. How many black sixes do you see? If you "see" 7, you are correct.

Most types of data visualization will include a numerosity effect, however those that take advantage of data reduction processes will be most beneficial for numerosity. Consider scatter plots, histograms, and other clustering visualizations.

Neuroscientists at Utrecht University in the Netherlands have recently investigated how the human brain maps numbers. Previous studies in monkeys have shown that certain neurons in the parietal cortex, (which is located at the back of the brain, beneath the crown of hair) activate when these animals viewed a specific number of items. Could the human brain also produce such a recognizable, topographical map of numerical quantity in the brain study? Such a map has been long suspected to exist, but yet to be discovered. The answer, as the study details—which were outlined in the September 2013 issue of the journal *Science*—is yes.

The science is overwhelming complex, but here is a digestible recap: researchers placed participants under an MRI and showed them dots of various groups over time (one dot, three dots, five dots, two dots, etc.). They used an advanced, high-field MRI—known as fMRI, which allowed them to see fine-scale details of brain activity, and gather the data needed to analyze neural responses. The brain acted like an abacus (in laymen's terms: a device for making calculations—or, that cool toy with the beads on wires that many of us remember playing with back in our elementary school days) (Lewis, 2013).

To include an image here without color would never do an illustration justice, but imagine a heat map—or some beautiful storm system on your nightly weather forecast—blanketed over part of your brain, and you will imagine something very similar to the data visualization provided by the researchers. Thus, the topographical counting map of legend. As it "saw" dots, the posterior parietal cortex responded and organized them by their count: small numbers in one area, larger areas in another. These findings are in line with previous research that has shown that number sense becomes less precise as quantity of items increases (a finding, which has been the catalyst behind things like reduction techniques that are so prevalent in many data visualization taxonomies). They also suggest that our higher cognitive functions might rely on the same organization principles (eg, face recognition) as do our other sensory systems.

8.3 COLOR 101

With the earlier discussions on color already top-of-mind, let us dig a bit deeper. We talked about the use of color in visuals already, so for this next section let us tackle a few specific applied color contingencies that affect data visualization design. This begins with a cursory overview of very basic color theory, which most of us are at least superficially aware of. We are taught primary, secondary, and tertiary colors in elementary school, and how together these colors make up the basic color wheel.

With the color wheel (see Figure 8.4), we can make purposeful choices of color combinations depending on what we are trying to accomplish—like contrast, blending, or other effects. In our basic color education, we are also taught the purpose of

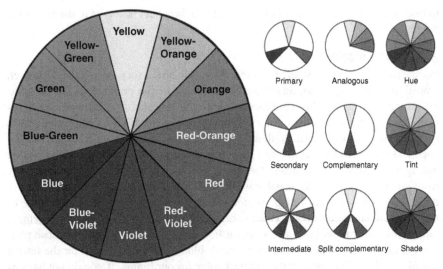

FIGURE 8.4 A Gray Scale Modified Traditional Color Wheel

complementary colors—those opposite each other on the color wheel—and how they provide the most contrast, or noticeable level of difference between two colors. More contrast means more visibility, which is why you often see highly-contrast colors used together (for example, these black words printed on a white page background). The opposite of the complementary colors are the analogous colors. Unlike complementary colors, analogous colors are those that neighbor each other on the color wheel and therefore have very little contrast and, instead, are nice harmonious blends (for example, orange and red). Finally, our basic color education also teaches us that colors often come with feelings, moods, and other cultural associations—like red for danger or warning; green for go or good; or even purple for royalty—that we infuse into the meaning of the color. This is related but separate from the warm versus cool color schema that segregate "cool" colors (those that are general considered calm and professional, like blues, greens, and purples) from "warm" colors (those that reflect passion, happiness, and energy, like reds, oranges, and yellows).

Of course, there are many more facets to studying color, but for the basis of our conversation, a simple nod to the color wheel and a few of its most common facets will suffice. Now, let us move on to color contingencies.

8.3.1 COLOR CONTINGENCIES

Beyond the basics of color theory, there are a few pockets of color contingencies we should pay special attention to. These are a sample set of color-based issues most commonly experienced when designing for data visualization, and thus worthwhile to briefly explore. There is a lot of truth to the saying that "beauty is in the eye of the beholder."

8.3.1.1 Color blindness

For the most part, we all share a common color vision sensory experience. However, "most" does not equal all, and there is a segment of the population—as many as 8% of men and 0.5% of women (according to the National Eye Institute (2015))—that suffer from some kind of color vision deficiency (or, CVD). Color blindness is typically the result of genetics, though in some cases it can result from physical or chemical changes in the eye, like vision deterioration, medications, or other vision damagers. Basically, this means that these individuals perceive colors differently from what most of us see, usually without knowing that it is different. There are three main types of color blindness: red–green (the most common), blue–green, or the complete absence of color vision—or, total color blindness, which is extremely rare. While our brains have about six million color cones (the term for those photoreceptors in the retina that perceive color), blue color cones are by far the fewest (Mahler, 2015). Thus, blue is the trickiest color for our brains. If you do not have as many blue cones, you may see the color as white, whereas if you have plenty, you may see "more" blue. This could have been one of the reasons behind one of the Internet's most recent color controversies on a certain mother of the bride's dress (see Box 8.1).

This is not the time or place to go into a lengthy discussion on the intricacies of color blindness or the science behind it. For now, it is enough to take away the fact that some people do perceive colors differently, and this has serious design implications on data visualization. Each flavor of CVD lends its own set of challenges when trying for consistent visual experiences. This affects everything from being

---

BOX 8.1 THE WHITE/GOLD—OR MAYBE BLUE/BLACK—TUMBLR DRESS

In February 2015, a Tumblr user swiped a picture of a dress (specifically, by member of a Scottish wedding party who was concerned over the color choices of the mother of the bride) with a question that would stump the Internet: "What color is this dress?" Opinions on the color combination of the dress—from everyone from fellow Tumblr users to Hollywood celebrities and even politicians—ranged from suggested white-and-gold and blue-and-black combinations to rainbow (courtesy of Miley Cyrus) to some very convincing color palettes provided by Adobe (Marquina, 2015). It would be an understatement to say that the picture went viral: within hours, it had been viewed more than 28 million times with 670,000 people simultaneously viewing a related Buzzfeed post (Mahler, 2015).

The dress debate hinged, very simply, on a matter of perception and how our brains processed visual information. Various theories floated about the Internet on why the dress looked different to different people—everything from depression, to color cones (suggested by Dr. Duje Tadin, an associate professor for brain and cognitive sciences at the University of Rochester), to optical illusions (by Dr. Joseph Toscano, an assistant professor in the Villanova University Department of Psychology), to cues about ambient light. Whatever the cause, the dress—sold by Roman Originals in Birmingham, England—was responsible for 60% of the companies' business by the Friday after the photo went viral.

able to read color-coded information on bar or pie charts or visually decode more complex visualizations like heat maps or tree maps. Color blindness can also be material specific—some people may have a harder time distinguishing color on artificial materials than on natural materials—thus a difference in digital displays versus on paper. So, obviously we want to take color blindness into account when crafting a data visualization to ensure that everyone is seeing the same data story unfold as everyone else.

There are a few tricks of the trade for designing to mitigate the affects of color blindness. Consider these:

- Avoid situations that could be tricky for color blindness factors. For example, rather than relying on color alone, make use of shapes (or even symbols) to supplement color-schemes without worrying too much on color perceptions.
- Be wary of similar-intensity colors and how they might look (or not look) in close proximity. For example, colors used in choropleth, tree, or heat maps. For those times when those types of designs are the best way to communicate information, consider using labels or other visual cues to help separate areas and further distinguish colored areas.
- Fight back against color blindness challenges and know which color combinations that can be used to usurp color blindness issues.
- When in doubt, go with gray. Even those with total color blindness can typically distinguish between varied shades of black and white.

Some of these may seem abstract now, but keep these tips in mind in the next section on visual design building blocks, when we look at things like shapes and texture more closely.

8.3.1.2 Color culture

Beauty is in the eye of the beholder, but perhaps it is just as accurate to say that *color* is also in the eye of the beholder—and not just due to genetic visual differences. In addition to vision abnormalities that cause people to perceive colors differently, people of different cultures or even genders may also (and often do) "see" colors differently.

8.3.1.2.1 Color symbolism

The more obvious of the two may be color symbolism. This term, based on anthropology, refers to how color is used, symbolically, in various cultures. There is great diversity in how different cultures use colors, in addition to how color is used within the same culture in different time periods or in association with holidays or other iconic associations. Let us have an example to illustrate how color symbolism is viewed on a larger cultural scale. Imagine this scenario: you are at a wedding, and the bride steps out in her beautiful wedding gown. What color is her dress? Most of you would probably say white (or ivory). In western culture, the color white (which is technically the presence of all colors in the visible spectrum) is typically associated with things like brides, or angels, or peace, or purity and cleanliness. However, in China, white would not be an appropriate color for a wedding as it is culturally a color of mourning. Likewise, in India, if a married woman wears unrelieved white, she is seen to be inviting widowhood and unhappiness—not the expected attitude of a bride! Those of Celtic heritage might argue that green is the most appropriate wedding color, as in Celtic mythology the Green Man was the God of Fertility. In fact, in the 1434 Renaissance painting "Giovanni Arnolfini and His Bride" we see the bride wearing a green gown—and slouching in an imitation of pregnancy to indicate her willingness to bear children.

As we continue to become a more and more globally connected world, it is important to be aware of the cultural perceptions of color. For recommended reading, check out *Color and Meaning: Art, Science, and Symbolism* by John Gage or *Secret Languages of Color: Science, Nature, History, Culture, Beauty of Red, Orange, Yellow, Green, Blue, & Violet* by Joann and Arielle Eckstut, both of which are quite fascinating. Or, if you are looking for a quicker takeaway, think on this: the red circle on a scorecard that you think means a negative (ie, a warning or caution sign) if you are in America might actually be something much more positive—like good fortune if you are in China—or rouse a more sorrowful emotion, such as mourning, if you are from South Africa. How might that one simple indicator change on a globally-accessed dashboard environment?

8.3.1.2.2 His and hers colors

It should be no surprise that if people from different cultures "see" colors differently, then so would people of different genders. If men are from Mars and women from Venus, then seeing colors different would almost certainly make sense. But, whether it is politeness or a sense of decorum, men and women do apparently perceive color differently.

A 2010 color survey hosted by XKCD.com generated 222,500 user sessions to name over five million colors based on RGB color samples (see the full color survey results at http://blog.xkcd.com/2010/05/03/color-survey-results/). The results were hilariously honest, and provided some interesting data on to how men and women look at colors differently. For example, a brownish-yellow color that men would describe as "vomit" is one that women might more diplomatically name "mustard" (Swanson, 2015). Analyzing the survey results, there was a noticeable trend that women also tended to be very generous (and somewhat overly-descriptive) in naming different color shades, with a disproportionally popular naming convention of things like "dusty" teal or "dusky" rose. (Another interesting find in the study is that spelling was a consistent issue across everyone—men, women, the color blind, and so on—which is probably a larger issue on vocabulary issues.)

Of course, there were some issues with the survey and it was by no means academic—though it was certainly a fun thought experiment. For one, being an informal distribution there is almost certainly some noise and bias built in. The researchers did use filters to drop out spammers and other outliers or scripts that junked up the data (like one spammer who used a script to name 2400 colors with the same racial slur). Secondly, since the survey was conducted online, it is right to assume that the monitor display of color would vary, especially since RGB is not an absolute color space. However, the difference in how colors appear across various monitors is in itself quite important when we think in terms of data visualizations, which are almost always presented digitally.

In early 2015, Stephen Von Worley of the data visualization blog *Data Pointed* visualized 2000 of the most commonly used color names mapped by gender preference. It is a stunning, interactive data visualization that could never done justice in black and white print, but you can view it online at www.datapointed.net. Ultimately, the takeaway here is simply that color comes with perception, and we must be aware of the opportunities and limitations of these as we create visualizations meant to resonate and engage.

8.4 VISUAL DESIGN BUILDING BLOCKS

When you first look at a data visualization, you may not realize just how much careful thought and effort went into crafting it. Data visualizations are multifaceted, not just because of their ability to represent multiple types of data and layer it in a meaningful visual way, but because to craft the visualization itself requires attention to every detail—from its carefully curated color pallet, to the methods in which the important pieces of information are connected into patterns, to the layout and chosen typefaces used throughout the graphic.

In the previous section, we focused on key preattentive features—color, patterns, and counting—that form the basis of a visual dialog with data. In this section, we will take a deeper look into how to curate visual meaning in the data through more specific elements. These—lines, textures, shapes, and typography—are some of the visual cues that influence how your eyes move around a visual to separate areas of importance from nonimportance. More important, they are the visual cues that guide us to create meaning and organize visual information in the way that is necessary for visual discovery.

8.4.1 LINES

The most basic building block of visual analysis, lines facilitate several purposes in data visualization. They are used to create complex shapes (discussed in the following section), to lead your way visually through (or to) different areas of a visualization, or as a way to layer texture upon a visual surface.

Lines are especially potent tools to reinforce patterns. This is because they offer powerful cues for the brain to use to perceive whether objects are created. Consider a diverse group of different colored shapes. With its preattentive capabilities, the brain will automatically group them by shape and color. Adding a line to connect certain shapes will add more connectedness, and produce a more powerful pattern (see Figure 8.5). As another example, consider a graph where distance, shape, and other elements are laid along one axis. The brain will perceive them as a single set of data, but lines—particularly curved lines, as opposed to sharp-angled lines—will

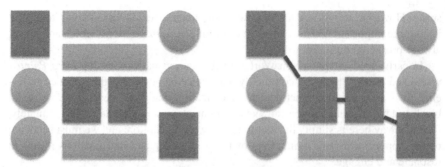

FIGURE 8.5 This Figure Shows the Added Patterning Influence of a Line as a Visual Vue

provide closure and logically group sets of data into a recognizable pattern (this is the pattern principle of continuity).

Lines can be used as labels, direction cues, or they can also be used as a way to create texture in data visualization. Texture is one of the more subtle (and easy to misemploy) design elements, but worth a mention due to its relation to line (and our previous discussions on color).

Texture is defined as the surface characteristics (or, the feel) of a material that can be experienced through the sense of touch (or the illusion of touch). It can be used to accent an area so that it becomes more dominant than another, or for the selective perception of different categories. Colors, shapes, and textures can be combined to have further levels of selection (see Figure 8.6). Finally, textures of increasing size

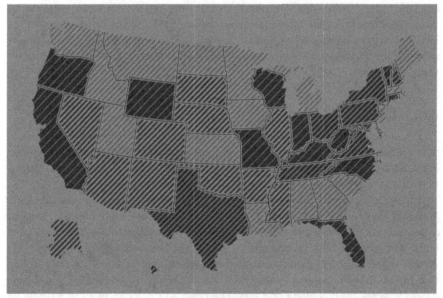

FIGURE 8.6 Even in Gray Scale, This Image, Created by Designer Riccardo Scalco, Shows How Colors, Shapes, and Lines can be Combined Together to Create Texture and Areas of Selection

can represent an order relation. Because it is usually accompanied with real adjectives like rough, smooth, or hard, texture may seem intrinsically three-dimensional (real). It can also be two-dimensional.

In data visualization, lines are one of the best ways to represent texture. For example, when used in tandem with color, lines can create texture through what is called "color weaving" to produce a tapestry of woven colors to simultaneously represent information about multiple colocated color encoded distributions. As an example, color weaving is similar to the texturing algorithms and techniques used to visualize multilayer in weather maps and other climatology visualizations. That said, texture can be a tricky and easily misused element of data visualization, and thus should be employed sparsely and with careful discretion.

8.4.2 SHAPES

In his late 19th-century article "The Tall Office Building Artistically Considered," Louis Sullivan (2012) made a statement that has forever impacted how we approach the premise of shapes and forms. He said:

> *"All things in nature have a shape, that is to say, a form, an outward semblance, that tells us what they are that distinguishes themselves from another...It is the pervading law of all things organic and inorganic of all things physical and metaphysical, of all things human and al things superhuman, of all true manifestations of the head, of the heart, of the soul, that the life is recognizable in its expression, that form ever follows function."*

Over the years, this "form follows function" refrain has been taken both as gospel verbatim as well completely misinterpreted (it has also been described as "coarse essentialism" by data visualization design gurus like Albert Cairo). Today, in visual design, it is a powerful mantra primarily applied to the relationship between the forms (of design elements, ie, shapes and lines) and the informational function it is intended to serve.

As forms, shapes are one of the ways that our brains create patterns. This is a time saving technique: we will immediately group similar objects and separate them from those that look different. So, shapes and forms should be driven by the goals of what the visual is communicating about the data.

Shapes are formed with lines that are combined to form squares, triangles, circles, and so on. They can be organic—irregular shapes found in nature (circles, etc.)—or geometric—shapes with strong lines and angles (like those used in mathematics). Likewise, shapes can be two-dimensional (2D) or three-dimensional (3D). These 3D shapes expand typical 2D shapes to include length, width, and depth—they are things like balls, cylinders, boxes, and pyramids. In data visualizations like pictograms, infographics forms and shapes take on an entire new catalog of options through the issue of icons and other symbolic elements as extensions of traditional shapes (consider using the shapes of people in lieu of dots or other shape). Some visualizations, like D3.js, made liberal use of nontraditional visual shapes. Further, like so many other elements of design, color has a hand in shape selection, too. This is particularly relevant in two ways: (1) Make sure you are using color priority in choosing a shape (if you want to use circles to emphasize areas of opportunity for sales agents on a map use green circles instead of, say red or orange), and (2) Be aware of color contrast and luminance among shapes. The higher the luminance contrast, the easier is it to see the edge between one shape and other. If the contrast is too low, it can be difficult to distinguish between similar shapes—or to even distinguish them at all.

Like many visual cues, there is often no "one right way" of encoding visualization properly through the use of shapes and forms. Many times it becomes less a question of "correct" and more a consideration for what is easier for the view. As an example, both a scatterplot and a bar chart can be used to represent absolute variables. But, to represent correlations using absolute variables, one scatterplot can essentially tell the same story as a pair of bar charts. Do not limit your thinking on shapes to just 2D or 3D. Some data visualizations—for example, bubble charts—can invoke another data dimension from bubble size when on an *x-y* axis. Here, color can add a 4th dimension of data to represent buckets or thresholds. Animation can add a 5th dimension. Remember: humans can visually process three to five dimensions of data.

8.4.3 TYPOGRAPHY

There is a large vocabulary when it comes to typography, and often times those unfamiliar with the nuances of each term will make use of them interchangeably. While they are compounding and interrelated terms, they do carry different meanings and should not be used synonymously. Thus, for the purposes of our discussion let us take a moment to define clearly three of the most commonly confused of these terms: typography, typeface, and font. These definitions will serve us well going forward.

> *Typography* itself is the study of the design of typefaces, and how they are laid out to best achieve the desired visual effect while conveying meaning to the reader
> *Typeface* is the design of the type itself (ie, Helvetica or Arial or Times New Roman)
> *Font* is a specification for a typeface (ie, 12pt bold Helvetica)

Generally speaking, when we think of typography within the context of a data visualization, we think in terms of two choices of typeface categories: serif versus sans serif. While the origin of the word "serif" is unknown, a common definition for it has come to be "feet"—small lines that tail from the edges of letters and symbols, and are separated into distinct units for a typewriter or typesetter. The concept of serifs as feet actually has a cognitive origin: feet were created to allow for ease of reading by providing continuity along letters, words, and lines/sentences in long bodies of text. Thus, *serif* typefaces—like Times New Roman or Baskerville, are those with "feet." Building on the previous, the word "sans" comes from the French "without." Thus, *sans serif* typefaces are those "without" feet. Serif fonts are usually considered to be more traditional, formal typefaces, while sans serif typefaces tend to have a more contemporary, modern feel. There are no absolutes of when—or when not—to use a serif versus a sans serif typeface, though a rule of thumb is that serif is better for print while sans serif is better for web (see Box 8.2).

In fact, in his book *Data Points: Visualization That Means Something*, Nathan Yau (2013) pointedly noted that while there has been much discourse on the best typeface, there has yet to be any true consensus. This goes to emphasize further that typeface selection is highly variable and depends much on personal preference. That said there are couple of important points to keep in mind when making a typeface or font selection. First, typography, like another other visual element, is no stranger to bias. There are some typefaces—for example, Comic Sans—that have been reduced to a sort-of comic strip application and are not taken seriously. Others—like Baskerville and Palatino—conjure up nostalgia imagery due to their historical use in vintage graphics. New fonts are being created while others are being improved specifically for readability on smaller devices (like phones and/or tablets) where real estate is reduced and a higher premium on typeface clarity is required. Some typefaces have been custom-created for use in advertising—like those fonts used in Star Wars or Back to the Future, for example, and are pigeonholed into their use in genre-related opportunities (which is not necessarily a bad thing, but one to be aware of). Many typefaces are also said to have personality. Like Comic Sans, others may come with a more light-hearted or conservative personality. Matching type personality with the tone of the message in the visualization is certainly not an exact science. A good technique to see if you are choosing appropriate fonts is to use a font that seems completely opposite of what you are trying to convey. Seeing how "wrong" a typeface can look will help you make a more appropriate selection. And, it is always

BOX 8.2 FONT WARS: SERIF VERSUS SANS SERIF

If you have ever seen me present anywhere, or seen me on my serif-soapbox, you will know that I am a very committed member of Team Sans Serif. Luckily, I am not alone in my war on serif. Actually, there is a satisfying amount of debate—scholarly or otherwise—on the use and rivalry between these two typography choices.

The crew at UrbanFonts, a hub of downloadable freeware, shareware, and linkware fonts, spent some time working up a research-based infographic that covered everything from dots per inch (or, DPI, a measure of spatial printing or video dot density, particularly the number of individual dots that can be placed in a line within the span of 1 in.) to classification (most typefaces can be classified into one of four basic groups—with serifs, without serifs, scripts, and decorative styles–and some have subgroups, too), with a guiding principle for when to use serif or sans serif fonts. This infographic, much too large to include in text here basically comes down to salient piece of wisdom based on the genesis of both types of typography. Serifs are used to guide the horizontal "flow" of the eyes and increase contrast and spacing between letters while binding characters into cohesive word wholes. This reduces eye fatigue when reading. Sans serifs, meanwhile, survive reproduction better due to their simplicity and are better for early readers just learning shape recognition. They maintain shape when enlarged—thus better for emphasis—and are more versatile. The best typography choice, then, is predicated on when and how it is used. For print and longer reading, serif has the upper hand. But, for web, emphasis, and reading development, sans serif takes the prize (Figure 8.7).

So, I will offer this caveat (and agree with UrbanFonts): The best font choice is where the reader does not notice the font, but the message.

USE

SERIF

IN NORMAL

BODY COPY

AND USE SANS

FOR SMALL TEXT

FIGURE 8.7 Serif Versus Sans Serif

worthwhile to sanity check a typeface and font across a few different types of devices to double check readability and compatibility.

(*Interesting tidbit on type:* If you have ever created a text document from a predesigned template, you are probably familiar with the phrase "Lorem Ipsum." Since the 1500s, the printing industry has used this text to demonstrate what a font will look like without having the reader become distracted by the meaning of the text itself. Although the term resembles ancient Latin, it is not actually intended to have meaning.)

The most pointed advice one can be given on typography is this: use typeface shrewdly and fonts with a purpose. It is easy to dismiss the importance of these selections, possibly because we are so conditioned to read text that we have become accustomed to focusing on the content of the words and not what they look like visually. However, the visual appearance of words can (and does) have just as much effect on how a document is received as the content itself. Fonts can create mood and atmosphere; they can give visual clues about the order a document should be read in and which parts are more important than others. Fonts can even be used to control how long it takes someone to read a document. Like colors, typefaces are typically chosen in corporate style guides and other branding design decisions. Hopefully now you better understand why typography is as important in data visualization as any other design element (not to mention the fun that can be had with word clouds as a visualization itself!).

For a few tips on type, apply the following guidelines:

Like colors and shades, limit type choices in graphics to one or two—perhaps a solid, thick one for headlines, and a smaller more readable one for copy

Remember visual hierarchy—headers should be larger and stand out, whereas tick labels or other content copy should be smaller and demand less attention (sans serif fonts work well for body copy because they are more easily readable in confined spaces)

Make sure the typeface and font chosen for the visualization work together to clearly convey the message of the data as well as the "feel" of the message (a data visualization on mortality rates in impoverished countries would look mighty silly (or even offensive) if delivered in Comic Sans)

8.5 VISUALIZATION CONSTRAINTS

You might have noticed a theme in many of these brief discussions on visual cues. They all seem to tie back to one or more preattentive features. It is easy to see how visual cues like line, textures, shapes, and typography are elements that build upon cognitive preattentive features that make our brains so important in visual analysis. Hence, these are only the building blocks of visual discovery, intended by design to be layered upon each other and used in mix-and-match fashion to make the most of our visual capacity for data visualization.

However, one important caveat to remember is that there is such a thing as "too much" design. The point of visual design is to communicate a key message clearly and effectively: the best data visualizations are those where nothing stands between the visual's message and its audience. When thinking in terms of design, reflect on the minimalistic design mantra "less is more." Most visualization purists advocate for minimalistic graphics stripped of gratuitous elements with concentration on the data itself. However, used correctly, visual cues can bring the data to life and give more context, meaning, and resonance to information. Data visualizations should be simple, balanced, and focused, and they should use visual enhancements (like hue, saturation, size, and color) judiciously—and for emphasis rather than explanation. Every graphic is shaped by a triangle of constraints: the tools and processes that make it, the materials from which it is made, and the use to which it is to be put.

This idea of design constraints as a triangle of forces comes from historian Jacob Bronowski (1979) and his discussions on context and visualization. In his essay on aesthetics and industrial design entitled "The Shape of Things" (which was first printed in *The Observer* in 1952 and later reprinted in the 1979 collection of essays, *The Visionary Eye*) Bronowski wrote: "The object to be made is held in a triangle of forces. One of these is given by the tools and the processes which go into make it. The second is given by the materials from which it is to be made. And the third is given by the use to which the thing is to be put. If the designer has any freedom, it is within this triangle of forces or constraints." We can thus visualize the triangle in the following way (see Figure 8.8).

Remember, this triangle is not a fixed triangle—each of its axes can move and, consequently, adjust the others along with it. But, because they do not move in isolation, every move of one axis puts strain on the other two. Therefore, it is important to

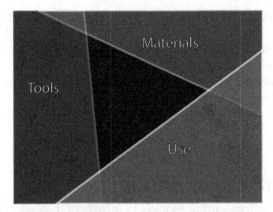

FIGURE 8.8 Bronowski's "Triangle of Forces" of Design Constraints

not only recognize the parameters of the triangle of forces, but to strive for balance within it.

8.5.1 THE EYE (CANDY) EXAM

The downside to being able to create visually so quickly and efficiently is that our brains can betray us and leave us with a wrong idea—visual bias. In the context of data visualization, these types of visuals are intended to communicate the correct information and insight clearly and effectively. Thus, we should pay close attention to recognizing the key cognitive elements in visualization, and how these should be used together to craft a meaningful representation of data in a visual way that avoids, or at least mitigates, bias. While we will explore best practices in data visualization in a later chapter, it is worthwhile to apply conversations in this chapter, albeit briefly, within the context of a triangle of forces for data visualization. The worst thing we can do is to spend a ton of time designing something that ends up in the realm of "too much" and distorts, over-embellishes, or otherwise confuses the visual story we are trying to tell by heaping on pretty colors or icons or flashy lines and symbols. Art and science, data visualizations require balance between information and design to be most useful.

To gage the effectiveness of any data visualization, we can ask the three following questions:

Is it visually approachable? First and foremost, make sure the visualization is straightforward and easy to understand by its intended audience. Then, capitalize on the fact that people perceive more aesthetic design as easier to use by including design elements—color, shapes, etc.—to make it visually appealing. This *is* visual design, or the practice of removing and simplifying things until *nothing stands between* the message and the audience. In visualization, the best design is the one you *do not* see.

Does it tell a story? At its core, a visualization packages data to tell a story. Therefore, they require a compelling narrative to transform data into knowledge. Make sure your visualization has a story to tell—*a* story: one. Too often people want to present *all* the data in a single visualization that can answer many questions—tell many stories—but effective visualizations are closer to a one-visualization-to-one-story ratio. Focus on one data visualization per story; there is no need for a mother all visualizations.

Is it actionable (or, to use a design concept: does it have affordance)? In other words, does the visualization provide guidance through visual clues for how it should be used? Visualizations should leverage visual clues—or establish a visual hierarchy—to direct the audience's attention. This is the "happy or uncomfortable" test: before you even know what the numbers say, the design of the visualization should make you feel something—it should compel you to worry or to celebrate.

A well-designed, meaningful, *non*eye candy data visualization that leverages colors, shapes, and design can not only display, but can *influence* the way we receive insights into data—which is something we all can benefit from. And that is a tasty win–win for everyone (Box 8.3).

The use of these principles to guide your design and representation of data will improve the efficacy of your visualization, ultimately creating understanding of the data story you are presenting.

It is easy to see how quickly a "scientific" view blurs into a design—or artistic—one. Regardless, whether we approach data visualization first from a scientific perspective or a design perspective, we are ultimately working to ensure that it relies on core visual and cognitive design principles intended to direct viewers' comprehension of visually encoded information.

This is where the value proposition of data visualization as a tool to communicate complex information really comes into play. Being able to truly see and understand that data requires more than simply drawing a collection of graphs, charts, and dashboards. It is not simply being able to represent the data, but doing so in a way that

---

BOX 8.3 THE VISUAL DESIGN CHECKLIST

This paper has taken an aggressive approach into condensing a vast amount of information into just a few pages. However, each of the sections above are especially relevant when we think about how to design a visual—any visual—whether it is intended to communicate data or any other type of information.

When determining how to make the most out of a data visualization, consider the following three bullets as guiding principles on a visual design checklist to leverage cognitive science and visual design to enable optimized visual dialog:

Emphasis: The use of colors, shapes, lines, etc., should direct/guide audience toward a particular part of the image or outcome (insight)

Balance: Color, forms/shapes, and other building blocks are harmonious

Unity: When principles of analysis (the mechanics of visualizing data) are in sync with its design

conveys a message. Data visualization is a creative process, and we can learn how to enrich it by leveraging years of research on how to design for cognition and perception. First, think of successful data visualization from a visual science perspective to ensure you are capitalizing on the right preattentive features to capitalize on the processing horsepower of the brain. Then, consider the careful balance of the art of visual design and curation alongside the observations and insights of data science. The most meaningful data visualizations will be the ones that express unity and correctly present complex information in a way that is visually meaningful, memorable, and actionable.

Beyond the visual design elements that go into making a meaningful data visualization are those best practices that tell us which types of visualizations are best for which type(s) of data, which visual features to highlight, and when it is appropriate to use traditional visualizations versus when customize for a better representation or deeper insight. Remember, a graphic can be functional and aesthetic without correctly using crafted color pallets and other curated elements of visual design. Likewise, it can be beautiful without meaning, or can be meaningful without necessarily being beautiful. As I asserted at the onset of this chapter, it truly is subtle science and exact art.

The key is to avoid overemphasis on trendy chart types that do not add insight beyond what a basic chart would provide—instead, focus on keeping it simple and optimized. Data visualization itself—similar to visual design—depends on both simplicity and focus with the goal of shortening the path to insight as much as possible. This is how data visualizations can achieve unity—when principles of analysis are in sync with those principles of design.

In the next chapter, we will stitch together this discussion of design consideration into the application of information visualization and thus move into more technical discussions on data visualization best practices and graphicacy techniques.

REFERENCES

Bronowski, J., 1979. Visionary Eye: Essays in the Arts, Literature and Science. MIT Press, Cambridge, MA.

Cairo, A., 2013. The Functional Art. New Riders, Berkley, CA.

Lewis, T., 2013. Is 'numerosity' humans' sixth sense? Livescience. Available from: http://www.livescience.com/39441-is-numerosity-humans-sixth-sense.html.

Mahler, J., 2015. The white and gold (no, blue and black!) dress that melted the Internet. The New York Times. Available from: http://www.nytimes.com/2015/02/28/business/a-simple-question-about-a-dress-and-the-world-weighs-in.html?_r=0.

Marquina, S., 2015. Tumblr dress debate: Is this dress white and gold or blue and black? Every celeb – and person – on the Internet is freaking out. US Magazine. Available from: http://www.usmagazine.com/celebrity-news/news/tumblr-dress-debate-white-and-gold-or-blue-and-black-2015262.

Medina, J., 2014. Brain Rules: 12 Principles for Surviving and Thriving at Work, Home, and School. Pearl Press, Seattle, WA.

National Eye Institute, 2015. Facts about color blindness. Available from: https://nei.nih.gov/health/color_blindness/facts_about.

Sullivan, L., 2012."The Tall Office Building Artistically Considered," Lippincott's Magazine, March, 1896. Available from: http://academics.triton.edu/faculty/fheitzman/talloffice-building.html.

Swanson, A., 2015. A fascinating visualization of how men and women see colors differently. The Washington Post. Available from: http://www.washingtonpost.com/blogs/wonkblog/wp/2015/02/05/a-fascinating-visualization-of-how-men-and-women-see-colors-differently/.

Yau, N., 2013. Data points: Visualization That Means Something. John Wiley & Sons, Inc, Indianapolis, IN.

The data visualization continuum

9

"There is a magic in graphs. The profile of a curve reveals in a flash a whole situation — the life history of an epidemic, a panic, or an era of prosperity. The curve informs the mind, awakens the imagination, convinces."
—Henry D. Hubbard

We began the last chapter with a simple parable—a quote from Harry Potter's potion master, Severus Snape, if you remember—that provided a useful analogy of the *"subtle science and exact art"* that can be applied to building and designing data visualization. The point, again, was simply this: the best data visualizations are, like potions, a carefully curated blend of art and science, and thus require equal attention to be paid both to the visualization method (the science) as well as to how the data is visually presented (the art).

These are highly interrelated but separate concepts that should be understood individually on their own merit, and together insofar as how they work together when applied to data visualization. When building a visualization to create meaning and communicate visually with data, nothing happens in a vacuum—not art, or science, or even storytelling for that matter. Each of these elements work in tandem and are, to some degree at least, contingent on each other for the whole to be successful. This is a holistic view of data visualization that takes into account how each of these parts become something intimately interconnected and understood completely only by reference to the whole, or by the outcome—the visual itself. (This view, for what it is worth, is conceptually similar to that of systems thinking, a holistic approach to analyses that focuses on the way a system's constituent parts interrelate within the context of a larger ecosystem whole (Senge, 2006). This is a practice requisite of the learning—or within our context, the discovery-oriented—organization.)

Chapter: The Importance of Visual Design, provided a high-level overview of some of the most important and deliberate of design considerations—like color, size, shape, typography, and so on—that go into curating meaningful design applied in data visualization. The intent of that chapter was to earn a basic understanding of how these features can make the best use of our brain's cognitive functions to help us better see and understand information. However, there are many designers who know the principles of design yet lack the understanding of how to visualize data effectively in a way that properly presents the information clearly and effectively, for maximum impact and communication. The opposite, of course, is true, too. There are just as equally a number of statisticians, data scientists, and other analysts with deep knowledge of data and context, but less knowledge of how to create engaging and actionable graphics.

If the previous chapter was the art, then this chapter is the other half of the coin: the science. However, this chapter is not meant as a field guide on how to create a data visualization, though we will touch on a diagnostic of some of the most prolific chart types and where they fit into the data visualization continuum. Nor is it intended as lesson in data visualization graphicacy mechanics. There are many references available that go deep into the weeds of those practices. What this chapter is an exploration of the purposes and processes of various forms of information visualization, with a focused discussion on what we can consider the "golden rules" that guide the process of building a successful data visualization.

9.1 DATA VISUALIZATION DEFINITION

If you ask a room full of people with varying backgrounds in data science, graphic design, analytics, or any other assortment of skills and experiences for the definition of "data visualization," chances are you are going to receive just as varied a response as the personalities in the room. Chances are, too, that you will also uncover some resonant themes and understandings, as well as some very contrary opinions. If you do a quick Google search online, or ask a number of leading minds in the data visualization space, you will likely get a similar result. As with any type of tool or principle, a level of disagreement is to be expected—encouraged even, as a consequence of greater discussion is (generally) more engagement, clarity, and thoughtful consideration into supporting components. Even in my journey, I have worked with companies and data scientists who are building visualizations so scientific and its almost hard to believe that they are data visualization. At the other end of the spectrum, I have also seen organizations where graphic designers are responsible for building data visualizations that sometimes are more suitable for artistic display, than in any corporate boardroom. I have seen dashboards both glorious and banal. I have even met people who have metaphorically lived by data visualization, and others than snub their nose at it. When it comes to any area of data, we are a mightily opinionated group.

Most broadly, the term data visualization generally describes any effort to help people understand the significance of data by placing it in a visual context. Some define data visualization purely as an analytical tool. Others are more liberal in their definitions, and probably the vast majority are those who draw the proverbial line in the sand between the artistic and scientific qualities of data visualization and dance between the two. And, regardless of the chosen definition, there are always likely to be distinctions that exist between data visualization and other subsets of visual information graphics, particularly infographics.

So, what is the definition of data visualization? Is it information art? Is it science, dependent on strict graphicacy guidelines for analytical use that benefit from intentional design process? Is it design, a creative endeavor to foster visual data storytelling or exploration? Is human science, or computer science, or both? The lines are blurry at best. And, the reality is that unlike the 20 magical Rings of Power, there is no one absolute definition to "rule them all." It would seem that definitions for data visualization are as diverse and dynamic as the people who use them—and as the visualizations themselves, which exist on a continuum from explanatory to exploratory, simple to complex, traditional to innovative.

Now is not the time to sort out all the arguments on data visualization, but that is not to say that we can dismiss the necessity of a guiding definition by which to frame conversations on data visualization. There is an obvious need to articulate what a data visualization is, even if it is an umbrella term with a smattering of subcategories beneath it.

Before definition let us first acknowledge the core value of data visualization in a culture of visual data discovery. Data visualization has been widely acknowledged as key to the democratization of data, primarily because it is really the only meaningful way to consume and digest large quantities of diverse information. Effectively—and creatively—built data visualizations support information literacy by painting a picture by which to assemble data points in relevant and expressive ways to depict quantitative information in a way that leverages our visual communication abilities; cognitive hardwiring and the perceptual powers of our brains; and our intrinsically human need to tell stories.

Thus, we can define data visualization as a visual display of information that is transformed by the influence of purposeful design decisions with the intent of encoding and conveying information that would otherwise be either difficult to understand or unlikely (or impossible) to connect with in a meaningful way. We can further elaborate on that definition by considering the following:

It is a *process* (as described by Scott Murray (2013), Assistant Professor of Design at the University of San Francisco and author of *Interactive Data Visualization for the Web*) of "mapping values to visuals," and blending visual design and information graphicacy to connect ideas, illuminate patterns, or answer or invite questions.

It is a *tool* by which to translate data into easier and better ways to see and understand in order explore patterns, trends, correlations, and relationships in data and convey results and insights. It can be built by any number of visualization tools or technologies, some of which are automated software while others require a large degree of human interaction and discretion in each step of the visualizing process.

It is a *communication mechanism* by which to explore or explain data. As an output, a data visualization can be used to build a narrative around, and communicate— or tell a story—about what is represented visually in the data. This can be achieved by using one data visualization to support text or persuade an audience (like in data journalism) or within a collection of several visualizations intended to provide a more complete picture of multiple pieces of related information (like in a data dashboard or scorecard).

9.2 THE POWER OF VIZ

Perhaps the most quintessential of examples of the power of data visualization comes from what is known as Anscombe's Quartet, four seemingly identical data sets constructed in 1973 by statistician Francis Anscombe. The data sets, shown in a table (Figure 9.1), appear to be identical when compared by their summary statistics. Each set has the same mean of both X and Y, the same sample variance, the same correlations between X and Y in each case, the same linear regression, and so on.

However, when each of the data sets is graphed (Figure 9.2), we can see beyond the limitations of basic statistic properties for describing data. You would expect that since each data set has the same summary statistics, they would also look very similar when visualized. But, as you can see, they actually look entirely different, and the effects of curvature and outliers drastically throw off summary statistics. This illustrates the power of visualization: simply by plotting the four data sets on an x/y coordinate plane, we get very distinctive results, demonstrating how important it is to plot your data—visualize it—rather than relying on a table or summary statistics alone. We can see the real relationships in the datasets emerge. Likewise, we can pick out trends, patterns, and outliers.

While a similar procedure to generate data sets with identical statistics and dissimilar graphics has since been developed, another more modern example of the power of visualization was another personal data experiment conducted by graphic designer Chelsea Carlson (whose work on social media addiction habits was shared in chapter: Separating Leaders From Laggards).

Carlson began her experiment—titled "Netflix & Chill" by doing what many of us do today: organizing information in Microsoft Excel. She listed the 27 television shows that were her favorites, including supporting information that quantified them across genres, budgets, and languages (see Figure 9.3). As a tool, the spreadsheet helped her to understand the correlation of the categories that showed interesting trends (number of seasons, popularity of IMDB, award winners, etc.) and those that

	Set A		Set B		Set C		Set D	
	X	Y	X	Y	X	Y	X	Y
0	10	8.04	10	9.14	10	7.46	8	6.58
1	8	6.95	8	8.14	8	6.77	8	5.76
2	13	7.58	13	8.74	13	12.74	8	7.71
3	9	8.81	9	8.77	9	7.11	8	8.84
4	11	8.33	11	9.26	11	7.81	8	8.47
5	14	9.96	14	8.10	14	8.84	8	7.04
6	6	7.24	6	6.13	6	6.08	8	5.25
7	4	4.26	4	3.10	4	5.39	19	12.50
8	12	10.84	12	9.13	12	8.15	8	5.56
9	7	4.82	7	7.26	7	6.42	8	7.91
10	5	5.68	5	4.74	5	5.73	8	6.89
mean	9.00	7.50	9.00	7.50	9.00	7.50	9.00	7.50
std	3.32	2.03	3.32	2.03	3.32	2.03	3.32	2.03
corr	0.82		0.82		0.82		0.82	
lin. reg.	$y = 3.00 + 0.500x$		$y = 3.00 + 0.500x$		$y = 3.00 + 0.500x$		$y = 3.00 + 0.500x$	

FIGURE 9.1 Anscombe's Quartet, in Table Form

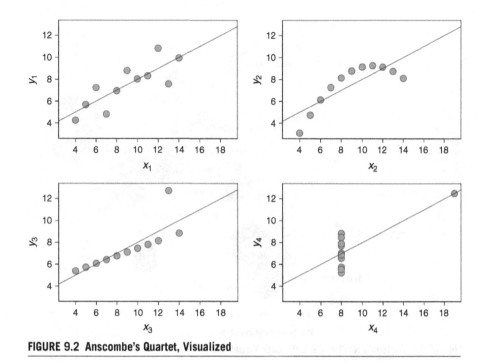

FIGURE 9.2 Anscombe's Quartet, Visualized

	show name	time period	main character	length	costume drama	# of seasons	years on the	IMDB us	IMDB # of users	golde	show creator
2	Mad Men	mid 20th	man	45	yes		7	2007-2015	8.7	211,187	4	Matthew Weiner
3	Velvet	mid 20th	ensemble	90	yes	4+		2013-	7.9	879	0	Ramon Campos, Gema R. Neira
4	Scandal	present	women	45	yes	5+		2012-	7.9	45,209	0	Shonda Rhimes
5	UnREAL	present	woman	45	no	2+		2015-	7.8	3,732	0	Marti Noxon, Sarah Gertrude Sha...
6	The Office	present	ensemble	20	no		9	2005-2013	8.6	178,906	1	Greg Daniels, Ricky Gervais, Ste...
7	Parks & Recreation	present	woman	20	no		7	2009-2015	8.6	133,112	1	Greg Daniels, Michael Schur
8	Downton Abbey	early 20th	ensemble	90	yes		6	2010-2015	8.7	98,053	2	Julian Fellowes
9	Sherlock	present	man	45	no	4+		2010-	9.3	433,533	0	Mark Gatiss, Steven Moffat
10	Empire	present	ensemble	45	yes	2+		2015-	8	20,544	0	Lee Daniels, Danny Strong
11	Firefly	future (2517)	man	45	yes		1	2002-2003	9.1	174,257	0	Joss Whedon
12	Arrested Development	present	man	20	no		5	2003-2013	9	199,522	1	Mitchell Hurwitz
13	Bates Motel	retro present	woman	45	yes	3+		2013-	8.1	49,920	0	Anthony Cipriano, Carlton Cuse,
14	Freaks & Geeks	1980s	women	45	no		1	1999-2000	8.9	32,813	1	Paul Feig
15	Twilight Zone	assorted	ensemble	45	no		5	1959-1964	9	39,253	1	Rod Serling
16	Broad City	present	woman	20	no	3+		2014-	8.5	10,164	0	Ilana Glazer, Abbi Jacobson
17	Pushing Daisies	retro present	couple	45	yes		2	2007-2009	8.4	42,479	0	Bryan Fuller
18	My-So-Called Life	present	woman	45	no		1	1994-1995	8.4	14,541	1	Winnie Holzman
19	Orange Is the New Black	present	women ensemble	45	no		4	2013-	8.4	105,373	0	Jenji Kohan
20	American Horror Story	assorted	ensemble	45	yes		5	2011-	8.3	173,856	1	Brad Falchuk, Ryan Murphy
21	Dead Like Me	present	woman	45	no		2	2003-2004	8.2	33,669	0	Bryan Fuller
22	The Riches	present	couple	45	no		1.5	2007-2008	8	7,004	0	Dmitry Lipkin
23	The Tudors	17th century	man	45	yes		4	2007-2010	8.1	47,512	0	Michael Hirst
24	Buffy the Vampire Slayer	present	woman	45	no		7	1997-2003	8.2	96,018	0	Joss Whedon
25	Dollhouse	present	woman	45	no		2	2009-2010	7.8	38,314	0	Joss Whedon
26	Project Runway	present	relationship	45	yes	14+		2004-	7.3	7,881	2	n/a
27	The Grand Hotel	early 20th	ensemble	90	yes		3	2011-2013	8.5	2,079	0	n/a

FIGURE 9.3 Carlson's Netflix and Chill Data Spreadsheet, in Table Form

did not (age and race of lead, setting, length of show, etc.), however this was the extent of meaningful analysis that could be done when limited to rows and columns.

Like Anscombe's Quartet, when visualized, Carlson was able to earn a deeper level of insight into the same data that already existed in Excel (Figure 9.4). As she worked through a visual discovery process, Carlson used a variety of graph

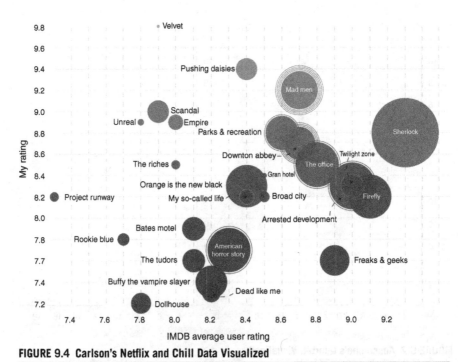

FIGURE 9.4 Carlson's Netflix and Chill Data Visualized

See more at https://www.umbel.com/blog/data-visualization/netflix-chill-little-data-experiment-understanding-my-own-taste-tv/

types—including scatterplots, packed bubble charts, timelines, and even pie charts—unified with a few consistent elements. She also used visual elements like size and color to provide additional visual cues to assign meaning to the visualization. As a result, she was able to come away with a few key realizations, including her bias for costume dramas, female leads, and genre-bending storylines.

The power of visualization goes beyond how powerful graphs are to better represent the intricacies of relationships within data, and extends to how audiences perceive and are influenced visually by data visualization, too. For example, researchers from Cornell found that merely including a graph in an article significantly increases reader persuasion. The researchers found that only 68% of participants believed a scientific claim without a graph, whereas 97% believed the same claim when a graph was included (Tal & Wansink, 2014).

The power of data visualization, whether for discovery or for persuasion, is obvious. However, as remarked a few times throughout the course of this text, along with that power comes great responsibility. Visualizations should be used for good—not to mislead or misconstrue information. And, they should work to leverage the incredible capabilities and bandwidth of the visual system to facilitate the movement of information into the brain very quickly in order to identify patterns, communicate relationships and meaning, inspire new questions, and incite further exploration.

9.3 TO EXPLAIN OR EXPLORE—OR BOTH?

While there is a vast host of different visualization types, there are generally three categories of visualizations. Each serves a different purpose, and because of this, it is important to understand the distinctions between each category and how they can be used to accomplish the goal for the data visualization. We will explore each type (with a relevant example for context) in the subsequent sections (Figure 9.5).

9.3.1 EXPLANATORY

As its title implies, explanatory data visualizations are intended to explain, thus they are the visualizations most efficient in telling a story to an audience or otherwise communicating insights to others who are likely not as familiar with the data, its context, or its meaning.

In an explanatory graphic, the goal of the visual is to communicate some kind of information—a story, an insight, an invitation to action—to the viewer. It is the responsibility of the designer to craft a visual that will facilitate this explanation, and typically the visualization will follow a well-defined narrative structure that begins with the main story point and trickles down through each part of the visual. Explanatory visualizations should be able to make a point effectively at a glance to facilitate and support a story told from the perspective of a designer.

For example, take a look at Figure 9.6. Created using the same data set on America's favorite pie flavors that was the inspiration behind the #onelesspie chart highlighted in chapter: The Data Science Education and Leadership Landscape, this simple bar chart plots an assortment of pie flavors (axis X) arranged according to percentage of Americans who selected the flavor as their favorite (axis Y). The main narrative in the simple chart is to show the most preferred pie flavor by Americans: apple. As an explanatory graphic, we are only concerned with highlighting the flavor with the highest value. The process that the designer and the receiver follow when designing and subsequently interpreting this chart is remarkably similar. First, ask a question of the data—"which pie flavor is most preferred?"—and then answer this question.

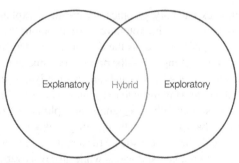

FIGURE 9.5　Three Categories of Data Visualization

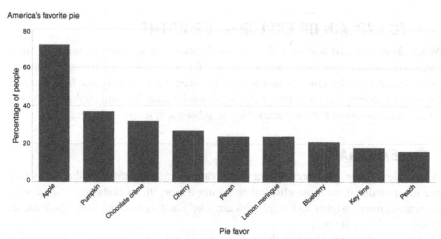

FIGURE 9.6 Explanatory Bar Chart Showing the America's Favorite Pie Flavors

Explanatory graphics are fundamentally intended to share information that is already known on the side of the designer. Therefore, they are editorially driven. Since the goal is to bring out a single story most clearly, the value of the visual is on simplicity. Thus, as much noise—distractions, points for discovery, etc.—are stripped from the visual, taking care not to remove the visual cues that emphasize the salient point of the story. Explanatory graphics, wherein visual discovery and exploration is discouraged, tend to be static and not interactive, which also puts more control in the hands of the designer.

Consider these scenarios in which explanatory visualizations are likely to be used:

- Answer a question
- Prove a point
- Support a decision
- Communicate information

9.3.2 EXPLORATORY

As you might expect, if explanatory graphics are meant to explain, then exploratory graphics are meant to explore. With exploratory visualization, the goal is to uncover stories that can later be explained. You, as the designer, are interested in exploring the data to find the story that it is telling you—the premise of using data visualization to enable visual discovery. Thus, exploratory visuals are inherently not editorially driven, but the emphasis is instead on plucking through the visual to discover one valuable story or perhaps even many small stories. When designing an exploratory graphic, it is unlikely that the designer knows what the story is, though they may know a point of interest or have a hypothesis they would like to investigate further. It is aimed at presenting the data in a way that the viewer can notice the obvious while also discovering something new.

Contrary to the stativity of explanatory visuals, exploratory visualizations work best when they are interactive and allow the viewer to follow train of thought thinking

Discoveries, by year

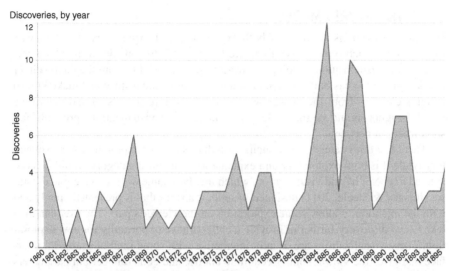

FIGURE 9.7 An Exploratory Visual Showing the Number of Important Discoveries Made in the Second Half of the 19th Century

to dig deeper to discover trends, patterns, or problems as they think through various questions or points of interest in the data presented to them. They should compellingly invite the viewer to get an overview of the visual at a high level, ask questions along the way, and find answers to those questions as they move visually through the data.

For example, see the visual in Figure 9.7. Created using a publically available data set on the yearly number of important discoveries from years 1860–1895, this area chart plots the sum of discoveries (axis Y) according to year (axis X). The most obvious narrative in the chart is the period of time in which a number of important discoveries were made: 1884. But, taking the entire visual into account, there are many more questions that almost immediately come to mind. By exploring the visual, and interacting with the data in various ways (including drill down or further sorting and refinement), we can take guesses at questions that we would need answers to in order to tell a deeper story and find answers to many salient story points. For instance, what kinds of discoveries were these? Who made them? Where did they occur? By laying on additional data too, such as the invention of new technologies, we could put together some hypotheses in the trends that enabled a general rise in important discoveries after the peak in 1884.

Exploratory visuals work best when there is a high volume of data to be visualized and when the visuals are interactive and contextualized. As with any type of data discovery, exploratory visualization-led discovery can by cyclical, iterative, and without a specific end point. It may yield one insight, or many, or none at all. Thus, consider scenarios when exploratory visualizations are likely to be used:

• Pose new questions
• Discover new areas of interest
• Explore previously unknown or unexplored data

9.3.3 THE HYBRID MODEL

Hybrid visualizations are a bit of both exploratory and explanatory. The best way to determine which type of visual you are looking at is to consider from which perspective the visualization is doing the work to reveal insights from the data—either the designer, who has built the visual in a way to facilitate a story and make known insights clear, or from the viewer who needs to explore the visual and determine which insights should be made clear. Inevitably, most visualizations probably fall somewhere in between.

There is a third category of visualization that is neither exploratory nor explanatory while it is both exploratory and explanatory. This third category would be considered a type of hybrid visualization, which involves some degree of a curated dataset (Iliisnky & Steele, 2011) designed to support a story that is presented openly and with the intention to allow some exploration on the viewer's part. The user can then take visual discovery further or provide a collaborative opportunity for new exploration. These visualizations are usually interactive with some kind of graphical interface that gives the viewer some freedom to choose and constrain certain parameters and thereby personalize the discovery experience.

Figure 9.8 is an example of an everyday hybrid visualization. It is a screen shot of the Google Hot Trends screen, grabbed on November 5, 2015, which is both celebrated as Guy Fawkes Day and the day of a major NASA headline (and hoax—I hope no one was bothered by that pesky 15 days of darkness in November 2015), both of which are represented in the grab. Google Hot Trends (view online in plain text or visual format at https://www.google.com/trends/) visualizes Google search queries in real-time in the form of a colorful, tree map-like grid. The queries, shown as they change, update every second to keep pace with the rate of change in what users are searching for online. This visualization does not highlight any single search

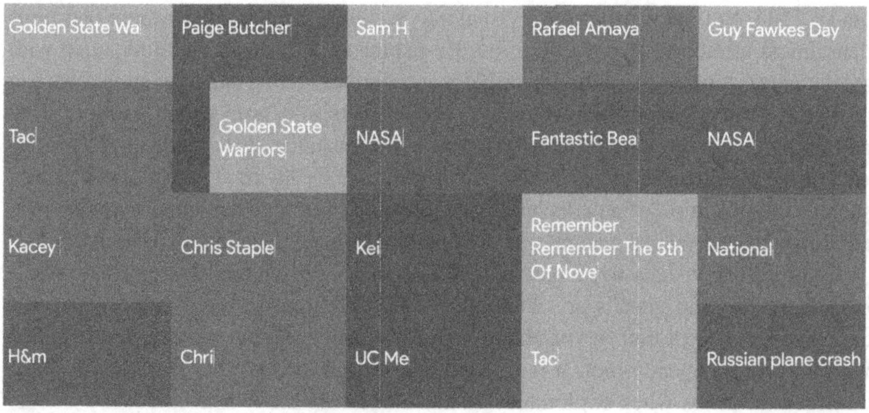

FIGURE 9.8 This Screen Grab of the Google Hot Trends Screen, Taken on November 5, 2015, is an Example of a Hybrid Visualization

query, but invites the viewer to explore any part of the visual at will. The story is left to the viewer to discover by interacting with the visualization.

In summary, the two main categories of visualizations—which may or may not be tempered by the actual visualization medium chosen—are to explain or to explore data. In the end, the distinction between the two comes down to the application and how the designer puts the visualization into use. If the visual is designed to tell a story that is already known then it is probably an explanatory visualization. Instead, if the visualization is a vehicle for the designer (or the viewer) to discover a new story to tell or to learn some other new insight into the data, it is likely an exploratory graphic. The balance between from which side—the designer or the viewer –the visualization is to be used by, and what degree of freedom or interaction is to be allowed by the visual.

Many visuals are a hybrid of both categories of visualization, and are designed to orient the viewer with an idea or engender them with a curiosity to further explore the visual in order to come to new conclusions or discover new insights and new stories.

9.4 **THE RISE OF THE INFOGRAPHIC**

One of the best depictions of hybrid data visualization can be found in the infographic.

An infographic both is and is not a data visualization. As a mechanism to communicate and convey information, it tends to fall somewhere along the continuum as a subset of data visualization, and it follows many of the same design principles. However, it does not meet the specific standards of data visualization as we have traditionally defined them, and it stands apart from what many would consider a "true" data visualization due in part to its design process, visual abundance (minimalistic approaches are definitely not par for the course in infographics), and use cases. It could be an exercise in semantics, but the use of an infographic could be best described as an activity to "illustrate" information, rather than to "visualize" it. Nonetheless, the consensus seems to be that while different, infographics do play an important role in data analysis—perhaps especially (or, perhaps only) for its storytelling qualities.

In Nathan Yau's blog, *FlowingData*, Yau took a stab at articulating the difference between an infographic and a data visualization, saying, "a visualization is the representation of data via geometry and math while infographics are a subset of visualization where an actual human being had a hand in explaining the (hopefully interesting) points in the data in question" (Yau, 2011). Further, in *Designing Data Visualizations,* Iliinsnky and Steele (2011) define it as: manually generated around specific data, tending to be shallow, and often aesthetically rich. To add to this, infographics tend to be almost always static and put a premium on creative representations of data, sometimes at the sacrifice of accuracy. Probably the most striking demarcation between a data visualization and an infographics is this: data visualization is a discipline, while infographics are merely a deliverable (or an item). While infographics present data and solicit a conclusion on the data, true data visualizations just present the data. The job of analyzing it and coming to a conclusion is left to the viewer.

Unlike data visualizations, which are typically designed with the intent to explore or explain information, infographics are generally created for the purpose of telling, and will thus usually be intended for a specific audience. Infographics, then, are subjective, self-contained, and discrete: it is information designed and presented in a way that is accessible for an audience.

Infographics are highly curated and the graphic design work is obvious. Often iconography and other graphical flair is used to illuminate the content, along with multiple approaches to visualization—including various chart and graph types, both traditional and more advanced. Because of this level of complexity, infographics are usually constructed by hand and digitally developed through graphic design tools (like Adobe Illustrator) as opposed to any standard data visualization solution (like Tableau). Many templates also exist to fulfill infographics needs, too, and can be purchased from stock photography portfolios.

9.5 CHOOSING THE CHART: A QUICK DIAGNOSTIC

In chapter: Improved Agility and Insights Through (Visual) Discovery, a conversation on the forms of visual discovery, we reviewed—at a very basic level—traditional forms of visual discovery (forms that provide simple, straightforward visual representations of data) and the more innovative visualizations (like heat maps or network visualizations) that take the next step to advancing visual data discovery through visualization.

While, there are many types of charts and graphs to choose from—far too many to cover all with any useful level of depth and application (see Figure 9.9 to explore a larger variety of graphics routinely used for data visualization purposes)—this section is aimed to include a diagnostic of some of the most commonly accessible and most familiar chart types available today. Many, if not most, of these are visualization types included in visualization tools of all calibers—from Microsoft Excel to Tableau and beyond. For the most part, these graph and chart types fall into the bucket of the more traditional types of visualizations, and thus serve as a good starting place for those users just beginning the journey to visually working with data, however some do tiptoe the line crossing over into the more advanced visualization types as well.

As a sample set, this section will look briefly at:

- The bar chart
- The line chart (and area charts)
- The pie chart (and its newer cousin, the donut chart)
- The scatter plot
- The bubble chart

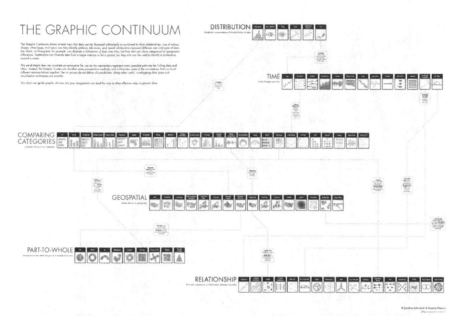

FIGURE 9.9 The Graphic Continuum, Conceived by Jonathan Schwabish and Severino Ribecca

(Note: This graphic should be given an entire page and oriented vertically)

- The histogram chart
- The treemap
- The heat map

1. The bar chart

   One of the most common ways to visualize data, the bar is a traditional favorite that can be used to quickly compare information and reveal highs and lows (trends) at a glance. This type of chart is best suited for numerical data that can be divided cleanly into distinct categories. Bars can be oriented on either the vertical or horizontal sides of the axis. This can be especially helpful for spotting trends, when both positive and negative data are plotted along a continuous axis.

   There are a few ways to spice up a simple bar chart. On a dashboard, several bar charts could be added to help a viewer quickly compare information side by side without moving through several charts in isolation. On the design side, overlaying bars with highlight colors or with texture. Finally, additional layers of information can be added to bar charts by either using side-by-side (or, clustered) bars, or by stacking related data on top of each other, or by adding a reference line to indicate a key value. These tactics give depth to an analysis and have the propensity to address multiple questions at once.

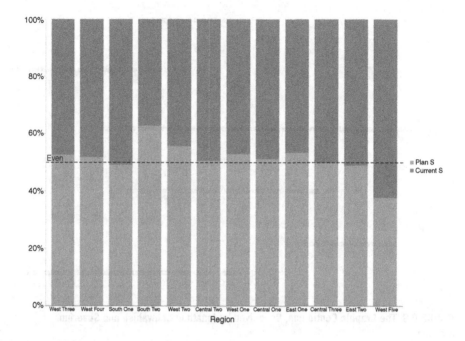

2. The line chart

   Like the bar chart, the line chart is another of the most frequently used chart types (which can also be paired with bar charts, too, to show trends). These charts connect individual numeric data points to visualize a sequence of values. The best use cases for a line charts involve with displaying trends over a period of time.

   When two or more lines are present, line charts can be transformed into area charts by filling the space under each respective line to extend the analysis and illuminate the relative contribution that a line contributes to the whole.

3. The pie chart/the donut chart

   We all love to hate the pie chart, and to a lesser extent, its shiny new(ish) cousin, the donut chart. Both are great options to visualize proportions (part of a whole). Unfortunately, they are also among the most misused (and overused) of chart types.

   The donut is basically the same idea as the pie, but with a hole cut in the middle that can be fun emphasizing a key metric of KPI. In either, the circle represents the whole, and the size of the wedge—the largest starting on the upper right—represents a percentage of the whole. Combined, each wedge in the pie should add up to equal 100%. Both charts are best used for comparing a few values, and viewers should not be asked to translate wedges into relevant data or compare one pie to another.

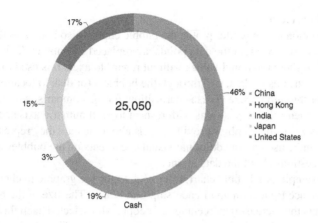

4. The scatter plot

   Scatter plots (also known as a scatter diagram, scattergram, scatter chart, or scatter graph) are an effective way to compare two different measures and visualize data points to quickly identify patterns, trends, concentrations (clusters), and outliers. These charts can give viewers a sense of where to focus discovery efforts further, and are best used to investigate relationships between variables.

   Adding a trend line to a scatter plot can be helpful to guide the eye and better define correlation. Incorporating filters can also reduce noise and prompt viewers to limit their investigation to the factors that matter most to their analysis.

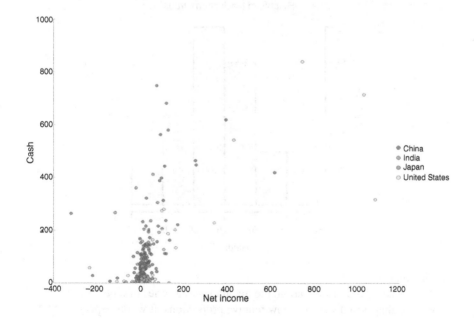

5. The bubble chart
   One variation of the scatter plot is the bubble chart—also known as the packed
   bubbles view—wherein the data points are replaced by bubbles. This is a
   method to show relational values without regard to axes. It is used to display
   three dimensions of data, two through the bubble's (or disk's) location and
   the other through its size. These charts allow for the comparison of entities in
   terms of their relative positions with respect to each numeric axis and size. The
   various sizes of the bubbles provide details about the data they represent, and
   colors can be used as an additional visual cue to encode the bubbles and answer
   many questions about the data at once.
   As an example of a bubble chart, refer back to the pie graphic in chapter: The
   Data Science Education and Leadership Landscape. The size of the bubble
   represents the increasing percentage of people who selected each flavor as
   their favorite, while the bubbles themselves are "colored" as the topping of
   each pie to visually showcase the flavor itself. As another technique for adding
   richness to bubble charts, consider overlaying them on top of a map to put
   geographically-related data quickly in context.

6. The histogram chart
   A different take on the bar chart, histograms can be used to understand the
   distribution of data by grouping data into categories and plotting them with
   vertical bars along an axis. These charts can be used to test different groupings
   of data, too, and can—like scatter plots—benefit from the use of filters to drill
   down into different categories and explore many data views quickly.

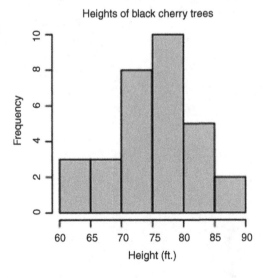

7. The treemap
   A more advanced visualization, the treemap uses a series of rectangles of
   various shapes and sizes to show relative proportions. It works especially well

if the data being visualized has a hierarchical structure (with parent nodes, children, etc.) or when analyzing part-to-whole relationship. As its name suggests, a treemap works to divide and subdivide based on parts of a whole by breaking down into smaller rectangles, often of a different color or different color gradient, to emphasize its relationship to the larger whole.

The treemap also provides a much more efficient way to see this relationship when working with large amounts of data by making efficient use of space. It is ideal for legibly showing hundreds (or perhaps even thousands) of items simultaneously within a single visualization.

8. The Heat Map

Among the more advanced visualizations is the heat map. This type of graph is a great way to compare categories of data using color and size as visual indicators to quantify the individual values through a matrix of colors. Similar to treemaps, a heat map represents the values by a variable in a hierarchy. They are similar in concept to the type of complex visual data representation that you might see used on your local weather forecast by the meteorologist to illustrate rainfall patterns across a region.

Tip for navigating this type of visualization would include adding a size variation for squares to show the concentration of intersecting factors while adding a third element, or even using a shape other than a square to convey meaning in a more impactful way.

9.6 DATA VISUALIZATION GOLDEN RULES

It was data visualization pioneer Edward Tufte (1983)—referred to by *The New York Times* as "the da Vinci of Data" (Shapley, 1998) who wrote, "Graphics reveal data. Indeed, graphics can be more precise and revealing than conventional statistical computations."

In Tufte's opinion, data visualization should show the data while inducing the viewer to think about the substance it is presenting rather than about methodology, graphic design, the technology of graphic production, or anything else. It should make large data sets coherent by incorporating design principles to present many numbers in a small space in a way that leverages the brain's natural visual processing horsepower. It should encourage the eye to compare different pieces of data, while revealing the data at several levels of detail—from a broad overview to a fine structure.

When bringing together the art, the science, and the story of any data visualization you should take into account the following as 10 Golden Rules of data visualization.

9.6.1 RULE #1: VISUALIZE WITH GOALS IN MIND

Goals come first. Creating an effective data visualization should begin first with knowing the purpose that the visualization is intended to serve. A clear goal in mind will shape how the designer will build a visualization that brings together all the necessary ingredients in alignment with one specific purpose. If the goal itself is unclear, it can be useful to start by thinking about how the visualization will be used once it is completed. For example, is it intended for strategic reasons, for analytical, for operational? Or, will it explain a specific insight, or be used as a tool for others to explore and discover new insights? Answering these questions will determine its purpose, and help to reverse engineer the approaches which may work best to build the visualization in order to meet its goal.

Separately, the goal of the data visualization is not the same as its message (which comes in a later step), though the two work in tandem so it is useful to mention this upfront, too. Whether the visualization is designed with the goal of prompting decision or action, or with the goal of inviting an audience to explore the data to find new insights, the designer of the data visualization is tasked with identifying the relationships and patterns of the data that support their goal. Then, pivot the perspective to think from your audience's point of view. Knowing both sides of the story will make sure that the goal of the data visualization is the same from the viewpoint of the designer and the viewer.

9.6.2 RULE #2: KNOW YOUR DATA

Almost anything can be turned into data and encoded visually, but before a designer can successfully create (or recreate) a data visualization, they must understand the underlying data. This includes the type of data, its context, and its meaning.

At a basic level, data can be classified into two primary groups: quantitative and qualitative. Qualitative data, measurements that are expressed by natural language description rather than numbers (eg, favorite color = yellow) can be further divided into two subsets: categorical and ordinal.

> *Quantitative* data are variables that are expressed in exact numbers and always associated with a scaled measure. These are metrics that can be counted, ordered, and aggregated. They can be discreet or continuous. *Example: life expectancy, income per person, year*
> *Categorical* (also, *nominal*) data are variables that do not conform to natural ordering, though they can be logically organized into groups (or categories). These may take on numerical values, but these values do not necessarily carry any mathematical meaning. *Example: gender, sport, geographical location (regions or states)*
> *Ordinal* data is similar to categorical data, except these can be counted and ordered (or ranked) in some way yet still cannot be aggregated.*Example: count bins (0-100, 101-200), rankings (easy, medium, hard), grades (A, B, C)*

Other factors—like data cardinality—also affect classification of data. Beyond data type, there are graphs, charts, and other visualization types best suited for specific types of data, as well as key data features most important to visualize. However, these decisions should come after the data itself and its context are well understood.

9.6.3 **RULE #3: PUT YOUR AUDIENCE FIRST**

The goal of the data visualization can be lost if it is not designed to suit its audience. Therefore, data visualizations should always be customized to fit the unique and diverse needs of its audience and only include what they need to know (message) in alignment with the visualization's purpose (goal) in a clear and focused way that is compelling and meaningful. What is relevant or needed by one group may be irrelevant or overwhelming to another. Too much information can cause information overload (drowning in data) or too little, increasing the likelihood that key points may be lost in data visualization noise or, conversely, stripped out or lost.

A helpful guide to determine the needs of the audience is to consider the following questions:

- Who is looking at the visualization?
- How will they be looking at it—in a static report, an interactive dashboard environment, on a mobile device?
- How will they be given its message?
- What kind of action might be taken?
- Does the visualization provide the right level of detail?
- Does it include the right type and amount of data to justify action?
- Does it tell a compelling story? Is it clear?
- What assumptions or bias might affect design choice?

9.6.4 **RULE #4: BE MEDIA SENSITIVE**

While it is not especially critical to think mobile-first, when designing a data visualization you should be aware of form factor bias and rethink the way storytelling is performed via mobile devices. One way to think about this is to consider how the visualization will be used on a mobile device—will it only be consumed, or is it intended to be exploratory, shared, or presented? If a desktop-based data visualization is anticipated to transform to fit a mobile device—whether a laptop or a smartphone—there are important design concerns to keep in mind. For example, how will the visualization orient on a mobile screen? Will it be large enough to convey meaning without losing depth of analysis? Will color gradients appear with clarity? Will headings and labels make sense, or will they be removed completely? Will users expect and/or desire to interact with the visualization the same way on a mobile device as they would on the desktop?

9.6.5 **RULE #5: CHOOSE THE RIGHT CHART**

For each type of data there is a diagnostic of visualizations best suited for specific analytic needs. Among these are: contribution analysis, time-series analysis, correlations, and so forth. For each, there are appropriate ways to visualize data and intended visual takeaways. Line charts, for example, are used to track changes or trends over time and show the relationship among variables. Bar charts are used to compare quantities of different categories; scatter plots to show joint variation of two data items; and the pie chart to compare parts of a whole. Many other advanced visualization types—like heat maps, treemaps, and histograms—span the continuum of exploratory and explanatory graphics. We explored some of these in the previous section, and there are many guidelines and practices that can guide the selection of the appropriate method. There are also key features to visualize, and best ways in which to visually represent them.

Regardless of the type of graph, chart, or other visualization method chosen, the designer must be keenly aware of its strengths and limits. They must know what kind of data it is best suited to visualize, and employ whatever type of graphic best conveys the story as simply and succinctly as possible. And, they should only include relevant visuals that deliver important information to the target audience. Remember, too, how data visualizations can work together if more than one is presented in story succession or on a dashboard. However, be careful because using too many different types of graphs, charts, or graphics that can leave the audience unsure of the message, and deterred from the goal.

9.6.6 RULE #6: PRACTICE RESPONSIBLE CHARTING

Understanding of data and an awareness of the most appropriate ways to visually represent them are the first step in building an effective data visualization, but beyond that comes the following mandate: chart with integrity. The ability for a visualization to lead us to answers can also occasionally lead us to the wrong answers. Data visualizations should not be used—intentionally or unintentionally—to distort, mislead, or misrepresent information. It is as important to avoid cherry picking of data to manipulate a visual representation. One should not treat all data equally nor force the data to fit a message that is untrue.

First, understand bias, and work to avoid it. There are several types of biases (confirmation, social, hindishgt, and priming, to list a few), and, to quote Jock Mackinlay, Vice President of Research and Design at Tableau Software, the "smarter you are, the stronger your cognitive biases are." Exploring data effectively is what protects you from cognitive biases.

Second, avoid Simpson's paradox, or a trend that appears in different groups of data but disappears or reverses when these groups are combined. One of the best-known real-world examples of Simpson's paradox occurred when the University of California Berkley was sued for a perceived bias against women in the 1970s based on analysis that suggested that women who applied for admission to graduate schools were admitted at significantly lower rates than men. Data for the fall of 1973 showed that the male applicants (a total of 8442) were admitted at a 44% admission rate, compared to female applicants (4321) who were admitted much lower, at a 35% admission rate. The illustration in Figure 9.10 shows how significant this difference appears at a surface glance.

However, by exploring the data deeper, and understanding additional levels of categorization of the data (see Figure 9.11), we can actually see that this is not so significant after all, and that we have fallen prey to a contradiction in probably and

FIGURE 9.10 Male Versus Female Applicants to UC Berkley Graduate School in 1973

Department	Men		Women	
	Applicants	Admitted	Applicants	Admitted
A	825	62%	108	82%
B	560	63%	25	68%
C	325	37%	593	34%
D	417	33%	375	35%
E	191	28%	393	24%
F	272	6%	341	7%

FIGURE 9.11 A Deeper Look at the UC Berkley Admission Data, by Department, Applications for Each Gender, and Percentage of Applicants Admitted

statistics—Simpson's paradox. In fact, depending on the academic department, women's admissions rates were actually higher than the men's in many cases, and each unit was dependent on the number of applications received.

The visual in Figure 9.12, presented by Visualizing Urban Data Idealab (or, VUDlab, a student-led organization formed at University of California-Berkeley) revisualizes this data in a much more appropriate way.

9.6.7 RULE #7: USE LABELS WISELY

This is less of a design conversation and more of an emphasis, again, on context. When labeling visualizations, include a compelling headline to orient the viewer and communicate the main focus of the visual—this is your title—and do it as clearly and concisely as possible. Headers are not the place to get fancy with typographies, keep them simple and do not capitalize every letter or go to unnecessary extremes to force attention. Label axis's horizontally so that they are easy to read, and again, be clear and concise. Minimize the use of legends and other explanatory elements, and instead design your visualization to communicate visual meaning without additional layers of description and clarification.

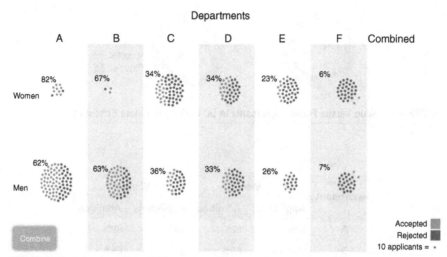

FIGURE 9.12 A Better Look at UC Berkley 1973 Admission Data From VUDlab.

Available at http://vudlab.com/simpsons/

Using labels wisely amounts to providing source information and leveraging supporting elements—like story points and annotations—with discretion. Do not be cryptic or clever, and do not over embellish. Just explain what the graphic is intended to do. This will help to put the visualization immediately into context.

9.6.8 RULE #8: DESIGN WITH CARE

Without revisiting a host of design considerations for data visualization, a good rule of thumb to designing with care is to make sure everything on the visualization serves at least one purpose. The design effort should be focused on showing the data above everything else. Therefore, design to the point: be straightforward and do not feel the need to fill every space on the page. Too much clutter makes the important information harder to find, harder to remember, and easier to dismiss.

Edward Tufte calls this "maximizing the data-ink ratio." Eliminate all extra ink—including chart features, unnecessary headers, etc., and redundant information, including background colors, borders, and grids—that add visual complexity to the graphic. Always choose the simplest, clearest, most efficient way to convey information correctly. Use color, size, position patterns, etc., discriminately to help the reader see what is important. Color adds emphasis, highlights the particular data points, and draws connections between graphs. The hue, value, and intensity of the color are significant and may have cultural or social connotations that you should be aware of, too.

Size and position draws attention to particular data points and hierarchy. The top of the charts and larger objects tend to draw the eye first, and this rule of thumb applies both to the individual data visualization, how visualizations are grouped together in a dashboard, and the dashboard layout itself. Cultural reading conventions also determine how people read charts (similar to how they read text).

Capitalize on the best features of data to visualize. As a guideline, consider the below:

- Categorical data: position, color hues, shape, clusters, boundaries
- Ordinal data: position, size, color intensity, color hues, shapes
- Quantitative data: position, length, size, color intensity, orientation (to communicate change)

9.6.9 RULE #9: LET THE DATA SPEAK

The most important component of a data visualization is (and always will be) the data. No matter what visual elements are included, or what chart or graph type best presents the data, the data itself should be the focal point of the visualization. Therefore, when viewers or analysts interact with a visualization, the data should be let speak first. So, when building a visualization, distracting elements should be avoided so they do not get in the way of the data. Rather than being force-fed a visualization users should be allowed to interact with the graphic on their own as they move through the visual discovery process.

Visual cues and story points are important aspects of a visualization, but come secondary to the data. Use visual cues strategically as indicators or visual cues to guide the audience and draw their attention, but let the data tell the story, not the design. While interaction and animation can assist the discovery experience, special effects—like 3D—should be avoided. Likewise, if the visual is intended to tell a story, make sure it does so in a way that is in line with your strategy. Narratives help to explain the data in words and adds depth to the story while contextualizing the graphics and embellishing on key points or implications. Aligning the visualization's story with the organization's strategy provides support on both sides, and helps the data speak within a larger, more meaningful, context.

9.6.10 RULE #10: EDIT AND REVISE BEFORE YOU SHARE

The more you design, the more you learn. The better you know your data, the better you can represent it appropriately. It is important to give yourself time to revise and edit iteratively, as well as take the opportunity to share data visualization drafts with other business experts or with candidates from the intended audience. Use this feedback to refine and fine-tune your graphic.

Mistakes are a normal part of life as well as a fundamental part of how science works. Researchers publish their findings along with their data so that other scientists can look for mistakes, flaws, or future areas of research opportunity.

9.7 CONCLUSIONS

This chapter concludes the depth of discussion that we will take on the mechanics and best practices (or, golden rules) of data visualization. More resources can be found in the Appendix. The point here was simply to provide a distilled look at some of the criteria for successfully crafting an accurate and appropriate visualization, and beginning to understand the plethora of options available and the undercurrent of meanings and uses behind them, as well as how some of the visual design principles of the previous chapter are applied and affected when putting data at the forefront of a visual conversation.

Moving forward, the final section of this book focuses on building a foundation for data visualization within a visual culture of data discovery. We will approach this by stitching together each of the conversations of the preceding chapters into meaningful applications on architecting for discovery and establishing data visualization as a core competency within the organization, and, further, how both of these work together to enable visual data discovery by design as part of a visual, data-centric culture.

REFERENCES

Iliisnky, N., Steele, J., 2011. Designing Data Visualization: Intentional Communication From Data to Display. O'Reilly Media, Inc, Sebastopoal, CA.

Murray, S., 2013. Interactive Data Visualization for the Web. O'Reilly Media, Inc, Sebastopoal, CA.

Senge, P., 2006. The Fifth Discipline: The Art and Practice of the Learning Organization. Doubleday, New York, NY.

Shapley, D., 1998. The da Vinci of data. The New York Times. Available from: http://www.nytimes.com/1998/03/30/business/the-da-vinci-of-data.html.

Tal, A., Wansink, B., 2014. Blinded with science: Trivial graphics and formulas increase ad persuasiveness and belief in product efficacy. Public Understanding of Science, 0963662514549688.

Tufte, E., 1983. The Visual Display of Quantitative Information. Graphics Press, New York, NY.

Yau, N., 2011. Open thread: What's the difference between a visualization and an infographics. Flowing Data [blog]. Available from: http://flowingdata.com/2011/01/03/open-thread-whats-the-difference-between-a-visualization-and-an-infographic/.

Building the foundation for data visualization

This section dives into the technical and organizational aspects of building the foundation for data discovery through people, processes, and technologies focused on enabling a culture of visual data discovery and data visualization.

III

Building the foundation for data visualization

This section invites to the foundation for data visualization. It explains the foundation for data visualization and the principles and techniques involved in making effective visual design and data visualization.

Architecting for discovery 10

"Simplicity, is the ultimate sophistication."
—Henry David Thoreau

Today's most disruptive and innovative companies are transforming into data-driven companies, leveraging vast amounts (and new forms) of data into processes that span from research and development to sales and marketing and beyond. In many industries the data is explosive: already the rate of data generation in the life sciences has reportedly exceeded that of even the predictions made by Moore's Law itself, which predicts the steady continuance of technology capacity to double every two years (Higdon et al., 2013). With every piece of detailed raw data now able to be affordably stored, managed, and accessed, technologies that analyze, share, and visualize information and insights will need to be ubiquitously operated at this scale too, and at the performance level required for visual analytics.

For many, this transformation is challenging. Not only is the very fabric of business evolving, but there are many technical considerations that must be addressed if organizations are to continue to earn a competitive advantage from their data, while simultaneously giving their business analysts, data scientists, and other data workers the level of enablement and empowerment they need to contribute meaningfully within the data discovery paradigm. These challenges are not limited to the sheer volume of data to manage, but to other key information challenges that affect everything from data integration agility, to governance, to the discovery process itself, and to using data visualizations successfully across the organization. Much of the traditional (and even new) approaches to data architecture have led to complex data silos (or, isolated data copies) that offer only an incomplete picture into data, along with slowing down the ability to provide access or gain timely insights. Further, the control of intellectual property and compliance with many regulations also poses a bevy of operational, regulatory, and information governance challenges. And, the continued push toward self-service with an emphasis on data visualization and storytelling has resulted in the concept that is at the heart of this book: the visual imperative. When buzzwords like "self-service" or "discovery" come up, they imply a certain amount of freedom and autonomy for analysts and data users of all shapes and forms to be able to work with and shuffle through data to earn new insights. These challenges are only exacerbated by the gradual shift to focus on visual analytics, a form of inquiry in which data that provides insight into solving a problem is displayed in

203

an interactive, graphical manner. Today as data architectures morph and evolve into modern data architectures, their success hinges on the ability to enable governed data discovery coupled with high-performance, speed, and earned competencies in how to leverage meaningful data visualization.

While this text is largely nontechnical, this will undoubtedly be by far the most technical chapter of the book, as we explore key information challenges, architectural considerations, and necessary elements of information management and governance that are top-of-mind for many. That said, I will endeavor to break down these concepts and make them as approachable as possible for those not well-oriented with things like discovery-oriented data architectures, while still adding substance and new learning to those who are.

10.1 KEY INFORMATION CHALLENGES FOR DATA DISCOVERY

Future business successes and discoveries hinge on the ability to quickly and intuitively leverage, analyze, and take action on the information housed within data.

Today's analytic challenges can be separated into three distinct categories: the integration challenge, the management challenge, and the discovery challenge. The answer to these challenges, however, is not the development of new tools or technologies. In fact, the old ways—replication, transformation, or even the data warehouse or new desktop-based approaches to analytics—have met with limited or siloed success: they simply do not afford an agile enough process to keep up with the insurgence of data size, complexity, or disparity. Nor should companies rely on the expectation of increased funding to foster additional solutions. Rather, they should turn to collaborative and transformative solutions that already exist and that are rapidly gaining adoption, acceptance, and use case validation.

Core data challenges have noted that existing data tools and resources for analysis lack integration—or unification of data sources—and can be difficult to both disseminate and maintain (both in terms of deployment and maintaining licensing and upgrades) (Higdon et al., 2013). Further, research literature and testimonies describe another research-impeding challenge: the management challenge posed by defining access rights and permissions to data, addressing governance and compliance rules, and centralizing metadata management. Finally, balancing the need to enable freedom with new data sources and data discovery by the business, while controlling consistency, governing proper contextual usage, and leveraging analytic capabilities are other challenges becoming increasingly in need of mitigation. In this section we will review each of these challenges, and then offer more in-depth solutions in the section after.

10.1.1 THE INTEGRATION CHALLENGE

Having access to data—all data—is a requirement for any data-driven company, as well as a long-standing barrier. In fact, a core expectation of the scientific method—according to the National Science Board data policy taskforce—is the "documentation and sharing of results, underlying data, and methodologies (National Science Board, 2011)." Highly accessible data not only enables the use of vast volumes of data for analysis, but it also fosters collaboration and cross-disciplinary efforts—enabling collective innovation.

In discovery, success depends largely on reliable and speedy access to data and information, and this includes information stored in multiple formats (structured and unstructured) and research locations (on-premise, remote premises, and cloud-based). Further, there must exist the ability to make this data available: to support numerous tactical and strategic needs through standards-based data access and delivery options that allow IT to flexibly publish data. Reducing complexity—smoothing out friction-causing activities—when federating data must also be addressed, and this requires the ability to transform data from native structures to create reusable views for iteration and discovery.

Ultimately, the ability to unify multiple data sources to provide researchers, analysts, and managers with the full view of information for decision-making and innovation without incurring the massive costs and overhead of physical data consolidation in data warehouses remains a primary integration challenge. Thus it is a pertinent barrier to overcome in the next-generation of data management. Further, this integration must be agile enough to adapt to rapid changes in the environment, respond to source data volatility, and navigate the addition of newly created data sets.

10.1.2 THE MANAGEMENT CHALLENGE

Another challenge is the guidance and deposition of context and metadata, and the sustainment of a reliable infrastructure that defines access and permissions and addresses various governance and compliance rules appropriate to the unique needs of any given industry.

Traditional data warehouses enable the management of data context through a centralized approach and the use of metadata, ensuring that users have well-analyzed business definitions and centralized access rights to support self-service and proper access. However, in highly distributed and fast changing data environments—coupled with more need for individualized or project-based definitions and access—the central data warehouse approach falls short and prioritizes the need of the few rather than the many. For most companies, this means the proliferation of sharing through replicated and copied data sets without consistent data synchronization or managed access rights.

In order to mitigate the risks associated with data, enterprise data governance programs are formed to define data owners, stewards, and custodians with policies to provide oversight for compliance and proper business usage of data through account-abilities. The management challenges for data environments such as these include, among others: permission to access data for analysis prior to integration, defining the data integration and relationships properly, and then determining who has access permissions to the resulting integrated data sets. These challenges are no different for data warehousing approaches or data federation approaches; however there is a high degree of risk when environments must resort to a highly disparate integration approach where governance and security are difficult—or nearly impossible—to implement without being centralized.

Management challenges with governance and access permissions are equally procedural and technological: without a basic framework and support of an information governance program, technology choices are likely to fail. Likewise, without a technology capable of fully implementing an information governance program, the program itself becomes ineffective.

10.1.3 **THE DISCOVERY CHALLENGE**

Finally, a third information challenge could be referred as a set of "discovery challenges." Within these challenges are balancing the need to enable the discovery process while still maintaining proper IT oversight and stewardship over data—or, freedom versus control (see Box 10.1)—which is different than the information or management challenge in that it affects not only how the data is federated and aggregated, but in how it is leveraged by users to discover new insights. Because discovery is (often) contingent on user independency, the continued drive for self-service—or,

BOX 10.1 FREEDOM VERSUS CONTROL PARADOX

Data governance is a framework for enabling data-related decision making and accountability that is driven by business needs for risk management, efficiency, and consistency. It is the accountability metric by which organizations make sound decisions and derive business value from their data. Governance is a carefully cultivated combination of people, processes, and technology policies to establish a quality control framework that ensures data is safely and effectively leveraged as an enterprise asset. Ultimately, data governance is a principal component of overall enterprise information management.

As a process, data discovery is sometimes an extension of traditional BI—which focuses on analyzing and verifying data against pre-defined business logic and definitions—with the goal of exploring data to discover, verify, and institutionalize new insights into the enterprise. The fundamental difference between BI and discovery is that BI *begins* with a definition, and discovery *ends* with one (or many). Data discovery requires that analysts pair unique business knowledge with intuitive, self-service tools to power a "fail fast" frictionless process that enables them to access, blend, and move through all available enterprise data both with agility and iteratively. And, among the biggest drivers in discovery is the power of patterns hidden inside the data: the more analysts and users empowered to do data discovery, the more insight opportunity, and thus the more potential business value. Therefore, data governance must be able to scale effectively while maintaining the speed of time to insight.

As constructs, data governance and data discovery seem inherently at odds: IT is held accountable by the business data owners for ensuring that data is accurate, complete, and secure, while users want to freely explore data without IT handcuffs. This is the "freedom versus control" paradox that puts the goals of IT and analysts at a crossroad as CIOs (and CDOs) are charged with balancing data opportunity and risk. However, rather than approaching governed data discovery as rivals, discovery-oriented organizations should instead approach it as a collaborative and proactive process between data owners, business analysts, and IT that sets clear requirements and expectations, opening lines of communication to better understand needs and priorities on both sides.

self-sufficiency—presents further challenges in controlling the proliferation generated by the discovery process as users create and share context. A critical part of the challenge, then, is how to establish a single view of data to enable discovery processes while governing context and business definitions.

Discovery challenges go beyond process and proliferation, too, to include further challenges in providing a scalable solution for enabling even broader sources of information to leverage for discovery, such as data stored (and shared) in the cloud. Analytical techniques and abilities also bring additional challenges to consider, as the evolution of discovery and analysis continues to become increasingly visual, bringing the need for visualization capabilities layered on top of analytics. Identifying and incorporating tools into the technology stack that can meet the needs of integration, analytics, and discovery simultaneously is the crux of the discovery challenge.

10.2 TACKLING TODAY'S INFORMATION CHALLENGES

By embracing a data unification strategy through the adoption and continued refinement and governance of a semantic layer to enable agility, access, and virtual federation of data, as well as by incorporating solutions that take advantage of scalable, cloud-based technologies that provide advanced analytic and discovery capabilities—including data visualization and visual analytics—companies can continue on their journeys to becoming even more data-capable organizations.

10.2.1 CHOOSING DATA ABSTRACTION FOR UNIFICATION

Data abstraction through a semantic layer supports timely, critical decision-making, as different business groups become synchronized with information across units, reducing operational silos and geographic separation. The semantic layer itself provides business context to data to establish a scalable, single source of truth that is reusable across the organization. Abstraction also overcomes data structure incompatibility by transforming data from its native structures and syntax into reusable views that are easy for end users to understand and developers to create solutions. It provides flexibility by decoupling the applications—or consumers—from data layers, allowing each to work independently in dealing with changes. Together, these capabilities help drive the discovery process by enabling users to access data across silos to analyze a holistic view of data.

Further, context reuse will inherently drive higher quality in semantic definitions as more people accept—and refine and localize—the definitions through use and adoption. The inclusion of a semantic layer centralizes metadata management, too, by defining a common repository and catalog between disparate data sources and tools. It also provides a consolidated location for data governance and implementing underlying data security, and centralizes access permissions, acting as a single unified environment to enforce roles and permissions across all federated data sources.

10.2.1.1 Digging into data abstraction

Data abstraction—or, as it is also referred to, data virtualization (DV)—is being recognized as the popular panacea for centralization, tackling challenges for manageability, consistency, and security. For database administrators, data abstraction is good for data management.

At a conceptual level, data abstraction is where a data object is a representation of physical data and the user is not (nor needs to be) aware of its actual physical representation or persistence in order to work with that object. The data abstraction becomes a "mapping" of user data needs and semantic context to physical data elements, services, or code. The benefits of data abstraction, then, are derived from the decoupling of data consumers and data sources. Data consumers only need to be concerned about their access point, and this allows for managing physical data—such as movement, cleansing, consolidation, and permissions—without disrupting data consumers. For example, a database view or synonym mapped to a physical database table is available unchanged to a data consumer, while its definition may need to change, its records reloaded, or its storage location changed.

Since abstracted data objects are mappings captured as metadata, they are very lightweight definitions. They do not persist any data and therefore are quick to create, update, and delete as needed. Data abstraction is so valuable because of its agility to define quickly and relate data from multiple data sources without data movement and persistence. This also represents fast time-to-value, ease of updating and dealing with change, and poses less risk to the business.

The growing reality is that there are more and more data sources of interest available for companies to manage. Integration and consolidation can no longer keep up with the demands of a single repository of integrated, cleansed, and single version of the truth (SVoT). Whenever a technology becomes too complex or numerous to manage, abstraction is the solution to detach the physical world from its logical counterpart. We have seen this trend in nearly every other layer in the technology stack; storage area networks manage thousands of disk drives as logical mount points, and network routing and addresses are represented by virtual local area and private networks (VLAN and VPN). Even operating systems are now virtualized as hypervisors running on servers in the cloud. Databases are no different when it comes to the benefits of abstraction.

With a single data access point—whether persisted or virtualized—companies can ensure data consistency and increase quality through reusability and governance to better monitor and enforce security in a single location, while providing data consumers with simplified navigation.

10.2.1.2 Putting abstraction in context

On the heels of centralization comes the concept of context. A semantic context layer is defined as an abstraction layer (virtualized) where some form of semantic context—usually business terminology—is provided to the data abstraction. Virtualizing database tables or files does not provide semantic context if the virtual data object still represents its original application specific naming of data elements. Semantic context exists when the virtualized data objects represent the context in which the user—or, business user—needs to work with the data. Semantic context layers are considered to be "closed systems" when they are embedded into other applications that benefit from having centralized semantic context and data connectivity, such as in BI tools.

Semantic context layers can exist without virtualized databases. Once again, this centralized repository of business context is used to represent data elements of underlying disparate databases and files. From the users' perspective, the data objects are in familiar business context and the proper usage becomes inherent, while metadata is used to mask the complexity of the data mappings. This is why information delivery applications that have user self-service capability and ad-hoc usage must rely on an abstracted translation layer. Additionally, exposing these "business data objects" drives reusability and therefore consistency across information applications and business decisions, while minimizing rework and the risk of reports referencing the same context utilizing different code.

Another benefit of a semantic context layer is its ability to handle the realization that SVoT is highly unlikely. Realistically, there are multiple perspectives of data, as multiple business context(s) (or abstractions) can be created on the same set of base data. This enables more business specific data objects to be created without having data duplication and transformation jobs to manage. An example is different business interpretations of a customer depending on the business unit or process involved. While data from several operational sources are integrated, the perspectives of a financial customer, sales customer, order management customer, or customer support customer may all have slight variations and involve different attribution of interest to that particular business unit or process.

10.2.1.3 The takeaway

Ultimately, data abstraction is a technique that is a fast and flexible way to integrate data for business usage without requiring data migration or storage. The inclusion of a semantic context layer focuses on business consumption of abstracted data objects in a single, centralized access point for applications within the system where the data stays firmly ensconced in business context.

10.2.2 CENTRALIZING CONTEXT IN THE CLOUD

The growing amount of data not only emphasizes the need for integration of the data, but for access and storage of the data, too. Cloud platforms offer a viable solution through scalable and affordable computing capabilities and large data storage—an Accenture research report that was released in 2013 predicted the cloud trend aptly, stating that cloud computing has shifted from an idea to a core capability, with many leading companies approaching new systems architectures with a "cloud first" mentality (Accenture, 2013). More recently, the International Data Corporation's (IDC) Worldwide Quarterly Cloud IT Infrastructure report, published in October 2015, forecasted that cloud infrastructure spending will continue to grow at a compounded annual growth rate (CAGR) of 15.1% and reach $53.1 billion by 2019 with cloud accounting for about 46% of the total spending on enterprise IT infrastructure (IDC, 2015). This growth is not limited to the scalability and storage cost efficiency of the cloud, but is also influenced by the ability to centralize context, collaborate, and become more agile. Taking the lead to manage context in the cloud is an opportunity to establish much-needed governance early on as cloud-orientation becomes a core capability over time.

With the addition of a semantic layer for unification and abstraction, data stored on the cloud can be easily and agilely abstracted with centralized context for everyone—enabling global collaboration. A multitude of use cases have proven that using the cloud drives collaboration, allowing companies' marketing, sales, and research functions to work more iteratively and with faster momentum. Ultimately, where data resides will have a dramatic effect on the discovery process—and trends support that eventually more and more data will be moved to the cloud (see Box 10.2). Moving abstraction closer to the data, then, just makes sense.

10.2.3 GETTING VISUAL WITH SELF-SERVICE

Providing users with tools that leverage abstraction techniques keeps data oversight and control with IT, while simultaneously reducing the dependency on IT to provide users with data needed for analysis. Leveraging this self-service (or, self-sufficient, as I defined it in chapter: From Self-Service to Self-Sufficiency) approach to discovery with visual analytic techniques drives discovery one step further by bringing data to a broader user community and enabling users to take advantage of emerging visual analytic techniques to visually explore data and curate analytical views for insights. Utilizing visual discovery makes analytics more approachable, allowing technical and nontechnical users to communicate through meaningful, visual reports that can be published (or shared) back into the analytical platform—whether via the cloud or on-premise—to encourage meaningful collaboration. Self-sufficient visual discovery and collaboration will benefit greatly from users not having to wonder where to go and get data—everyone would simply know to go to the one repository for everything.

While traditionally most organizations have relied heavily on explanatory and reporting graphics across many functional areas, there are significant differences in these types of visualizations that impact the ability to visually analyze data and discover new insights. Traditional BI reporting graphics (the standard line, bar, or pie charts) provide quick-consumption communications to summarize salient information. With exploratory graphics—or, advanced visualizations (such as geospatial, quartals, decision trees, and trellis charts)—analysts can visualize clusters or aggregate data; they can also experiment with data through iteration to discover correlations or predictors to create new analytic models. These tools for visual discovery are highly interactive, enabling underlying information to emerge through discovery, and typically require the support of a robust semantic layer.

BOX 10.2 THE CLOUD, CIRCA 2015

Over the past few years, the choice for implementing cloud technologies into the data infrastructure has been primarily limited to the black or white options of public versus private clouds. While private clouds are essentially an optimized, on-premises version of cloud computing, public clouds are generally subscription-based "as-a-service" hosted options that offer additional benefits like readily available, on-demand capacity and the outsourcing of infrastructure management costs. To date, a primary roadblock to public cloud adoption has been trepidation over security—with a laundry list of concerns that involve data breaches, data loss, and potential risks associated with multitenancy.

It is true: a few years ago, cloud security was not great. Today, it is improved through a combination of more mature user requirements and governance processes for cloud access. Even so, recent research has found that security remains at the top of big data concerns for the cloud—with almost 40% of respondents still "extremely concerned."

Concerned or not, cloud adoption inevitably continues as every organization finds its balance. In fact, in research we have conducted at Radiant Advisors throughout the past several years, we have seen decreased security reservations and growing cloud adoption among two traditionally cloud-hesitant, high-security industries: government agencies and the life sciences (in this case, including healthcare). While previously aligning security policies with federal security requirements has been a challenge for government agencies, collaborative efforts between cyber-security and cloud experts are overcoming that through increased confidence in cloud security and the consistent application of security practices that have created a baseline of standards to meet agency expectations. For example, recent joint efforts in federal agencies—like that of FedRAMP (see http://cloud.cio.gov/fedramp), a collaborative effort with cybersecurity and cloud experts from the several US government agencies (including the GSA, NIST, DHS, DOD, NSA, OMB, and the Federal CIO Council) to accelerate the adoption of secure cloud solutions through increased confidence in cloud security and the consistent application of security practices—have helped to create a baseline of standards to level-set cloud service providers to understand federal security requirements and establish a level of confidence for agencies.

Ultimately, we are finding the answer to cloud—public or private—is not all or nothing: it is both. Companies want a blend of the best of both the scalability and cost efficiency of public cloud and the security of private clouds. This is where hybrid cloud technologies—defined as those that provide the resources of the public cloud with the security and management control in the private cloud—are quickly gaining traction.

The IT industry unanimously predicts an increase in hybrid cloud deployments, and hybrid cloud maturity and adoption topped the list of cloud predictions for 2015 and beyond. In December 2014, Accenture and Microsoft launched the Accenture Hybrid Cloud Solution for Microsoft Azure to help enterprises build and manage enterprise-wide cloud infrastructure and applications. Likewise, Cisco began 2015 by introducing its InterCloud Fabric to support multi-hypervisor and multicloud with the freedom to place workloads as-needed with the same network security and control polices in public clouds that are enforced in the data center. This points not just to hybrid cloud maturity, but also its role in infrastructure optimization. "Because Internet-as-a-Service, Platform-as-a-Service, and Software-as-a-Service optimize point requirements wonderfully, adoption has been tremendous. But now that your apps, data, and infrastructure are everywhere, optimizing this hybrid mix is your next opportunity," Bob Eve, Director of Technical Marketing in Cisco's Data Virtualization business unit, mentioned to me in email. "From business down, start by connecting your data. From infrastructure up, start by aligning system management."

While there are many options to explore, the choice will be *which*—not *if*—cloud type has a place in your enterprise. Of course, it is important to remember that hybrid cloud is new and complex, and capable organizations are likely to still be looking for instructions, rules, methodologies, or success case studies prior to adoption.

10.3 DESIGNING FOR FRICTIONLESS

Friction, and the concept of frictionless, was introduced earlier in chapter: Improved Agility and Insights Through (Visual) Discovery. To revisit it here briefly, friction is caused by the incremental events that add time and complexity to discovery through activities that slow down the process. These are activities that IT used to do for business users and which add time and complexity to the discovery process, interrupting efficiency and extending the time to insight. For example, in discovery, these friction-laden activities could be requesting access to new data or requesting access to an approved discovery environment.

Friction, then, is a speed killer—it adds time to discovery and interrupts the "train of thought" ability to move quickly through the discovery process and earn insight. Friction*less* is the antithesis of friction. As friction decreases, so, too, does time to insight (speed increases). Therefore, to decrease friction is to increase the speed at which discoveries—and thus insights—can be made. That is the concept of frictionless—to pluck out as many of those interruptions as possible and smooth out the discovery process.

We can conceptualize iterative discovery as a continuous loop of five compounding activities, where the goal is to remove as much friction from the process as possible (see Figure 10.1).

In the first stage, analysts get access and begin working with data. While they cannot yet justify the value of the discovery process as insights are yet to be discovered, they nevertheless expect access to data in a low barrier process that requires high-performance (like speed, access, and diversity of data source). After accessing data, analysts begin to explore and require tools to quickly assess, profile, and interrogate data—including big data. As they move into blending, analysts require agility and access to integrate various sources and types of data to enhance and unify it, and ultimately enrich insight opportunities.

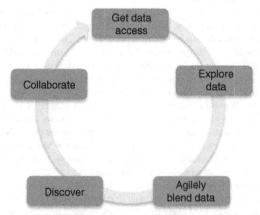

FIGURE 10.1 This Visual Illustrates the Five Compounding Steps in an Iterative, Frictionless Discovery Process

These first three steps are the initial preparation phases that fuel discovery (though they typically take the most time). Only after data can be accessed, explored, and blended, can analysts begin to build data and analytic models and visually work with data. Once insights are discovered (or not), analysts can then collaborate with other users for verification to find additional insights, story-tell, and cross-learn. This collaboration is how analysts share knowledge; validate insight accuracy and meaningfulness; and leverage peer knowledge and insights to avoid potential errors and inaccuracies. It is also the governance checkpoint in the discovery process to engage in postdiscovery assessment processes. We will discuss these checkpoints in the following sections.

10.4 ENABLING GOVERNED DATA DISCOVERY

Business-driven data discovery is becoming fundamental for organizations to adapt to the fast-changing technology landscape in nearly every industry. Companies must explore, iterate, and extract meaningful and actionable insights from vast amounts of new and increasingly diverse internal and external data. A formalized discovery process fills the gap between business and IT: subject experts are empowered in their business domain, and IT actively supports and takes a data management role in facilitating the needs of the business. Without recognizing and governing this process, business users struggle—or worse, to work around polices for data governance and IT data management.

Recent technologies, like Apache Hadoop, have significantly lowered the technical barriers to ingesting multiple varieties and significant volumes of data for users. However, one of the biggest barriers to discovery is still providing controlled access to data, and data governance remains a charged topic. To achieve the maximum benefits of discovery, analysts must be able to move quickly and iteratively through the discovery process with as little friction—and as much IT-independence—as possible. Empowered with new discovery tools, more data, and more capabilities, ensuring data and analytics are both trustworthy and protected becomes more difficult and imperative. This becomes a careful balance of freedom versus control, and brings the role of governance to the forefront of the discovery conversation.

Data governance is not a one-size-fits-all set of rules and policies: every organization (or even various groups within organizations) requires its own rules and definitions for discovery for its unique culture and environment. Enabling governed data discovery begins with robust and well-planned governance to support rather than hinder discovery. Likewise, governance programs will continue to evolve, and discovery-oriented policies should be designed with the least amount of restrictions upfront as possible, and then refined iteratively as discovery requirements become further defined. This section discusses and explains how to manage the barriers and risks of self-service and enable agile data discovery across the organization by extending existing data governance framework concepts to the data-driven and discovery-oriented business.

10.4.1 GOVERNANCE CHECKPOINTS IN DISCOVERY

Data governance frameworks rely on the active participation of data owners, data stewards, and data management (IT) as cornerstones of accountability, knowledge, and implementation of policies. In my work with Radiant Advisors, we identified three critical checkpoint areas in the data discovery cycle where data governance should be in place to enable as self-sufficient and frictionless an experience as possible (Figure 10.2).

The first checkpoint opportunity is at the beginning of data discovery. This involves streamlining data access to data with the ability to grant, chaperone, and receive access rights, thereby enabling faster data exploration in an approved discovery environment. The second collaboration checkpoint occurs after discovery and is necessary to verify and validate insights, and determines the designation of context for new data definitions, relationships, and analytic models. In the third and last checkpoint, governed discoveries are intended for the purposeful and appropriate sharing of insights (both internally and externally) to ensure that they are leveraged, continued, and communicated appropriately. Now, we will explore each of these areas in detail.

10.4.1.1 Checkpoint #1: to enable faster data exploration

Data discovery begins with an analyst's need for unfettered access to search for insights hidden within untapped data, relationships, or correlations. This need for access is compounded by the expectation for quick, unrestricted access to data in

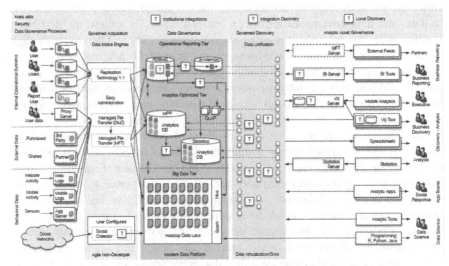

FIGURE 10.2 Radiant Advisors' Modern Data Platform Enabling Governed Data Discovery

---

BOX 10.3 SMALL OR BIG DATA FOR DISCOVERY?

Older data science routines promised that proper statistical sampling of a population data set was enough to make accurate predictions. Outliers were aggregated and prediction could focus on more significant data clusters. However, data-driven companies are now very interested in the outliers themselves as business opportunities to discover, understand, and exploit in the long-tail strategy. With today's data discovery horsepower we now have the ability to do descriptive analytics on the entire population and take a larger perspective into analyzing data. The more data available to access, use, and blend for discovery, the more ability to extract and exploit valuable meanings and insights. Therein is the advantage of big versus small data for discovery: outliers have more meaning than they used to. Data-driven companies will think beyond the curve and place a larger premium on looking at the data overlooked by old statistical sampling methodologies to find new opportunities for the business in previously unexplored data.

---

discovery environments while working through the discovery process. For faster data exploration, policies should be designed related to the discovery environment itself—how, when, where, and under what circumstances analysts should leverage personal desktops, temporary discovery workspaces, virtual environments, or even cloud-based environments. Each environment has its set of benefits and drawbacks, and some environments may be rendered inapplicable simply because they are not already a part of an organizational data infrastructure and cannot justify additional effort or expense.

First, from Microsoft Excel to the current generation of easily adopted desktop discovery tools, the personal desktop is a long-standing discovery environment. Its use for discovery grants instant environment access for users but is inherently limited by space restrictions and likely unable to facilitate all data needs (see Box 10.3) and requires data download or extraction. Also, personal desktop use for discovery must also be policed by supplemental security policies (like desktops not allowing data be taken off-site, or procedures for IT remote wipe capabilities). Beyond personal desktops, users may request a temporary workspace within an existing database (like a sandbox or section of the data lake) to act as an isolated and quarantined area for discovery. Of course, to leverage these low technology barriers for discovery, the database must already exist in the architecture. If not, a data virtualization discovery environment could be designed to access and integrate disparate heterogeneous physical databases. However, again if these are not already part of the existing technology architecture they can be timely and cost-intensive to establish. Finally, cloud-based discovery environments can be sanctioned for low-cost on-demand discovery environments. While beyond personal desktops clouds may be the fastest time to enable a discovery environment, they will likely come with other governance implications, such as moving internal data to a cloud environment or the eventual inability to bring external data back into the enterprise until it has been validated. For any governed discovery environment, there must be timelines in place for permitted data access in discovery. Once this timeframe has expired, processes and rules for properly purging sample data sets must be established. There is more than one way for discovery to exist and prosper in the enterprise, and comprehensive governance ensures that friction is able to be contained by data management.

Beyond policies for discovery environments, access policies should also be defined for individual data source categories. These include requesting access to internal systems (relational databases, proprietary databases, web logs, etc.), third party acquired data sets, public data (eg, social), and other Internet data sources. The role of personally-collected, independent user data in discovery will also require consideration for its validation and restriction, as will policies and processes for access related to fetching data from disparate sources.

Defining policies for data access and discovery environments may expand the roles of existing data owners and data stewards, as well as bring to light the possibility of defining these new roles for new types of data, like social data and data generated from the Internet of Things (IoT). An interesting paradigm for data ownership and stewardship is that the analysts doing discovery may already be the unofficial stewards of previously "unowned" social or IOT data. While social data acquisition vendors and solutions may already address concerns regarding privacy and retention in social platforms, new data owners and stewards will need to pay close attention to social data used in discovery. Moreover, it will be the data owners' responsibility to decide and define how (or if) blending of data sets should be created. For instance, there may be situations where data blending is outlawed by data source contracts, or there may be concerns about blending anonymous, invalidated, or other social data with internal data for discovery purposes. The level of governance and veracity of data changes within the realm of big data will depend on the data source, as well as the analyst using the data and the context in which it is being used. There should also be considerations for data masking and decisions on which data fields should be hidden, the level to which data should be obfuscated, and how this impacts the usability of the data for analysis and discovery.

10.4.1.2 Checkpoint #2: at the time of insight

Once users have been given data and access to a discovery environment and an insight has been discovered—whether a new context or definition, extending an existing data model, or a new correlated subgroup of data of interest—a governance checkpoint should be in place for verification and validation. Before an insight can be broadly consumed and leveraged throughout the enterprise, it must be reviewed to ensure it is true, accurate, and applicable.

This postdiscovery governance assessment is the catalyst that begins the movement of an insight from discovery to institutionalized definition. A collaborative approach to verification is one option. In this approach an insight is sourced among peers, subject matter experts, and others in the organization to validate that it is meaningful, correct, and free of errors. Data stewards may also be involved to build consensus on definition(s) and verify context and where context is applicable. Data owners (and/or stewards) may also be asked to bless insights with approval before they are shared or consumed (meanwhile the insight remains in local usage adding value to the business in quarantine until this assessment is completed).

Following postdiscovery assessment comes postdiscovery designation of new definitions and context. This is twofold: new context should be given designation within the enterprise (local vs global) along with a shelf life (static vs dynamic) for applicability. To the former, a continuum of enterprise semantic context exists that ranges from local, to workgroup, to department, division, line of business, or enterprise. The more global the definition in the enterprise, the more broadly the data will be consumed and a data owner should be involved with the verification and designation process. To the latter, an insight may only be valid for a project or other short-term need, or it may be a new standard within long-standard enterprise key performance indicator (KPI) metrics. Over time, as underlying data changes the definitions and integrations behind the context, the discovery's shelf life will be an important determinant in how data management integrates the discovery.

Being discovery-led enables the decoupling between business users and data management. However, once postdiscovery governance is complete and the designation of semantic context defined, data management must decide how to manage the definition going forward. Data management will make the decision whether the discovery should live physically or virtually in the integration architecture (ie, move an abstracted discovery into a physical database, or take a discovery done physically in a lake and abstract it), and how best to shift a discovery from a discovery environment to a production environment and maintain ongoing data acquisition so that a long-term insight will continue to be valid.

10.4.1.3 Checkpoint #3: for institutionalizing and ongoing sharing

Once an insight has been discovered, vetted by the data owners and stewards, and moved under the purview of data management, a governance checkpoint should be included before new discoveries are communicated into the organization. While this may already exist as part of the normal governance process, consider these three key areas to focus on as checkpoints for new discoveries.

First is capturing newly discovered insight metadata (from reasoning, to logic, to lineage) for search and navigation in order to ensure that the people who need the data can find it—including other (and future) discoverers. Data owners need to define the continued access and security of the insight, including its use in exchange with partners and suppliers. This is a valid point to consider because while discovery may have identified a special cluster or group, the new data may be unable to be shared with others externally. Finally, with transparency both internal and external to the organization continuing to earn a sharpened focus in an increasingly data-dependent culture, additional policies and guidelines on how data can be shared and through what means should be defined. One relevant example is how data is shared via live, public social streams, and decisions on what—if any—filters should be in place. Internal collaboration technologies and/or platforms are likely to be required, too.

10.5 CONCLUSIONS

Evolving existing data governance programs to enable architected governed data discovery provides the opportunity to leverage proven principles and practices as guidelines to provide governance-in-action that effortlessly empowers discovery-oriented analysts, project, and business needs instead of restricting them unnecessarily due to a lack of a well thought out approach. The new discovery culture brings along with it a set of expectations by analysts who want to move with agility through data that is acquired from all types of data in order to iterate, integrate, and explore a frictionless discovery process. Designing data governance to enable governed data discovery should be approached as an agile and collaborative process between data owners, users, and IT with a common goal. In order for discovery to reach its maximum potential, there is an inherent amount of freedom required, and policies should enable speed, access, and exploration, rather than restrict it. Therefore, as data governance policies are defined, they should focus on writing rules that are looser and higher-level, while providing the intent and the framework for how to conduct discovery.

Of course, data governance is a continuously evolving process that identifies new policies, modifies existing ones, and retires policies and roles as they become obsolete or out-of-date. As companies begin to enable governed data discovery across the organization, they should expect this to be a starting point. Like discovery itself, new data governance policies will also be discovered based on the iterative discovery model and data governance principles. Fortunately, the data governance evolution is being aided by tools and products in the market that are also tackling these challenges for their customers to produce the necessary capabilities and artifacts being required by data governance programs. Therefore, a tool's data governance capabilities are becoming an essential part of evaluations and no longer optional to its primary purpose. With some tools, you will find a thorough data governance strategy that infuses your in-house program with new ideas and proven best practices.

10.6 ANATOMY OF A VISUAL DISCOVERY APPLICATION

When we begin to think about architecting for visual discovery, perhaps it is more efficient to pick through the pieces necessary to build the correct framework, rather than trying to assemble it from the ground up. We can consider this as a more surgical approach, if you will, to pull apart the anatomy of a visual discovery application, based on the several tightly coupled components (or interdependent layers) between the data and the end user that are required to leverage advanced analytics algorithms and advanced visualizations for business analytics.

Some companies will have data engineers, mathematicians, and even visualization experts working with their own tools to create advanced analytic visualizations because a specific solution might not otherwise exist in the market. However, this is a slow, costly, and risky approach (for maintainability) that may be undertaken by companies that either have the infrastructure to support the initiative, or possibly by those that simply do not realize the risks and complexity involved. Typically, a company will have one or two layers already to leverage and will instead seek out the advanced visualization or analytics tool, and then create more custom code to move and transform the data between data stores. Here are the core three layers of architecture needed for a visual discovery application:

Advanced visualizations layer: Basic visualizations are simply not powerful enough to see the richness and colors within massive amounts of data. While there are many basic and proven chart and graph types available in common tools, the ability to see more data with the most visual intuitive diversity is needed. Advanced data visualization types employ "lenses" to componentize the visual, yet still have it tightly integrated with the output of the proper data analytics routine.

Advanced analytics layer: This layer and capability represents the complexity of employing the correct analytic routines, SQL data access, and mapping the output with the advanced visualization. Shielding the customer from complex SQL (ie, both correct and properly tuned to execute well) is highly valuable to the user experience.

Data access layer: The reality for most companies is that the required data sets are still in disparate systems—possibly in a data mart or data warehouse. There can be data integration routines developed to consolidate the needed data into a consolidated database or analytic sandbox; however this has proven to be highly inefficient in dealing with system/data volatility and incurring additional time and cost. The appropriate solution is to have a data virtualization layer with proper implementation to maintain a data object repository.

10.7 THE CONVERGENCE OF VISUAL ANALYTICS AND VISUAL DISCOVERY

Over the past few years, the data industry has become increasingly visual with the maturity of robust visualization tools geared toward enriching visual analysis for analytics and visual data discovery. In many ways, visual discovery has been seen as the catalyst to breaking open the potential of data in the most intuitive and self-service way possible. However, as an interactive process of exploration that embodies the use of visual technologies to augment human capabilities and prompt the user to uncover new insights and discoveries, there is still much to define in terms of the use cases for and core competencies needed in visual data discovery. Likewise, there are still lingering ambiguities over the nuances, roles, and processes of visual analysis as a function that uses visual data representations to support various analytical tasks.

While this chapter has touched lightly on data visualization and visual analytics, the next chapter will dive into this in more detail with the introduction of the Data Visualization Competency Center™.

REFERENCES

Accenture, 2013. Technology Vision. "Every Life Sciences Business is a Digital Business."

Higdon, R., Haynes, W., Stanberry, L., Stewart, E., Yandl, G., Howard, C., Broomall, W., Kolker, N., Kolker, E., 2013. Unraveling the complexities of life sciences data. Big Data 1 (1), 42–50.

IDC, 2015. Worldwide Quarterly Cloud IT Infrastructure Tracker. Available from: http://www.idc.com/getdoc.jsp?containerId=prUS25946315.

National Science Board, 2011. "Digital Research Data Sharing and Management."

Data visualization as a core competency

11

"Design is a way of life, a point of view. It involves the whole complex of visual communications: talent, creative ability, manual skill, and technical knowledge. Aesthetics and economics, technology and psychology are intrinsically related to the process."
—Paul Rand

Data visualization offers a tremendous opportunity to reach insights from data by leveraging our intrinsic hard-wiring to understand complex information visually. A well-designed, meaningful visual delivers immediate, actionable, and aesthetically intriguing insights at a glance and offers a tool to tell an engaging and meaningful data story. With increasing self-service capabilities and functionality available in the many accessible and intuitive tools today, more business-oriented users are being enabled to independently create and share their visual discoveries.

However, successful data visualization goes beyond providing a visual representation of data. It requires using the right kind of graphicacy technique to correctly interpret and analyze the data, as well as employing the right combination of carefully distilled design principles to curate a meaningful story. Ineffective or poorly designed data representations delivered by users who lack formal data analysis and design education can distort the message of the data, or lose the attention of the stakeholder altogether. This creates business risk: incorrect or inadequate visual communication can squander the opportunity to take action on a new insight or worse—cause the business to take action in the wrong direction. Further, with the consumerization of approachable data visualization tools, users have more tool choice and a bigger say in purchase decisions, and vendors can accommodate more pervasive tool deployments by providing near-immediate value department by department (commonly referred to as a "land and expand" strategy). Combined, these have a significant impact on the maturity of data visualization in the organization as well as how they are incorporated as information assets while mitigating the potential risks of self-service data visualization.

This chapter collapses our previous discussions on visual design and the Golden Rules of data visualization, along with the need for governance, guided visual discovery, and earned competency in using data visualization, to introduce the role of the Data Visualization Competency Center (DVCC). We will discuss how data-driven organizations can articulate a set of core competencies focusing on visual design principles, data visualization best practices, and by cultivating a culture of collaboration, and how to begin the journey to socializing and implementing a productive DVCC within the organization.

221

11.1 DATA VISUALIZATION BUSINESS BENEFITS AND RISKS

The rapid introduction of user-friendly features and functionality in business intelligence and analytics solutions is enabling more users than ever before to explore, create, and share insights. This makes data visualization a must-have tool for the modern data analyst. We know that data visualizations foster visual data literacy; we know that they can be useful mechanisms to tell a meaningful, actionable data story. We also know that visual discovery is affected by the power of numbers, and that the more users that are empowered to work with visualizations as part of the discovery process, the more opportunities to discover insights exist. This puts a premium on self-service. Unfortunately, it also creates risk, and alongside creative freedom comes with a required awareness of the importance of visual design principles as well as how to appropriately and effectively use visualizations to represent data accurately to deliver unique and purposeful analytic assets.

To make the most of the promise of data visualization, businesses must find a way to manage the risks of self-service data visualization while still capitalizing on its potential to allow a broader, more diverse group of analysts to reach interactive insights at the speed of thought and communicate new insights and discoveries directly back to the business. To begin a fruitful discussion on how any organization can benefit from an organized competency around data visualization, let us start off by taking a moment to compare both the business benefits and the risks of using data visualization.

11.1.1 BENEFITS

Data visualization is one of the most significant technologies of the 21st century, providing an approach to reimagining data as a whole—how to read, interpret, and understand all sorts of new data—and collectively introducing companies to a new way of seeing and interacting with data. With a higher premium on self-service, data visualization tools allow analysts to reach interactive insights at the speed of thought and reduce the burden on IT. We can use data visualizations to tell evocative data stories and communicate new insights and discoveries directly back to the business. Further, the ability to rapidly generate meaningful data visuals is one way that organizations are earning actionable insights needed to immediately take action on a business problem or opportunity. And, with the availability of more visualization tools than ever before, best practices are evolving and clear business use cases are becoming solidified. In an article penned by TIBCO Spotfire's Senior VP and General Manager, Brian Gentile (2014) eloquently summed up this host of benefits by remarking that data visualization "fosters a new business language" by engaging users with data to open up new ways of looking at the business and enabling a broad audience of analytic users in the "quest for greater performance."

Some of these specific benefits include the ability to:

- Reach interactive insights at the speed of thought
- Reduce the burden on IT

- Tell stories and communicate new discoveries
- Fingerprint new information assets
- Foster a new business language

11.1.2 RISKS

In addition to the list of benefits and opportunities provided by self-service data visualization there is also a set of emergent business risks that demand attention. For one, without awareness of visual design principles, unbalanced visuals created without consideration for color use, pattern recognition, or other visual design cues may unintentionally distort the meaning of the data—or lead to the generation of chart junk or eye candy devoid of true value. Second, with more enablement and access to data through optimized self-service tools, users who lack formal education in data analysis may introduce the risk for the business to take action on poorly designed visualizations that misinterpret or misrepresent data. Because of tool prolificacy and the emergence of freemium models and other easily accessible tools, a data visualization democracy within the organization may result in an oversaturation of visual assets. Worse, competing user priorities, compounded by the consumerization of tools, may bloat the tool ecosystem in the organization, causing confusion, inconsistency, and a lack of oversight that govern how data visualizations are created, used, and shared within the business.

11.2 INTRODUCING THE DATA VISUALIZATION COMPETENCY CENTER

As data visualization continues to take an increasingly important seat at the data table, now is the time to introduce the Data Visualization Competency Center—the DVCC—to take BI further, provide best practices, and fingerprint data visualizations as unique digital assets in the business (Box 11.1).

The DVCC should be seen as an extension of the Business Intelligence Competency Center (BICC)—a permanent, formal organizational structure tasked with advancing and promoting the effect use of BI (or in the DVCC's case, data visualization) in support of the organization's overall BI strategy that includes data visualization. Similar to how the BICC is a cross-functional organizational team with defined tasks, roles, responsibilities, and processes designed to support the use of BI across the organization, the DVCC should likewise focus on how data visualization is designed, created, and leveraged. Its central location is pivotal in driving and supporting an overall information strategy, and serves as a beacon by which to organize and coordinate efforts, reduce redundancy, and increase infectiveness that can be coordinated throughout the entire organization. And, like the BICC, the knowledge amassed in the DVCC should be balanced with how it is embedded into the business. This will help to avoid the "ivory tower" effect that may cause the business to reject a competency center and open lines of communication and collective learning by providing an environment by which to share successes as well as lessons learned going forward.

BOX 11.1 INSPIRATION FOR THE DVCC

The original DVCC research began as the result of a seminar I delivered in Rome, Italy for Technology Transfer in November 2014 when an attendee posed the question: "how do I govern all of the visualizations being rapidly created and shared within my organization?" With this question top-of-mind, the embryotic framework for what a DVCC could be was framed, and in January 2015 an Insights-as-a-Service provider helped to take the research to market. When the original research was aired via a webinar, several hundred live listeners joined to hear the release (some of which have gone on to build their own DVCCs).

During the initial webinar, I asked the audience to participate in a live poll and select which of the three competency areas of the DVCC—design, graphicacy, or collaboration—they felt was the most pertinent to data visualization success within the organization. The results of the poll as collected in the webinar are shown in Figure 11.1. While collaboration (represented by a feedback loop icon on the far right) received a noticeably lower amount of responses than the other two options, design (with the icon of a person standing in front of a visualization) and graphicacy (with the icon of a person inside a cogged wheel) received relatively equal results. These results coincide with a more universal industry standing, because while there is a wealth of long-standing literature that covers the technical aspects of both design and visualization, the collaborative, social, and organizational aspects are less studied. It would be safe to assume, then, that these are the two areas that demand the most in-depth level of attention for which the DVCC should respond and react to.

Which do you feel is most important for the DVCC?

🖵 Respond at PollEv.com/lindyryan
∞ Answers to this poll are anonymous

FIGURE 11.1 Live Poll Results From the Initial DVCC Research Release

The establishment of a DVCC serves a trifold mission.

First, this competency center provides education on visual design principles so users will understand the role of design and the key cognitive elements affected by data visualization.

Second, it leverages data graphicacy best practices to facilitate guided data discovery through recommendations and proven standards for understanding types of data and the best ways to visually present them.

Third, a competency center focused on the effective use of data visualization should cultivate a collaborative learning culture that enables a review network for newly created data visualizations before they are provided to the business.

A DVCC will support the use of effective self-service data visualization by providing best practices, standards, and education on how these information assets should be designed, created, and leveraged in the business. Ultimately the DVCC houses the essence of governed data visualization, but replaces the red tape of policies with a culture of education and collaboration.

And, though the exact mission statement of the DVCC will be adapted to fit the needs and culture of any individual organization to some extent (which we will look at in further detail later in this chapter), the mission of the DVCC frames three unchanging areas that support its mission in developing and fostering continued development and competency in the business. These can be articulated as follows:

- Educate users on visual design principles and the cognitive elements affected by data visualization, and document decisions to provide standards on how design should be used uniformly across the organization in accordance with its corporate culture and brand.
- Provide best practices and proven standards for understanding types of data and how to visually present them according to the analytical processes and tasks they are intended to support.
- Foster a culture of communication, collaboration, and collective learning that enables a review network for newly created data visualizations, consistency, and reliability of visual assets (including individual visualizations and dashboards), and fosters enterprise-wide communication and sharing of resources and learning opportunities.

Each of these areas will be discussed in the sections that follow.

11.2.1 DECISION DESIGN STANDARDS

When thinking in terms of design, a token of advice is this: do not mistake beautiful data visualization for effective data visualization. Remember, visual design hinges not on embellishment, but on removing and simplifying until nothing stands between the visual's message and its audience. Be alert not only to cognitive biases, but also to designer bias as visualization designers, too, have their own ideas about what constitutes good design and build these assumptions into how they visually represent data (Dix et al., 2010). Personally, I have an affinity for working with circles—they please me—and tend to gravitate toward things like donut charts or arc, network, or sunbursts diagrams, while some of my peers actively shy away from these chart types.

Chapter: The Importance of Visual Design was dedicated to reviewing, in greater detail, many of the important elements of visual design that should be accounted for within visualization, and to discuss them again would only be redundant without adding any additional value. Instead, let us simply take the opportunity to briefly revisit a few specific design elements worthy of making a decision on when establishing design standards for the DVCC to help guide thinking on a tester set of important decision points later.

First, color activates the visual cortex of the brain—a process called perceptual pop-out—and is one of the first cognitive processes enlisted when analyzing visual imagery. The wrong colors can mislead, confuse, or misinterpret information. Color, too, should not be relied upon to convey meaning; likewise, it should not be used for decorative or noninformational purposes. Instead, use color sparingly and understand the importance of color selection. Beyond color, consider the layout of visual elements according to the visual processing horsepower of the brain. Organize visuals in a manner that facilitates natural eye movement—or, reading gravity. If this concept is difficult to grasp, think of it as the narrative flow of dashboards: how analyses can be grouped together based on the logical sequence of layered data understanding. This is data hierarchy, which places high-level visualizations to the left and detail visualizations to the right and bottom. Finally, use white space to avoid visual clutter and reduce unnecessary visual elements, like redundant chart labels or overused boxes or lines to separate data. Here, consider Gestalt principles that emphasize simplicity in shape, color, and proximity and look for continuation, closure, and figure-ground principles.

When establishing your design standards, ask and make decisions on the following questions:

- How color will be used? How will we select our color palette? (Custom? Default in the tool? Aligned to corporate colors?)
- How will we set standards for other design elements, like lines or shapes?
- How will visuals be organized on a dashboard? What is most important?
- When/where/how will we use lines in visualizations, in dashboards?
- What shapes will we use, and how will they be used as visual cues?
- Which typography choices will we use, and how will they be assigned for various purposes?
- Will we use icons? If so, which ones?
- Are there standards for photos versus illustrations? How will they be used?

11.2.2 ESTABLISH INTERNAL DATA VISUALIZATION BEST PRACTICES

While design is an integral part of effective data visualization, the data should always come first. And, though data visualization does not equal visual analysis, a good visual begins with understanding data. (The important differentiator between the two comes down to action. Data visualization is a tool, which uses charts and graphs to depict information, whereas visual analysis is a process—one that is interactive and requires participation (action) on behalf of the user or business analyst to discover new insights.)

There are many types of data and ways to visualize them, but we can distill that conversation down to two key best practices to keep in mind when visualizing data. Moreover, given the vast array of visualization choices available, it can be a challenging task for users (especially those who are less familiar with visual data analysis) to choose the most appropriate one. Some are highly information intensive and very complex, whereas others give less information but are more informative for a novice (Dix et al., 2010). In either case, first, understand the data you want to visualize and, second, know what kind of information you want to communicate. At a basic level, data can be classified into three primary groups. We reviewed these in a bit more depth in chapter: The Data Visualization Continuum, but let us briefly summarize them here again. Qualitative data—often used interchangeably with categorical data—is a measurement expressed by natural language description (eg, favorite color = orange). This type of data can be further broken down into nominal data—categories where there is not a natural ordering (gender, state, sport, etc.), and ordinal variables, where a category does have order (size, attitudes, etc.) but cannot be aggregated. Unlike qualitative data, quantitative data is expressed in numbers and is always associated with a scale measure—these are metrics that can be counted, ordered, and aggregated.

For each type of data there is a diagnostic of visualizations best suited for specific analytic needs, and we reviewed a sample in this text already. To develop a core competency, the DVCC should leverage mechanisms to provide guided data visualization as guardrails for users without (or with limited) data analysis background. This includes the use of collective intelligence and/or recommendation engines alongside established best practices to "self-check" graphic selections, and to ensure that the best visualization option is selected for the data and the insight goal in mind. Truly guided visual discovery will also be an education enabler by providing learning opportunities for nontechnical analysts to understand their analysis step-by-step.

As decision points for building a set of internal best practices that align to proven data visualization principles, the following questions are helpful:

- What types of visualizations will be used?
- What type of analytical purpose(s) are visualizations intended to serve?
- Are these the same types of visualizations for desktop-based dashboards as for mobile?
- Who will educate users on data types and graphicacy standards?
- Who will verify data is used in context?
- Who will "approve" a data visualization is designed accurately and correctly?

11.2.3 DEVELOP A COLLABORATIVE, COLLECTIVE CULTURE

As with any type of information, data visualizations created and used in isolation can become their own version of data silos, and we should not overlook the need to collaborate with subject matter experts and engage in group critiques before publishing new—or revised—visuals. A successful data visualization should be able to be understood by its intended audience from a position of personal insight and experience—this is how the visualization tells a meaningful story. Collaboration helps ensure the visualization does tell a story—and the one the author anticipated it to tell.

The benefits of collaboration have long been a part of organizational leadership strategies. Collaboration fosters continuous improvement and collective learning, and it provides an embedded feedback tool to elaborate and expand on ideas across the organization in a meaningful way. Organizations that have a genuine passion for data are more likely to cultivate a culture of collaboration to uncover more, better, and faster data correlations and reveal new answers and insights from their data. This is driven by the willingness to ask questions, engage in discussion, and approach data visualization in a way that furthers collaborative learning within the organization. Further, from a data management perspective, for any analysis tool to be truly useful to an organization it must be updated constantly to account for changes, and it must be protected from falling out of sync when a number of collaborators access the same data. This, too, applies to the advent of data visualizations as unique information assets in the business. Of course, it may not be feasible or practical to put every single new visualization through a quality-check or review process, but at a core library of governed visualization assets should be maintained—perhaps at the enterprise level, or those used to measure key strategic KPIs.

The DVCC should provide an environment that fosters a collaborative culture and engages the organization as a community. Many experts agree that community effort is required for visualization (Dix et al., 2010). Mechanisms for peer feedback—like the ability to leave comments, favorite or like designs, and share insights—provide the opportunity for users to identify and address issues with data visualizations before presenting them to the business, and to put the audience first in storytelling by crafting data narratives with goals in mind. This is also where collaboration provides a framework for quality—by giving users (and data owners) the opportunity to sanity check new data visualizations.

11.2.4 A BRIEF WORD ON MOBILE

The priority of and use case for mobile will differ from industry to industry, and from company to company. It may even exist on a broad spectrum within any single company, as different needs from different audiences are reflected within how they approach and use mobile capabilities for data visualization—from executives who want to see and consume data on a mobile-optimized dashboard while traveling, to field reps who need to visually interact with data to perform analysis on the go, to users who regularly interact with dashboards or visual reporting on their smartphones, and anywhere in between. Even mobile itself is not limited to one form factor, and the use of mobile as a conduit for data visualization can be further constrained by device (tablets, smartphones, and so on).

It would be overly insistent to suggest that data visualization decisions or standards should be approached from a mobile-first perspective, so we will not spend a substantial amount of attention on them here. However, this does not mean that mobile (again, depending on its priority within the organization) should not be considered at all. For example, think about how mobile might alter or affect different dashboard layouts—how will filters align to individual visuals or the dashboard as a whole, or how will elements like shapes, lines, or other visual cues translate to the confines of a mobile screen? Are the data visualizations themselves optimized for mobile delivery, or would another chart type be better suited? These are just a few of the types of questions that warrant attention when making decisions and setting standards to be carried out by the DVCC.

11.3 **TOOLS FOR THE DVCC**

As with any data-oriented tool, from architecture to storage to analytics, there is no one "magic bullet" solution that can be pulled straight out of the box and put into practice. Relying on any industry vendor or tool to support the DVCC would be an irresponsible oversight on behalf of the business for many reasons. Many tools provide support on design consideration (like snap-to-grid dashboarding widgets that align charts and add white space buffer, or default color palettes that are programmed to react to measures and dimensions accordingly) or provided guided analytics or recommendations for building data visualization (such as recommending visualization types based on the data selected for analysis, or remove the capability to select certain chart types based on the same). Some do even offer robust collaboration environments with governance features (including security, data management controls, and internal monitoring as well as the ability to like, share, or comment on drafted visualizations). However, a tool alone is simply not a vehicle for leading or providing the ongoing care and feeding of a rich visual data culture such as facilitated by the DVCC.

While the strengths of any tool should be leveraged into the operations of the DVCC, the organization itself should actively act to bolster these internally as well as to proactively and aggressively fill gaps. If the decisions discussed in the previous sections are the "processes," and the DVCC itself the people, then these next four areas would qualify as the technology part of the trifecta. Whether fulfilled in part by a tool or wholly by the organization, we can break down these key tool-based areas as:

- Recommendation and collective learning engines that focus on use cases in the business to develop internal standards, best practices, and collaborative abilities. This is an important mechanism to foster continuous learning and improvement within the organization, and to fully understand opportunities to address gaps and/or provide further training, communication, or socialization of established design and visualization.
- Interconnected discovery environment to capture feedback and provide guided analytics to business analysts. In addition to a continuous improvement method that can guide future education and communication activities, keeping the discovery environment connected can help illuminate areas that could benefit from more enablement, such as more tool support, or be candidates for new tiers within a larger DVCC community.
- A documented, maintained, and accessible library of DVCC-based assets, including training materials and pedagogies that facilitate foundational and

ongoing knowledge transfer. Because the DVCC is an ongoing, centralized practice area, the ownership of assets and succession plans of the core DVCC team members, roles, and responsibilities should be planned and articulated to ensure continuity and stability.

- Monitoring environment to understand how users are consuming and interacting with visualization and visual discovery, and uncover educational and performance-optimizing opportunities. In addition to the people-centric opportunities of this function, it also provides a technology or instrument by which to monitor and scrutinize the data itself—from where it is being sourced, who owns it, how it is governed, how often (or rarely) it is accessed, etc.

Again, remember that it is unwise to expect any tool to perform any or all of these activities in whole though many do have strengths and benefits that can be leveraged to support them. All visualization tools are not created equal, and many offer a bevy of abilities to click and create stunning data visualizations at will without guiding analytics and visual discovery. Likewise, business analysts or other data users and business application developers have varying degrees of visual design and data analysis skills and education, and can learn from a standardized set of best practice and design principles to facilitate the curation of meaningful, accurate visualizations. And, all users across the organization can benefit from an environment that facilitates sharing and collective learning while providing a review network to fine-tune newly created data visualizations before they are shared back to the business (Figure 11.2) (Box 11.2).

FIGURE 11.2 The Four Tenets of the DVCC

BOX 11.2 RESPONSES TO THE DVCC

Over the course of development and research to define the DVCC framework and competency areas, I had the opportunity to work hands-on with several companies across many industries of verticals. Since the release of the original research in summer 2015, I also have had the great pleasure to put this methodology into practice to help companies build DVCCs in their organizations from the ground up. I am happy to report that the DVCC is a competency center that has been welcomed and embraced by all of these companies.

> *"Self-service data visualization capabilities are giving users more power and flexibility. We now need a framework to guide and support the users to use the datasets, features and tools the right way. This is where the Data Visualization Competency Center can help."*
>
> **—Director of Information Services at a pharmaceuticals research and experimentation company**

> *"Like data governance, which has certain standards and policies, data visualization should also have a set of standards for design, development, and storytelling – these are the core competencies of the DVCC."*
>
> **—Senior Manager of Data Assurance at a large drug retailing chain**

> *"The DVCC is a concept that completely resonates with what we see in the market and in our approach to making self-service data visualization core information assets – we are effectively becoming a DVCC."*
>
> **—VP of Product Management at a computer security software company**

11.4 SOCIALIZING THE DVCC

By now we have a clear understanding of what the DVCC is, its mission and tenets, and the value of what the DVCC can support, provide, and promote in the business as part of a larger shift to a visual data culture. However, while the journey to building, implementing, and the ongoing maintenance and backing of a DVCC is long, establishing a productive and well-grounded competency center begins with taking the first steps of formally adapting behavior to the norms of an organizational culture: socialization.

Socialization is critical for awareness, engagement, and proliferation of an idea across a wide spectrum of users with varying needs, priorities, and drivers that push behaviors. Developing a DVCC socialization plan is paramount to translating the DVCC from a concept to an achievable framework and articulating its value proposition in a way that facilitates constructive conversations that are tailored to various audiences within the business.

There are many corresponding elements that should be connected and built upon in layers in order to develop a robust DVCC implementation kit, and these pieces are where we will spend the remainder of this chapter. However, a well-organized socialization plan begins with two essential things: a vision and a core team of people dedicated to that vision.

11.4.1 CRAFTING A VISION STATEMENT

There is a common quote, attributed to an anonymous author that states, "Dissatisfaction and discouragement are not caused by the absence of things but the absence of vision." In plainer words, a vision is a powerful thing.

Earlier we discussed the mission of the DVCC, but equal attention should be paid to the development of a vision statement that is in line with the overall visual data culture goals of the organization, and speaks to the part that the DVCC will play as the organization continues its path to realizing that culture. After all, a mission and a vision are complementary but not the same. A mission statement is, in effect, an organization's summary of its goals and objectives. It concentrates on the present, and what the organization wants to do "now"; it defines customers, critical processes, and sets an expectation for the desired level of performance.

For example, the mission of the DVCC is to support the use of effective self-service data visualization by providing best practices, standards, and education on how these information assets should be designed, created, and leveraged in the business. In this concise sentence, we can clearly see goals (to support the use of self-service visualization), customers (the business as a whole), critical processes (best practices, standards, and education), and—lastly—the expected performance level (effective). It is not remarkably enthusiastic, but it meets the purpose of a mission statement.

A vision statement takes a look further ahead. It focuses on the future and provides a source of inspiration and motivation about what the organization desires to accomplish, and the change it hopes to evoke. When working with teams to craft a vision statement, ask a series of thought-provoking questions to tweeze out vision in pieces, and then work collaboratively to sew it together. These are questions like:

- Why do you want a DVCC?
- What do you want a DVCC to accomplish?
- What does the DVCC look like now, in 6 months, in 1 year, in 5 years?
- What are the top three desired outcomes you want to accomplish with the DVCC?

Vision is personal, and it will vary depending on the desires and necessities of those who set the vision. As examples, the following are two vision statements for the DVCC recently written in workshops delivered on-site at clients:

To accelerate visual data discovery by increasing the breadth of data availability, empowering users to achieve proficiency with data visualization tools and best practices, and enabling rapid time to insight leveraging data visualization.
To act as stewards for data visualization and to model the values of quality and consistency in order to prioritize the use of data visualization across the organization so it serves as a communication body to foster cultural change.

Take a moment to review these vision statements and see how they resonate with you. Notice that both the statements seem to hover around a common theme, that is, the DVCC should empower (or serve) others in the mission to enable the organization to realize the tangible business of using the power of data visualization for insight and discovery.

11.4.2 BUILDING THE CORE TEAM

To enact a vision requires a core team of dedicated people to take the vision and—as Captain Jean Luc Picard of the *USS Enterprise* would say—"make it so." These visionary leaders are those who have both the vision and the conviction, as well as the energy, to put the vision statement into action.

When building a core team to carry out the vision for the DVCC, it may be helpful to think of it through the lens of proven project management approaches. In other words, think like a project management office (PMO) and bring together a cross-functional team of leaders that can speak to various angles of the project and communicate clearly across functional and departmental lines. This DVCC PMO, if you will, is charged with building, supporting, and maintaining the integrity of DVCC research and documentation, as well as evangelizing data visualization best practices. As the first official DVCC entity, they will likely be the first data visualization governance checkpoint to ensure all visual information assets shared conform to recommended best practices as data visualization is adopted throughout the organization, as well as the first group of tool super users. Assembling a cross-functional team is especially important because these teams bring the most to the table in terms of the abilities to:

- Speak knowledgably to various parts of the organization
- Represent the business' interests in decisions being made for the DVCC
- Communicate decisions made, standards, tools and progress of program to users, and business groups
- Be accountable for a wide array of project timelines and milestones
- Identify data owners as need arises in projects
- Prioritize projects when resource conflicts come up
- Bring forth internal best practices

The core team should include at least five people. There should be a project champion, or sponsor, that has executive authority and can lead socialization among the appropriate executive audience, generate leadership support, acquire funding, and has signing authority that will be necessary to initiate things like tool acquisition, external training resources, and so forth. In addition, there should be a project manager assigned whose primary responsibility is to facilitate forward momentum on the project as a whole, driving each representative party or action toward a common goal. This person will likely fall on the business side of the organization, but should be able to clearly and effectively communicate to both executive and technical audiences and serve as the focal point of the project to audiences that are external to the DVCC PMO. While the project manager likely comes from the business side, another person should take on the role of the voice of the business. This person will be responsible for keeping the business goals, outcomes, needs, and drivers at the forefront of the DVCC roadmap and implementation strategy. (In many instances, this person should be from a functional area that has an obvious use case for data visualization, and may have unique insight into some organizational standards, like color palettes or corporate communication guidelines, that would be an added value to the core team.)

On the more technical side, a technical expert is necessary. This would be someone who is deeply familiar with the overall enterprise architecture and can be relied upon to lead technical decisions and conversations that will arise, as well as be familiar with the organization's data management policies, processes, and procedures. Finally, an initial power user should be the person designated to have the most robust hands-on knowledge of data visualization best practices, tool valuation, and eventually, tool use and capabilities.

Along with the individual roles and responsibilities of each designated person within the core group, the group as a whole has a central set of essential responsibilities. These include:

Align vocabulary: By developing a common set of terms that will enable DVCC communication

Drive accountability: While this team may not be responsible for making decisions, they do own the accountability for ensuring decisions are made and ensuring that they are institutionalized into the DVCC vocabulary

Be experts: Expose members to resources available to foster a level of group knowledge so that everyone knows enough about every other piece to have a holistic knowledge

Be the first tester group: Members of this group should be those who establish processes as well as sanity check through trial and experimentation to make sure they are whole, sound, repeatable, and manageable

11.5 THE IMPLEMENTATION ROADMAP

Once the mission, vision, and a core team dedicated to carrying out these have been identified, the next step in a socialization plan for the DVCC is to build an implementation roadmap. This is the step that puts action around a vision, and works to distill data visualization into key business outcomes (goals) and to align these with business drivers (needs) and technical efficiencies to be earned (wants). From there, we can pave a milestone-driven path to success by beginning with quick-win opportunities to rapidly demonstrate the value of the DVCC to the business while planning the prioritization of ongoing opportunities. Finally, the implementation roadmap should also include a tiered, all-inclusive communication plan to plot both top-down and bottom-up communication to engender continued support, awareness, and engagement in a long-term, strategic data visualization cultural migration.

11.5.1 ALIGNING BUSINESS OUTCOMES TO DRIVERS AND EFFICIENCIES

Aligning business outcomes to drivers and technical efficiencies involves making sure that a desired outcome meets real and valid needs for both the business-at-large as well as offers an improvement in technical efficiency (see Figure 11.3). This exercise is helpful to validate that goals are worthwhile within the larger context of the business, and provide a tangle and useful benefit back equally to business and IT (a symbiotic relationship crucial to the DVCC).

Desired business outcomes should speak to what is important for the business to accomplish, and when building the roadmap you should work to identify at least three attainable and relevant business outcomes. Often, these can span from data unification needs, to centralized information management, to business agility. As an example, let us explore that last—agility—to better understand how a DVCC can support it as an outcome, or goal, of an organized competency center for data visualization.

As a business outcome for data visualization, agility could be qualified as the goal of aligning visual data exploration and discovery with data governance and IT data management. Business drivers, then, speak to the "needs" of the business, and to support agility could include things like (1) increase the speed of discovery and insights, (2) enable all users to work with data in an organized and efficient way that is suitable for users of varying types and skillsets, and (3) reduce the dependency on IT by providing approved visual discovery environments with requirements for data governance, security, access, and so on already defined and implemented. On the technical efficiency side, business agility could be quantified to address technical "need" statements like providing a secure environment to ingest, integrate, and visually analyze new data, to empower users while maintaining governance, and to support the sharing of new insights in a safe way. To repurpose the previous visual with a practical application, consider Figure 11.4.

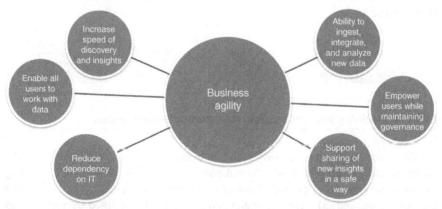

FIGURE 11.3 Aligning Business Outcomes with Business Drivers and Technical Efficiencies

FIGURE 11.4 Business Agility as a Desired Business Outcome for the DVCC

11.5.2 ESTABLISHING SUCCESS CRITERIA FOR EACH PHASE

The implementation roadmap includes three stages: platform delivery (which includes both the tool platform as well as the foundational set of DVCC decision documents and training materials); an index of quick-win opportunities to provide immediate business value; and a robust, enterprise-wide communication strategy.

Regardless of the specific outcome assigned, it should be qualified with success criteria that set the precedent for when and how a deliverable can be marked as successfully achieved. This success criteria is then the catalyst for working backward, step-by-step, to ensure that the goal is reached in achievable, incremental steps along the way that add value. And, an articulated success point acts as a guiding light that defines the end point in which the outcome can be checked as completed and a clear timeline in which to do so.

For example, if the roadmap calls for internal design standards to be decisioned and data visualization best practices to be established, we can set the success criteria as these being defined, documented, approved, and ready for user training. Following the model mentioned later, we can logically break the larger outcome down into four steps (Figure 11.5):

FIGURE 11.5 Defining Steps and Stages to Meet Outcome Success Criteria

This same logic can be applied to any outcome within the DVCC roadmap. The important thing to keep in mind is to make sure that all steps on the path to meeting success criteria have (1) estimated costs (if any) and clear benefits, (2) incremental business value, and (3) clear ownership and accountability defined by someone on the DVCC core team.

11.5.3 IDENTIFYING QUICK WINS TO PROVE VALUE

Quick-win opportunities are where emerging DVCCs can capitalize on low-hanging fruit. These opportunities should fit the purpose of data visualization and have minimal obstacles or ambiguity. In other words they should be quick to deliver, easy to implement, and highly visible to influential groups within the business whose support will be valuable for ongoing success. While other outcomes on the roadmap may have timelines requiring six or more months of work, organize quick win opportunities that are "bite size," taking from two weeks to two months to accomplish. Start proving value as quickly as possible by tackling them from shortest to longest, so that there is near-immediate and continuous value being delivered back to the business on its investment in the DVCC.

Identifying quick wins are an easy place to start by thinking in terms of what challenges users or departments in the business are currently struggling with, and devoting DVCC resources to overcoming that challenge. For example, perhaps there are dashboards already being used that could benefit from applying (or acting as test cases) new design decisions or improving to be in line with data visualization best practices. Or, perhaps there is a need for a new dashboard to meet an upcoming high visibility executive reporting event or an internal corporate briefing event. These are just a few sample situations that could benefit from being prioritized as a quick win opportunity, and often these quick wins are already top-of-mind for various members on the core DVCC team.

As with any outcome on the roadmap, quick wins also need a clear timeline and assigned ownership. In addition to the opportunity, justification and business impact should be articulated to validate the opportunity is a quick win (see Figure 11.6).

11.5.4 ARCHITECTING AN ALL-INCLUSIVE COMMUNICATION PLAN

Nobel-prize winner George Bernard Shaw was once quoted as saying, "the single biggest problem in communication is the illusion that it has taken place." He was right: communication as a critical part of change leadership is often a stumbling block. Often we assume that because a project or initiative of any type has funding, executive sponsorship, and a footprint in the organization, that it has been communicated appropriately throughout the organization, in the best way, and both to and from the right people. Unfortunately, this is often also a faulty assumption.

	Business Opportunity	Business Impact and Quick-Win justification, minimal risks to quick delivery	Business Owner
1	Integrated visual reporting for Sales Activity monitoring of Top 10 accounts	Provides business reporting without having to build a data mart or multiple reports for several business metrics	Joe, Director of Something

FIGURE 11.6 Outlining an Example Quick-Win Opportunity for the DVCC

Architecting an all-inclusive communication plan involves two streams of communication: top down and bottom up. These streams should be two-way, too, and the DVCC should be outputting communication as well as receiving and incorporating feedback—or, listening to the voices of their customers. In the same way we must take our audiences into consideration and customize visualization outputs and storytelling paths; we must also customize communication as needed to fit the needs of its receiving audiences and make sure they are receiving the information they need.

For a community path, deliver communication that builds up the entire organization. Make information accessible and approachable. Offer training opportunities, networking events (like meet ups or user group meetings), or even make the most of digital platforms like online communities, Wiki sites, or gamification elements that can be earned through interaction and engagement with the DVCC and/or data visualization.

For an executive audience, create a data visualization scorecard that speaks to the metrics that the business needs to know, is quick and digestible, and provides proof points that they can share from a leadership level back to the enterprise. Leadership will need the right information at the right time to make informed decisions, plan strategically, and provide trickle down communication from the heart of the organization.

11.6 **FOUR TIPS TO DVCC SUCCESS**

The above sections have provided a framework by which to organize a successful rollout of a DVCC in a clear, structured, and manageable way that provides incremental value and keeps all tiers of audience active and engaged. This socialization and implementation roadmap can be organized into a set of documents or presentations that can be shared in order to earn executive sponsorship and user participation. Likewise, the set of standards, best practices guides, and training pedagogies developed are also corporate assets that will serve as the foundational components of a DVCC library of information.

While the sections earlier provided a practical, step-by-step guide to getting started, this final section is more generalized and will provide some general tips to success that should be kept in mind during the initiation and follow-through of any DVCC activities and initiatives. Many questions and considerations will arise during the formation of DVCC, but the four tips below are those that should live top-of-mind from day one. These are:

1. Take time to conduct due diligence
2. Establish a common business vocabulary
3. Know who your data stewards are
4. Respect the limitations of self-service visualization

11.6.1 TAKE TIME TO CONDUCT DUE DILIGENCE

Any tool or technology cannot be relied upon to carry out the mission of the DVCC— or to perform data visualization tasks and processes in a vacuum. It is the organization's responsibility to take time to thoroughly compare tool offerings and evaluate their strengths and weaknesses in line with the needs of the organization to be able to get footing on how the tool will fit into the environment before purchasing and beginning tool or platform implementation. Visualization tools do not function in isolation and are part of a larger data architecture, and knowing how a tool fits within this overall picture will help you to maximize the value of your investment and minimize unpleasant surprises going forward. Not only is it important to have a clear idea of how the technology will fit within the existing organizational infrastructure, but also it is necessary to know how users throughout the organization will apply the tool to solve business issues and where use cases, training opportunities, or specific requirements may exist that will affect how tools are compared, too. Crafting a mission and vision statement prior to embarking on tool evaluations will help to ensure that tools are evaluated in line with the organization's plans for now, and for the future.

Knowing how any given tool (or stack of tools) will fit within these discussions prior to purchasing or implementing a solution will give you the insight you need to proactively capitalize on strengths and plan to fill gaps when working through the initial phases of an implementation plan. Performing comparative due diligence, testing (proof of concept or pilot activities), as well as bringing together the right evaluation group for a tool decision are crucial. Industry comparative reports or ranking assessments are a helpful guide in surface-level analysis, but when reviewing a tool organizations should weight areas of importance by what matters most within the current culture as well as the larger visual data cultural vision. Some of the areas you should be looking to compare tools on include:

- Analytics/data science capabilities
- Range of visualization options
- User experience/guided analytics
- Customization options
- Self-service abilities
- Collaboration/sharing abilities
- Security/governance capabilities
- Storytelling capabilities
- Mobile capabilities
- Enterprise scalability

11.6.2 ESTABLISH A COMMON BUSINESS VOCABULARY

A common phrase that swirls around the larger computer science industry is the technical concept of single version of truth (SVOT) that describes the idea of having a single centralized database that stores all of an organization's data in a consistent, nonredundant form. While many argue the possibility, reliability, and even the accuracy of a SVOT approach, it is a concept that can be applied within the context of how the DVCC should set consistently understood definitions of data and a reasonable level of quality.

While the goal of a DVCC does not have to be quite so lofty as a formal SVOT initiative, there is a need to establish a common business vocabulary—or, business glossary—to construct a shared understanding as to what data means that is understood, trusted, and utilized by individuals and groups. It is less a matter of absolutes than of standardization. Variations in definitions cause confusion, inconsistency, recreating of the wheel activities, and overall reduce the validity of analytic activity. On the other hand, standard definitions promote consistency, streamline visualization activities (eg, a common visualization or dashboard can be shared and used by many rather than each group recreating the same visual), and can facilitate fruitful conversation because everyone is working on the same set of assumptions and meanings of the data, its use by the business, and its context.

Additionally, expectations for version control and updating of this business glossary should be established, too, so that there is a level of assurance that this tool will continue to be of value within the business. Determine how often and who will be responsible for leading efforts to make sure the vocabulary stays up to date and accurate. This does not necessarily need to be the person who "owns" the data, but the person who will be responsible for keeping the glossary up to date and current—the "editor," if you will.

11.6.3 KNOW WHO YOUR DATA STEWARDS ARE

With more users given access to and the ability to work with data, the need for data ownership and oversight becomes even more important. Of course, data visualization tools and efforts are only one facet of this conversation, but it serves as an additional opportunity to highlight the importance of robust data governance and management for both the data and for data visualization, too, as reliable information assets. Using data visualization as a pathway to the democratization of data does not loosen the need for proper governance and data management, but in fact it highlights the need for even clearer boundaries and data dissemination, tracking, and monitoring—especially among those who have the ability to make changes to the data sources or write back to the system of record through their visual discovery activities.

Data stewards do not necessarily "own" the data, but they are the go-to person for questions, concerns, or doubts on the data's use, quality, or context—they are also probably those that can be counted on to contribute a meaningful definition of the data back into the business vocabulary. These stewards are often intermediaries between business and IT and can speak to both sides to know both the business drivers and needs and how the data supports them, as well as be versed in the entire lifecycle of the data itself, from generation or acquisition, to where it lives (source) in the data architecture, to how it is administered and what its security and access controls look like.

11.6.4 RESPECT THE LIMITATIONS OF SELF-SERVICE VISUALIZATION

As we have seen in the pages of this text, data visualization is a powerful means of enabling visual analysts to find trends, patterns, and more in the data. However, we have also seen how it can be used incorrectly to either intentionally or inadvertently misrepresent, misconstrue, or otherwise misinterpret information and pass off visual insights, no matter how accurate, correct, or meaningful, as truths. We know that different users will rely upon and use data visualization for different needs, through different forms and devices, and each will have different levels of expertise in things like visual design, data visualization best practices and graphicacy, and storytelling. There will always be users who desire to be hands-on and deeply involved in building data visualizations, and there will always be those who only want to review and consume approved visual assets. Aptitude gaps and a spectrum of user group aspirations are to be expected, and not something startled or distressed by. It is simply a reality that should be proactively planned for.

While the demand for self-service is a something of a battle cry heard loud and clear through the data industry and all tiers of data users, it carries with it an undercurrent of warning. As we discussed in chapter: From Self-Service to Self-Sufficiency, there is a broad continuum from making all users empowered by self-service and making all users proficient as self-sufficient. Thus, it is important to know both the audience of data visualization—how they will consume it, and how they will need to be visually presented data—which will help as you encourage adoption and promote enterprise-wide use of visual analytics, and the audience of those who will be hands-on with the tools, too. More often than not there is a learning curve in both tool and mindset, and the core DVCC team will be tasked with meeting that curve with customized and user-appropriate training and education in all aspects and for all designated audience types, as well as developing ongoing and dynamic training methodology that account for things like new users and system upgrades and new tool capabilities, and upholds the move toward a deeper commitment to visual data discovery.

Let us continue this conversation into the next chapter, where we build upon architecture considerations and competency areas to review how the organization can combine these in a concreted effort to truly enable visual data discovery by design and nurture the shift to a visual data-centric culture. As a capstone chapter, chapter: Enabling Visual Data Discovery by Design will go back through the entirety of this text, plucking out the most pertinent and core elements of our discussions to sew them a single application that touches base on the three most important elements of a visual data culture: people, processes, and technologies.

REFERENCES

Dix, A., Pohl, M., Ellis, G., 2010. Mastering the information age. EuroGraphics.

Gentile, B., 2014. The top 5 business benefits of using data visualization. Data Informed. Available from: http://data-informed.com/top-5-business-benefits-using-data-visualization/.

Visual discovery by design

12

"Design must be functional, and functionality must be translated into visual aesthetic without any reliance on gimmicks that have to be explained."
—Ferdinand Porsche

Each chapter in this book has taken us on a journey through the various elements that make discovery so overwhelmingly visual. We have trekked through the history of visual communication and how it has paved the way to how we think about visual design today. We have talked about why we tell stories with visualization, how to tell these data stories in meaningful ways, and why visualization itself is a compelling narrative. We went through a high-level debrief on the key cognitive ingredients needed to have a visual dialogue with data. And, we have explored important design considerations and evolving data visualization best practices.

We have stayed close to the tip of the iceberg in each of these subjects, just glazing the surface to cherry pick those most pertinent of details and valuable information nuggets most relevant to our purposes here. Now, we can sew those discussions together into a quilt of new purpose. You will find that this chapter serves as a purposeful convergence of these previous conversations, collapsing them into one synthesized application—visual data discovery by design. Essentially, this is the climactic moment of the text because enabling visual data discovery by design is the essence of the entire book: it is the organizational design of data-centric companies and how that flows through its people, processes, and technologies. It is how to "design" data visualization from a communication, design, and storytelling perspective. And, it is approaching visualization as a discovery-centric mechanism, whether in static visualizations, or animated, mobile, streaming, or wearables in the coming Internet of Things.

Okay. So, I have made a big deal about building up the excitement of the discovery by design idea. The next question, then, is: what is so important about it?

That is the easy part, so let us start there. In today's emerging discovery culture, business users demand more independence to acquire, analyze, and sustain new insights from their data. We saw that in chapters: Improved Agility and Insights Through (Visual) Discovery; and From Self-Service to Self-Sufficiency, when we talked about how discovery is moving up to the adult table of data management, and how self-service is also maturing into self-sufficiency driving a cultural change that ripples all the way back to IT. Focusing on self-sufficiency and high-performance in emerging discovery tools is key to earning the business value through discovery demanded by the data-driven business.

243

The next question: how do we do it? FDR taught us that, in politics, nothing happens by accident—"if it happens, you can bet it was planned that way." Building visual discovery by design is likewise nonaccidental. It takes diligence, determination, and design thinking—a method for the practical and creative resolution of problems that is custom-built to meet an intended result. And, it takes effort to continue curating and refining to keep pace with fluid changes in a fast-paced data economy, disruptive tool marketplace, and competitive environment. Consider the words of Aristotle: We are what we repeatedly do. Excellence, then, is not an act, but it is something deliberately planned and designed. It is intended.

With technological speed, performance, and agility forming the backbone for discovery, layering on the muscle of intuitive self-sufficiency, interactive sharing environments, rich visualization, and a strong mobile-delivery orientation will provide data-centric companies with the power they need to enable true "discovery by design" and empower everyone in the organization with the ability to earn valuable insights into their data.

In this chapter, we will discuss how data-centric companies are leveraging disruptive tools to find more ways to capitalize on "discovery by design" and:

- Balance user intuition and self-service capabilities with high-performance environments for sharable, actionable timeframe insights
- Facilitate increased time to insight through speed, agility, and self-sufficiency
- Leverage a scalable, quickly adapting solution that is powered by visualization, collaboration, and mobility

12.1 DATA DISCOVERY BY DESIGN

As we all have come to terms with by now, the data industry has changed. And, this change is not limited to tools or technologies—or even by the data itself, but it includes the people as well.

Today's business users are exponentially more data savvy. They may or may not be digital natives, but they are more comfortable with technology and more familiar with key analytics concepts. Further, they better understand the context of their data and their requirements for how they want to work with it on every day basis. Data is quickly becoming more of a mindset than a tool, and—as I have said before—today's most innovative and disruptive companies are those whose people treat data like gold—or, even better, like oxygen. No longer a handy asset, you now need data to survive.

Technology itself has become more economical: the price of hardware is not as expensive, and solutions are more flexible and customizable than ever before with more emphasis on user experience (or UX, the overall experience of a person using a product such as a website or computer application, especially in terms of how easy or pleasing it is to use) and user interface (or UI, the means by which a user and a computer system interact, particularly the use of input devices and software) design for simplicity and user intuition. Here, we see the effects of the democratization of data that was discussed in chapter: Navigating Ethics in the Big Data Discovery: in the data democracy, everyone can do what was once reserved only for the big corporations with big pockets for technology. Business users, too, have a larger say in purchase decisions, thanks to the advent of freemium options (or other low-barrier pricing models) and the continued consumerization of traditional BI, discovery, and data visualization tools. Of course, with the mainstream adoption beginning for big data for business analytics, companies are becoming increasingly more data-centric, and are finding more ways to exploit data for competitive advantage and enable more users across the organization to participate in the business process of discovery. This is, again, that shift from self-service to self-sufficiency, and one way in which organizations are enabling as many users as possible within the organization to participate in the data discovery process likewise meeting that business user demand for more independence to acquire, analyze, and sustain the discovery of new insights from their data. Like we discussed in chapter: From Self-Service to Self-Sufficiency, being truly self-sufficient requires that technical and nontechnical users alike have the tools, environment, and access, they need to contribute and collaborate in the discovery environment. And, again, because the discovery process is one of exploration that hinges on the ability of users to combine data sources and experiment with data within their unique business context. The self-sufficient business user requires independence from IT to define their own discovery experience. Consider discovery by design as a guiding light in the discovery resolution. The reality is that people will do what they need to do to achieve business goals. If they are not provided with tools, they will download on their own; if they are given no discovery environment, they will use the cloud or their desktops. With or without IT, business users are empowered to embark on discovery. So, the question becomes how organizations can most efficiently and effectively guide that process.

As discovery continues to reshape how we earn insights from our data, discovery tools must also continue to balance user intuition and self-sufficient capabilities. More important, these must be balanced against high-performance for sharable, actionable timeframe insights across the organization. We will continue to see that true (or at least the most successful) discovery tools will be differentiated from traditional BI tools by their ability to facilitate discovery by design and increase time to insight through speed, agility, and self-sufficiency inside a scalable solution that can quickly adapt to changing business needs. Going forward, we will take a look at the power of disruption again—this time in the context of the discovery tool landscape, and not the industry as a whole—and the value of speed in enabling data discovery by design that is powered by visualization, collaboration, and mobility.

12.1.1 POWER OF DISRUPTION (IN THE TOOL LANDSCAPE)

The fundamental extension of traditional BI to include discovery is one that has been shaped not only by the evolving needs and data aptitudes of the business, but by changes and disruption in the industry—and its emerging technologies, vendor marketplace, and tool ecosystem—too.

The story goes like this: in years past, traditional BI tools were routinely blamed for being "too slow" but in reality, it was typically the database behind the tool responsible for latency issues. The acquisition of the then-major BI vendors—including Cognos, Business Objects, and Hyperion (who were acquired by IBM, SAP, and Oracle, respectively)—left a gap in the BI tool marketplace, which provided the opportunity for new vendors to spring up and capitalize on previously unaddressed weaknesses. In response (or perhaps as part of an impending tool revolution), incumbent vendors were quick to move data in-memory to achieve high-performance analytics and iteration through caching and ultimately provide a better user experience. The next-generation of disruptive BI tools, then, focused on addressing performance through speed, integration, and agility; advanced visualization capabilities; and intuitive UX design and self-service. This is where many tools are circling and trying to differentiate in the ecosystem today.

These disruptive tools were not—and still are not—just concerned about addressing the weaknesses left exposed by some of the more traditional BI tools. They are also offering lower barriers of adoption without IT—like the downloadable Tableau desktop (or free Tableau Public), or (also free) self-service Software-as-a-Service (SaaS) data blending applications (like Informatica Rev), or cloud-based analytical tool (like Birst and Qlik Cloud). With more emphasis on low-barrier adoption and freemium models, we continue to see lower and more efficient pricing SaaS models for users to "pay for what you use." This make tools more affordable for business departments—and easier to embrace without having to find an allowance in IT's shared resource pools.

As we continue to include discovery as an increasingly fundamental process, today's disruptive vendors focus on providing tools that facilitate true discovery by design. They will be all about providing tools and technology solutions that make the end user—technical and nontechnical alike, or that "modern data analyst"—more independent, which is the crux of self-sufficiency in the new discovery culture. However, self-sufficiency does not happen in a silo, nor does it relate to making only singles users self-sufficient—it is a broader concept that puts a higher premium on interconnectedness and enablement. Therefore, true discovery tools provide users the ability to connect to large volumes of new data without scripting and to join different data sets together easily to filter, query, and visualize at will to explore data in detail without choking the system or relying on IT, thus circumventing data discovery friction.

As a caveat, be aware that the user independence that powers discovery within the organization is not only influenced by the disruptive nature of the tool itself, but is just as much contingent on the vendor and its ability to innovate, adapt, and listen to the voice of the customer in how it continues to enhance the user experience of their core tool(s) and solutions portfolio. This is where buying companies can benefit by erring on the side of simplicity. While the larger, more mature vendors (and their software) have their place in the architecture, these unfortunately have the tendency to fall victim to the trifecta of doom: overdesigned functionality and features, difficult to manage incremental updates, and slow response times for support. When choosing a vendor to bring into your technology stack for discovery by design, think about their DNA—what they were originally designed to accomplish. You will find that some of these vendors were created to solve enterprise reporting problems and can find it hard to evolve into something else. Just like in ecology, sometimes things (products) have to move aside to make way for new growth. This is where smaller, more specialized, and disruptive vendors are driven by customer needs to continuously refine the scope of their core product in a way that deepens the tool's value without bloating the software in a way that loses sight of the original need it was initially designed to address. Disruptive vendors, too, will pay attention to the feature priorities that are most important to the consumer.

Ultimately, navigating the "new breed" of traditional tools versus truly disruptive discovery tools means that we must concentrate first and foremost on the elements that make a tool designed for discovery—a robust, agile IT-independent and user-centric approach that has better access to data, agile high-performance, and is designed with collaboration as a top priority. Additionally, to capitalize truly on the power of disruption, the vendor behind this tool should be dedicated to continuing to innovate and provide perpetual competitive advantage to its customers through its core technology. Vendors do so through technological advances. Just as important, by paying attention to customer feedback—what they want, need, like, dislike, their pains, and how they do things. Luckily, with the boom right now in the tool ecosystem, several vendors are popping up that are committed to this mission and are already proving value at customers within all verticals of industry with modern adoption business models that lower the barrier for would be self-sufficient customers.

12.1.2 **THE VALUE OF SPEED**

As always, speed tops the list of needs in the data discovery culture. To quote that famous *Top Gun* line, when working with data and discovery today, we feel the need—"the need for speed!"

Because the discovery culture is at its heart a fail-fast environment, it places an inherent premium on speed and performance. Of course, there are different perspectives of speed, such as the difference of "speed" between query performance and "speed" of data latency ("I need data *faster*"). And, there is a need for "speed" to meet business demands, and thus the rise of battling in-memory platforms—like Spark vs. MapReduce (see Box 12.1)—for speed in real-time data analysis.

It is an important note to add that this need for speed, has the prerequisite of being able to quickly harness large amounts and varieties of data with agility for exploration to enrich the discovery process. Remember, in the era of disruption of the BI marketplace, emerging new vendors were eager to fill and capitalize on the exposed weaknesses of the large mega-vendors. One of these was speed for response time between the database and the tool stack, which was the catalyst for many vendors to move data into local in-memory to achieve high-performance analytics at the user's desktop and iteration through caching for a better user experience.

BOX 12.1 THE RISE OF SPARK

Spark is an open source Apache Foundation project that enables organizations to perform in-memory analytics on big data sets. With hundreds of involved contributors, Spark has recently overtaken Hadoop as the most active open source big data project today (Marr, 2015).

As an alternative to MapReduce, Spark is a next-generation generalized processing engine for large-scale data processing. It was originally developed in 2009 at UC Berkeley's AMPLab to perform in-memory analytics on big data sets. Because it is *"generalized"* for flexible workflow processing the Spark programming model allows other computational engines to be easily abstracted and accessible via a simple programming API. Therefore, the Spark environment provides big data developers and data scientists a quicker way to build advanced analytics programs that require multiple iterative processing and data flows. Spark's reputation for faster performance comes from its Resilient Distributed Datasets (RDDs), a collection of elements partitioned across the nodes of a cluster that pull data into memory from HDFS, NoSQL databases (such as Cassandra and Hbase), or local and distributed file systems like Amazon S3.

Spark is quickly becoming a standard for writing deep analytics that need to leverage in-memory performance, streaming data, machine learning libraries, SQL, and graph analytics. While advanced analytics and performance needs drive Spark's development focus, its data processing idioms are a fast way to develop data processing flows while abstracting much of MapReduce's complexity. For companies that have been previously leveraging Pig as an abstraction away from MapReduce, Pig-on-Spark—or "Spork"—is gaining traction as a way to maintain that, too. Developers can chain together data functions to filter, sort, transform, and leverage SQL all in-memory with RDDs and gain performance over equivalent MapReduce applications.

Again, let me pin in a quick caveat. While speed is a criterion to successful data discovery, speed for the sake of speed on its own provides little more than an enticing thrill ride—fun and fast while its happening, and over too quickly (and leaving you with a little bit of vertigo). The real value of speed to drive discovery has a direct relationship with the ability to quickly earn insights on data and facilitate interactive and immediate reaction. The value of speed, then, can be found at the intersection of actionable time to insight and the ease of the discovery process (remember that Google search engine result from chapter: Separating Leaders From Laggards).

Think back to our earlier discussion on the role of friction in discovery as a way to better understand influencers on speed. Speed is what we achieve by reducing friction-causing activities—those incremental events that add time and complexity to discovery through activities that slow down the process, like those that IT used to do for business users (like connecting data sources, generating visualizations, or sharing insights back through dashboards and reports—all of which can be reduced or removed completely with robust self-service, visualization, collaboration, and sharing capabilities). As friction decreases, time to insight increases, thereby reducing the barriers to discovery and subsequently increasing time to insight—or, speed. Speed, then, is a function of friction: the less friction in the discovery process, the more value speed can deliver to the business. Simply put, time to insight minus friction equals speed (or Time to Insight—Friction = Speed).

12.1.3 DISCOVERY BY DESIGN

Finally, the design of the discovery environment is just as critical to the success of discovery as is either disruption or speed.

Discovery is an iterative "many cycles" and "fail fast" revolving process wherein data is abstracted or extracted into in-memory—integrated, derived, modeled, and then visualized to see insights into the data. Once new insights have been discovered (or not discovered, as the case may be), discovery continues on an exploratory "lather, rinse, and then repeat" cycle until new insights are eventually uncovered and can be shared back into the business. Sometimes, even failed discoveries can be valuable, too, and these also should be institutionalized (added into the organizational fabric). This is the exploratory nature of data discovery: the path is not always clear and rarely does the discovery process end up where the original idea was headed. Along the way, mini-insights may change the approach, cause the consideration of new data sources, or illuminate that data quality and stability may not be available and another discovery path is needed. This is also where collaboration, sharing, and collective innovation input can spark new ideas and insights.

For example, pretend for a minute that you are stuck in rush hour traffic on your way home from the office. You know where you are, and where you hope to end up, but the way you take to get there is influenced by how bad the traffic is in certain areas along the way, or if you have an errands to stop off at on your way home. Maybe you will take the interstate if it is not too backed up, or maybe you will weave through the back roads depending on what strikes your fancy. And, maybe you will not end up at home at all (at least not when you expected to), and instead you decide to meet up with some friends for dinner. It may be a little colorful, but this is a fitting way to illustrate the discovery process—its adaptive and iterative, and many times the path you think you are taking is not the direction you end up going at all.

Discovery is more important in today's business environment for two main reasons: business analytics and data science are driven by algorithms and data to discover a business solution that is currently unknown to the conscious business, and new, high volume, high velocity data needs to be analyzed to be understood. Having speed—coupled with performance and agility—as the backbone for discovery creates the foundation for a valuable discovery experience. After understanding the importance of the power of disruption, the need for speed, and a core focus on how to design bottom-up for discovery, we can move into the four elements of design that enable self-sufficient discovery by design. Self-sufficiency, interactive and collaborative sharing environments, visualization, and a strong mobile-orientation are key elements to achieve true discovery by design and overcome barriers to empower everyone in the organization with valuable insights in real-time. This is, of course, the modus operandi of our data needs today. We have explored these in more depth in earlier chapters, but let us summarize them applied into context now.

12.1.3.1 Designed for self-sufficiency

The shift from self-service to self-sufficiency is a paradigm shift that is fundamentally intertwined with the extension of BI to discovery in that it changes the impact of the user from being able to consume something that has been predefined and provided to having the ability—through tools, environment, and access—to discover it independently. In its entirety and at length, this was the premise of chapter: From Self-Service to Self-Sufficiency, of this book.

In the scope of visual discovery by design, the exponential growth in the volume, variety, and velocity of data generated today, requires users with business knowledge to become partners in discovery to engage collaboratively in the discovery and analytical opportunities brought with mass amounts of new and diverse data. Equipped with better tools, users are earning greater autonomy and IT independence. At the core of the concept of self-sufficient discovery by design is that true discovery tools should be designed specifically with the business user in mind. It should remove barriers for adopting a BI tool by providing a simple, intuitive user interface and functionality that is designed to empower the self-sufficient user to contribute, share, and discover their own insights—from easily unifying disparate data to building reports, designing visualizations, and sharing back to the larger community.

12.1.3.2 Designed for collaboration

Collaboration is an investment strategy, and designing discovery for collaboration is two-fold.

First, pairing self-sufficient discovery with collaborative capabilities fosters collective innovation. It builds a more robust discovery environment by providing the ability for technical and nontechnical users to communicate through meaningful reports, dashboards, or visualizations that can then be shared back into the analytical platform to encourage meaningful collaboration and shared insight. Further, these drive higher quality in context definitions; encourage cooperation and sharing between cross-functional units; and, ultimately, enjoy the benefit of having a broader network of creativity, constructive criticism, and business knowledge and awareness.

Second, collaborative discovery closes the gap between business users and IT to nurture data democratization and facilitate the shift of IT (as central management and control) from Information Technology to Enablement Technology (ET)—where IT's role is less that of a technology administrator, and instead is primarily responsible for enabling more self-sufficient opportunities for business users to gain more actionable insights that brings value to the business, while simultaneously educating the business on IT processes and governance. Creating a collaborative environment also establishes transparency by supporting the sharing of current and relevant information between units. And, it provides a consolidated location for data governance and implementing underlying data security to centralize access permissions and act as a single unified environment to enforce roles and permissions across all federated data sources.

12.1.3.3 Designed for visualization

By now we have detailed at length how, as humans, we are intrinsically hardwired visual creatures—from the way we learn and remember, to the way we perceive and interpret information. Keeping discovery visual leverages our intrinsic visual capacities and empowers even the most nontechnical user with the ability to meaningfully ingest, synthesize, and take action from their insights. Visualization, within the discovery environment, makes analytics significantly more approachable to the self-sufficient business user by providing a powerful venue to access huge volumes and varieties of data and convey knowledge in a way that would not otherwise be possible. In fact, visualization vastly improves discovery in some cases and, in others, is the only way to work with and communicate large data sets. Visualization within discovery is the vehicle to move from shared understanding to shared insight.

Robust visualization capabilities—whether through dashboards, traditional charts and graphs, or advanced visualizations—endow business users with the ability to access data and build well-designed, meaningful visualizations to visually explore data and discover insights at a glance through the careful distillation of images, color and design. Making visualizations interactive allows the exploration process to continue visually—a premise at the heart of visual discovery—and leverages our cognitive abilities of visual communication to enrich the discovery process and follow train-of-thought thinking to insights through discovery.

12.1.3.4 Designed for mobility

Today, in a rapidly more and more interconnected and mobile world with the growing Internet of Things (or, Internet of Everything, as it is sometimes called), mobility does not just provide new opportunities for consuming and interacting with data and analytics: it fundamentally alters the paradigm by which we expect to consume and interact with data and analytics. Mobile data discovery, then, demands an intuitive, hands-on, and second nature "touch" approach to visually interact with data in a familiar, compelling, and meaningful way. Going mobile makes discovery a portable experience, too, and brings it with the expectation of a responsive, secure, and device-agnostic mobility through consistent, cross-platform experiences for continued discovery that is irrespective of the device with the ability to launch a discovery session on-the-fly.

While mobile is a topic we will pay special attention to in our next and final chapter, the important takeaway here is that having a mobile-first stance is the catalyst to enriching visual analytics and enabling self-sufficient, on-the-go business users in a new era of discovery. The continued increase in the mobility of secure and managed data access ensures that self-sufficient, IT-independent business users have immediate time to insight and action with access to relevant, live data no matter their physical location or device of preference. Because of the choice of multiple devices and form factors and usage patterns, mobility is a personalized experience for each user, too, and further supports the need for disruptive discovery tools to continue to focus on the individualized user experience.

12.1.4 TYING IT TOGETHER

As mainstream adoption of big data continues to progress, focusing on self-sufficiency and high-performance in emerging discovery tools is the key to earning the business value through discovery that is demanded by the data-driven business. With speed, performance, and agility forming the backbone for discovery, we can layer on the muscle of intuitive self-sufficiency, interactive and collaborative sharing environments, visualization, and a strong mobile-delivery to provide data-centric companies with the power they need to enable true discovery by design and empower everyone in the organization with valuable insights in a low friction, actionable timeframe (Figure 12.1). To recap the first section, consider these core takeaways:

> *Self-Sufficient:* More and more, self-service is being redefined to be less about access and more about ability. This paradigm shift from self-service to self-sufficiency fundamentally changes the impact of the user from being able to consume a predefined something to discover it independently. Equipped with

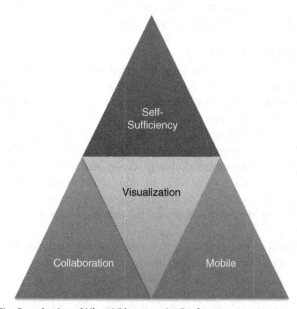

FIGURE 12.1 The Four Angles of Visual Discovery by Design

better tools, users are earning greater autonomy and IT independence to become true partners in discovery. There is a hard line between programming-oriented and user-oriented in tool design that does not change. What does change is the vendor's ability to create tools that enable nonprogrammers to do the same things as the programmers. Eventually tools (and technologies) also mature to the point, where the paradigm shifts from innovative, to optimize, and to commoditize. (The extract, transform, load—or ETL—industry went through this revolution in the 90s, too, as it moved from programmer-oriented to 3GL tools for the masses.)

Collaborative: Collaboration gives users the ability to communicate in ways that enable shared insight; drive higher quality in definitions; encourage cooperation and sharing between cross-functional units; and, ultimately, enjoy the benefit of having a broader network of creativity, constructive criticism, and business knowledge and awareness. It also improves the originator's confidence, and, eventually their proficiency and is contagious for collectively inspiring the groups brainstorming. Collaborative discovery also closes the gap between business users and IT, nurturing data democratization and facilitating the shift of IT to ET.

Visual: Keeping discovery visual leverages our innate visual hardwiring and empowers even the most nontechnical user with the ability to meaningfully ingest, synthesize, and take action from their insights through the careful distillation of images, color and aesthetic design. Visualization moves discovery from shared understanding to shared insight, and interactive visualizations allow the exploration process to follow train-of-thought thinking to insight. The ability to think visually encourages the artisan within all of us to express ourselves through visual communication.

Mobility: Today, having a mobile-first stance is the catalyst to enriching visual analytics and enabling self-sufficient, on-the-go business users in a new era of discovery. Mobile data discovery puts an inherent premium on an intuitive, interactive "touch" approach to interact visually with data in a familiar, compelling, and meaningful way. And, ultimately, mobility means discovery a portable experience that is personalized for the user

Ultimately, it boils down to this:

- The data-driven business demands value from discovery
- Self-sufficiency and high-performance are invaluable in the discovery process
- Speed, performance, and agility are the backbone of discovery
- Self-sufficiency, collaboration, visualization, and mobility are the muscle

To return to the opening of this chapter and the story of disruption in the tool landscape, we can say this: moving forward, as more and more discovery tools enters market, those that continue to concentrate first and foremost on the elements that enable discovery by design—a robust, agile, IT-independent and user-centric approach that has better access to data, agile high-performance, and is designed for collaboration—will continue to be disruptive in the market and allow companies to truly capitalize on the business process of discovery.

12.2 LEVERAGING VISUALIZATION FOR ASSESSABLE, MEANINGFUL, ACTIONABLE

Visual data discovery by design is the path by which we can use visualizations to reach new insights and discoveries. Let us switch gears from talking about how to curate discovery by design and ruminate on what data visualization should be used for. While some data visualizations are at the level of art (and even commissioned to be so by companies), others are more deliberate, carefully crafting a story to tell the user through the orchestration of images, information, and/or animation.

To derive true value from visualizations they must be dynamic, preferably interactive, and always actionable. They need to augment the message of the data without overshadowing it. And, myriad results from recent studies on the subject of data visualization and cognitive recall have found that data visualizations need to be memorable, blending accurate data with influential features like color, density, and content themes.

Yet while it is easy to get swept away in the "prettiness" of visualizations, it is important not to forget their purpose. Visualizations should foster the easy consumption of large amounts of data: they should leave the consumer with an understanding of information, or give them new inspiration. The goal of a visualization—any visualization—is to provide a data consumer with the insights they need to make effective decisions quickly through a well-designed, visual end user experience. At the end of the day, visualizations need to not only display information, but they must also be actionable—they have got to initiate a response that adds value to the business.

Consider this example: Aaron Koblin monitored US flight patterns (141k of them, actually) over a 24 hour period, and then used open-source language processing to crunch and munch the data and Adobe After Effects products to create an advanced data visualization. The Flight Patterns visualizations led to the Celestial Mechanics project—a "planetarium-based artwork installation that visualizes the statistics, data, and protocols of manmade aerial technologies"—by Scott Hessels and Gabriel Dunne of UCLA.

This award-winning project—while incredible (and super, super cool)—lacked the actionable piece that makes visualizations useful and therefore could be perceived as incredible artwork opposed to effective data visualization and meaningful visual communication. Compare that to FlightAware, a global aviation software and data services company that tracks private and commercial aircraft in the US and abroad. As the largest flight-tracking website in the world, FlightAware provides online flight planning, airport information, and airport fuel prices to data consumers. One of their tools, Misery Map, is a "real-time weather and flight data visualization that overlays Nexrad radar imagery on a map of the country, with red-green graphs showing the pain at major airports." This visual tool incorporates data from various sources to make the information valuable and actionable, and easily understood, for consumers.

12.3 THREE KEY POINTS TO A USEFUL DATA VISUALIZATION

To get the most value out of your data visualization—to ensure it is not only communicating data but is also doing so in a useful way—keep these three points in mind:

- Resist the urge to play—or tinker—with what is pretty in visualizations without knowing your message first. Just because something is pretty does not mean that it is effective—or useful. Be vigilant to cut out the "noise" in data visualizations, and focus on what is important and how to communicate that effectively. Remember the simplifying mantra of "less is more," and that visual design ultimately hinges not on embellishment, but on removing and simplifying until nothing stands between the visual's message and its audience.
- Educate yourself in visualization, and know which visualizations are appropriate for communicating different data sets (such as time-series, comparisons, and multidimensionality). Think about the key relationships among data sets, and let this guide you to selecting the right visualization for the data you want to display. Refer again to chapters: The Data Visualization and Continumm; and Data Visualization as a Core Competency, but expect these to evolve and potentially change as new types of data and visualizations continue to arise. There is certainly more education on the mechanics of data visualization than what we covered in this text that will be worthwhile. Recommendations for further study are included in the Appendix.
- Continue to put the conversation at the heart of the data visualization. Understand storytelling with visualizations, and the importance of memorability. Data visualizations are about telling a story—using visual solutions to communicate a narrative that make the context tangible and digestible by the consumer. Successful data visualization should be able to be understood by its intended audience from a position of personal insight and experience—they should put the audience—and its goals and needs—first.

As with any project, focusing on the end goal is important to guide the creation of your visualization: a good plan is the foundation of a good design.

REFERENCE

Marr, B., 2015. Spark or Hadoop – which is the best big data framework? Forbes Tech. Available from http://www.forbes.com/sites/bernardmarr/2015/06/22/spark-or-hadoop-which-is-the-best-big-data-framework/.

The need for visualization in the Internet of Things

13

"Dreams about the future are always filled with gadgets."
—Neil deGrasse Tyson

Data is powerful. It separates leaders from laggards and drives business disruption, transformation, and reinvention. Today's fast acceleration of big data projects is putting data to work and already generating business value. The concept of achieving results from big data analytics is fast becoming the norm. Today's most progressive companies are using the power of data to propel their industries into new areas of innovation, specialization, and optimization, driven by the horsepower of new tools and technologies that are providing more opportunities than ever before to harness, integrate, and interact with massive amounts of disparate data for business insights and value. Simultaneously, with a resurgence of the role and importance of data visualization and the need to "see" and understand this mounting volume, variety, and velocity of data in new ways we—business people, knowledge workers, and even for our personal data use—are becoming more visual. The premium on visual insights is becoming increasingly dominant in all things information management, as well as in every day business life. This is the heart of the imperative that is a driving force for creating a visual culture of data discovery. The traditional standards of data visualizations are making way for richer, more robust, and more advanced visualizations and new ways of seeing and interacting with data, whether on the desktop or on the go. In a nutshell, that has been the core premise of this entire book, and the imperative to create a visual culture of data discovery is something that will only continue as the era of the Internet of Things (IoT) unfolds.

As we have progressed through each chapter of this text, we have focused primarily on how the data industry as we know it *has* changed, or how it *is* changing. Now, as we embark on our final chapter and bring this book to a close, I would like to take another step forward and set our sights on the future—how the world of data *will* continue to change in the days going forward, and the important emerging technologies that will pave the way to getting us there—and those that we are just now beginning to catch glimpses of the most bleeding edge of technology. These highly visual technologies will be those that turn human data into meaning, both for the business and for the individual.

This final chapter will take a high-level look at advanced and emerging visual technologies and the need for data visualization in the Internet of Things. We will look at data in motion through animation and streaming, explore highly interconnected mobile strategies and an interconnected web of wearable devices, and, finally, take a look into gameplay and playful data visualization backed by machine learning and affective computing technologies, including augmented reality.

13.1 UNDERSTANDING "DATA IN MOTION"

Now, there are a few ways to interpret the phrase "data in motion" that warrants a bit of upfront clarification so that we are all on the same page. One definition of "data in motion," and perhaps the more traditional, is a term used for data in transit. It speaks to the flow of data through the analytical process as it moves between all versions of the original file, especially when data is on the Internet and analytics occur in real-time. This definition of data in motion represents the continuous interactions between people, processes, data, and things (like wearable devices or online engagement modules) to drive real-time data discovery. While this definition is certainly important, as we discuss emerging technologies and the predictive value of analytics in the IoT, think of data in motion a bit more visually and beyond a simple process movement. If you are familiar with the concept of "poetry in motion," consider how it could be applied to describe data in motion as the ability to watch something previously static (in the case of poetry, the written word) move in a way that brings out all the beautiful feelings and touches on multiple senses. To illustrate this a bit more clearly, think back to storytelling. We have explored the rationale for the old colloquialism "a picture is worth a thousand words" in several ways throughout this text; however, that has typically been in regard to a static image, whether one or many. Now, consider the story that could be told through a picture that moves. Like poetry in motion, think for a moment about how watching a visualization move might elicit additional emotions, or touch on multiple senses as you watch a story unfold through movement.

As an example, consider the image depicted in Figure 13.1. Drawn by the late American artist, writer, choreographer, theatre director, designer, and teacher Remy Charlip, this visual is a dance annotation, the symbolic representation of human movement drawn to guide dancers to learn and replicate dance positions. The visual, beautiful on its own, is nothing compared to the effect of watching a pair of dancers move off of paper and in the flesh. On paper it is static, or as Edward Tufte wrote in his 1990 text *Envisioning Information*, a "visual instant." In motion—whether on stage, on film, or even in a practice ballroom—is something else entirely.

To visually see data in motion is to watch as trends take shape or as patterns form or dissolve. With data visualization, we can watch this movement through stop and play animation, or online on an app, as you watch your heart rate keep pace with your exercise routine through the sensors in your Fitbit, or even move as you interact and play with information and swipe your hand to literally move data with your fingertips for train-of-thought analysis on the screen of your mobile tablet.

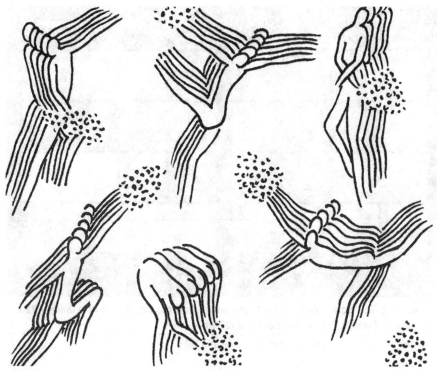

FIGURE 13.1 "Flowering Trees," Remy Charlip's *Air Mail Dances*

13.2 THE INTERNET OF THINGS PRIMER

Before we look at some of the visual technologies and advances that will contribute to the growth and dynamism of the IoT, let us take orient ourselves to understand a little bit more about what the Internet of Things is and exactly how much of an impact it holds in our data-centric future. Without this context, the importance of later discussion could be too diluted to earn the appropriate meaning.

Coined by British entrepreneur Kevin Ashton in 1999, the IoT is defined succinctly in Wikipedia as "the network of physical objects or 'things' embedded within electronic, software, sensors, and network creativity, which enables these objects to collect and exchange data." It allows objects to be sensed and controlled across existing network infrastructure. It creates opportunities between the physical world and the digital. And, it applies to everything—from human generated data, to built in sensors in automobiles, to medical devices like heart monitoring implants and sensors in neonatal hospital units, to biochip transponders on farm animals, and household thermostat systems and electronic toothbrushes. It is fair to say that the IoT is fast becoming the Internet of *Everything*, which itself is another term quickly becoming enshrined as part of the data industry vernacular.

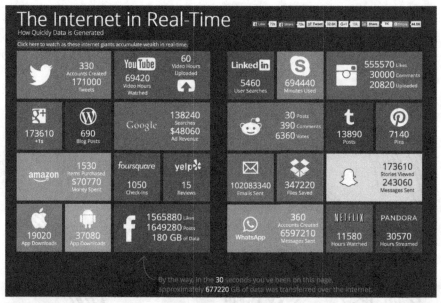

FIGURE 13.2 This Screenshot, Grabbed From www.pennstocks.la, Shows How Quickly Data is Generated Through User Interactions and Activities Online

Approximately 677,220GB was Transferred Within 30 s

Beyond the huge amount of new application areas, the IoT is also expected to generate large amount of data from diverse locations that will need to be aggregated very quickly, thereby increasing the need to better collect, index, store, and process data—particularly unstructured data—that go above and beyond traditional data management infrastructure and are partially responsible for the ongoing maturation of public, private, and hybrid cloud technologies. According to a 2014 study, approximately 77% of all newly generated data is unstructured, including audio, video, emails, digital images, social networking data, and more (Hitachi Data Systems, 2014). More important: previous predictions that unstructured data will double every three months are being realized today (Gartner, 2005) (Figure 13.2).

In fact, the World Economic Congress forecasts that, over the next ten years, another 2 billion people will get online, and along with them, over 50 billion new devices (World Economic Forum, 2015). Even sooner than that, IoT data generation is going to exceed 400 ZB by 2018—nearly 50 times higher than the sum total of data center traffic (Cisco, 2014). To break that down a bit, 1 ZB is 1,000 EB; 1 EB is 1,000 PB; 1 PB is 1,000 TB; and 1 TB is 1,000 GB.

For many who are not in the trenches of these types of measurements, they are probably unintuitive and isolated, too big and too foreign to grasp conceptually, so let us break it down. Again, 1 ZB is approximately 1,000 EB. 1 EB alone has the capacity to stream the entirety of the Netflix catalog more than 3,000 times; it is roughly equivalent to about 250 billion DVDs. And 250 billion is a huge number, no matter what it counts. If you took every spoken word in the human language over time, and

---

BOX 13.1 PREDICTIVE VALUE IN IoT

Everything starts with a business priority, so let us spend a moment considering the tangible business value of the IoT. Today, advanced analytics are surging, and, along with it, advanced visualization. A recent Forrester report qualified this as a growth in advanced visualization use from 22% in 2014 to 43% in 2015 (Forrester, 2015). Every industry is graced with more data—richer transactional data from business apps; usage and behavioral from web/mobile; social data; log data; sensor data, and so on—and everyone is looking for better ways to visualize and understand it.

With more data pouring in through the IoT, the opportunities to use this data to our advantage and push our advanced analytical models along the continuum from predictive (models that can anticipate outcomes with a significant probability of accuracy though not absolute) to prescriptive (adaptive and able to act in real-time—in this case, contextualized as "business time" and can be micro seconds or tens of seconds, depending on the business need, on that which you predicted). With the power of prediction comes the desire and initiative to take action, and the insight needed to take the best action that will influence the customer's decision and, thus, the outcome. Such prescriptive analytics can be linked to the idea of "perishable insights"—those insights that are only valuable when we see them immediately—now—to take immediate action. These can vary on level of criticality, but wherever they fall, are no less perishable. For example, think of health monitoring devices for infants in neo-natal unites that requires immediate and urgent attention. Less critical but no less perishable, Spotify has implemented an idea to use the accelerometer in smart phones to detect, if you are moving, gage the tempo of your run, and deliver a piped music experience.

---

put it into a database, you would still only stock up about 42 ZB of language, a small fraction of the 400 estimated in the IoT by 2018.

So, with all these data, devices, and people, where is the return on investment for the costs and efforts of data infrastructure and management for the data-driven business? Industry research says that the economic value of the IoT is to the tune of $6 trillion (though some have numbers as high as $7.1 trillion). The breakdown looks something like this: predictive maintenance ($2 trillion), smart home and security ($300 billion), smart cities ($1 trillion), and smart offices and energy ($7 billion) (McKinsey Global Institute, 2015).

While this is not the place to go further into the mechanics of the data lake or the value of analytics that we can leverage the mass amount of information into, in order to make better decisions and predictions (see Box 13.1), what I want to focus on is the value of people in the IoT and how data visualization (and other visual technologies) will lead the way in change. Some of these have to do with making visualizations even more powerful through techniques like streaming an animation, others are more human-centric in design to provide the consumer value proposition to contribute even in deeper ways to data generation through wearables and personal analytics, and even still some are more interactive and focus on things like gameplay, augmented reality, or what are becoming known as "playful visualizations" (Box 13.2).

13.3 THE ART OF ANIMATION

Seeing information in motion ties back to our visual capacities for how we learn, communicate, and remember—which provides fodder to the old saying, "seeing is believing." To provide the optimal example of the visual benefits of data in motion,

BOX 13.2 DEVICES CAN MEASURE DEPRESSION, TOO

A recent study by researchers at Northwestern Medicine, published in the *Journal of Medical Internet Research* in summer 2015, suggested that phone usage data can be used to diagnose mental states, particularly depression, by tracking daily usage and geographical location information. As a result, scientists can identify depressive symptoms with 87% accuracy (McDonald, 2015).

The study, which led to these findings, was conducted by researchers who analyzed GPS data and phone usage for 28 individuals over two weeks. These participants were also given a standardized questionnaire (the PHQ 9), and half the respondents illustrated symptoms of depressions that ranged from mild to severe while the other half did not. Then, with specifically designed algorithms, the aforementioned data were then correlated with depression test results. Lead research author, Sohrob Saeb, noted that the smartphone data was more reliable in detecting depression than the standardized questionnaire. So, what were the predictors? According to the study, one major contributor was the amount of time spent using the smart phone. The average daily usage for depressed participants was about 68 minutes, compared to 17 minutes for nondepressed participants. Other data, like those users who spent more time at home or in fewer locations, were also depression indicators.

let us return again to the construct of visual storytelling. When you think of visual stories that move, the first thing that comes to mind is very likely of television or movies and how stories are told in films. Thus, let us use that to our advantage and talk about storytelling in the language of perhaps the most innovative, visual storyteller: Hollywood.

In chapter: Visual Storytelling with Data, I shared an anecdote on storytelling from entertainment legend Francis Ford Coppola. Now, let me share another example to set the stage appropriately. A few years ago, I had the opportunity to meet actor Cary Elwes (heartthrob of the 1987 cult classic, *Princess Bride*, but also celebrated for his other roles in films including *Twister*, *Liar Liar*, and *Saw I & II, and* as maybe-maybe-not art thief Pierre Despereaux in TV's *Psych*). I mention Elwes' film credits to emphasize his breadth of experience in bringing stories—whether the fantastical or the gruesome—to life. When I met Elwes we did not talk about data—we talked about making movies, his movies specifically. But, in between his stories from the set (including when Fire Swamp flames leapt higher than anticipated and nearly caught Robin Wright's hair on fire, to point out a photo of Wallace Shawn's face, when he was certain that he was going to be fired from the film for his portrayal of Vizzini), the Man in Black made a remark that stuck with me as he considered the stunts they had managed to pull off with limited technology and a heavy dose of creativity and courage on the set of *The Princess Bride*. He said—and I am paraphrasing—"we didn't have a green screen, as you know, so we just did it [special effects]." (FYI, though the green screen was invented by Larry Butler for special effects in the 1940 film, *The Thief of Bagdad*, the entirety of *The Princess Bride* was filmed on live sets in the UK).

Currently, it is almost hard to imagine a movie being made without the benefits of digital sorcery to fabricate everything from stunts to skin tones to entire landscapes and story settings. Even still, it is no great secret that Hollywood is now and has always been an inherently visual place: through various forms of visualization—sets, costumes, props, special effects, etc.—Hollywood has been telling us stories for years. And, they did it as effectively in the grainy black and white of old silent films (think 1902 French silent film *A Trip to the Moon*) as in today's most special effect riddled blockbusters (Avatar comes to mind). When you strip away the shiny glamour and boil it to roots, this capacity for engaging visual storytelling is the direct result of one thing: they know how to bring our imaginations to life through animation. With animation, whether through capturing actors on film, using a green screen to enable special effects, or even newer technologies like computer graphics (more commonly, CG) that uses image data with specialized graphical hardware and software, we are effectively watching data in motion. The heart of animation is movement.

If the Dread Pirate Roberts is a bit outside of your movie repertoire, think instead of another prime example of visual animation: Walt Disney. It would be an understatement to say that Disney has set the bar for how stories are animated. Whether Walt himself or the Disney as we know it today, the company has been upping the anty of animated storytelling since its beginning with the release of the animated cartoon *Snow White and the Seven Dwarves* in 1937. Seven decades later, with films like *Frozen* (its most lucrative cartoon ever) and its recent purchase of the *Star Wars* franchise, Disney's animation legacy continues.

Of course, the data industry is no stranger to visual stories—or to Hollywood for that matter. Vendors such as IBM, Microsoft, Oracle, and Teradata all have strong ties in the media and entertainment industry. When it comes to in-house, Hollywood-grown talent, data visualization solutions provider Tableau has put a formidable entertainment industry stake in the ground with its cofounder, early Pixar employee Pat Hanrahan, former LucasFilm CTO Dave Story, and fellow LucasFilm special effects guru Philip Hubbard. Of course, Tableau is not the only visual analytics technologies leveraging showbiz talent into doing its part to facilitate the evolution of an increasingly visual, data-centric culture in the IoT. Disruptive start-ups are taking the cue, too. For example, Visual Cue, an Orlando-based data viz start up with the mantra "pictures are a universal language" creates mosaic tile-based dashboards to tell a data story. Its founder, Kerry GIlger, spent time earlier in his career building animatronic robots and doing camera work for the Osmonds. Such examples demonstrate the ability to take a rich storytelling and/or animation heritage and bring it off the silver screen for the benefit of the data-driven business.

Animation has proven its popularity in user interfaces due to its intuitive and engaging nature. Data science research suggests that data visualization in motion through animation improves interaction, attracts attention, fosters engagement, and facilitates learning and decision-making. It also simplifies object consistency for changing objects in transition, including changes in position, size, shape, and color. For visual discovery and analysis, this gives rise to perceptions of causality and intentionality, communicating cause-and-effect relationships, and establishing storytelling narratives. However, animations can also be problematic and should not be used without a clear understanding of design principles for animation, and many researchers recommend using animation to ensure that data tells a clean story, as too

---

BOX 13.3 ANIMATION EXAMPLE: GAPMINDER TRENDALYZER

Probably one of the most common examples of animated data visualization floating around the data industry today is that of Gapminder Trendalyzer (http://www.gapminder.org/tag/trendalyzer/), which has been featured at TED, both in 2006 and 2007. If you are unfamiliar, Gapminder Trendalyzer, founded in Stockholm by Ola Rosling, Anna Rosling Rönnlund, and Hans Rosling, is best described as a bubble chart using animation to illustrate trends over time in three dimensions: one for the X-axis, one for the Y-axis, and one for the bubble size, animated over changes in a fourth dimension (time). This technique appears to be very effective in presentations, where a presenter tells the observer where to focus attention by bringing the data to life and emphasizing critical results.

For as successful the Gapminder Trendalyzer animation is for storytelling, it can be more problematic for analysis. In fact, researchers have found that one key aspect of presentations that feature animation was having a narrator explaining and highlighting features in the data (Robertson et al., 2008). Conversely, when an animation is used for analysis on unfamiliar data, an analyst does not know what points will be salient and will likely spend a significant amount of time exploring the animation before any meaningful insights or conclusions can be achieved. This is one area where Gapminder Trendalyzer has come under criticism, too.

---

many data points can confuse an audience (see Box 13.3) (Robertson et al., 2008). Further, we must understand which type of visualizations can benefit most from animation, and when to use animation for maximum advantage. Academic analysis of data visualization has indicated that participants feel engaged and enabled to collaborate using data visualization—and thus build on previously existing knowledge to earn strong support for gaining insight with an overview, patterns, and relationships in data easier to discover. In particular, animation has been found to offer significant advantages across both syntactic and semantic tasks to improve graphic perception of statistical data graphics (Heer & Robertson, 2007). However, there are many principles and design considerations for correctly using animation for data visualization, and while animation has proven its popularity in user interfaces in part to its intuitive and engaging nature, it can also make solo analysis challenging if data is not kept in context.

13.3.1 BEYOND ANIMATION TO STREAMING DATA VISUALIZATION

Seeing data in motion ties back to the inherent need of visually seeing information move through motion and storytelling. If animation data visualization is the younger, hip brother of static data visualization or even dashboards, then streaming data visualization is its adorable baby sister (this line, referring to Tableau's recent release of Vizable—a mobile app with the ability to edit and create new visualization on a tablet—is one I heard at the Tableau User Conference #data15 alongwith 10,000 other data users in October of 2015, and I loved it so much that I am happy to repurpose it here). In this section, let us consider how animation goes next-generation with streaming data visualization.

Within streaming visualization lies the power of not only insight, but also of prediction. When you see data move, you can see trends, anticipate changes, react immediately, and write your own data story. Traditional visualization—and even the emergence of advanced visualization for visual analytics—falls short of meeting the expectations of true visual discovery. Real-time, streaming visual analytics takes visual discovery to a previously untapped level through the ability to witness data in motion for immediate time to insight. More important, seeing data in motion through steaming visualization does what static visualization simply cannot: it fundamentally shifts the discovery process from reactive to predictive. It does this through animation—the ability to see trends moving in real-time within the data that provides the opportunity to visually identify, consume, and predict changes that can be proactively reacted by the data-driven organization. This will be increasingly more valuable within the IoT, too, as the addition of sensor and device data in streaming data visualizations will give businesses unprecedented predictive insight into their business in new ways.

The difference between animated data visualization and streaming data visualization can be subtle. While both visualization types use movement to show data move, animation shows a play (or replay) of data already formed to move in a predefined way. Streaming, instead, shows data as it moves in real-time. Back to our earlier examples of animation in film, the difference in these two forms on visualization could be the difference between watching a movie (animation) and watching events play out in live TV (streaming). As another example, think about the value of real-time quotes when stock trading. For example, on NASDAQ.com, a real-time quote page shows real time information for US stocks (listed on NASDAQ, NYSE, and AMEX). It provides investors with the securities' real-time NASDAQ Last Sale, Net Change, and NASDAQ Volume. There is tangible benefit for traders in seeing streaming data: rather than watching historical information to make the best decision possible, they can instead see information as it changes and respond immediately. Delays can result in missed opportunities and lost profits.

13.3.1.1 *Visual sedimentation*

One interesting way to facilitate streaming data visualization is through a process known as visual sedimentation. This process is inspired by the physical process of sedimentation, commonly understood as the deposition of a solid material from air or water, and provides a way to visualize streaming data that simply cannot be achieved in classic charts. While static charts cannot show live updates and thus natively loses the value of data in motion, our physical world is good at showing changes while preserving context (through elements like sediment, physical forces, decay, and barriers).

By definition, visual sedimentation as a visualization process is the result of deconstructing and visualizing data streams by representing data as objects falling due to gravity forces that aggregate into compact layers over time. Further, these layers are constrained by borders (walls) and the ground (see Figure 13.3). As an example, consider this: streaming data, like incoming tweets carried in through a Twitter stream, have several stages that are difficult to represent visually in a straightforward way, specifically when the effort is focused on smoothing the transition between the

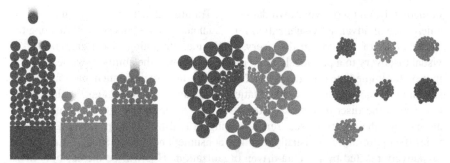

FIGURE 13.3 The Visual Sedimentation Metaphor Applied to a Bar Chart (Left), a Pie Chart (Center), and a Bubble Chart (Right)

(Source: Illustrated by Huron, Vuillemot, and Fekete).

data stream's focus—recent data—and the context, or older data. Within these stages, data may appear at unpredictable times, accumulate until it is processed, and need to be kept in aggregated form to provide ongoing historical and contextual significance. These challenges align to many characteristics of the visual sedimentation process as conceptualized, and with visual sedimentation, we can apply the metaphor to the visualization of data streams by mapping concepts to visual counterparts, including the following:

Tokens, a visual mark representing a data item arriving in the stream that has a four-stage lifecycle of entrance, suspension, accumulation, and decay
Layout, a two-dimensional geological cross-section of strata layers that houses tokens within walls, the ground, aggregated areas, and containers
Forces, like gravity, decay, and flocculation, that specify the behaviors of the tokens
Aggregated areas that represent the final state undergone by tokens that affect the visual representation of the data itself

In research presented at IEEE, researchers Huron et al., 2013 applied the method of visual sedimentation and demonstrated a toolkit for three different classic chart types: bar charts, pie charts, and bubble charts. They then demonstrated the effectiveness of this technique in a multitude of case studies, including Bubble T, an online tweet monitoring application. In Bubble T each token is a tweet filled with an avatar picture that is filtered into columns designated for each candidate. Visual sedimentation has also been used to monitor language edits on Wikipedia, to view birth and death rates in real time, and a project called SEDIMMS, a record of 20 k tweets containing both the words "M&M" and a color name name. Each tweet falls into an appropriately colored bin, and layers condense into previous dates in the bottom. (A visual sedimentation toolkit, which is an open-source JavaScript library that can be built on top of existing toolkits such as D3.js, jQuery, and Box2DWeb, is available at visualsedimentation.org.)

13.4 HUMAN CENTERED DESIGN IN MOBILE(FIRST) STRATEGIES

Data generation is becoming incredibly mobile, and everyday users are using mobile technologies to create and share more and more information about themselves—as well as having new expectations as to how they can explore their own personal analytics, too. Historically, most designers have approached the desktop side of any project first and left the mobile part as a secondary goal that gets (hopefully) accomplished later. Even with the rise of responsive design and the emphasis on mobile technologies, many designers sill begin with the "full size" site and work down to mobile. However, with the emphasis of "mobile first," there is a growing trend in the industry to flip this workflow around and actually begin with mobile considerations and then work up to a larger desktop version—or not.

As "on the go" becomes more of a mantra than a philosophy, mobile is becoming the new normal in a rapidly mobile world. And, it does not just give us new opportunities for consuming and interacting with data and analytics. Rather, it fundamentally alters the paradigm by which we expect to consume and interact with data and analytics. Going "mobile first" brings with it the expectation of responsive and device-agnostic mobility, and demands an intuitive, hands-on "touch" approach to visually interact with data in a compelling and meaningful way. Mobile is no longer a niche market. Recent mobile statistics show that there are 1.2 billion mobile users worldwide, and 25% of these are mobile only (meaning that they rarely use a desktop device to access the Internet or desktop-based software) (Code My Views, 2015). Further, mobile apps have been downloaded a total of 10.9 billion times and mobile sales are increasing across the board with over 85% of devices web-ready. Obviously, the desktop is not going away, but, just as obviously, mobile is here to stay.

Today, regardless of form factor, mobility is being used to enrich visual analytics and enable self-sufficient users in a new era of visual discovery. New features are being added, like increased security (including biometric access through platforms like MicroStrategy, which considers itself to be the most secure mobile platform) and bi-directional, write back capabilities (offered by pure mobile-first players like Roambi and iVEDiX). While mobile moves up the ranks of desired visualization features/functionality, it has yet to reach the top; our research at Radiant Advisors has seen that user experience and interactivity is the top priority for adopters at approximately 70% (see Figure 13.4). Other leading user priority features include native app design, visual analysis capabilities, and security.

In terms of chart types best suited for analysis on a mobile screen, traditional chart types are still on the top. Even reduced to the small constraints of precious mobile real estate, these still provide the best means of working with data visualization efficiently and intuitively, and they are among the most prolific either in mobile-first native tools or in mobile versions of popular desktop products. Among these are column charts, its cousin the stacked column chart, area charts, line charts, pie charts, comparison charts, waterfall charts, and scatter and bubble charts. There are many peripheral discussions of value in mobile but in our limited space, let us move onto

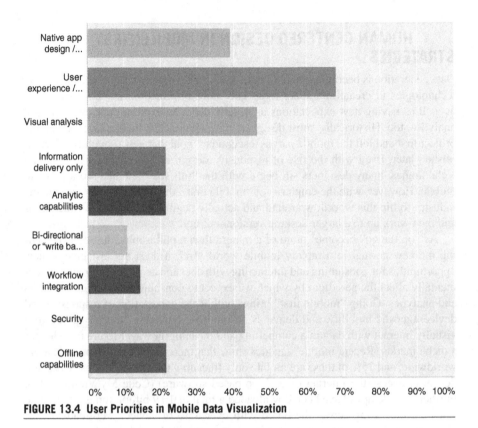

FIGURE 13.4 User Priorities in Mobile Data Visualization

look specifically at the role of the wearables market in the IoT, as well as how it is perhaps the largest contributor to the shift toward personal visual analytics (PVA).

13.4.1 WEARABLE DEVICES

A wearable takes mobile beyond smartphones and tablets. Devices that can be worn on the person—your wrist, neck, finger, or even clipped to your clothing (or *within* your clothing)—wearables are a category of devices that can be worn by a consumer and often include tracking information related to health and fitness, or that have small motion sensors to take snapshots of data and sync with mobile devices. In a 2015 BI Intelligence Estimates Tech Report (aptly titled The Wearables Report), released by Business Insider, wearables are shown to be on an obvious growth curve with a compounded annual growth rate (or, CAGR) of 35% between 2014 and 2019. In number of devices shipped, this translates to something like 148 million new units shipped annually in 2019, up from 33 million currently in 2015. Of course, there are many consumer challenges to overcome in the wearables market, most notably things like small screen size, clunky style, and limited battery life. There are many other challenges on the business and analytics side, too.

With a huge opportunity for manufacturers to carve out niche space and make new investments, there is already diverse assortment of wearable devices available in the market today. As a quick snapshot of the current options, the following are a few favorites, some of which were introduced already in chapter: Separating Leaders From Laggards. Though the wearables market is quite vast and diverse, we will limit this to three basic categories: convenience devices, smartwatches and communication devices, and fitness trackers. Many of these may be already familiar to you. In fact, I would wager to bet that you might have one or more of the devices—or one similar—from the selection mentioned later. While this section is only a static snapshot of the current wearables market and uses a few specific products to describe how wearables affect consumers and their personal analytics, they are representative of sample of products that address the personal needs, wants, and functions of the user. Thus in this debrief we will focus on how each technology works, how it is changing or advancing the wearables market, and what type of data is generated and collected.

13.4.1.1 Disney magicband

As a personalized park option and billion-dollar big data investment, Disney introduced its MagicBands in the last bit of 2013. The bands are RFID tag bracelets, personalized with a unique ID, monogram, and chip (think: user profile) for each designated park guest. When you register a guest with a MagicBand, you also include their name and birthday, which gives Disney the data it needs to provide custom birthday offers, including notifying nearby characters in the park to sneak over and say hello. The bands can be used, simultaneously, as room keys, credit cards, FastPass ride tickets (to reduce time spent waiting in line), photo logs for character snapshots, and more. Each MagicBand contains an HF radio frequency device and a transmitter, which sends and receives RF signals through a small antenna inside the MagicBand (Disney, 2015).

Through the band, Disney can more or less keep track of everything you do in the larger park ecosystem. It can track everything you do, everything you buy, everywhere you eat, ride, and go. It can build artificial intelligence (AI) models on itineraries, show schedules, line length, weather, character appearances, etc., to figure out what influences stay length and cash expenditure to maximize guest experience and park profit. With this information, Disney is working to better the park experience for every guest, as well as to increase the value of any individual customer within the parks by encouraging them to stay longer, spend more, and come back more often. This aggregated data helps the park understand crowd movement patterns and where, in real time, crowds may be slow moving and need to be dispersed by, say a parade, happening nearby. (www.disneystore.com/magicband)

13.4.1.2 Apple watch

In our research at Radiant Advisors, we have already seen that iOS takes the market share for user preference for mobile apps (in a mobile tech survey, nearly 60% of respondents said iOS was the preferred mobile platform, more than the sum of Android—39% and Windows 14%—combined). In September 2014, Apple's current CEO, Tim Cook, delivered his keynote introducing the Apple Watch, calling it a new relationship people have with technology—and Apple's most personal device to "connect and communicate" seamlessly from your wrist.

On the surface, the Apple Watch can more or less do most of the things the iPhone can through both touch interaction and the Digital Crown, a little dial on the side that acts like the iPod's clickwheel to scroll through a list or zoom in an out of a map. It has both a gyroscope and an accelerometer (to count steps and extrapolate distance, thus calculating pace and calories burned in a workout session), plus a custom sensor that uses visible-light and infrared LED along with photodiodes to determine heart rate. It works in tandem with your phone's GPS and Wi-Fi to determine your location and other geographical information, thus it can track daily activities as well as workouts between its sensors and the capabilities connected by the iPhone. As far as aesthetics, the watches boast everything from a sapphire crystal face, to a stainless steel case, or even 18-karate gold casting in yellow or rose (if you are willing to pay in the $10,000–$17,000 price range).

Going forward, smartwatches are expected to be the leading wearables product category and take an increasing larger percentage of shipments—rising by 41% over the next five years to ultimately account for 59% of total wearable devices shipments in the holiday season of 2015 and on to just over 70% of shipments in 2019 (Business Insider, 2015). Today, the Apple Watch is responsible for truly kick starting the overall worth in the smartwatch market, already taking 40% of adoption in 2015 and is expected to reach a peak of 48% of the share in 2017 (Business Insider, 2015). And, with Google joining Apple in the smartwatch market, estimates are that these platforms will eventually make up over 90% of all wearables, with some distinctions between smartwatches and other devices, especially with fitness bands, such as FitBit, which is next on the list below. (www.apple.com/watch)

13.4.1.3 FitBit

At its core, FitBit is a physical activity tracker that tracks much of a person's physical activity and integrates with software to provide personal analytics with the goal of helping health-conscious wearers to become more active, eat a more well-rounded diet, and sleep better. It is a sort of 21st century pedometer originally introduced in 2008 by Eric Friedman and James Park (Chandler, 2012). The device itself is only about two inches long and about half an inch wide, and can be easily clipped onto a pants pocket or snapped into a wristband. Like the sensors in the Apple Watch, the FitBit has a sensitive sensor that logs a range of data about activities to generate estimates on distance traveled, activity level, calories burned, etc. It also has an altimeter, designed to measure how much elevation is gained or lost during a day, which is an important contributor to physical activity metrics. The clip has a built in organic light-emitted diode (OLED) that scrolls current activity data, which alerts the wearer if they have not met daily fitness goal requirements via a little avatar that grows or shrinks depending on the wearer's activity level. For additional gamification, the device displays "chatter" messages to encourage the wearer to keep moving. The data is offloaded to a wireless base station whenever the wearer passes within 15 feet of the base, and is uploaded to the accompanying software where it converts raw data into usable information through its proprietary algorithms.

FitBit and other wearable fitness devices have come under some scrutiny as to whether they actually work or not (there is a relatively high degree of error, though the FitBit itself has one of the lowest at only around 10%) (Prigg, 2014), yet they nevertheless are anticipated to continue catering to niche audiences due to their appeal to those interested in health and exercise. However, research suggests that Fit-Bit and similar devices aimed only at fitness tracking (as opposed to, for example, smartwatches that include these in their lists of capabilities) will see their share of the wearable device market contract to a 20% share in 2019, down from 36% in 2015 (www.fitbit.com)

13.4.2 WEARABLES FOR HIM/HER

The evolution of wearables does not stop at increased capabilities and customization (like what clips to add on your MagicBand or which metal band of Apple Watch to get). Luxury designers are getting in on the wearables market—like Swarovski, Montblanc, Rebecca Minkoff, Fossil, and Tory Burch, to name a few—often by partnering with device makers. These devices are becoming even more personal and designed to fit the customer. Within this is what I like to call the "genderfication" of wearables: narrowing the market to better segment and meet the unique needs of customer demographics. Here is a quick look at how these devices are being designed for him and for her.

13.4.2.1 Wearables for her

The fashion conscious techn-anista could benefit from wearables jewelry accessories, such as Ringly, a gemstone ring device that connects to your phone and sends customized notifications through a smartphone app (available currently for both iOS and Android devices) about incoming emails, texts, calendar alerts, and more through a choice of four vibration types and light. Rings are made from genuine gemstones and mounted in 18-karate matte gold plating. (www.ringly.com)

13.4.2.2 Wearables for him

Recently, designer clothing line Ralph Lauren has been sharpening its chops in the wearables apparels market, releasing its PoloTech™ shirt to the public. According to the site, silver fibers woven directly into the fabric read heart rate, breathing depth, and balance, as well as other key metrics, which are streamed to your device via a detachable, Bluetooth-enabled black box to offer live biometrics, adaptive workouts, and more. (www.ralphlauren.com)

13.4.3 PERSONAL VISUAL ANALYTICS

A discussion on wearables is a necessary predecessor in order to fully grasp the importance and possibilities of personal visual analytics (or, PVA). Data surrounds each and every one of us in our day lives, ranging from exercise logs, to records of our interactions with others on various social media platforms, to digitized genealogical data, and more. And thanks in part to things like wearable devices that track and record data from our lives we are becoming more and more familiar and comfortable with seeing and working with information that is intrinsically personal to us. With corresponding mobile apps that link directly to wearable-collected data, individuals have begun exploring how they can understand the data that affects them in their personal lives (Tory & Carpendale, 2015).

There is a Quantified Self movement to incorporate technology into data acquisition on various aspects of a person's daily life in terms of outputs, states (moods, vital signs, etc.), and performance by comparing wearable sensors and wearable computing. Also known as life logging, the Quantified Self movement is focused on self-knowledge and self-tracking that is enabled by technology to improve daily functioning. This self-monitoring activity of recording personal behaviors, thoughts, or feelings is made exponentially more approachable and intuitive with visual analytics tools (Choe et al., 2014). In fact, there is an enormous potential for us to use our personal data and personal analytics in the same way as we might interact with any other data, and through the same types of visualizations and visual discovery processes. This is a concept referred to as PVA, the science of analytical reasoning facilitated by visual representations used within a personal context, thereby empowering individuals to make better use of their personal data that is relevant to their personal lives, interests, and needs (Tory & Carpendale, 2015). As an example, consider the image in Figure 13.5, which shows a snapshot of the visual dashboard of personal data corresponding to one smartwatch currently available in the market.

Of course, if designing visual analysis tools for business users who lack formal data analysis education is challenging, then designing tools to support the analysis of data in one's nonprofessional life can only be compounded with additional research and design challenges. These go beyond supporting visualization and analysis of data in nonprofessional context, but also are constrained by other personal factors, like form factor preferences or resource budgets to acquire such devices. An emergent field today, PVA is an area currently undergoing a call to arms from researchers in the space. Many—perhaps most—believe that integrating techniques from a variety of areas (among these visualization, analytics, ubiquitous computing, human-computer interaction, and personal informatics) will eventually lead to more powerful, engaging, and useful interactive data experiences for everyone—not just formal data users (Huang et al., 2015).

13.5 INTERACTION FOR PLAYFUL DATA VISUALIZATION

PVA is one way that people are taking a more intimate interest in seeing and interacting with data on an individual level. And, while many users may not have a deep knowledge of how to navigate the analytics provided on their wearable app

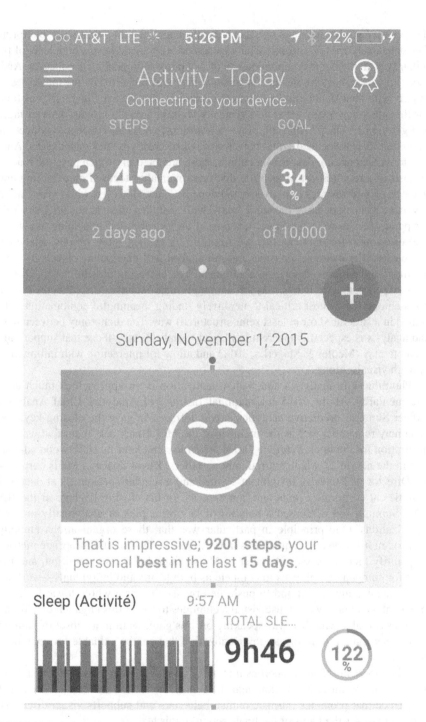

FIGURE 13.5 A Snapshot of Personal Visual Analytics, Taken From a Smartwatch Correspondent App

dashboards (or other personal visual analytics venues, including things like platforms for social analytics for various social web activities), they do have a high level of familiarity with the context, a prerequisite of any purposeful analytical endeavor. And, more important, because the data is personal they are compelled by the innate desire to *play* with their data to find answers to questions like—to use Figure 13.5 as food for thought—how many steps do I typically walk in a day? Or, what time of night to I get the best sleep? After all, play—a notoriously difficult concept to define—is important: it is associated with characteristics like creativity and imagination. And, in our ever-expanding data-driven culture, these are the traits which pave the road to curiosity—a requirement of an agile discovery mentality focused on exploring and uncovering new insights into diverse and dynamic data. However, while many might shy away from associating the word "play" with analytics, there is nonetheless a role for playfulness even in the more daunting of analytical tasks. Imagining a new visual orientation for data can then be followed by further, more serious, analytical approaches. For example, consider how an analyst will manipulate objects by sorting them into patterns, theorizing about meanings, exploring possibilities… Though these experimental activities may be seemingly unproductive (discovery), they are often among those most critical to iteratively finding meaningful combinations (insights) in a structured (or at least semi-structured) way. The dichotomy between play and analysis is especially apparent in playful visualizations—those that support and promote play (Medler & Magerko, 2011) and allow for interaction with information through visualizations.

Playfulness in analytics and with visualization is an approach as much as it is a mentality. At the 2015 International Institute of Analytics Chief Analytics Officer Summit, predictive analytics expert Jeffrey Ma gave the closing keynote. (You may remember Jeff as the member of the MIT Blackjack Team that was the inspiration for the book *Bringing Down the House* and later its Hollywood adaptation in the movie *21* which starred, among others, Kevin Spacey.) Ma is currently the Director of Business Insights at Twitter and a regular speaker about data and analytics at corporate events and conferences. In his closing keynote at the IIA CAO Summit, Ma discussed a handful of key principles of analytically minded organizations. One principle in particular was that these organizations embody intrinsic motivation and channel this motivation into the use of appropriate metrics to quantify their successes. Another of Ma's principles was competition, and the need for company employees to compete as both teams and individuals—working for personal achievement and to push the organization as a whole toward a common goal—and how we can use visual techniques to foster this engagement. To the latter, essentially what Ma was speaking on was gamification, a subset of gaming techniques applied to information visualization that can be valuable for analytical insight.

While there are many properties that make up playful data visualization, among the most important is interaction, and this—how interaction delivers a rich visual experience that promotes intrinsic human behaviors and supports visual discovery through play—is the focus of the final section of this text.

13.5.1 **GAMIFICATION AND GAMEPLAY**

When we think of visual, "playful" interaction with information, one concept that bubbles to the top is gamification and how it can be used as a paradigm of rewarding behaviors within a visual analytics system. However, it is important to note here the distinction between gamification and gameplay because, though it is probably the more recognizable of the two terms, gamification alone is only one piece of the overall architecture of truly playful visualizations that benefit from the gaming techniques. Gameplay, too, has important influencers in how it contributes to playful visualization and visual data discovery.

First, gamification generally refers to the application of typical elements of game playing (like point scoring, competition with others, rules of play) to other areas of activity, typically with the goal of encouraging engagement with a product or service. Applications of gamification include things like earning virtual badges or other trophies of interactions within a gaming environment that are awarded based on accomplishing milestones along a journey to proficiency. It is also often used as a recruitment tool in human resources environments—for instance, the US Army's transportable "Virtual Army Experience" units are taken to recruiting environments to attract and informally test potential recruits—to motivation and goal tracking applications used everywhere from virtual training academies (see Treehouse.com) to engendering customer loyalty and rewards (see Recyclebank.com).

Gameplay, on the other hand, is a bit more ambiguous to define, but generally refers to the tactical aspects of a computer game, like its plot and the way it is played, and is distinct from its corresponding graphics and sound effects. It is commonly associated with video games and is the pattern (or patterns) defined through the game rules, the connection between different player types and the game, and game-related challenges and how they are overcome. While the principles of information visualization can inform the design of game-related visual analytic systems (like monitoring player performance over time), gameplay practices themselves are also being used to offer a unique perspective on interactive analytics, too, and how video game data can be visualized. This was a used case presented by researchers Medler and Magerko and the focus of a 2011 paper in information mapping (Medler & Magerko, 2011).

13.5.2 **INTERACTIVITY**

Gamification, gameplay, and playful data visualization are not synonymous (or even close to being synonymous for that matter); however, the undercurrent of interactivity is a mutual enabler of them all, and reinforces our key emphasis within these discussions.

At the core of any type of data visualization tends to appear two main components: representation—how the data is represented through visual cues and graphicacy techniques—and interaction. This interaction is a part of a visualization's overall visual dialog (introduced in chapter: Visual Communication and Literacy, which refers to the exchange of information—or, dialog—between the designer of visual, the visual itself, and its recipient). Unfortunately, aside from things like drill-down or expand activities, or animation and streaming conversations, interactivity is often deemed secondary to representation. And, while static images offer expressive value, their usefulness is limited by design. In contrast, interactive data visualization can be used as stimuli to prompt insight and inspire creativity.

Depending on the users' intent, there are several different categories of interaction in data visualization that have been articulated within the literature. These are:

Select: to mark something as interesting for deeper exploration and/or analysis
Explore: to actively engage in investigative behaviors with the visual
Reconfigure: to arrange the data or the visual differently
Encode: to provide a different illustration of the data
Abstract (or elaborate): to show more or less detail
Filter: to show something conditionally with the removal of certain aspects
Connect: to show related items and explore new correlations (Yi et al., 2007)

As a related aside, it is worth to remark that many—if not all—of these categories of interaction are those most capitalized on by the gesture-based methodology of mobile-first visual discovery applications, such as those provided by Roambi or Tableau's new app, Vizable.

Ultimately, interactivity supports visual thinking which drives visual discovery. Without interactivity, visual discovery falls short of its intended purpose, yet with the right interactivity, data visualization becomes a natural extension of the analyst's thought process. Interactivity, then, is the element that allows analysts to "play" with data: to manipulate information into patterns, theorize about meanings, project interpretations, explore possibilities—all while balancing the fixed content, context, and relationships of the data with creativity and imagination. Playful visualizations are where the dichotomy of discovery—or, play—and analysis disappears (Boxes 13.4, 13.5, and 13.6).

BOX 13.4 THE PNNL MURAL PROJECT

Wouldn't it be great if you could have the benefit of a giant, wall-sized, interactive, and animated data visualization that encompasses the human-centered and gesture-based design of a mobile device? The Pacific Northwest National Laboratory's Interactive Power Wall—referred to as MURAL—is located in the Multidisciplinary Research and Analysis Lab of PNNL's Computational Science Facility and is just that. MURAL provides a unique capability to explore the boundaries of collaborative scientific and information visualization research on large, high-density displays (PNNL, 2015).

In a nutshell, MURAL is a multiprojector, multitouch interactive display system with a total resolution of 15.4 million pixels (or 7.4 times 1080P HD) on a 7-ft high by 16-ft wide continuous high-quality glass display screen. It is used within a general-purpose space that can accommodate up to sixty people for research projects, meetings, working groups, and/or presentations.

BOX 13.5 THE USE CASE FOR AUGMENTED REALITY

Between the ability to perform personal visual analytics from the comfort of your own smartphone, to interacting with massive visual information displays, the new visual data culture is edging nearer and nearer to fulfilling some of our wildest science fiction fantasies for working with data. Now, it is beginning to go even further with the introduction of augmented reality (AR).

As one example, data visualization vendor, Visual Cue is blending infographics, symbolism, and data visualization mechanics to develop an augmented reality feature as a game-like add-on to their visual analysis tool. Like gameplay or other playful visualizations, augmented reality has been found to be appropriate in instances that offer people data in an environment that makes it a little less like data analysis and a little more like a game. With AR, users can use a device—like a tablet or even a smartphone—to see data "floating" above a machine or a person's, making abstract data become connected into its origin in a relatable way. Right now the most solid use cases for augmented reality have been in areas such as call centers and with machine data in production environments (depicted in Figure 13.6). The nature of the technology, which is still maturing, tends to work best with things that do not move around too fast.

With AR, the goal is transparency. "If it's visible in the data, can make it visible in the real world," says Visual Cue's Nathan Snow. "The future of data viz is bringing abstract information and making it consumable by everyone in every context." Snow is right: in many ways, modern data can no longer be limited to using the same visualizations that were created 200 years ago. Yes, charts and graphs are still very valuable, but for modern information streams, the data is so immense we need new ways of looking at it. Augmented reality is one way to abstract data and make thousands of rows and columns of numbers real.

BOX 13.6 GAMEPLAY IN THE CLASSROOM

A really interesting application of visual gameplay to produce results has been brought to light through Classcraft, an online educational role-playing game that teachers and students play together in the classroom. The platform uses play, engagement, and collaboration to create a truly positive force in the classroom—in other words, to gamify learning—and is not intended to replace existing school curriculum but rather to supplement classroom learning by encouraging teamwork and increasing student motivation and discipline. The platform works by allowing teachers to transform their classrooms into role-playing game environments.

Today Classcraft has been introduced by educators from elementary classrooms to college lecture halls, and has proven successful at reimaging learning for all grade levels. The testimonials are impressive. Of a sampling of the hundreds of teachers using Classcraft over the past twelve months, 98% report playing increased student engagement, 99% report a positive impact on classroom behavior, and 89% have noticed an overall increase in classroom efficiency. More important: Classcraft seems to be living up to its intended purpose: 88% of teachers report an increase in academic performance by students that have had the opportunity to introduce visual play into learning. More at www.classcraft.com.

This book begins and ends with a bit of a personal touch: from the larger picture of how we—as consumers—are affected by the shift of data-centric companies to a progressively visual culture of data discovery, to how we—as individuals—can contribute to that discovery and participate as part of a more holistic visual data culture. In effect, we all are part of the ongoing visual imperative to see and understand data more clearly, and to interact with this information in a way that makes the most sense: visually. From top to bottom, from the most data-driven organizations that are

FIGURE 13.6 An Example of How Visual Cue's Augmented Reality Platform

(Source: With permission from VisualCue Technologies LLC).

leading every niche of industry, disrupting, transforming, and reinventing the way we do business, to the most personal analytics captured and reported through commonplace wearable devices, the ability to visually understand complex information through curated data visualization is making analytics more approachable, more insightful, and more valuable.

So as this text draws to a close, I will leave you with this—a call to action. Be aware of the visual imperative and incorporate the tools, tips, techniques that we have reviewed and discussed in this book within your work and personal lives to better understand the world around you and affect positive change. And, go beyond awareness and find new opportunities and opportunities to engage, too. Be a leader by fostering and nourishing a culture of visual data discovery in your organization. It is of the utmost importance now, and will continue to play an even larger and more critical role in the future.

REFERENCES

Business Insider., 2015. The wearables report: Growth trends, customer attitudes, and why smartwatches will dominate. Available from: http://www.businessinsider.com/the-wearable-computing-market-report-bii-2015-7.

Chandler, N., 2012. How FitBit works. HowStuffWorks.com. Available from: http://electronics.howstuffworks.com/gadgets/fitness/fitbit.htm.

Choe, E., Lee, B., Kientz, J., 2014. Personal visual analytics for self-monitoring.

Cisco, 2014. Cisco Global Cloud Index: Forecast and Methodology, 2013–2018. Available from: http://www.cisco.com/c/en/us/solutions/collateral/service-provider/global-cloud-index-gci/Cloud_Index_White_Paper.pdf.

Code My Views, 2015. Mobile first design: Why it's great and why it sucks. Available from: https://codemyviews.com/blog/mobilefirst.

Disney., 2015. Available from: https://disneyworld.disney.go.com/faq/my-disney-experience/my-magic-plus-privacy/.

Forrester., 2015. Global Business Technographics® Data And Analytics Survey, 2015. Available from: https://www.forrester.com/Global+Business+Technographics+Data+And+Analytics+Survey+2015/-/E-SUS2955.

Gartner., 2005. "Introducing the High-Performance Workplace: Improving Competitive Advantage and Employee Impact," Gartner, May 16, 2005.

Heer, J., Robertson, G.G., 2007. Animated transitions in statistical data graphics. IEEE Trans. Vis. Comput. Graph. 13 (6), 1240–1247.

Hitachi Data Systems., 2014. In the age of unstructured data, enterprise-class unified storage gives IT a business edge: 7 key elements to look for in a multipetabyte-scale unified storage system. Available from: https://www.hds.com/assets/pdf/enterprise-class-unified-storage-in-the-age-of-unstructured-data-white-paper.pdf.

Huang, D., Tory, M., Aseniero, B., Bartram, L., Bateman, S., Carpendale, S., Tang, A., Woodbury, R., 2015. Personal visualization and personal visual analytics. IEEE Trans. Vis. Comput. Graph. 21 (3), 420–433.

Huron, S., Vuillemot, R., Fekete, J.D., 2013. Visual sedimentation. IEEE Trans. Vis. Comput. Graph. 19 (12), 2446–2455.

McDonald, G., 2015. Depressed? Your phone already knows. Discovery News. Available from: http://news.discovery.com/tech/gear-and-gadgets/depressed-your-phone-already-knows-150715.htm

McKinsey Global Institute, 2015. The Internet of Things: Mapping the value beyond the hype.

Medler, B., Magerko, B., 2011. Analytics of play: using information visualization and gameplay practices for visualizing video game data. Parsons J Inf. Mapping 3 (1), 1–12.

PNNL., 2015. Available from: http://vis.pnnl.gov/research.stm#tsg.

Prigg, M., 2014. Does your fitness band really work? Scientists Does your fitness band really work? Scientists analyse tracking tech and find Fitbit and others 'no more effective than a $25 pedometer'. Daily Mail UK. Available from: http://www.dailymail.co.uk/sciencetech/article-2653178/Does-fitness-band-really-work-Scientists-analyse-tracking-tech-Fitbit-no-effective-pedometer.html#ixzz3qSJs7Q2D.

Robertson, G., Fernandez, R., Fisher, D., Lee, B., Stasko, J., 2008. Effectiveness of animation in trend visualization. IEEE Trans. Vis. Comput. Graph. 14 (6), 1325–1332.

Tory, M., Carpendale, S., 2015. Personal visualization and personal visual analytics. IEEE Comput. Graph. Appls. 35 (4), 26–27.

World Economic Forum. 2015. http://www.weforum.org/projects/digital-infrastructure-and-applications-2020.

Yi, J.S., ah Kang, Y., Stasko, J.T., Jacko, J.A., 2007. Toward a deeper understanding of the role of interaction in information visualization. IEEE Trans. Vis. Comput. Graph. 13 (6), 1224–1231.

Appendix

RECOMMENDED READING

During the course of research for this book I have read, reviewed, and consulted a variety of texts and resources. Many of these offer deeper exploration and analysis on several of the areas that were introduced in the various chapters throughout this book.

If you are interested in exploring areas of interest further, I would like to recommend the following books from my personal bookshelf that may guide you in your quest for more information. I have categorized them loosely by interest are below:

On Storytelling
The Seven Basic Plots by Christopher Booker
Useful Fictions by Michael Austin
On the Origins of Stories by Brian Boyd

On Visual Design
Design for Hackers by David Kadavy
Infographics: The Power of Visual Storytelling by Jason Lankow and Josh Ritchie
Interactive Design by Andy Pratt and Jason Nunes
100 Things Every Designer Needs to Know About People by Susan Weinschenk

On Data Visualization
Designing Data Visualization by Noah Iliinsky and Julie Steele
Interactive Data Visualization for the Web by Scott Murray
Data Points by Nathan Yau
The Functional Art by Albert Cairo
Envisioning Information by Edward Tufte

On Data and/or Business Leadership
The Visual Organization by Phil Simon
The New IT by Jill Dyché
The Fifth Discipline: The Art & Practice of The Learning Organization by Peter Senge
Crisis & Renewal: Meeting the Challenge of Organizational Change by David Hurst
The New Ecology of Leadership by David Hurst
A Sense of Urgency by John Kotter
Big Data by Victor Mayer-Shönberger and Kenneth Cukier

On Ethics
Socrates Reloaded by Frank Buytendijk
You Are Not a Gadget by Jaron Lanier
The Man Who Lied to His Laptop by Clifford Nass

Miscellaneous
The House Advantage by Jeffrey Ma and Ben Mezrich
The Signal and the Noise by Nate Silver
The Highest Rung of the Latter by Deane May Zager

Subject Index

Printed in the United States
By Bookmasters